THE AUTHOR

Spencer J. Rosie is an Orcadian and lives in the heart of Kirkwall, a short walk away from St Magnus Cathedral. He was educated at Kirkwall Grammar School, where history was a favourite subject, and then went to Aberdeen University to study geology. In 1979, he returned to his native islands to work at the Flotta oil terminal and became involved in local politics, becoming a founding member of the Orkney Movement, and was later elected to Orkney Islands Council. He is a past chairman of Kirkwall Community Council.
He is married to Erica, a teacher, and they have a grown-up family of five.

Picture taken from the roof of the author's home in Victoria Street.

Saints and Sinners

Published by The Orcadian (Kirkwall Press)
Hell's Half Acre, Kirkwall, Orkney, KW15 1GJ
Tel: 01856 879000 Fax: 01856 879001
www.orcadian.co.uk

Book sales: www.orcadian.co.uk/shop/index.php

ISBN No: 978-1-902957-78-4

All rights reserved. The contents of this book may not be reproduced in
any form without written permission from the publishers,
except for short extracts for quotation or review.

Text © Spencer J. Rosie, 2015

Photographs:
© The Orcadian
© Orkney Library Photographic Archive
Other copyright as shown.

Printed in Orkney by The Orcadian, Hatston Print Centre,
Hell's Half Acre, Kirkwall, Orkney, Scotland, KW15 1GJ

Saints and Sinners

Memorials of St Magnus Cathedral

Spencer J. Rosie

*To all those, like my father and
his uncle, ex Provost James Flett,
who loved St Magnus Cathedral,
but are not commemorated
in the building.*

CONTENTS

Introduction	xiii
Acknowledgement	xv
Heraldic Terms	xvi
Chapter 1 The Eleventh Century	**1**
1. Olaf II Haraldsson of Norway c995-1030	1
Chapter 2 The Twelfth Century	**3**
2. Magnus Erlendsson c1070-1117	3
3. Kol Kalisson	4
4. Rognvald Kali Kolsson 1103-1158	5
5. Erlend Haraldsson (Earl of Orkney 1151-1154)	7
6. William I the Old (Bishop of Orkney c1102-1168)	7
Chapter 3 The Thirteenth Century	**9**
7. Bjarni Kolbeinsson (Bishop of Orkney 1188-1223)	9
8. Hakon IV Hakonsson of Norway 1203-1263	10
9. Thirteenth Century Warrior Grave Slab	11
Chapter 4 The Fourteenth Century	**13**
10. The Paplay Tomb	13
Chapter 5 The Fifteenth Century	**17**
11. Thomas Tulloch (Bishop of Orkney 1418-1461)	17
12. Andrew Pictoris (Bishop of Orkney 1477-c1505)	18
Chapter 6 The Sixteenth Century	**21**
13. MF c1500	21
14. VP c1522	22
15. Edward Stewart (Bishop of Orkney c1505-1524)	23
16. Thomas Murray 1527 (1577?)	23
17. Robert Maxwell (Bishop of Orkney c1524-1540)	24
18. Robert Reid (Bishop of Orkney 1541-1558)	25
19. The Seal of the Chapter of Orkney	26
20. Nicolas Halcro c1550	27
21. William Halcro c1565	28
22. Edward Sinclair c1564	28
23. Unidentified Sinclair	30
24. Lawrence Sinclair 1564	30
25. Lord Adam Stewart 1575	31
26. William Henryson 1582	32
27. Robert Stewart (Earl of Orkney 1581-1593)	32
28. James Monteith 1574/Patrick Monteith 1597	34
29. William Kincaid 1594	35
30. William Maine 1592/Mariore Thomson 1609	35

Chapter 7 The Seventeenth Century	**37**
31. James Law (Bishop of Orkney 1605-1615)	37
32. George Graham (Bishop of Orkney 1615-1639)	39
33. Andrew Honeyman (Bishop of Orkney 1664-1676)	41
34. Murdoch Mackenzie (Bishop of Orkney 1676-1688)	42
35. Tomas Reid 1603	43
36. Isobel Calcrit 1612/William Bannatyne of Gairsay	44
37. Catherine Craigie 1612/Magnus Pottinger	45
38. RC 1612 and Kirkwall Incorporated Trades	46
39. AB post 1613	46
40. William Irving of Sebay 1614	47
41. Hew Halcro of that Ilk (Wooden Panel) (1644)	48
42. William Craigie (1652)/Margaret Halcro (Wooden Panel)	48
43. Edward Sinclair/Ursula Foulzie (Wooden Panel)	49
44. David MacLellan/M. Groat (Wooden Panel)	50
45. Edward Pottinger of Howbister c1642	51
46. Thomas Sandison 1656/Walter Sandison	51
47. Yenstay - AY/GY 1652 (or 1625?)/EY 1663	52
48. George Sinclair 1643	52
49. Marjorie Smyth 1666/Beatrix Smyth1669/Patrick Smyth	53
50. George Drummond 1653 1660 1662	54
51. Mary Drummond 1664/Patrick Blair	56
52. Blair/Buchanan	57
53. John Cuthbert 1651 1668 1669/Margaret Chalmaer	58
54. Thomas Taylor 1666/Jennet Pottinger	59
55. Marjorie Pottinger 1669/Thomas Dishington	59
56. Patrick Prince 1673/Margaret Grott	60
57. John Sinclair 1676/James Adamson 1682	61
58. Mort Brod- Robert Nicolson	62
59. Robert Irving 1679/Barbara Williamson	64
60. James Black 1675/Helen Richan	65
61. Robert Richan 1679/Isabella Bellenden	65
62. John Richan 1679/Janet Loutit	67
63. John Kaa 1679/Agnes Loutit	68
64. Thomas Baikie 1665	68
65. James Baikie 1679/Sibilla Halcro	69
66. Peter Winchester 1677/Jean Baikie 1674	70
67. Elizabeth Elphinstone 1680/Thomas Loutit	72
68. Elizabeth Irving 1681/George Traill	72
69. George Liddell 1681	74
70. John Edmondstone 1682/Elizabeth Mowbray	75
71. Barbara Irving 1682/Mitchell Rendall	76
72. Margaret Hendersone 1683/David Forbes	77
73. Robert Leigh 1683/Hugh Leigh	78
74. David Monroe 1684/Jean Richan	78
75. Patrick Murray 1687/Anna Linay	79
76. Elizabeth Cuthbert 1685/James Wallace 1688	79
77. Nicola Traill 1688/David Covingtrie	80
78. Jean Grahame 1694/David Craigie	81

Chapter 8 The Eighteenth Century — 85
79. Mary Young 1750/John Riddoch — 85
80. James & Janet Spence 1781 — 87
81. The Groat Memorial — 88
82. Traills of Westness & Woodwick — 89

Chapter 9 The Nineteenth Century — 95
83. James Watson 1770-1808 — 98
84. Thomas Smith c1778-1811 — 99
85. George Omond c1760-1813 — 99
86. James Riddoch c1746-1818 — 100
87. Robert Yule 1763-1824 — 101
88. Margaret Riddoch c1740-1825 — 102
89. Malcolm Laing c1763-1818/ Samuel Laing 1780-1868 — 103
90. George William Traill 1792-1847 — 106
91. William Logie 1786-1856 — 107
92. James Robertson 1799-1876 — 108
93. James Stuart 1834-1883 — 111
94. William Balfour Baikie 1825-1864 — 112
95. John Rae 1813-1893 — 115
96. Charles Clouston 1800-1884 — 118
97. Thomas Peace 1832-1892 — 119

Chapter 10 The Twentieth Century — 121
98. Buckham Hugh Hossack 1832-1902 — 121
99. George Thoms 1831-1903 — 122
100. Frederick William Traill-Burroughs 1831-1905 — 124
101. James David Marwick 1826-1908 — 127
102. Robert Garden 1846-1912 — 127
103. Margaret Jolly 1856-1938 — 129
104. Pat Shearer 1914 — 129
105. Benjamin David Craigie Bell 1859-1915 — 130
106. Thomas Clouston 1840-1915 — 131
107. Archibald Garden Robertson 1898-1917 — 132
108. William Baikie Watson 1918 — 133
109. Great War Memorial — 134
110. James Scarth Spence Logie 1820-1920 — 138
111. Margaret Manson Graham 1860-1933 — 139
112. HMS Royal Oak 1939 — 140
113. Alfred Baikie 1861-1947 — 141
114. Caroline Cumming Spence 1879-1924 — 142
115. Andrew James Campbell 1875-1950 — 143
116. William Barclay 1888-1958 — 144
117. P. C. Flett 1878-1960 — 145
118. Harald Leslie 1905-1982 — 146
119. R. A. A. S. Macrae 1915-1999 — 147

Poets' Corner **148**

120. J. Storer Clouston 1870-1944   149
121. John Mooney 1862-1950   150
122. Hugh Marwick 1881-1965   151
123. Edwin Muir 1887-1959   152
124. Robert Rendall 1898-1967   154
125. Eric Linklater 1899-1974   155
126. Stanley Cursiter 1887-1976   157
127. George Mackay Brown 1921-1996   160

Glossary   **163**

Abbreviations   **164**

Appendix: The Windows of St Magnus Cathedral **165**

Index   **167**

Endnotes   **175**

LIST OF ILLUSTRATIONS

Figure 1	Plan showing position of memorials	x
Figure 2	Paplay tomb	14
Figure 3	Paplay graveslab	14
Figure 4	Arms of Steven Paplay	14
Figure 5	Gravestone of MF	21
Figure 6	Depiction of St Michael fighting Satan	23
Figure 7	The Seal of the Chapter of Orkney	26
Figure 8	The Seal of James Law, Bishop of Orkney 1605-1615	38
Figure 9	The Seal of George Graham, Bishop of Orkney 1615-1639	39
Figure 10	The Seal of Andrew Honeyman, Bishop of Orkney 1664-1676	41
Figure 11	The Seal of Murdoch Mackenzie, Bishop of Orkney 1676-1688	43
Figure 12	Arms of the current Chief of Clan Marjoribanks	47
Figure 13	Extract by Arthur Buchanan of Sound, Sherriff Depute of Orkney, registering sheep mark for Mitchell Rendall of Breck, 1668.	76
Figure 14	1769 floor plan of the nave	96
Figure 15	Plan of nave showing burials 1792-1824	97

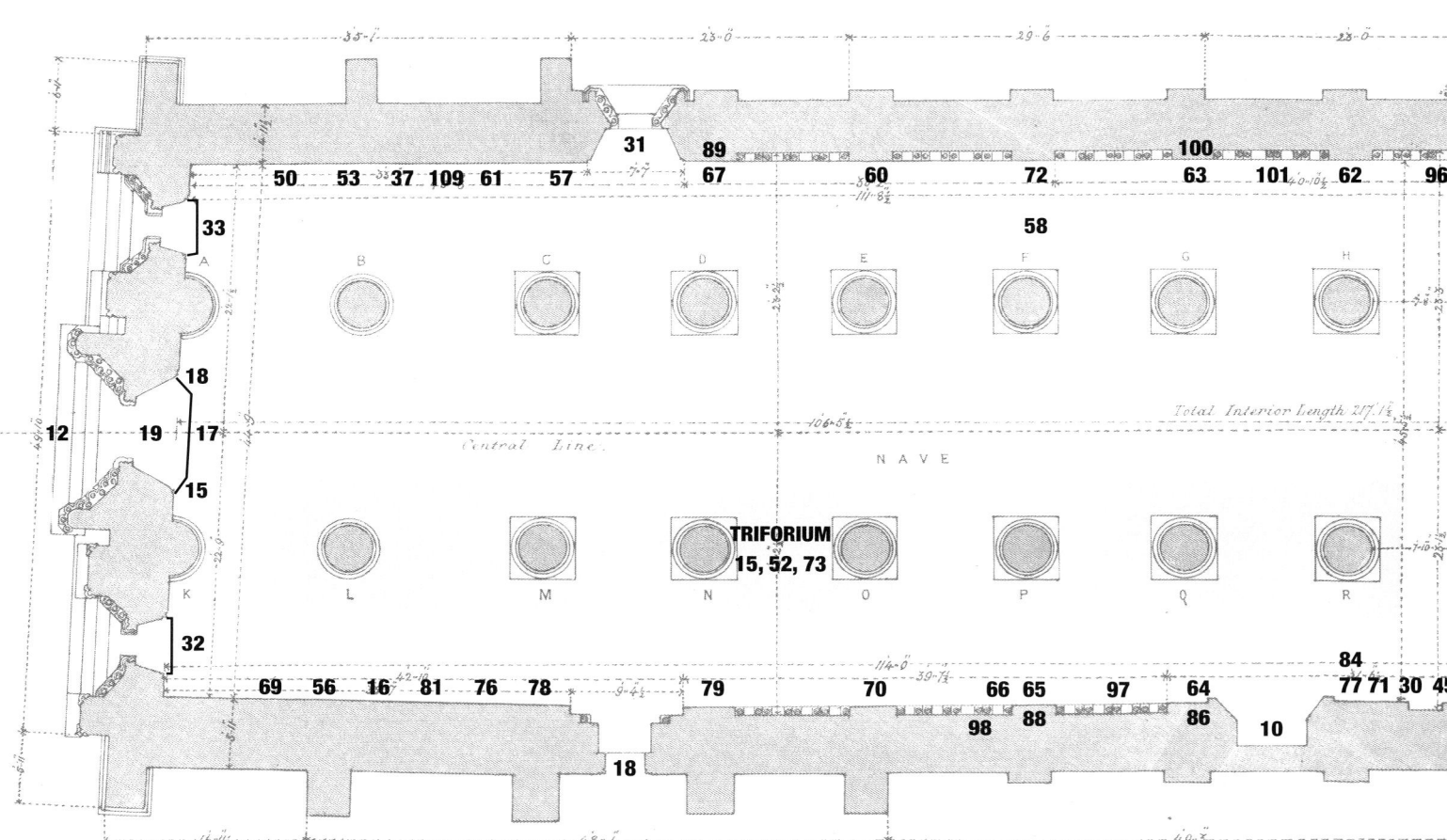

Figure 1 Plan showing position of memorials.

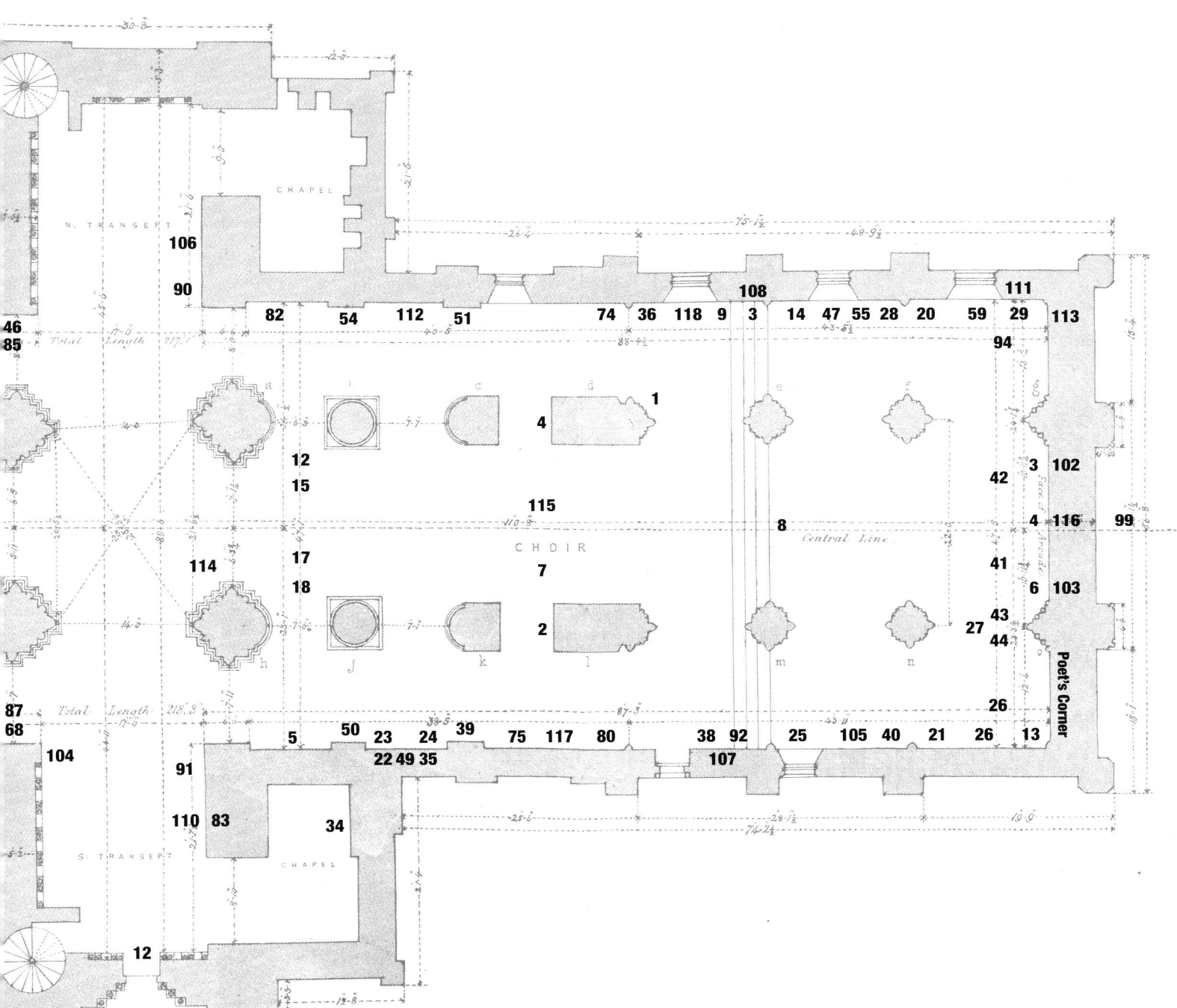

INTRODUCTION

St Magnus Cathedral has been at the heart of the Orkney community for nearly 900 years and has fulfilled an amazing variety of functions in that time. These include being a place of pilgrimage, a sail store, a place to conduct business, a stronghold, a stable, a barracks, a parliament, a court, a prison, a burial site, a drinking den, a library, a wood store, a place to elect councillors, a concert hall, a place of worship and a major visitor attraction. It has also seen murder take place within its hallowed walls.

The focus of this book is the vast number of memorials and dedications the building has accrued over the centuries. It seeks to throw some light on the people being commemorated. Their stories provide a link, not only with the history of the Cathedral, but also the wider history of Orkney and beyond during the last 1000 years.

The people commemorated within the Cathedral were, in the main, the elite of Orkney society. Many were decision makers, being part of the church, earldom or town council. Just as Earl Rognvald traded in his younger days, many of these people were also merchants, who traded across the North Sea, exporting Orkney produce and bringing back commodities Orkney did not have, notably timber. In later centuries, some indulged in the illicit activity of smuggling. With the guilds having the right of a seat on Kirkwall Town Council, tradesmen are also well represented, their professions occupying a higher status in former times than perhaps they do today.

The gravestones preserved within St Magnus Cathedral are only a fraction of the many that were at one time inside the building. The gravestones were laid flat over the burial plots and, over time, their surfaces wore away with the tramping of many feet. Following the Reformation, around 1560, the rich adornments of the Catholic era were removed or covered over and the choir was used as the place of worship. The nave, along with the crossing, was screened off and used for burials until well into the nineteenth century. Between 1794 and 1823 alone, there were 138 interments. In the mid nineteenth century, the Government took over the building and dug up all the graves, placing the bodies in a communal grave in the churchyard. Any tombstone from which the inscription had worn away was discarded and, once the new floor had been laid, those remaining were erected around the inside walls of the Cathedral. In this way, some of the best examples of sixteenth and seventeenth century gravestones to be found in Britain have been preserved. In his monumental book, *Kirkwall in the Orkneys*, B. H. Hossack, himself one of the recipients of a memorial in the Cathedral, describes a tombstone thus:

No work of human hands has a more monotonous existence than a tombstone. There it stands recording the name of the occupant of the grave below. The monuments of contemporaries and successors speedily crowd round it, and at length a generation arises to whom the epitaph conveys no information. The memory of the man has gone, and only the name remains. At last the old thing decays into illegibility and crumbles away or is removed. This is the natural history of tombstones[1].

Hossack certainly did his bit to preserve the identity of many of the people commemorated on the gravestones within St Magnus and it is to be hoped that this book adds to his great work.

The memorials described in this book include gravestones, plaques, wood carvings of historical figures, coats-of-arms and window dedications. The figures depicted in the stained glass windows, however, have not been included, but are listed in an appendix. In total, 127 memorials have been documented, commemorating or mentioning more than 300 individuals, not including the 834 names in the *Royal Oak* book of remembrance.

The presence of coats-of-arms has proved invaluable in identifying some of the gravestones in the Cathedral, which have little other identifiable features. Heraldry is the art of designing, displaying and recording arms. They were developed to help identify knights in tournaments or in battle and gradually these designs became more important when they were used in legal documents as seals. As a result, the use of these arms became strictly regulated. Officially, coats-of-arms were awarded to individuals, with modifications made for each new family member down through the generations. A whole new language was created to describe the designs, which, on first reading, seems totally unintelligible. A list of heraldic terms and explanations is included on page xvi.

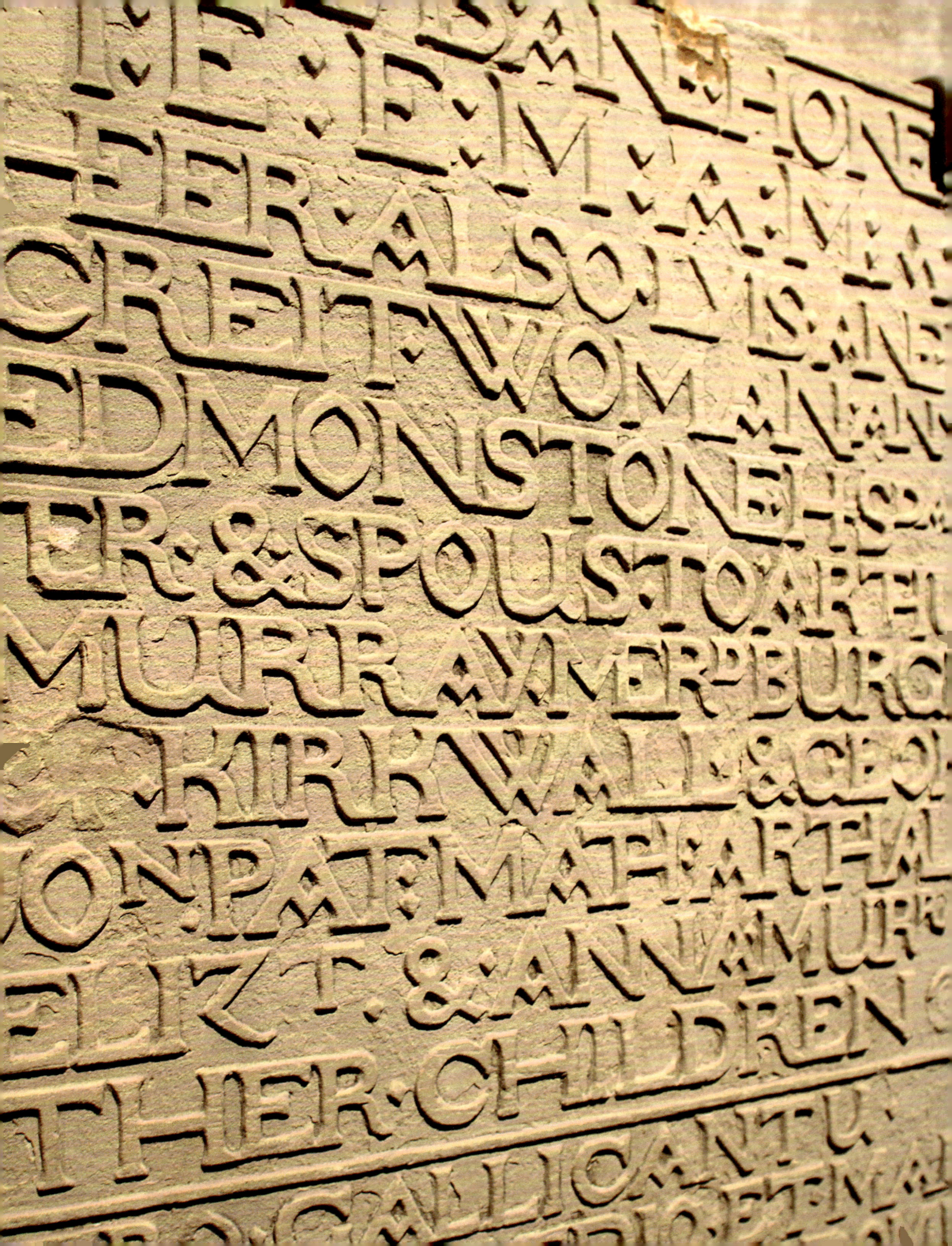

ACKNOWLEDGEMENTS

This book could not have been written without the work of other people. Orkney is fortunate to have had so many talented historians, without whose work I could not have proceeded. B. H. Hossack has already been mentioned. The brilliant historian, Joseph Storer Clouston (120), did much work on the gravestones of St Magnus Cathedral, as well as the coats-of-arms they displayed. In the summer of 1917, during restoration work on the Cathedral, he was able to examine them and take rubbings, while the slabs lay outside. The results of his researches were published in several well-argued articles for the Society of Antiquaries of Scotland.

I could not have done the research had Evan MacGillivray not established the Orkney Room collection or managed to preserve so much of Orkney's written record. The present Orkney Library and Archive has built enormously on Evan's pioneering work and is an excellent place to carry out research. I cannot praise highly enough the helpfulness and patience of the staff and to David Mackie, in particular. I have also to thank the assistance of members of the Family History Society, who, very handily, are based next door to the Archives.

Much praise is also due to the custodians of St Magnus Cathedral, who have taken a great interest in my project and provided much useful information. I never tire of going on a tour of the upper floors of the Cathedral and always come away with a new fact learnt.

Being able to decipher and read old documents is a skill I am unlikely to master. Fortunately there were a number of talented people who worked on Orkney records. In the past, A. W. Johnston and William Spence were notable examples. More recently, Morris Pottinger's editing of the Kirkwall Town Council Minutes from the last half of the seventeenth century has been particularly useful. Reading old documents has become a hobby for Mrs Jennifer Thomson, whom I would like to thank for interpreting a small document relating to Mitchell Rendall of Breck (71).

Thanks must be given to Willie Thomson and Ray Fereday for their advice and encouragement, as well as shining much light on Orkney's past, making research for this book more straightforward. Thanks are also given to Shetland's Archivist, Brian Smith, for clarifying the identity of the coat-of-arms above the west door of the Cathedral.

St Magnus Cathedral contains the gravestones of a number of the associates of the Stewart Earls of Orkney. This period of history has been admirably covered by Peter Anderson in various publications.

For providing descriptions of the individuals on the World War 1 Memorial, I would like to thank Brian Budge. He certainly deserves praise for all the work he has completed on Orcadians who gave their lives in two World Wars. I would also like to thank Richard Shearer for his assistance on this subject matter.

Other people deserving special mention are Elizabeth Miller for her memories of her aunt, Caroline Cumming Spence (114), Margaret Flaws for sourcing a number of Norwegian texts and helping with translations, James Irving for his proof read and for his very useful comments, Victoria Whitworth for some Latin translations and James Miller for agreeing to publish this book.

Last, but by no means least, I would like to thank Alan Bichan for the many hours of proof reading he has undertaken over the past few years. He has made this book a much better read than it otherwise might have been.

Heraldic Terms

Annulet: a circle.

Bend: two lines drawn from dexter chief to sinister base.

Billet: brick-shaped charge.

Bougets: a charge representing a leather vessel for carrying water.

Checky: a field divided into small squares.

Chevron: an inverted V-shape.

Componee: single row of alternating squares.

Counter-componee: two rows of alternating squares.

Cross-crosslet: cross with its ends crossed.

Dexter: the left-hand side looking at the shield or the bearer's right-hand side.

Engrailed: a line composed of semicircular indents, with the teeth or points facing outward

Erased: torn off leaving jagged edges.

Ermine: representation of fur indicated by black spots on a white field.

Escutcheon: shield.

Fess: horizontal band across the middle of a shield.

Fitchy: cut to a point.

Fleur-de-lys: flower of the lilly, associated with the Kings of France.

Goutte: the shape of a tear drop.

Gules: the colour red.

Helm and mantling: helmet with drapery, leaves etc.

Impale: two coats-of-arms joined, very often used to show husband and wife.

In chief: the upper part of the shield.

Invected: the reverse of engrailed

Martlet: a small bird without feet.

Mascle: a lozenge-shaped bearing.

Mullet: five-pointed star.

Pale: broad stripe from top to bottom of the shield.

Passant: shown sideways as walking past.

Pheon: barbed head of a dart or arrow.

Pile: inverted pyramidal figure.

Saltire: St Andrew's cross.

Sinister: the right-hand side looking at the shield or the bearer's left-hand side.

Trefoil: stylised clover.

Vulned: act of wounding, commonly associated with the pelican picking its breast.

CHAPTER 1

The Eleventh Century – Early Beginnings of Kirkjuvagr

By the start of the eleventh century, Orkney was the centre of a powerful Norse Earldom, nominally under the King of Norway, but whose ruling family perpetrated a policy of expansion against its southern neighbours. Powerful earls, such as Sigurd Eysteinsson, Einar Rognvaldsson (Turf-Einar) and Thorfinn Einarsson (Thorfinn Skull-Splitter) gradually expanded their territories to the south and west. As a result, by the start of the eleventh century, Sigurd Hlodvirsson (Sigurd the Stout) controlled not only Orkney and Shetland, but also the Western Isles and large areas of northern and western mainland Scotland.

The eleventh century saw Christianity being gradually re-established in the islands (the indigenous Pictish people the Norse invaders supplanted were Christian). For the sake of a good story, *The Orkneyinga Saga* records that the conversion of Norse Orkney happened in 995, when King Olaf Tryggvasson of Norway, who had been campaigning in Britain for a number of years, was on his way back to Norway. He surprised Earl Sigurd at Osmundwall (Kirk Hope in Walls) and, according to the Saga, Earl Sigurd was enticed at the point of a sword into being baptised.

If anyone could be said to be the founder of Kirkwall, it would be a descendant of Sigurd, Rognvald Brusisson.[2] Kirkwall, or Kirkjuvagr as it was known in Norse times, had already developed as a small trading post in the eleventh century. When Rognvald eventually came back to Orkney as Earl, after many years in Scandinavia and Russia, he founded a church in Kirkwall, in the area of Bridge Street, and dedicated it to his foster father, St Olaf (1). This was the church that gave Kirkwall its name.[3] The parish name of St Ola also comes from this source.[4] The first mention of Kirkwall in the saga is when Rognvald decided to winter there about 1046. "Earl Rognvald took up residence at Kirkwall and gathered in all the provisions he needed for the winter there. He had a great retinue and lived in grand style."[5] Rognvald was eventually killed by his uncle and rival, Thorfinn Sigurdsson, who, by the time of his death, around 1064, had become the most powerful of all the Norse Earls of Orkney.

Olaf II Haraldssonn, the King and patron saint of Norway. In death, his cult status helped unify the country.

1. Olaf II Haraldsson (c995-1030)

Situated in the north side of the choir is the statue of Saint Olaf Haraldsson, King and patron saint of Norway, standing on a dragon-shaped creature with a human head, which symbolises paganism. A plaque gives the following text:

> This statue, a replica of one modelled for the Cathedral of Nidaros, was gifted by the Church of Norway "in the spirit of ancient kinship and lasting friendship" to the Provost, Magistrates and Councillors as representing the inhabitants of the City and Royal Burgh of Kirkwall on the occasion of the octocentenary of this cathedral. July 1937.

Olaf was a warrior king, who continued the work of his

predecessor, Olaf Tryggvasson, by forcibly converting his country to Christianity and unifying it. He was a son of Harald Grenske, petty king in Vestfold, who was burnt to death trying to woo another woman while Olaf was still in his mother's womb. His mother, Asta Gudbrandsdatter, later remarried and had more children, including Harald Hardrada, a future King of Norway. Olaf spent much of his formative years abroad, spending time in England and Normandy, where he was influenced by their Christian laws and values. He was baptised in Rouen, France, and saw it as his destiny to unite Norway and to impose Christian rule. Olaf returned to Norway in 1015, declared himself king and, after some forceful persuasion, managed to unite the various petty kingdoms under his rule.

Olaf was able to assert some authority over the Orkney Earldom when Earls Brusi and Thorfinn failed to agree to the division of the earldom. Both earls visited Norway and appealed to King Olaf, who gave each a third, forfeiting the remaining third to the crown. Unable to maintain direct rule, King Olaf entrusted the royal third to Earl Brusi, but kept the earl's son, Rognvald, as a guarantee of his obedience.[6]

In uniting the kingdom and imposing his rule, Olaf created many enemies and was forced to flee Norway when many Norwegian nobles supported the invasion of their own country by Canute the Great of Denmark and England. He tried to regain his kingdom in 1030, helped by his foster son, Rognvald Brusisson, but was defeated and killed at the Battle of Sticklestad. Five years later, Rognvald Brusisson helped Olaf's illegitimate son, Magnus the Good, gain the throne.

The death of Olaf Haraldsson was followed by an outpouring of veneration and within a year he was canonised. Olaf was much more successful in death than in life, and the cult of Saint Olaf not only unified the country but completed the conversion to Christianity.

Among the shrines to saints in St Magnus Cathedral was one to St Olaf. During renovations, an early fifteenth century statue of Norway's patron saint was found in the building and can now be seen in the Orkney Museum.

The arms of Norway consist of a lion with the battle-axe of St Olaf in its paws. The importance of Orkney in Norwegian history, and vice versa, is amply shown by the presence of the Norwegian lion on Orkney's coat-of-arms.

CHAPTER 2

The Twelfth Century – Construction begins

Conflict caused by disputes within the ruling families of the Orkney Earldom was a recurring theme of the twelfth century, starting with tensions between the cousins, Magnus (2) and Hakon, which led to the killing of the former on Egilsay. It continued in the time of Rognvald Kolsson (4), when all-out civil war broke out for a while.

By the time Earl Rognvald Kolsson gained control of the Earldom, it made perfect sense to choose Kirkwall for the site of the new minster and to move the episcopal seat from Birsay. Trade was growing and Kirkwall was already established as a small urban centre with a central position in the islands and a good natural harbour (the Peerie Sea was then partially open to the sea). Ships could also be brought right up to the construction site, bringing in the supplies of stone.

While the Earldom of Orkney militarily reached a peak in the eleventh century under the warlike Earl Thorfinn Sigurdsson, the twelfth century saw an artistic and cultural high under the rule of Rognvald Kolsson.

The death of Rognvald in Caithness, in 1158, left Harald Maddadsson, who had been made earl as an infant, in sole charge of the Orkney Earldom. Harald was the son of Earl Maddad of Atholl and Margaret, the daughter of Earl Hakon Paulsson, and owed his position as an Earl of Orkney to the complicated alliances into which Rognvald had to enter to gain the Orkney earldom.

Having a knack of intervening disastrously in both Norwegian and Scottish politics, Harald Maddadsson's long reign saw the earldom begin to decline. His support of a rival claimant to the throne of Norway saw Shetland being removed from Orkney control and the imposition of a sysselman or royal official in Orkney. His policy of supporting enemies of the Scottish kings led to a decline in Orkney's influence over the northern part of mainland Scotland.

2. Magnus Erlendsson (c1070-c1117)

St Magnus Cathedral was built as a memorial to Magnus Erlendsson and to house his relics. Magnus was the son of Earl Erlend Thorfinnsson and Thora, daughter of Sumerlidi Ospaksson of Iceland, the union displaying the close connection between Iceland and Orkney at this time. Magnus received a good schooling, which included learning 'holy writings'.[7] In his early manhood, however, he is said to have kept evil company with Viking marauders, participating in their plundering and killing.[8] By the time he was 18, he seems to have moved on from this period of plundering, which possibly had been part of his military training, and, as will be seen, outrightly refused to take part in such Viking activity.

The sons of Earl Thorfinn, Erlend and Paul, ruled the Earldom together for many years and relations were said to have been good between the two brothers until their children, Magnus Erlendsson and Hakon Paulsson, grew to adulthood, rivalries between the two causing friction amongst the ruling families. Their rule came to an abrupt end with the arrival, in 1098, of King Magnus Barelegs of Norway. He took Erlend and Paul prisoner and sent them to Norway, where they both soon died. Magnus Barelegs' young son, Sigurd, was made ruler of Orkney in their place.

Now cup bearer to the king, Magnus Erlendsson, along with his brother, Erling, and his cousin, Hakon, accompanied Magnus Barelegs on his Viking cruise down the west coast of Britain. According to *Orkneyinga Saga,* Erling was either killed in battle during this expedition or died with King Magnus in Ulster a few years later. If we are to believe the saga, Magnus was to show his nonconformity to the standards of the time when he refused to fight in a battle in the Menai Strait against two Norman Earls, who had seized Anglesey from the Welsh. Magnus proclaimed he had no quarrel against these people, so he sat on the deck of his ship, reading from his psalter, while the battle raged about him. This angered the king and soon Magnus took his chance to slip away one night while his ship was anchored off the Scottish coast. He spent time at the court of the Scottish King, Edgar, where he was granted the Earldom of Caithness.

Once King Magnus Barelegs had died and Sigurd had returned to Norway to rule jointly with his brothers, Hakon was able to recover his inheritance by being made Earl of Orkney. Magnus returned to Orkney to claim his share of the islands. For a while they co-operated well together, but relations soon began to break down.

There is reason to believe Magnus left Orkney for a time but his return led to a showdown with Earl Hakon.

The two men, along with their armed followers, met at an assembly or ting. Mutual friends intervened to avoid bloodshed and another meeting was arranged between the two, to be held on the island of Egilsay, to confirm peace between the two sides. Each was to bring two ships, an agreement with which Magnus complied, but when Hakon arrived with seven or eight large warships filled with men, Magnus knew he was unlikely to survive the meeting. He offered Hakon three options, but only the death of Magnus would suffice for Hakon's supporters, who wanted to ensure the islands were ruled without the dissensions caused by a split leadership. Magnus faced his demise with bravery, telling Lifolf, Hakon's cook, to stand in front of him and strike him hard on the head with an axe. Magnus believed it was not fitting for a chieftain to be beheaded like a thief.[9] While Hakon was described in the *Orkneyinga Saga* as a fine administrator, bringing peace to the land,[10] it was Magnus who has been revered and celebrated down through the ages and will continue to be, so long as the building that is his lasting memorial still stands.

Hakon was prevailed upon by Thora, Magnus's mother, to allow her son to be buried within the minster at Birsay. The nature of his death soon led to reports of miraculous cures associated with his grave. Initially Bishop William resisted these stories, not wanting to upset Earl Hakon. It was only after Hakon's death and after supposedly being on the receiving end of one of Magnus's miracles that he had Magnus canonised. The saint's remains were taken to St. Olaf's Church in Kirkwall, before eventually being housed in the new cathedral being built by his nephew, Rognvald. The cult of St Magnus spread to Norway and other parts of the Norse world, his fame making Orkney an important place of pilgrimage. Numerous churches were dedicated to him, including five in Shetland, two in Caithness, seven in Iceland and another St Magnus Cathedral in the Faroe Islands, which was given a finger bone of the saint. There is even a church dedicated to him in London.

Magnus's remains were found in a pillar in the south side of the choir in the early part of the twentieth century, the unmistakable cleavage in the skull confirming the dramatic events of the saga. Most of the bones of the skeleton were found to be present. The missing bones included the mandible, right clavicle, right ulna and most of the hand bones. These would have supplied relics to the many churches dedicated to St Magnus. His height is estimated at 1.75m (5ft 9in), with long forearms and lower legs.[11] This supports his description given in the saga.[12] A plaque now marks the pillar where his remains still lie.

3. Kol Kalisson

At the east end, in what is now St Rognvald Chapel, are three wooden figures carved in 1965 by local cabinet maker, Reynold Eunson. Kol is the left hand figure holding the plumb line to symbolise his involvement in the first phase of construction. There is also a plaque on the north side of the choir, toward the east end, which says:

> GRIMSTAD COUNTY BOROUGH, AGDER, NORWAY FJAERE CHURCH FROM AB. 1150. BUILT IN STONE IN ROMANESQUE AND GOTHIC STYLE.
>
> THE CHURCH WAS BUILT AND OWNED BY THE FJAERE FARMERS.
>
> FJAERE CHURCH IS SITUATED AB. 2 KILOMETRES FROM BRINGSVAERD ESTATE WHERE THE EARL OF ORKNEY, RAGNVALD KALE KOLSSON WAS BORN AND BROUGHT UP. BRINGSVAERD IS BELIEVED TO HAVE CONTRIBUTED RICHLY TO THE BUILDING OF THE CHURCH.
>
> THE DECORATIONS IN THE CORNER OF THIS PLAQUE ARE COPIES OF CARVINGS FROM THE SOUTHERN PORTAL OF FJAERE CHURCH.
>
> THE PLAQUE IS PRESENTED BY GRIMSTAD COUNTY BOROUGH TO ST MAGNUS CATHEDRAL ON THE OCCASION OF THE 850 YEARS ANNIVERSARY OF THE CATHEDRAL'S FOUNDATION, AS A GREETING TO THE PEOPLE OF THE ORKNEYS.
>
> GRIMSTAD WISHES TO HONOUR TWO GREAT MEN. EARL RAGNVALD KALE KOLSSON, WHO INITIATED THE ERECTION AND HIS FATHER, KOL KALESSON, WHO SUPERVISED THE BUILDING OF ST MAGNUS CATHEDRAL FROM 1137.
>
> ST RAGNVALD'S DAY
>
> 20TH AUGUST 1987

Kol Kalisson was an important chieftain in Agder in Norway, who, along with his father, Kali Saebjarnarsson, accompanied King Magnus Barelegs in his military expedition to reinforce Norwegian power over the western seaboard of Britain. In compensation for the death of his father on the expedition, Kol was given the hand in marriage of Gunnhild, Earl Erlend's daughter (Magnus Erlendsson's sister). She came with a dowry of some land in Orkney, including a farm at Paplay.[13] Kol returned to Agdir in Norway, where his son Kali and daughter Ingirid were born and brought up.

Kol Kalisson, St Rognvald's father, who supervised the early stages of building the Cathedral.

in the planning for Rognvald's second expedition.[16] He caused confusion among Rognvald's opponents in Orkney by tricking the watchers on Fair Isle to light the beacon, setting off a chain of beacons in Orkney, and resulting in the muster of Earl Paul's forces. Later, when Rognvald was ready to sail with his forces, Kol arranged for the Fair Isle beacon to be doused, ensuring that Rognvald's arrival in Orkney remained unannounced.[17]

Once Rognvald had been established as Earl of Orkney, Kol supervised the initial building phase of the new cathedral. Masons, who had worked on Durham Cathedral, were procured through Dunfermline Abbey and quarries were opened up at the Head of Holland and on the island of Eday to supply the different colours of sandstone required. Progress was initially rapid until Rognvald's assets began to run out. It was Kol who solved the problem of funding,[18] by proposing that the law be changed to allow the leading farmers to buy back their odal lands, which in the past had been inherited by previous Earls.[19] This they readily agreed to do and there was no lack of funds for the building of the church. By the time of his death, Rognvald had richly endowed the Cathedral with land to provide a good income for the future. Furthermore, a cathedral that housed the relics of so well known and popular a saint could only grow in wealth and prestige. The medieval belief in the power of saints' relics was very strong and those who were cured by Magnus' intervention gave rich gifts to the Cathedral.

Kol was described as a man of exceptional intelligence. This is borne out by the reliance Kali placed on his father. Kali, who adopted the name Rognvald, had strong backing in Shetland, but support in Orkney was very much for Earl Paul, who had rebuffed any thought of sharing the Earldom. It was Kol who told his son to promise to build a stone minster in Kirkwall dedicated to his maternal uncle, Earl Magnus, to help win over hearts and minds in Orkney.[14] Rognvald lacked a patrilineal claim to the Earldom, so Kol's strategy was to use the cult of St Magnus as a means of providing a religiously based legitimacy in Orkney, where Rognvald was at first regarded as a foreign invader.[15] Bishop William, a previous supporter of Hakon's side of the family, became crucial in ensuring the success of this strategy.

Rognvald's first attempt at gaining the Earldom ended in failure, after Paul surprised his forces in Shetland. According to *Orkneyinga Saga*, Kol encouraged Rognvald to try again, pointing out that the support of the Shetlanders had been won. Kol played a lead role

4. Rognvald Kali Kolsson (1103-1158)

Orkneyinga Saga tells the story of the Norse Earls of Orkney from the beginning of the earldom in the tenth century through to the start of the thirteenth century, but the undoubted star of the saga is Rognvald Kali Kolsson, skald, warrior, man of many talents and founder of St Magnus Cathedral.[20]

Kali was the son of Kol and Gunnhild, Magnus Erlendsson's sister, and was brought up in Agder in Norway. When he was fifteen, he joined a trading vessel and sailed to Grimsby, where he met and became friends with Harald Gilli, a future King of Norway. In 1129, King Sigurd granted the same half share of the Orkney Earldom that used to belong to his uncle, Magnus. It was at this time he adopted the name Rognvald, after Rognvald Brusisson, who was regarded by Kali's mother as the most able of all the Earls of Orkney.[21] When Sigurd died, Rognvald helped his old friend Harald Gilli gain the throne and maintain it against his half brother. It was only when Harald Gilli's position was secure and he had confirmed

Saint Rognvald, who started the building of St Magnus Cathedral.

Rognvald's entitlement to a half share of the Orkney Earldom, that Rognvald attempted to take this share from Earl Paul Hakonsson. Rognvald had an uphill struggle. Paul was well established in Orkney, while Rognvald, having been brought up in Norway, was an outsider and unknown to Orcadians. Rognvald had to use all the help he could obtain, proceeding to secure a network of alliances which would isolate Paul. This included the enlisting of support from Frakok and her son, Olvir Rosta in Sutherland.

A two-pronged attack was planned for the summer of 1135, Rognvald coming from Shetland and Olvir Rosta moving up from Sutherland. The plan went awry when weather delayed both fleets, giving Paul time to discover what was afoot. He first of all defeated Olvir Rosta in a sea battle off Tankerness and then surprised Rognvald in Shetland, scattering his fleet. Rognvald tried again the following year and, with the beacon on Fair Isle doused, Rognvald's fleet arrived in Westray without being seen by Paul's forces. Major conflict was avoided by the kidnapping of Paul by the notorious Sweyn Asleifsson, who took him to Atholl, where, under the less than sisterly care of Margaret, wife of Earl Maddad, he was never to be seen again.[22]

Rognvald fulfilled his promise to build a cathedral in Kirkwall and construction was begun in 1137. Rognvald provided not only funds for the erection of the Cathedral, but also endowments for its future maintenance.[23]

By 1151, with construction of the Cathedral sufficiently advanced to allow the housing of Magnus' relics, Rognvald was secure enough to set off on a crusade to the Holy Land, leaving the young Harald Maddadsson in charge. Rognvald sailed with 15 ships and took with him Bishop William, who commanded one of the ships. At least one castle was sacked, a number of vessels and their cargoes were taken and, after a love affair or two, the Holy Land was reached, where Rognvald bathed in the Jordan and visited Jerusalem. On the way back, they left their ships at Constantinople, visited Rome and returned to Norway overland. The expedition was a remarkable achievement, being testament to their navigational skills and knowledge of the then known world.

On his return to Orkney, Rognvald became embroiled in the War of the Three Earls. Erlend Haraldsson (5) had staked his claim to the Earldom. Being a son of a previous earl, he had a much stronger case than either Harald or Rognvald. After a number of changing alliances, Erlend eventually came off worst and was killed by the forces of Harald and Rognvald. With peace restored, Rognvald continued to rule in partnership with Harald.

In 1158, Rognvald was killed on a deer hunting trip in Caithness by Thorbjorn Klerk, whom Rognvald had recently banished and declared an outlaw. Thorbjorn had been foster father to Earl Harald and was one of his closest advisors. This placed Harald in a difficult position, but he did not intervene when retribution was being carried out on Rognvald's slayers.[24] Rognvald's body was taken back to Orkney and buried in the magnificent building he had started. He was canonised in 1192, with his relics being exhumed and placed on display alongside those of his saintly uncle. Rognvald met all the criteria to attain saintly status. He was very popular among his people, had provided the ecclesiastical community with a magnificent benefaction and had met a violent death as an innocent victim. His continuing popularity among the Cathedral community is shown by the placing of his statue on Bishop Reid's extension to the Bishop's Palace in the 1550s.[25]

His relics, consisting of a cranium minus the face and some other skeletal bones, were found in the early nineteenth century in a pillar in the north side of the choir. At first, they were thought to be those of Magnus, until his relics were found a century later in the opposite pillar on the south side of the choir. Examination of Rognvald's bones reveal that he was stockier than his uncle and slightly shorter, a height of 1.72m (5ft 8in) being estimated.[26] A plaque now marks the pillar where his remains are found. One of the aspects for which St Magnus Cathedral is unique is that it holds the remains of both its founder and the person to whom it is dedicated. Of the three wooden carvings in St Rognvald Chapel, Rognvald is the middle figure, who holds the model of the Cathedral as it was first envisioned, complete with twin towers at the west end.

5. Erlend Haraldsson (Earl of Orkney 1151-1154)

In a recess in the south wall of the choir, beneath the Cathedral's notorious prison cell, known as Marwick Hole, is buried the remains of what may be Erlend Haraldsson. A small card says:

> The burial place of Earl Erlend Haraldsson, who was slain by the forces of Earl Rognvald Kolsson in a sea fight off Damsay during the night of the 2nd December. He was buried here on the 23rd December 1154.

Erlend was the grandson of Earl Hakon Paulsson. According to the saga, his father, Earl Harald Hakonsson, had died when he seized a shirt meant for his half-brother, Earl Paul, but which had been poisoned by his mother, Helga, and her sister, Frakok.[27] The two rather sinister ladies were banished from Orkney and Erlend was brought up in Sutherland by Frakok. Being the son of a former earl, Erlend had a very strong claim to the earldom and he received support from King David of Scotland, who gave him half of Caithness.

While Rognvald was away on his crusade to the Holy Land, Erlend challenged Earl Harald for control over the earldom. A truce was fixed between the two, in which it was agreed that Erlend should go to Norway to seek Rognvald's share of the earldom from the king. Erlend's claim was eventually rejected by King Eystein, but he was given Harald's share instead. When Erlend returned to Orkney, he was reconciled with Sweyn Asleifsson, the two having been on bad terms since the killing, by Sweyn, of Frakok in Helmsdale. Sweyn agreed to help Erlend in his bid for power and, to begin with, was successful in ousting Harald from Orkney.[28]

Rognvald's return in the winter of 1153 saw him at first making an alliance with Erlend. Rognvald had little choice as he had come to Orkney ahead of his own forces, who would only return the following summer. The situation, however, soon changed when Rognvald came face to face with Harald. The bonds between the two were strong and they agreed to join forces against Erlend. After both men had narrowly escaped, following surprise attacks by Erlend and his forces, they, in turn, surprised Erlend on his ship moored at Damsay in the Bay of Firth. Sweyn had gone to Sandwick on other business and the young Erlend had been drinking heavily, resulting in such a state of drunkenness he could not be roused. During the attack, one of Erlend's men eventually picked up his comatose leader and escaped overboard. Erlend was later found dead with a spear through his body.[29] It is thought he was taken to St Magnus Cathedral and buried in the building.

We cannot be sure of the identity of the body buried in the south choir wall. The saga is very vague on the subject, merely saying that Erlend's body was "taken to church".[30] The grave was discovered during the renovations carried out in the early part of the twentieth century. It is 4 feet 8 inches long, 3 feet 9 inches from the floor, covered by a lintel 5 feet 8 inches long and is protected in the front by six blocks of red freestone.[31] The skeleton inside was confirmed to belong to a young man and it was speculated at the time that it might belong to Erlend Haraldsson.[32]

6. Bishop William I the Old (Bishop of Orkney c1102-1168)

Bishop William the Old is represented by two wooden carvings in the Cathedral, one on the north side of the organ screen and the other at the east end, in St Rognvald Chapel, the figure of a bishop standing next to the carving of St Rognvald.

William was reputedly the first resident Bishop of Orkney (previous incumbents were probably missionary bishops) and was possibly educated in France, being described in the *Orkneyinga Saga* as a 'clerk of Paris'. His origins have sparked much speculation, but it seems likely that he had local connections.[33] According to *Orkneyinga Saga,* William was bishop in Orkney for an incredible 66 years. Given that he died in 1168, William must have been consecrated at a very young age.

Bishop William may well have played a part in the dramatic events on Egilsay, which led to the death of Earl Magnus Erlendsson. William was likely appointed Bishop of Orkney by the Norwegian monarchy and was not the official choice of the Catholic Church. Control over the Orkney church at this time was being contested between the archbishops of York, who claimed supremacy over Scottish bishops, and those of Hamburg-Bremen, who had responsibility for Scandinavia.[34] The introduction of a rival bishop may have precipitated the conflict between Hakon

William the Old, Orkney's first resident Bishop.

and Magnus that eventually led to Magnus' death on Egilsay.³⁵ While William's episcopate seat at this time was still at Birsay, references in the *Orkneyinga Saga* would indicate that, at least some of the time, he resided on Egilsay.³⁶ It seems inconceivable, therefore, that the bishop did not participate in that fateful meeting on his island home. William's involvement in the events leading to Magnus' death may have been deliberately omitted from the sagas in order to conceal his connection with the saint's murder.³⁷ It would have been unseemly for the bishop who canonised Magnus to have been associated with his killing.

After the death of Magnus, William initially resisted the growing cult surrounding his remains. It was only after William visited Norway in 1134 that he changed his position. It is very likely that he was drawn into Rognvald's plans to obtain his share of the earldom and, importantly, his vow to build a magnificent stone minster in memory of his martyred uncle, Magnus. The *Orkneyinga Saga* says William was struck blind at the church in Birsay and only regained his sight after praying to Magnus and promising to translate his holy relics to Kirkwall.³⁸ This he did and Magnus was canonised in 1136, with his remains being taken up and set over the altar on the 13th of December, which became his feast day. The day normally set aside to remember him, however, is 16th April, the date of his death.

William's change of heart certainly paid dividends. As well as construction work beginning on the new minster for his episcopate seat, building work also started on a residence for the bishop in Kirkwall.³⁹ This was a rectangular-shaped, single storied hall. Only the foundations of the original Bishop's Palace can be seen today.

In 1151, William, who then must have been an old man, accompanied Rognvald on his crusade and was given command of one of his ships. This was essentially a military expedition under the guise of a religious pilgrimage.

William survived Rognvald by another ten years and was buried in the Cathedral.

His tomb was discovered during nineteenth century renovations in a small stone cist on the north side of the choir between the two east-most pillars. A number of artefacts were recovered, including a bone handle and an inscribed lead plate saying, "Here lies William the Old of happy memory, the first bishop".⁴⁰ It is a matter of great regret that his remains were not treated in the same manner as those of Rognvald and Magnus. As a result of subsequent renovations, his bones were removed from the building and buried in the kirkyard to the north of the Cathedral nave, mingled with the bones of other Kirkwall residents.⁴¹

CHAPTER 3

The Thirteenth Century – Norse Power Wanes

Earl Harald Maddadsson was succeeded by his sons, John and David, who ruled jointly until David's death in 1214. John was the last Norse Earl of Orkney, who came to a rather pathetic end in Thurso in 1231, being killed in a drunken attack by the sysselman, Hanef Ungi. It took a number of years before the succession was resolved in favour of a Scottish family in Angus. The reasons for this choice are unknown but several theories exist.[42]

Building work on the Cathedral continued under the dynamic Bishop Bjarni, with the construction of an extended east end, nave and north and south transepts. Two new chapels were also built and the tower and steeple were erected above the central crossing, which had to be rebuilt after a probable failure of the original crossing. The central tower was probably completed during the episcopate of a subsequent bishop, Henry, a one-time Cathedral canon. Work seems to have stopped around the middle of the thirteenth century and would not be restarted to any great extent for another couple of hundred years.[43] Impetus may have been lost as a result of Bishop Henry's involvement with the 1263 Norwegian expedition (see 8) to reassert authority over the Hebrides and Man, and with subsequent negotiations with the Scots.

The latter part of the century saw intense diplomatic activity with Norway over the Scottish Royal succession, following the death of Alexander III, who died prematurely after falling off his horse. The only surviving descendant was Margaret, the infant daughter of King Erik of Norway. This little princess, who was known as the Maid of Norway, eventually arrived in Orkney in 1290 but tragically died before arriving in her new kingdom, plunging Scotland into years of turmoil, better known as the Wars of Independence.

7. Bishop Bjarni Kolbeinsson (Bishop of Orkney 1188-1223)

On the south side of the organ screen, which was installed in the early part of the twentieth century, is a carving of Bishop Bjarni Kolbeinsson, who played a pivotal role in the development of the Cathedral.

Bjarni was the second son of Kolbein Hruga of Wyre and Herbjorg, the great grand-daughter of Earl Paul Thorfinnsson.[44] Bjarni's father was a Norwegian

Bishop Bjarni has been described as the greatest man Orkney ever produced.

nobleman, closely related to the Kings of Norway, who came to Orkney perhaps as some kind of representative of the king. It is possible that Bjarni was educated at the Benedictine abbey of Munkeliv, near Bergen[45] and, following the death of Bishop William II, he became Bishop of Orkney in 1188, his appointment being most likely due to the influence of his second cousin, Earl Harald Maddadsson. Bjarni was responsible for declaring Rognvald's sanctity, with Papal permission, and for moving his relics in the Cathedral from grave to shrine. While the cult of St Rognvald remained very much localised within the Orkney earldom, the promotion of a second saintly earl added enormously to the reputation of Orkney and further enhanced the status of the diocese. Bjarni oversaw several extensions to the Cathedral, including the choir to provide room for a second saintly tomb and also perhaps to house the secular canons required to run the affairs of the diocese.[46]

Like many of his successors (notably Robert Reid), Bishop Bjarni had secular duties to attend to, mainly as a diplomat. Earl Harald Maddadsson was lucky to have his services to help smooth stormy waters after he supported the disastrous invasion of Norway by an army raised in Orkney and Shetland in support of a rival claimant to the throne of Norway. In 1209, Bishop Bjarni was once again sent to Norway to negotiate another reconciliation, this time on behalf of Earls John and David.[47]

Bishop Bjarni continued the tradition of skaldic poetry, which had been adopted by Earl Rognvald. Two major works are attributed to him: the lay of the *Jomsvikings* and the proverb poem, *Malshattakvaedi*.[48] Bjarni also had close contacts with the intellectual community in Iceland and it is very probable that the Orkneyinga Saga was written at this time. Iceland's oldest use of a seal comes from a signet ring, bearing a raven, given by Bishop Bjarni to a wealthy chieftain in the far northwest of Iceland.

There is evidence that Bjarni may have inaugurated a church school in Kirkwall, which later became Kirkwall Grammar School and was supported by revenues derived from the island of Wyre, where he was brought up[49]. This endowment became known as the Prebend of St Peter, possibly named after the little Norse church in Wyre, dedicated to St Peter.[50]

Bjarni was a regular visitor to Bergen and his last known visits relate to the subject of the next memorial, Hakon Hakonsson. In 1218, Bjarni was present with all the Norwegian bishops at the great meeting of notables in Bergen, gathered to witness the trial by ordeal of Hakon's mother to prove the future king's parentage.[51] Bjarni was back in Bergen in 1223 for another important meeting, to decide finally on Hakon's right to the throne. It was following this meeting that Bjarni died suddenly and the new king quickly replaced him with a Norwegian bishop called Jofrey[52].

Bishop Bjarni has been described as the greatest man that Orkney has ever produced and many attribute the best architectural features of the Cathedral to his supervision.[53] It is certainly a pity he died away from Orkney as he missed out on being buried in the building he did more than most to progress.

8. King Hakon IV Hakonsson of Norway (1203-1263)

On the floor of St Rognvald Chapel, just to the east of

King Hakon IV Hakonsson of Norway. This memorial was commissioned by the Norwegian Government on the 700th anniversary of the king's death.

the choir partition, is a marble slab to the memory of this venerable king. The memorial was paid for by the Norwegian Government on the 700th anniversary of his death. The Cultural Attaché from the Norwegian Embassy unveiled the memorial tablet, with Provost James Scott accepting the gift.[54] The slab lies over the position where the king's body lay, before being taken back to Norway. The text of the slab is in Latin and translated says:

Hakon son of Hakon

King of Norway

AD1217-AD1263

He was buried here from the month of Dec AD 1263 to the month of March AD 1264

Hakon was the illegitimate son of King Hakon III and was born shortly after the king's death in 1203. For some time there had been internal conflict in Norway, exacerbated by confused succession laws. Hakon's mother had to prove his parentage by trial of ordeal and Hakon's right to the throne was only recognised in 1223. It was not until 1240 that Hakon's position was secure, after his main rival, Earl Skule, had been put to death.[55]

Hakon was then able to stabilise his country and bring to it a level of prosperity not witnessed for many years. He was also able to concentrate on extending his dominions abroad, in particular making a sustained effort to break down Iceland's independence. By 1261, Greenland had capitulated to Norwegian pressure and Iceland the following year. Ironically it was one of Hakon's staunchest opponents in Iceland, Sturla Thordarsson, who was commissioned to compile the king's biography after his death.[56]

Hakon's possessions in the Hebrides and the Isle of Man were coming under pressure from an increasingly aggressive Scotland. A number of small expeditions had been sent to keep control over the area, but in 1262 news arrived in Norway of an attack on Skye with reports of atrocities carried out by the Scots. The Norwegian levy was called out in the spring of 1263.[57]

The impressive expedition of 100 ships, led by the king, was joined in the trip across from Bergen by Earl Magnus III and Bishop Henry of Orkney. Particularly impressive was Hakon's own ship, the *Krossuden*, which had room for nearly 300 men.

In August, after securing the submission of Caithness, the fleet sailed west. Initially the expedition met with success, with Hebridean allegiance being restored and reinforcements arriving from the King of Man. The fleet based itself near Arran and negotiations were opened with the Scots, but it soon became apparent that they were stalling for time, hoping the change of season would force the Norwegians' withdrawal. Hakon broke off negotiations and started raiding, but the Scots' strategy began to work when a powerful south west gale struck at the start of October and lashed the fleet. Much superior Scottish forces won the subsequent Battle of Largs but it was hardly the great victory they claimed. The lateness of the season forced Hakon to withdraw without the diplomatic settlement he wanted.

By the end of October, Hakon was back in Orkney with twenty ships, allowing the remainder of his fleet leave to return home. With his health deteriorating, Hakon decided to overwinter in Kirkwall, staying at the Bishop's Palace. The *Hakonar Saga* gives a very moving account of his last days. He went to St Magnus Cathedral and prayed at the shrine of St Magnus. Once confined to bed, he had the sagas read to him, including the *Heimskringla*, written by Snorri Sturlasson, Sturla Thordarsson's uncle, whose murder Hakon had ordered some twenty years previously. Hakon died on 18th December and was temporarily laid to rest in St Magnus Cathedral until the following spring, when his body was taken back to Bergen for burial.

In the triforium of the Cathedral is a limestone coffin, which was obviously meant for someone of importance. Its intended purpose will perhaps never be known, but it is possible that the coffin once held Hakon's body. Interestingly, there are marks on the side of the coffin, which are thought to be from swords being sharpened against the stone of the sarcophagus for good luck.[58]

9. Thirteenth Century Warrior Grave Slab

The oldest gravestone in the Cathedral, estimated to date from the thirteenth century, is to be found on the north side of the choir, near the St Magnus pillar. The stone has been broken or cut along one side, but what can be seen are a sword and a cross on a base of three steps. The cross head is circular with three projecting

The oldest gravestone in the Cathedral.

arms, each shaped like fleur-de-lys. In the cross head is a deeply incised pattern, which is a common religious symbol found throughout Europe, being used by early Christians to represent Jesus. A similar pattern can be seen on a stone near the Paplay Tomb (10). The carving is very faint and a torch is required to reveal its detail.[59] When the antiquarian, Sir Henry Dryden, studied the slab in the nineteenth century, he found on the opposite side of the cross from the sword, a shield with a bordure (a band around the edge) and no charge.[60] The initials PC or TPC, carved above the cross, are thought to have been added at a much later date when the slab was likely to have been reused.[61] The geometric pattern was also likely to have been added in post-Reformation times to detract from the popish cross.

CHAPTER 4

The Fourteenth Century – The Black Death

The middle of the fourteenth century saw an event which had a catastrophic impact on Orkney and seriously weakened Norway's ability to hold on to its overseas dominions. The onslaught of the Black Death in Orkney is recorded in a brief entry in the Icelandic Annals and it is known from later rentals that much land went out of cultivation.[62] The effect in Norway was more marked, with the country losing between a third and a half of its population.[63] The plague was no respecter of social position and the nobility in Norway was decimated. By the end of the century political power had shifted across the water to Denmark, with the amalgamation of the crowns. The scarcity of clergy in post-Black Death Norway accelerated the infiltration of Scots into the ruling class in Orkney.

The death of Earl Magnus V, around 1321, saw the end of the Angus line, with the earldom eventually passing to Malise, Earl of Strathearn. With five daughters and no male heirs, a complicated succession dispute followed his death around 1350 which took nearly 30 years to resolve, when Henry Sinclair was installed as Earl of Orkney, Henry being a son of Isabella, eldest daughter of Earl Malise's second marriage.

The Sinclair era saw Orkney pass into the hands of one of Scotland's most powerful families, whose seat was at Roslin in Midlothian. Henry, the first Sinclair Earl of Orkney, seems to have been responsible for the building of a castle on the shores of the Peerie Sea in defiance of Norwegian royal decree. This castle would play a significant part in events in Orkney over the next couple of centuries. It was originally built as a tower house 'on the Scottish pattern',[64] around which a strong curtain wall, linking blockhouses at each corner, was added at a later date.

10. The Paplay Tomb.

Built into the south wall of the nave is a very impressive arched-tomb with a recumbent slab lying loose in the recess. This slab is thought to have been originally located elsewhere.[65] Above the arch is a shield with three gouttes (tear drops). A similar design, though this time with the points of the gouttes converging, is also carved on the recumbent slab, beneath a helmet.

The identity of these memorials has inspired much interest and speculation. Such an imposing tomb

The Paplay Tomb has prompted considerable academic interest and speculation. The traditional story is that it was built by a husband to thwart his nagging wife's promise to dance on his grave.

Paplay arms on the tomb.

Paplay graveslab.

could only have been erected for someone of great importance, for example an earl or bishop, though the lack of any religious insignia would seem to rule out the latter. Indeed the nineteenth century antiquarian, Sir Henry Dryden, who made a close study of St Magnus Cathedral, thought the tomb belonged to a member of the Strathearn family. A seal of Gilbert, Earl of Strathearn, from about 1200, bears nine gouttes reversed on the shield.[66] Storer Clouston (120) dismissed Dryden's theory and, instead, linked the coat-of-arms on the tomb and grave slab to the Paplays, through the identification of a later seal, attached to a court record from 1584, belonging to Steven Paplay.[67]

Fig.2 Paplay Tomb   Fig.3 Paplay graveslab   Fig.4 Arms of Steven Paplay

Given the similarities in the heraldic shields of the tomb and graveslab, two closely related individuals are being commemorated. Today the tomb and gravestone are described as belonging to two 'Paplays', but it has to be remembered it would be at least a century after their lifetime before the earliest surviving records of the surname appear.

Expert opinion on the architecture of the tomb and the style of the heraldic shields has estimated the date of the tomb as the fourteenth century and, more specifically, the latter half of that century.[68] The slab is thought to be slightly earlier. Having ruled out an earl or bishop, Clouston speculated Lawmen might be the recipients of these memorials. The Lawman presided over the Lawting or head court and was the chief magistrate, acting as the principal spokesman and representative of the island community. The name Sigurd of Paplay crops up in a document from 1369, describing the arbitration of a dispute between the Bishop of Orkney and the King's chief official or sysselman in Orkney. The arbitration was carried out under the authority of the Lawman and Lawting. In 1338 Sigurd Sigvatsson was Lawman of Orkney and before that his father Sigvat Kolbeinsson was Lawman in 1325. Clouston speculated that Sigurd Sigvatsson and Sigurd of Paplay could be the same person. The estimated date for the tomb is consistent with the time period for both men. Similarly the date of the slab fits with the time period of Sigurd's father, Sigvat Kolbeinsson. At that time, it would have been sufficient for the two Lawmen to be identified by their distinctive seals carved on the tomb and the slab.

More is now known about these two individuals than in Clouston's day, which casts doubt on any link with Paplay. Sigvat Kolbeinsson belonged to an aristocratic family based in Bergen, which is described as being related to Bishop Bjarni Kolbeinsson. One of Sigvat's brothers, Einar, was abbot of Munkeliv Abbey, thus continuing the family connection with that religious institution. This link with Bjarni, who was related to Earl Paul, is at odds with the Paplays, whose link is very much with the Erlend dynasty, a previous Sigurd of Paplay having married Erlend's wife, Thora, the mother of St Magnus. The surviving seals of Sigvat's brothers, Olav and Jon, along with Sigvat's son, Gunnar, bear no resemblance to that shown on the tomb or grave slab.[69]

There is still, however, the strong possibility that the Sigurd of Paplay mentioned in the 1369 agreement is the person being commemorated by the tomb. This document describes how relations between the bishop and sysselman had deteriorated to such an extent that violence had arisen between their respective supporters.[70] A Commission was set up consisting of representatives of both parties and members of the Lawting. Both sides agreed to abide by the decision of the Commission, which resulted in the bishop having to pay the sysselman 141 gold coins plus all the butter he had impounded in his store.[71] Both sides had to release all those who had been arrested as a result of the dispute and restore their property. The bishop was instructed to have "good native men in Orkney and Shetland to serve him", a warning against employing Scottish clerics. Another decision of the Commission was that the bishop and the 'rikest men' (i.e. the members of the leading families who, by tradition, comprised the Lawting) should be first and foremost in all counsels. It would seem that the local Commissioners, among them Sigurd of Paplay, took the chance to speak out and gain some control. The agreement has been described as a home rule declaration aimed at curbing the controls exercised by the sysselman on behalf of remote government in Norway.[72] The Paplay tomb could, therefore, be seen as a memorial to a prominent Orkney politician of the Norse era, who did his best to preserve Orkney's autonomy. Moreover, with a family link going back to St Magnus himself, this Sigurd of Paplay had a strong case for having such a magnificent tomb in a cathedral dedicated to his distant relative. It is also perhaps worth pointing out that an important element of the endowment set up for the maintenance of St Magnus Cathedral, the Prebend of St John, consisted of teinds from the lands at Paplay in Holm.

The traditional story of the Paplay Tomb was that a husband, whose nagging wife had threatened to dance on his grave, built this low arched tomb in the wall to prevent her carrying out her threat. It was also supposed that a passage led outside from the tomb. Interestingly, Sir Walter Scott used this information on the passage for his novel *The Pirate*, providing the means for Norna of Fitful Head to secretly enter the Cathedral. The tomb was first opened by Sir Henry Dryden in 1846 but nothing was found. A deeper trench was dug on 15th November 1847, going down five feet three inches below the base of the pillars. A witness of the time said, "a few bones were found in the upper part of the earth, more than the bones of one or even two human beings, but there was no stone coffin, no pieces of wood, and no vaulted passage to the outside".[73]

CHAPTER 5

The Fifteenth Century – A Change of Ownership

This century saw two very significant events in Orkney. The first was the transfer of power from Denmark to Scotland, in 1468, the result of part payment of a wedding dowry, when King James III married Princess Margaret of Denmark. The Danish king was so penniless he could not afford the dowry. As a result, Orkney was pawned until such a time as the islands could be redeemed. Shetland was thrown in the following year when the remaining dowry could not be raised. It has to be said that there was no sudden break with the past. Trade with Norway continued, Orkney and Shetland merchants enjoying toll free status until 1580.[74] The second event was the elevation of Kirkwall, in 1486, to a Royal Burgh, with power over the city being transferred to the Provost, Magistrates and Councillors. In addition, it was gifted considerable tracts of surrounding land. The pawning of the islands in 1468 had left a vacuum where 'foreigners, forestallers and others' had encroached upon the liberties of the local merchants.[75] The 1486 Charter confirmed privileges that Kirkwall had enjoyed previously, stating that the city 'was erected a long time ago by our noble predecessors in a complete Burgh Royal'.[76] The powers vested in the Town Council included a monopoly of trade regulation, not only within the bounds of Kirkwall, but also throughout the whole County of Orkney. Supported by Royal Charter, the Town Council granted Burgess Tickets whereby the holders were allowed to conduct business as recognised free traders. In return, the holders were stented or taxed, with a proportion going to the Burgh and the remaining to the Crown.

The 1486 Charter included the gift of St Magnus Cathedral to the Burgh of Kirkwall. There is little doubt King James III had the right to give the building away. Previous to 1486, St Magnus Cathedral had been the private property of Earl Rognvald and his successors. In 1470, the Scottish king had acquired, from Earl William Sinclair, the title and rights of the earldom, which included control over the building. It is surprising that he did not give the Cathedral to the Church. It may have been in response to the rivalry between Bishop Andrew (12) and Lord Henry Sinclair, the leaseholder of the earldom and grandson of Earl William Sinclair, that he gave control of the building to a third party. Bishop Andrew does not appear to have objected to this arrangement and it has been suggested that, with church resources having been overextended to complete the west front, he was glad to be rid of any further financial responsibility for the building.[77]

11. Thomas Tulloch, Bishop of Orkney 1418-1461

Thomas Tulloch, Bishop of Orkney 1418 – 1461. It was during his time that the language of administrative documents changed from Norwegian to Scots.

Thomas Tulloch's magnificent tomb has long since disappeared from the Cathedral. There is, however, still a memorial to Thomas Tulloch consisting of his coat-of-arms carved in the west end of the north side choir stalls. The arms consist of three mullets on a fess between three cross crosslets fitchy. These arms are also carved above the inside of the south transept door.

Thomas Tulloch was a native of Angus, being the presbyter of the diocese of Brechin until his elevation to Bishop of Orkney in 1418 by Pope Martin IV.[78] Two years later, he was in Laaland in Denmark tendering his oath of fealty to King Erik III, and was given the governorship of Orkney at a time when David Menzies was acting as guardian for the young Earl William Sinclair.[79] When the unpopular Menzies replaced Tulloch as governor, a list of complaints was sent to the Danish king against his misrule,[80] followed by an appeal to Queen Phillippa, asking that the young Earl (William) be appointed governor.[81]

With the aid of the Chapter of St Magnus Cathedral (19), Tulloch drew up a genealogy to prove Earl William Sinclair's descent from the first Norse Earls to aid William's claim to the earldom, which was finally confirmed in 1434. The surviving text from this *Diploma*[82] suggests that there were extensive sources available in the library of the Cathedral at the time, which must have included versions of various sagas then in existence. The bishop was present in Copenhagen for the ceremony of William Sinclair's formal installation as Earl and sealed the document on behalf of King Erik.[83]

It was in Tulloch's time that the official language for administrative purposes changed to Scots, the last official document in Norwegian being written in 1425.[84] This change reflected the practical reality of the after effect of the Black Death, which led to a lack of Norwegian clerics and left the administration in Orkney being increasingly undertaken by clergy with a Scots background. Both Thomas Tulloch and his successor, William Tulloch, were well trusted by the Danish Crown and represented the country on several occasions.[85]

At the time of Thomas Tulloch, the inside of the Cathedral would have been very different from today, with the walls and ceiling covered in coats of plaster and decorated in rich colour. Part of this medieval floral decoration can still be seen today on the ceiling of the north aisle of the nave near the Mort Brod (58). The centrepiece in the Cathedral was the shrine to St Magnus, and in 1441 Bishop Thomas Tulloch petitioned the Pope to grant indulgences to pilgrims visiting the shrine on certain feast days.[86] The Cathedral also had a proliferation of side altars or prebends dedicated to a variety of saints.[87]

Thomas Tulloch remained as bishop until he resigned around 1461. This was at a particularly difficult time for his diocese, which, in the same year, suffered a devastating attack from Hebridean forces led by the brother of John MacDonald, Lord of the Isles. William Sinclair, who was then with the young King James III, was in dispute with the Lord of the Isles, who took the opportunity to attack Sinclair's domain while he was absent from Orkney. One of the first actions of the new bishop, a relative of Thomas Tulloch, was to write to King Kristian excusing his and the Earl of Orkney's absence from court due to the recent invasion and resultant devastation of Orkney.[88]

Thomas Tulloch died in 1463 and was buried in St Magnus Cathedral. Following the Black Death, people had, not unnaturally, become obsessive about death, with the rich and powerful arranging to be buried under elaborate tombs. Thomas Tulloch was laid to rest in one of the most splendid canopied tombs to be found in Scotland. It was situated in the choir of St Magnus Cathedral, between the easternmost piers of the choir arcade. This became the place in Kirkwall to settle debts and agree business deals; an agreement made at Tulloch's tomb was regarded as binding.[89] The tomb was badly vandalised in the time of Cromwell and the remnants were removed during the mid-nineteenth century restoration. Fortunately, these were preserved and can now be seen in the Orkney Museum.

12. Andrew Pictoris, Bishop of Orkney 1477-c1505

Above the outside of the main west door is a stone-carved shield, with a coat-of-arms of three escutcheons. Confusingly, these are similar to the arms of Sir George Hay of Kinfauns (later 1st Earl of Kinnoul), Lord Chancellor of Scotland, who had a tack of the Orkney Earldom and Bishopric in 1624.[90] The arms above the west door, however, belong to a bishop, as shown by the head of a crozier above the shield. It is thought these arms belong to Bishop Andrew Pictoris, perhaps confirmed by the discovery of an elaborately carved armorial stone at Kebister, in Shetland, belonging to Andrew's son, Henry Phankouth, Archdeacon of Shetland 1501-1529. These arms include two escutcheons in chief, as on the Cathedral stone.[91]

Andrew Pictoris probably came from Saxony, being ordained in the German diocese of Meissen. In a papal letter of 1472 he is described as Andreas Alamani, Andrew the German. He came to Scotland in 1469 in the company of Princess Margaret of Denmark, who had just married King James III of Scotland. Being skilled as a doctor of medicine, he prospered at the Scottish court, becoming James III's physician.[92]

Following the transfer of Bishop William Tulloch to Moray, Andrew became Bishop of Orkney in 1477. This appointment has been described as very appropriate, considering he came to Scotland with the Danish princess, whose marriage gave the Scottish crown rights in Orkney and Shetland.[93] For a time, Andrew was given a tack of the islands and custodianship of Kirkwall Castle, which led to strained relations with Henry Sinclair. Despite the economic conditions of the time, Bishop Andrew found enough money to complete the west end of St Magnus Cathedral, hence the presence of his arms above the west door. It is relatively easy to identify this west extension as it has small lancets instead of the much larger round-headed windows from previous building phases.[94] The completion of the Cathedral was extremely important in stabilising its structure; some of the pillars in the west of the nave were beginning to lean away from the transept owing to the lack of a supporting wall.

In 1494, Henry IV of England issued a safe conduct to Bishop Andrew for travelling through England to foreign parts. As has been said, Andrew had a son called Henry Phankouth. It is possible that, among the business Andrew had in Europe, he was seeking papal dispensations for the defect of his son's birth. He eventually procured letters of legitimization, allowing Henry to become Archdeacon of Shetland in 1501.

Towards the end of his tenure, Andrew was assisted by Edward Stewart (15), who represented the Bishop in disputes with Henry Sinclair and his uncle, Sir David Sinclair of Sumburgh. The appointment of Henry Phankouth as Archdeacon of Shetland was the cause of one dispute, with Sir David Sinclair supporting an alternative candidate, Magnus Herwood, presented by King Hans of Norway and Denmark. Only the intervention of King James IV of Scotland ensured the appointment of the Bishop's son.

The last record of Bishop Andrew was in 1505 when he might have been 85 years old.[95]

CHAPTER 6

The Sixteenth Century – Trouble and Strife

With Henry Sinclair's increasing absence from Orkney on state duties, his brother, Sir William Sinclair of Warsetter (in Sanday), began to act on his behalf. After Henry's death at Flodden, in 1513, Henry's widow received her husband's tack, but effective control in Orkney remained with Henry's brother.[96]

Trouble flared after Sir William's death when relationships deteriorated between his illegitimate offspring, James and Edward (22), and Henry's son, Lord William Sinclair, who came to Orkney to claim his birthright. This led to the Battle of Summerdale, where an army under Lord William and his cousin, the Earl of Caithness, was utterly defeated in Orphir by the Warsetter Sinclairs. It was said that the Earl of Caithness' head was brought back home by the few of his men who escaped, giving rise to the curse, which was still being used in the North Highlands centuries later: *Shuil mhorer Gaol do'Arcu dhuit, gun hian dachi ach en cann - I wish you Lord Caithness' journey to Orkney, only the head to return.*[97]

The victory at Summerdale left the Warsetter Sinclairs in charge of Orkney and Shetland, with the Scottish Government powerless to react. By 1535, James Sinclair styled himself 'Justice of Orkney'. King James V eventually gave in to the reality of the situation and knighted James, legitimised both James and Edward, and gave James a feudal charter of Sanday and Stronsay.[98] Kirkwall was also given a renewal of its Burgh Charter at this time. The Scottish Crown was anxious to resolve the situation in its northern islands and would not have wanted to see them drift back to Scandinavian control.

In 1541, Robert Reid (18) was appointed Bishop of Orkney. Although a major churchman of his day and staunch defender of the Catholic faith, even he could not stem the Protestant Revolution that was sweeping Europe. Scotland was one of the last countries to reject papacy, due, in no small measure, to French influence at the Scottish court.

In 1559, Adam Bothwell[99] became the last Vatican-appointed Bishop of Orkney and a year later the Reformation began in Scotland when the Scots Parliament agreed to break away from Papal Authority and ban the celebration of mass. Bothwell was sympathetic to reform and was able to guide Orkney through a difficult transitional period. However, he brought in his wake a band of particularly avaricious relatives, who were able to take full advantage of the break-up of the Bishopric estates caused by the Reformation.[100] Orkney's traditional and distinctive Norse institutions were doomed, particularly when the arrival of Robert Stewart, bastard son of King James V, and his entourage were added to the mix.

13. MF c1500

At the extreme east end on the south side stands this very attractive red sandstone monument, which has proved very contentious. It shows a shield containing two coats-of-arms above a stepped cross fleury with the initials MF in relief within square panels. The sinister coat-of-arms clearly belongs to Tulloch; three mullets on a fess between three cross crosslets fitchy. With the lack of any text and the presence of a stepped cross, an early date in the sixteenth century has been estimated.

Figure 5 The gravestone of MF   This memorial probably dates to the early 16th century and possibly shows the Flett coat-of-arms, though experts were divided on the veracity of this.

There are two opposing opinions regarding the dexter coat-of-arms. First of all, the author of *Orkney Armorials* (1902), Lieutenant H. L. Norton Smith, identified these arms, three trefoils slipped with a crescent in centre, as belonging to Bothwell.[101] He wrongly identified the initials as MB, having first inspected the gravestones in 1901, when the Cathedral was badly lit, but continued to maintain the arms belonged to Bothwell, saying the gravestone could have been re-used, with the B re-chiselled to make an F.[102]

Clouston, however, identified the crescent of the dexter arms as a drinking horn, a not uncommon charge on Norwegian seals, and suggested that the arms belonged to the Fletts.[103] In 1425, Kolbein Flett attached his seal to the Complaint of Orkney, but unfortunately the seal is too defaced to identify any coat-of-arms. Clouston further mentions Magnus Flett as a witness on a deed in 1480 and 1482, whom he supposed was related to the Fletts of Hobbister. He further hypothesised that the woman Magnus married was Begis Tulloch, a name that cropped up in a deed associated with Sir David Sinclair of Sumburgh,[104] who left much of his Orkney lands in a will of 1506 to William Flett of Hobbister.

14. VP c1522

This gravestone lies on the north side of the choir, toward the east end. The stone, which is in good preservation, has a shield flanked by the initials VP, on which is depicted two keys hanging from a spear between two dice with a dragon at its base. With a lack of inscription, a date in the early part of the sixteenth century is estimated.

It was Dr Craven, Rector of St Olaf's Episcopal Church in Kirkwall (1876-1924) and first President of Orkney Antiquarian Society, who suggested the shield design was an allegorical picture rather than a coat-of-arms. The keys symbolise St Peter, the spear and dice are indicative of the Passion Instruments (symbols of Christ's crucifixion) and the dragon symbolises the power of evil.[105]

Clouston suggests two possible candidates from records of the time. One was a chaplain, Sir William Parquer, mentioned as a witness in 1534 and 1536. The Sir is an ecclesiastic title equivalent to today's Reverend. Clouston's more favoured choice was William Thomas Peterson, who is mentioned in various early sixteenth century documents, which identify him as William of Ness, in Tankerness.[106] His grandfather was Peter of Ness, who is known to have died in or before 1447.[107] William adopted the surname 'Peterson' from his grandfather, so the symbolism on the gravestone for St Peter is very appropriate. Clouston thought that the Petersons and Petries, found subsequently in the parish of St Andrews, were descended from this family.

Clouston later added a bit of colour to the interpretation of this stone after writing about Orcadian involvement in the bodyguard of the French King.[108] Following

This stone is thought to date back to the 16th century and its origins have prompted speculation, including a French connection.

the defeat at Agincourt, in 1415, the French turned to Scotland for help. A Scots army of some six thousand men was sent to France and the advances made by King Henry V of England were stemmed. The French were very grateful and the young, future King Charles VII, who was to owe his crown to the efforts of Joan of Arc, founded an elite Scottish military unit which was to become the personal bodyguard of the Kings of France.

Orcadians appear on the muster rolls of these Archer Guards from very early on, with various members of the Clouston family being recorded, including a former Lawman of Orkney (1422-1425), who was given extra pay to support his elevated position. In addition to symbols of St Peter, the gravestone shows the device of St Michael, which has St Michael slaying the devil in the form of a dragon. This same device was worn by the French kings' Archer Guards. The symbol of St Michael is the balance scale, showing that he will weigh human souls on the Day of Judgement. The tombstone in St Magnus has substituted the angel slaying the dragon with two keys, symbols of St Peter, hanging from the spear but made to look like the balance scales of St Michael. A Guillaume (William) Patrisson is on the muster roll of 1507 and again from 1510 to 1516. Bearing in mind the names Patrick and Peter were interchangeable, it is likely that VP was in fact William Thomas Peterson, who is recorded in Orkney in 1522 as one of several Gudmen[109] (men of the highest social standing) and who may have had a fascinating career as one of the bodyguards of the King of France. His

Figure 6. Typical depiction of St Michael fighting with Satan. The Book of Revelation (12:7-9) ...*there was war in heaven. Michael and his angels fought against the dragon, and the dragon and his angels fought back. But he was not strong enough, and they lost their place in heaven.*

involvement in the French Archers may stem from a family link with the Cloustons, who had several family members registered in the French muster rolls in the latter half of the fifteenth century.[110]

15. Edward Stewart (Bishop of Orkney c1505-1524)

Up in the triforium is a stone with the coat-of-arms of Bishop Edward Stewart. This stone was found on opening an old aumbry in the south chapel of the Cathedral. His coat-of-arms, consisting of a chequered, horizontal band, is also carved on the west end of the north side choir stalls, as well as above the west door on the south side of the nave, and shows he could claim descent from King Robert II of Scotland. They are the same arms as the hereditary Sheriffs of Bute, the first of whom was John Stewart, natural son of King Robert II.[111] A stone bearing these arms was also found built into the walls of the Earl's Palace in Birsay.

The coat of arms of Bishop Edward Stewart shows he could claim Royal lineage from King Robert II.

Edward Stewart was appointed coadjutor (successor) to Bishop Andrew and represented the bishop in his disputes against Henry Sinclair. He became Bishop of Orkney after the death of the elderly Bishop Andrew. Once established as bishop, Edward seems to have spent most of his time outside Orkney, leaving the running of the diocese to his brother, William.[112] In November 1513, he was in Perth, attending a general council to consider the after effects of the disaster that had taken place at Flodden. About this time he dedicated the chapel of King's College in Aberdeen.[113]

It appears that Edward was frequently incapacitated with gout and by the end of 1523 was unable to perform the duties of his office, as shown in a letter from the Duke of Albany to Pope Clement VII.[114]

16. Thomas Murray 1527

Located on the south side of the nave near the west door, this gravestone has a coat-of-arms consisting of a chevron between three mullets and what is possibly a crescent (see 75 for a similar coat-of-arms). Below is a cross on a base of two steps, on which is incised a Z symbol. There is a faint inscription in Latin, which translated says:

> Here lies Thomas Murray burgess of Kirkwall who died 10th April 15(2)7.

The fact that this gravestone has a stepped cross would suggest a pre-Reformation date. Thomas Murray of Garth, who died in 1527, is likely to be the individual commemorated. The gravestone was perhaps later erected by his son Sir Magnus Murray, Vicar of Walls in Shetland, whose initials MM are carved either side of the cross. Various legal documents identify this Thomas Murray and his ownership of Garth, in Stromness Parish. They include a disposition dated May 10th 1567, transferring Sir Magnus Murray of Woodwick's share of Garth to his brother, James.[115] The disposition says that their parents were Thomas Murray and Kathleen Paplay.[116] As on the gravestone, Thomas Murray is often described in these legal documents as a burgess of Kirkwall.[117]

Sir Magnus Murray (again the 'Sir' is an ecclesiastical title) is recorded on a settlement on inheritance, from 1564, for lands in Holm.[118] He held the vicarage of St Ola and the subdeanery, and he had a feu charter relating to the lands of the prebend of Woodwick. He also became the vicar of the Shetland parish of Walls. He was considered competent by Bishop Adam Bothwell to serve in the Reformed Church and was accepted as a reader in 1562. Priests who were found unsuitable or unwilling to serve in the new church were still allowed to keep two-thirds of the vicarage income for their lifetime, the remaining third being part of the stipend paid to the replacement ministers or readers.[119]

This stone was probably erected by Sir Magnus Murray, in memory of his father. Murray junior became the Vicar of Walls in Shetland. The cross on the memorial is more obvious in this photograph than when viewed in 'real life'.

Magnus Murray was thus able to keep all the income of his vicarage of Walls, which was worth £60. He is thought to have died prior to 10th June 1567.[120]

17. Robert Maxwell (Bishop of Orkney c1524-1540)

In the tower are the three great bells of the Cathedral, all provided by Robert Maxwell and cast in Edinburgh in 1528 by Robert Borthwick, who had been King James IV's master gunner at Flodden. Borthwick had been casting weapons at Edinburgh Castle since 1498 and, with King James IV taking a keen interest in armaments, was "master melter of the king's guns" by 1512.

The inscriptions on the bells are as follows:

The treble bell: "Maid be maister robert maxvell, byschop of Orknay, ye second zeir of his consecration ye zeir of gode ImVcXXVIII zeris ye XV zeir of Kyng James ye V be robert borthvyk maid al thre in ye castel of Edyburgh." On a medallion is a figure of St Magnus, on a shield the arms of Bishop Maxwell and on another part of the bell are the letters "I h s". (These letters are the Roman form of the Greek contraction for Jesus).[121]

The second bell: "Maid be maister robert maxvell, bischop of Orknay, in ye second yeir of his consecration in the zeir of god ImVcXXVIII zeiris ye XV zeir of ye reign of King James V." On a medallion attached to the bell is a figure with a sword and under it, "Sanctus Magnus". Below is "robert borthvik". On a medallion are the arms of Scotland and on another part, the arms of Bishop Maxwell. There are also the letters "I h s".

The largest bell, the tenor: "Made by Master Robert Maxwell, Bischop of Orkney, the yaer of God MDXXVIII the year of the reign of King James V. Robert Borthwick made me in the castel of Edinburgh". The following inscription was added, "Taken et brought againe heir by Alexander Geddus marchant in Kirkwa, and recasted at Amsterdam, Jully 1682 years, by Claudius Fremy, city bell caster. It weighs 1450P." On a medallion is a figure with sword and under it, "SCT MAGNVUS". On a raised shield are the arms of Bishop Maxwell.[122]

Robert Maxwell's coat-of-arms can also be found carved on the west end of the south choir stalls as well as inside the main west door. The arms consist of a saltire with an annulet.

Robert Maxwell, son of Sir John Maxwell of Pollock[123], was appointed Bishop of Orkney around 1524 and his arrival in the islands, following his consecration around 1526, coincided with an upsurge in trouble between the Warsetter Sinclairs and Lord William Sinclair, whose followers had taken the Bishop's Palace. Lord Sinclair was instructed by the Lords of Council in Edinburgh to

Bishop Robert Maxwell's coat-of-arms can be found inside the main west door, on the west end of the south choir stalls and in the Cathedral tower on all three bells, which he donated.

relinquish his hold on the Bishop's Palace and have his followers hand it over to the new bishop.

As well as gifting a peal of three new bells for the Cathedral, Maxwell also provided elaborate new stalls for the cathedral clergy.[124] They were richly carved, including arms of former bishops.[125]

It was Robert Maxwell who entertained King James V and Cardinal Beaton, at his own expense, on their visit to Kirkwall in 1540. The king's main objective in making this voyage was to subdue rebellion in the West Highlands and Hebrides, but on his way he stopped in Orkney to make an impressive display of Scottish force and enhance royal authority. While in Kirkwall, the King lodged in a house in Victoria Street, which was owned by the bishop.[126] Maxwell died in the spring of the following year.

18. Robert Reid (Bishop of Orkney 1541-1558)

The coat-of-arms of Robert Reid, consisting of a stag's head, is carved on the west side of the south choir stalls and above the inside of the west door on the north side of the nave. It is thought that his coat-of-arms is also carved above the outside of the door on the south side of the nave of the Cathedral.

Robert Reid was the outstanding churchman of his day and also one of Scotland's leading diplomats. Born around 1495, his father, John Reid of Aikenhead in Clackmannanshire, was killed at Flodden in 1513. Robert had a distinguished academic career, being educated at St Andrews University, before being appointed Cistercian Abbot of Kinloss, and then, in 1531, commendator of the priory of Beauly. In both places he left his mark as a renovator and builder, as he was soon to do in Kirkwall.[127]

In 1541, Reid was appointed Bishop of Orkney, following the death of Robert Maxwell. Once established, he set about renovating the Bishop's Palace, which by this time was in a poor state of repair. He had the Moosie Tooer built, buttressed the western wall of the building, which appears to have been sagging, and fortified the bishop's own apartments with embrasures for firearms defence.[128] Whilst the Palace was being restored, it is likely Reid occupied a house in the Laverock. His coat-of-arms was found in a house in what is now known as Victoria Street.[129] He is also credited with restoring St Olaf's Church, which had been burned down by English marauders. The arched doorway of the church in St Olaf's Wynd is all that now remains. In addition, it is thought he was responsible for the bishop's door on the south side of the nave, and the dungeon, known as Marwick's Hole, is believed to date from his time in office.[130]

In 1544, he produced a formal constitution for the Cathedral Chapter, which provided for the appointment of a provost, archdeacon, chantor, chancellor, treasurer, subdean and succentor, seven other prebendaries, thirteen chaplains and six boy choristers.[131] In it he specified the roles and responsibilities of each office and listed the qualifications required. The principal clergy were required to build manses adjacent to the Cathedral to ensure they did not absent themselves too much. A string of church offices and manses were therefore built on ground reclaimed from the Peerie Sea, opposite the Cathedral. This was the origin of Tankerness House, which started life as the Archdeanery and Sub-chantry (home of the choir master and choir boys).[132] Education was to play an important part, with a new block of buildings for the Grammar School being built near Broad Street (next to the current Spence's newspaper shop). The principal chaplain, known as the Chaplain

Bishop Robert Reid was an important churchman and international diplomat in his day. He was responsible for building the Moosie Tooer in the Bishop's Palace.

of St Peter, was master of the Grammar School, while the Chaplain of St Augustine was master of the Song School.

The reforms were intended to strengthen the diocese against Protestant revolution, then sweeping Europe, and allowed Reid to concentrate on his many other state duties, leaving the running of the diocese in the hands of clergy well qualified for the task. They also had the effect of diverting income away from the parishes into a hierarchy in the Cathedral.[133] There was a token gesture in meeting the widespread need for Bible tuition, with the Provost and Archdeacon being required to preach in the vernacular four times a year within the Cathedral. Despite this, Reid's reforms showed that he was not a leader who gave priority to the spiritual needs of his people.

The revenues of the Prebend of St John, set up for the maintenance of the Cathedral, were put towards the stipend of Cathedral ministers.[134] Instead, Reid set up the post of prebendary of St Mary, which was to take care of the roof and glass of the church, and arrange for repairs to be done at the Bishop's expense. The Burgh Council appear not to have objected to this arrangement and Councillors were probably glad to be rid of the responsibility.[135] With building work nearing completion or not long finished, future maintenance of the building would not have been a big issue at the time. This was, however, to store up problems in the future, particularly during the following century, when the position of bishop would come and go.

Reid's state duties included embassies to the Court of Henry VIII in England, in 1533, and France in 1535-36, when he negotiated the royal marriage of King James V to Madelaine de Valois, daughter of Francis V of France. She sadly died within months of coming to Scotland. His skill as a lawyer saw him succeed, in 1549, to the Presidency of the College of Justice, the supreme court of Scotland. He helped to negotiate a peace deal in 1551 with the young English king, Edward VI. Reid's skill at diplomatic language backfired in 1557 when he helped to broker another peace treaty, this time in the reign of Mary I. The Scots promptly broke the treaty, which led the English to send a force to burn Kirkwall (see 22). Bishop Reid's last diplomatic mission was to France in 1558 to arrange the marriage of Mary Queen of Scots to the Dauphin. He died in Dieppe after successfully concluding his mission. It is alleged that he and his fellow commissioners from Scotland were poisoned.[136]

19. The Seal of the Chapter of Orkney

On the north side of the south choir stalls is a carving of the Seal of the Chapter of Orkney. Another similar carving is found at the main west door entrance. The seal shows three figures, the middle one being St Magnus with sword in hand standing in a church door and two monks kneeling and praying on either side of him. Round the rim is the Latin inscription:

SIGILLUM CAPITULI ORKADENSIS
ECCLESIA SMCTMAGNI

(*Seal of the Orkney Chapter of St Magnus Cathedral*)

Figure 7 The Seal of the Chapter of Orkney (from Craven J. B. 1901, *The Blazon of Episcopacy in Orkney 1421-1688*)

The seal probably dates back to the early days of the Cathedral Chapter, though very few medieval seals have survived from this time.[137] The figure of St Magnus holding a sword, a symbol of his martyrdom, formed a core element of the ensign of office for Orkney bishops over the centuries. Bishop Thomas Tulloch's seal, from 1422, includes this figure of St Magnus with sword.[138] The figure is also seen on the bells of the Cathedral.

The Cathedral Chapter was the college of clerics set up to advise the bishop and, in his absence, to see to the running of the diocese. From an early date, ecclesiastical appointments in Norway were made by the king with little consultation. In 1153, when Cardinal Nicholas Breakspear was organising the setting up of the Archdiocese of Trondheim, under which all the overseas dioceses, including Orkney, would be subject, he prescribed that bishops should be elected by chapters of secular canons associated with their cathedrals. These secular canons were clergy who were not members of any particular order. It was envisaged that there would be twelve canons in each chapter, supported by the tithes of specific parishes in the diocese.[139] Bishop Bjarni (7) appears to have begun to implement the Cardinal's proposals through changes to the original monastic plan of the Cathedral.[140]

For a while, the king continued to make church appointments, for example, replacing Bishop Bjarni with Jofrey. In 1247, however, the chapter of St Magnus Cathedral unanimously elected Henry as

Bishop from its own ranks. He was consecrated in Norway, after having received a special dispensation from the Pope for his illegitimacy, being the natural son of an ecclesiastic.[141] With Jofrey having been in poor health for many years, Henry is likely to have continued overseeing the construction work begun by Bishop Bjarni on the Cathedral. Despite the fact that the Cathedral was founded by Earl Rognvald and remained the property of his successors, it would seem that the supervising of building work was left to the church dignitaries.[142]

Henry's successor, Peter, was also from the ranks of the chapter, being Archdeacon of Shetland. While Peter's successor, Dolgfinn (1286-1309), was chosen and consecrated by the Bishop of Oslo, the Cathedral Chapter reaffirmed its right of election by choosing William, Archdeacon of Orkney, in 1309.[143] His election, however, led to deteriorating relations between the Orkney and Norwegian churches.

Scottish infiltration into the ranks of the Cathedral Chapter seems to have been well under way by the middle of the fourteenth century, which is perhaps understandable considering the effects the Black Death had on the local population. This infiltration must have caused some friction as one of the recommendations of the 1369 arbitration was that the bishop should choose "good native men in Orkney and Shetland to serve him".[144]

In the Orkney diocese, the chapter was presided over by the Archdeacon of Shetland, being the highest ranking official next to the bishop. An Archdeacon of Orkney was not recorded until 1309, when the above-mentioned William III was elected as bishop. The Cathedral Chapter was certainly well enough established by 1286 to be entrusted with accepting the annual payments from Scotland to the Norwegian crown as part of the Treaty of Perth. In the early 1430s, the Chapter used the resources available in its library to draw up a genealogy in support of William Sinclair's claim to the Earldom of Orkney (see 11).

As has been noted, Bishop Reid reformed and considerably enlarged the staff of the Cathedral from the previous arrangement of six canons and six chaplains. While religious reform was sweeping Europe, Orkney was relatively, though not entirely, untouched by the resulting divisions. One Orcadian, James Skea, was forced to flee to England in 1548 for fear of being burnt at the stake for his heretical views. Two years later, a chaplain of the Cathedral Chapter, called James Kaa, sought a respite for his "tenascite and pertinessite in halding of oppynionis concerning the faith contare the tenor of actis of parliament".[145]

20. Nicholas Halcro c1550

This much worn gravestone stands on the north side of the choir near the east end. It has a shield surmounted by a chalice. The shield is divided into quarters, which display a helmet, an indecipherable carving, a mount and a heart. The inscription is now illegible, but in 1917 Clouston read the name "nicolas hacro".[146]

It can be concluded that the gravestone commemorates Sir Nicholas Halcro, Parson of Orphir, who is frequently mentioned in documents from c1507 to 1545. From a testimonial, dated 29th May 1507, Halcro's father is identified as David Halcro of Thurregar in South Ronaldsay.[147]

The Halcros were a very important Orkney family, whose main estate was in South Ronaldsay, and many members of the family were heavily involved in the Church. During the time of Bishop Reid, a number of Halcros, including Sir Nicolas Halcro, held key positions in the Cathedral Chapter.

Nicholas Halcro was part of Bishop Reid's reform

This commemorates Nicholas Halcro, a member of a very important family in Orkney whose main estate was in South Ronaldsay.

of the Cathedral Chapter, being given the position of Precentor, a role in which he was responsible for the music, conducting the choir and regulating the celebration of mass. He was in charge of all the church services held throughout every day of the year and had a deputy, the Succentor, to assist him. He was required to be a Master of Arts or graduate in some other faculty and well versed in chant. The prebend of Orphir and vicarage of Stenness were appropriated to him.[148] He had a house near the 'Bridge of St Olave' (modern Bridge Street), which he bought from Henry Phankouth, Archdeacon of Shetland. After Bishop Reid's reforms, Nicholas gave the tenement to his servant, William Tulloch and his wife, Mariota Boswell.[149]

Records of Nicholas Halcro disappear about1550 and consquently his gravestone is estimated to date from about then. William Halcro of Aikers was the heir of Nicholas Halcro, so was likely to be a nephew or even a son.[150]

21. William Halcro c1565

This gravestone is found on the south side of the choir, the third slab from the east end. It bears two shields. The uppermost has the initials VH and has two gouttes below two mullets and a lion rampant, all above a lower compartment containing a flat based mount. The lower shield is flanked by the initials IS and consists of three bars wavy below a seal's head erased.

There is a faint Latin inscription, with much of it unreadable (shown within the brackets):

HIC IACET HO(N)EST(US VIR)
VILIELM(US HALCR)O
VIVO IN AUTERNUM

Here lies an honest man William Halcro.
I live forever.

The surname can be identified as Halcro from the coat-of-arms. This William Halcro does not appear to be the previously mentioned William Halcro of Aikers, who died in 1593 and whose two wives were Margaret Cragy and Margaret Bruce. Neither of their initials, nor their coats-of-arms match the lower shield. This William Halcro appears to have been the son of John Halcro, and a near relative of Sir Hugh Halcro, rector of South Ronaldsay, who died in 1554.[151]

The second coat-of-arms probably belongs to his wife. As the coat-of- arms is unknown in Scottish heraldry, Clouston concluded that it could be linked to a native Orkney family, his favoured candidate being the Skeas.[152] In 1562, a William Halcro supervised the division of the estate of Cara in South Ronaldsay, belonging to the deceased John Cromarty, whose

William Halcro's family originated in South Ronaldsay.

second wife was Janet Skea.[153] As Clouston stated, William Halcro appears to have been a trusted friend of the family at the time she was left a widow as he was also a witness to an agreement involving John of Cara, Janet Skea's eldest stepson, on 13th April 1561.[154] The identity of Janet Skea as William Halcro's wife certainly fits the IS (the I and J were indistinguishable at this time) on the gravestone.

The date of William Halcro's death is unknown, but would have been post 1562.

22. Edward Sinclair of Strom c1564

Part of Edward Sinclair's tombstone can be found in the south choir aisle not far from Marwick's Hole. His memorial is the top half of what, at first glance, looks like one gravestone, but is in actual fact two separate, though related, memorials. On the stone is a shield above the initials ES. Below this, the pommel of a double handed sword (a weapon Edward might well have used to great effect at Summerdale) can just about be made out. The shield is quartered. A mullet with crescent, an engrailed cross, a thistle and a buckle are depicted in the four sections. The legible inscription round the margin says:

"......LYIS ANE HONORABIL MAN EDVARD........".

The presence of the engrailed cross confirms it belongs to a Sinclair and the arms on the stone are the same as those found on a partially preserved seal of Edward Sinclair appended to a charter of 22nd September 1544.[155]

Edward Sinclair was the second illegitimate son of Sir William Sinclair of Warsetter in Sanday. His older brother was James of Brecks and his half brother was Magnus of Warsetter. Edward had estates in Shetland, at Strom in Whiteness.

The governance of Orkney was in the hands of Sir William Sinclair during the absence of his brother, Lord Henry Sinclair, and also after Henry's death at Flodden, when Henry's widow continued to collect the rents. Henry's death led to friction between the various branches of the Sinclair family, particularly when Henry's son, Lord William Sinclair came of age and began to seek his inheritance.

The situation remained reasonably calm during Sir William's lifetime, but conflict flared up after his death, around 1523. By 1528, Lord William Sinclair had been given custody of Kirkwall Castle with powers to administer justice. This was too much for the Warsetter Sinclairs, and, in a surprise night time raid, James and Edward took the castle, captured their cousin and put to death some of his followers. Lord William was ejected from Orkney and sought refuge in Caithness with his other cousin, the Earl of Caithness. Permission was sought for putting down what was effectively a rebellion and letters soon arrived from the king charging the rebels to give up the Castle. When it was discovered the messenger serving the royal letters had been imprisoned, an invasion was launched.[156]

James and Edward had a large force assembled from both Orkney and Shetland, and ambushed the invaders with great ferocity at Summerdale in Orphir. The Earl of Caithness was killed and Lord William was captured, along with his son, who died in captivity. The bloodletting did not stop there. Twenty-two sailors from the vessels that transported the invaders to Orkney were taken ashore and killed on the beach. Other refugees from the battle were dragged from sanctuary in St Magnus Cathedral and St Lawrence Kirk (probably Burray), and slaughtered. The brothers also dealt ruthlessly with the Shetlanders that had supported Lord William. Edward Sinclair slew Magnus Sinclair, son of Sir David Sinclair of Sumburgh, another relation, along with three of his followers. Shortly after this, James himself went to

Edward Sinclair of Strom was a skilled military man. In the Battle of Papdale he led Orcadians to repel an English expeditionary force, reportedly killing 500 men.

Shetland and executed the Lawman as well as hanging a number of others. This scale of gratuitous violence had not been seen since saga times.[157]

The brothers were now in complete command of the islands, with James describing himself as 'Justice of Orkney'. James, however, did not have long to enjoy his success as he committed suicide in 1536.[158] King James V was determined to end the feuds and, in 1539, he brought Lord William and Edward Sinclair together at his Falkland residence, and had them enter a legal contract of alliance so that they would co-operate in the good governance of the islands. Shortly after, Edward, together with thirty other named individuals, received a formal respite under the Privy Seal for all crimes committed.[159]

Following James V's visit to Orkney, the post of Lawman was abolished and was replaced with the Scottish position of Sheriff. Edward Sinclair became Sheriff-depute around 1542 and was still holding court as late as June 1559.

Edward's military prowess was called upon once more in his later life. Orkney and Shetland had long suffered from attacks from English shipping and, in turn, the islanders attacked English ships when the opportunity arose. In 1557, an English expedition was dispatched to the islands, perhaps in retaliation for Robert Reid's role in a failed piece of Scottish diplomacy. On 11th and 12th August, a large squadron of English ships arrived and put ashore at Kirkwall, burning part of the town, capturing the Cathedral and landing artillery pieces to bombard the Castle. By the time they came ashore on 13th August, they were met by a large force of islanders, led by Edward Sinclair. The ensuing Battle of Papdale led to the capture of the English guns, the death of three captains from the squadron and at least ninety-seven men. One report put the English dead at 500. The Admiral in charge of the squadron, Sir John Clere, was said to have drowned when his boat overturned while attempting to return to his ship.[160]

Edward was very friendly with Bishop Robert Reid, being one of the witnesses to the document setting out Reid's reforms of the Cathedral Chapter.[161] In 1549, Reid agreed to lease the lands of Skockness in Rousay to his 'friend', Edward and his wife, Margaret Dishington.[162] Edward also remained on good terms with Adam Bothwell, allowing the Bishop's reforms to proceed by not actively opposing the abolition of the Mass, though he found it difficult to 'thole that the mass were done'. The passage of time seems to have moderated Edward and it was Edward's sons, Henry and Robert, who led Catholic grass roots opposition to changes being brought in by Bishop Bothwell.

Margaret Dishington was Edward's second wife.[163] While the identity of his first wife is unknown, there is good reason to believe she was a daughter, or at least close relative, of Henry Phankouth, Archdeacon of Shetland. For a start, the Archdeacon made Edward his heir. The name of Edward's eldest son, Henry, is another clue. His son's coat-of-arms perhaps reflects his father's heritage. It consists of a shield quartered, the first and fourth showing the Sinclair arms, and the second and third quarters showing escutcheons, similar to those above the west door of the Cathedral (see 12).[164]

It is not known when Edward died, but his tombstone was found in the choir, very close to that of Lawrence Sinclair (24). The latter's death in 1564 coincides with Edward's disappearance from records, so the approximate date of 1564 for Edward's death can be given.[165]

23. Unidentified Sinclair

This stone stands underneath that of Edward Sinclair. Again only part of the tombstone is preserved, but the stone and style is very similar to that of its near

This memorial is unidentified but is probably related to Edward Sinclair (22).

neighbour and so a similar date can be estimated. Like Edward Sinclair's stone, there is a coat-of-arms and an inscription round the margin, which is too faint to read. The coat-of-arms consists of a shield quartered with an engrailed cross, confirming a Sinclair being commemorated. The first quarter consists of a heart, the second and third a galley and the fourth a buckle. It is likely that this person was another veteran of the Battle of Summerdale.

24. Lawrence Sinclair 1564

Two stones to the east of that of Edward Sinclair stands the gravestone of Lawrence Sinclair, a fellow warrior at the Battle of Summerdale. Again only the top half of the gravestone survives and has been placed beneath the one belonging to Tomas Reid (see 35). The stone has a shield with an engrailed cross in the upper compartment. In the dexter base is a star between two crosses fitchy and in the sinister base are two gouttes. The initials 'IS' flank the shield. Round the outside of the stone, in Latin, is the following text, which translated says:

Here lies an honourable man Lawrence (Sinclair) ....(January or February) in the year of our lord 1564.

Lawrence Sinclair was a Battle of Summerdale veteran.

their friends, kinsmen and adherents living in Orkney and Shetland who had participated in their misdeeds.

It is known from documents of the time that Lawrence Sinclair had a brother in Shetland, confusingly also called Lawrence, but described as "of Norbister".[169] Along with his wife, Janet Strang, a document from 1565-6 names a son called Arthur.[170] Another document, dated 6th June 1578, names his eldest son as David.[171]

25. Lord Adam Stewart 1575

This fascinating gravestone can be found on the south side of the choir, though its original position was on the floor of the north choir aisle, having been rediscovered on 5th October 1848, during the restoration work carried out by the Government.[172] It shows the initials 'LAS' about a shield charged with the Royal Arms of Scotland. The initial 'L' is above the shield, whilst 'A' and 'S' are at the sides. Incised around the margins in Gothic letters is a Latin inscription, which translated says:

> *Here lies Lord Adam Stewart son of the illustrious Prince James V King of Scots who died on the 20th June, in the year of our Lord 1575.*

On the dexter edge is an inscription in similar characters.

> *Lady Halcro daughter of the same had this tomb made at her own expense.*[173]

Although James V died relatively young and left only one legitimate offspring, Mary Queen of Scots, he was prodigious in the bed chamber, producing many illegitimate children, of which Orkney received its fair share. Information on Adam Stewart is sparse. It is likely he was one of James V's youngest illegitimate

The engrailed cross on the coat-of-arms leaves no doubt that this is a Sinclair. The tombstone commemorates Lawrence Sinclair of Sands (Deerness). burgess of Kirkwall, whose wife was Janet Strang – thus the initials 'IS'. Lawrence Sinclair belonged to the Sinclairs of Houss, one of the chief Shetland families of the name.[166] The two gouttes on the lower sinister third of the shield seem to indicate a link with the Paplay family. Lawrence was a Shetlander and neither his wife (Janet Strang) nor his mother (Marion of Houss) was a Paplay. The odal lands of Sands in Deerness belonged to the Paplays, but these only accounted for a part of Sands, the rest belonging to the bishopric. Lawrence was described as 'of Sands', implying that he held the bishopric land on tack. The use of the Paplay arms may stem from the fact that all of Sands had once been Paplay property.[167]

Lawrence, along with his father, William Sinclair of Houss, is mentioned in the respite of 1539 given to Edward Sinclair by King James V, forgiving him and thirty others for the murder of John, Earl of Caithness, and for other later crimes.[168] The respite included all

This stone commemorates Lord Adam Stewart, one of the many illegitimate children of King James V.

children and his mother is thought to be Helenor Stewart, daughter of John, 3rd Earl of Lennox (second creation). Adam received a pension from the Prior of the Charterhouse of Perth and probably came to Orkney as a result of his half brother, Earl Robert Stewart. Adam's widow is said to have been "gritlie burdynnit with many bairns".[174] He died in 1575 and was buried in the north aisle of the choir of the Cathedral. His tombstone was raised by his daughter, Barbara, who had married Henry Halcro of that Ilk.[175]

26. William Henryson 1582

This well preserved stone can be found at the east end of the south side of the choir. The initials 'VH' flank a shield with two coats-of-arms; dexter shows three piles and sinister, a saltire coupled with a decrescent. Also, inside the shield are the initials 'MB', which stand for Margaret Bonar, being the wife of William Henryson. Round the outside of the stone, in Latin, is the text,

Here lies William Henryson formerly Treasurer of Orkney who died on the 19th day of December 1582.

William Henryson (or Henderson) was a royal messenger, who first arrived in Orkney in 1563 with Patrick Bellenden, Bishop Adam Bothwell's cousin.[176] He acted as factor of land in Orkney belonging to Bellenden's brother, Sir John Bellenden of Auchinoull, the Justice Clerk.[177] His letters to both Bellendens cast a light on the events of the time, particularly concerning Robert Stewart, with whom he associated and occasionally served.

Henryson was with Earl Robert at Gorn in Sandwick at the time of the seizing of the Cathedral and the killings committed therein (see 28), and, in an attempt to exonerate Robert, wrote to Sir John Bellenden explaining what had happened.[178] He was granted a tack of land in North Ronaldsay by Earl Robert and, in 1578, was presented to the parsonage of Stronsay, putting him in charge of the finances of St Magnus Cathedral and so giving him the position of 'Treasurer of Orkney'. Under Bishop Reid's reforms, the Treasurer of the Cathedral Chapter was entitled to the Prepend of St Nicholas in Stronsay and the parsonage of that island. Henryson also became vicar of North Ronaldsay.

Henryson's legal experience saw him as a commissioner to hear Shetland's complaints against Laurence Bruce of Cultmalindie, Robert Stewart's half-brother and representative in Shetland.[179] Hundreds of ordinary Shetlanders turned out to make their complaints to the commissioners, the resulting report providing a remarkably detailed picture of life in Shetland at the time. These complaints included manipulating the local system of weights and measures to maximise income to the earldom, interfering with the Shetland legal system, taking bribes and abusing local hospitality.[180] It was Henryson who travelled south to lay the commissioner's findings before the Privy Council, which resulted in Bruce's removal from office. His fall from grace, however, did not last long and Bruce was soon in charge in Shetland once again.

William Henryson was succeeded by his brother, Cuthbert, as Treasurer of Orkney and vicar of North Ronaldsay.[181]

27. Earl Robert Stewart 1593

There is no physical evidence that Robert Stewart was buried in the Cathedral, though various writers, such as Peterkin, Tudor and Hossack, state that he was. A part of the north choir aisle was known as the 'Stewart aisle'. This of course may only refer to Lord Adam Stewart, whose tombstone was originally found there. It would be surprising if Robert had not been buried in the Cathedral, given that he died in the Palace of the Yards in Kirkwall (now known as the Bishop's Palace). Furthermore, there is the story of twelve hand bells, plus the Cathedral bells, being required for his funeral to ward away evil spirits.[182]

However, a memorial does exist to Robert Stewart in the Cathedral. It takes the form of a carved, wooden panel containing Robert Stewart's coat-of-arms. The panel can be found incorporated into the furniture of St Rognvald Chapel in the east end of the Cathedral, along with a number of seventeenth century panels, a few of which were loaned to the Scottish National Portrait Gallery in 1891 for a Heraldic Exhibition.[183] Orkney Museum has on display a similar wooden panel, originally found in the Cathedral, with Patrick

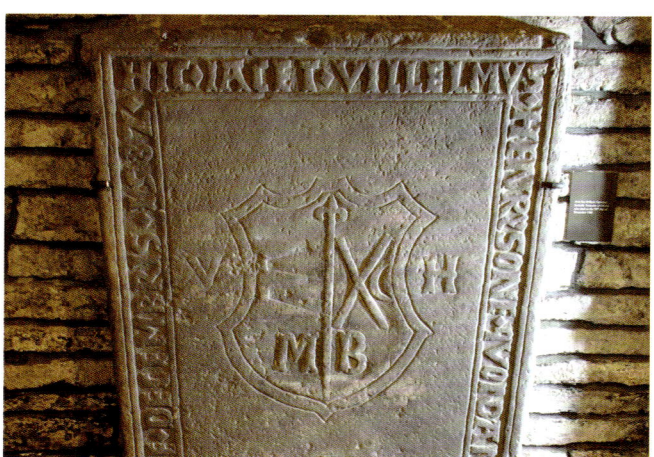

William Henryson was a close associate of Earl Robert Stewart and attempted to clear him of blame for the Cathedral murders in 1568 (see 26 and 28).

Stewart's coat-of-arms. Robert's panel has the date 1593, which suggests that his son, Patrick, had it made in commemoration of his father and incorporated it into the gallery he built for himself in the Cathedral.

Robert Stewart was born in 1533, the illegitimate son of King James V and Euphemia, daughter of the first Lord Elphinstone. In 1548, he was sent to France to be educated, along with his half-sister, the young Mary Queen of Scots. Following his return from France, Robert remained close to court for a number of years and, in 1561, was in Leith to welcome the return of Queen Mary to Scotland. Shortly after this, he married the sister of the Earl of Cassillis, Jean Kennedy, who later tried to divorce him on the grounds of adultery. In total, Robert had at least ten illegitimate children with three mistresses, Marjorie Sandilands, Janet Allardyce and Janet Gray. His wife seldom visited Orkney, being a poor sailor,[184] and spent most of her time in Edinburgh, where she had a house in the Canongate.[185]

With Mary Queen of Scots' return to Scotland, Robert remained at court and became friendly with Mary's husband, Lord Darnley. Robert was two-faced in his dealings with the Queen's husband, being on the fringes of the plot to assassinate him, while at the same time dropping hints to Darnley about the danger he faced.[186]

In 1565, Robert received a grant of Orkney and Shetland and was appointed Sheriff for the islands. He was, however, soon replaced by Gilbert Balfour and his rights to Orkney and Shetland were swept away a year later when Queen Mary married James Hepburn, Earl of Bothwell, giving him the title of Duke of Orkney. This title did not last long as Mary was forced to abdicate in favour of her son, James, and Hepburn fled to Scandinavia via Orkney and Shetland.

In 1567, Robert made his first appearance in Orkney, with a view to establishing himself in power. Through inducements and bribes, he soon persuaded Gilbert Balfour to give up the Sheriffship. He also gained occupancy of Kirkwall Castle, but not St Magnus Cathedral, which was in the possession of Bishop Bothwell. The following year, his followers seized the Cathedral, killing two of the Bishop's men. Robert was not present and was embarrassed by the deaths.[187] Robert eventually got rid of his rival, Bishop Bothwell. While Bothwell remained Bishop of Orkney, he gave up his rights to the Orkney Bishopric lands when he agreed to exchange them for Robert's Abbey of Holyrood. This gave Robert a secure legal status in the islands. Arguments over the details of this deal, however, would continue for the rest of their lives.

After Gilbert Balfour had left for exile in Sweden, Robert spent the next few years consolidating his position in Orkney by taking over Noltland Castle and by making himself Provost of Kirkwall (25th October 1569). He also began work on his palace in Birsay. In accepting the role of Provost, Robert made promises he had no intention of keeping. He said he had "compassion, pitie, respect and consideratioun to the commonweal of the burgh" and noted how its liberties were abused by strangers.[188] He was able to take advantage of the burgesses' commercial monopolies by securing for himself two thirds of any goods forfeited for violation of the burgh regulations. He forbade the burgesses to buy skins, hides, butter, oil and other wares without his leave. He was later accused of having seized the town's charter-chest and of having destroyed its contents.[189] During his later period of troubles (1586-1589), Robert demitted the office of Provost to his servant, David Scollay of Tofts, who was senior Bailie.

Following the assassination of the regent, his half-brother the Earl of Moray, Robert's position became more precarious. In 1575, after a catalogue of complaints had been set before the Privy Council,

Earl Robert Stewart definitely falls into the "Sinners" category in the title of this book.

he was forced to leave the islands and be warded in Edinburgh Castle. While in Edinburgh, Robert was able to recover his position by gaining favour with his nephew, the young James VI. In 1580, he became a Privy Councillor and, a year later, was created Earl of Orkney, Lord of Shetland and Knight of Birsay.[190] His tenure of the Bishopric was confirmed in 1585, giving him complete power in the islands, which he used to maximum effect to acquire much property.

By 1587, however, a maturing James VI was taking an increasing interest in maladministration on the part of some of his Sheriffs, including the land grabbing being perpetrated by the Orkney Earl. Realising the danger, Robert began giving back some of the land he had misappropriated from udal landowners. By this stage, he was becoming an embarrassment to the Crown and was described in official circles as the 'lait erle of Orkney'.[191] In previous years, Robert had been involved in treasonable contacts with Denmark, offering to restore Danish/Norwegian rule in Orkney and Shetland in return for control of the islands. The late 1580s saw negotiations between Scotland and Denmark for the marriage settlement between James VI and Anne of Denmark, and it was thought best to keep Robert out of harm's way, particularly when the Danes were expressing interest in redeeming the islands. One of Robert's staunchest opponents, Patrick Bellenden of Stenness, was sent by the king with three armed ships to collect taxes in the islands and take the Orkney Earl to Edinburgh. This plan was thwarted, however, when Robert mobilised local support, forcing Bellenden to withdraw empty handed, after being met by an armed band of islanders led by Robert himself. Memories of Summerdale remained strong in the islands and it would appear that Robert was able to stir patriotic fervour, particularly if it meant stopping the collection of taxes.[192] It would not be the last time that a Stewart Earl could muster local support.

Robert managed to maintain his position, though many of his powers were transferred to his legitimate son, Patrick. He also had to fend off attempts by Adam Bothwell to have him publically declared a debtor (put to the horn). He remained for much of the rest of his life in Orkney and died peacefully in his bed in the Palace of the Yards (Bishop's Palace) on 4th February 1593.

28. James Monteith of Saltcoats 1574 and Patrick Monteith of Fair Isle 1597

Towards the east end of the choir stand a number of gravestones marking some of the many servants Earl Robert Stewart took with him to Orkney. The first of these, which can be found on the north side of the choir, commemorates the Monteiths, Robert's chief henchmen. The stone has a shield, now much worn, in which buckles are depicted. The coat-of-arms of Monteith of Kerse is recorded in the Lyon office from 1570 as showing a shield quartered, which includes six buckles.[193]

The inscription reads:

> JAMES OF SALTCOATS AND
> PATRICK OF FAIR ISLE
> MONTEITHS IA 1574
> PA 1597

There is also an indecipherable Latin inscription around the margin.

James Monteith of Saltcoats and his brother, Patrick (later 'of Fair Isle'), were among Robert Stewart's closest followers. Even before they came to Orkney, they were in Robert's service and involved in 'troubill and debaitt' at Falkirk.[194] The bastard sons of King James V received rich ecclesiastical benefices. The Holyrood estates, much of which stretched along the banks of the Firth of Forth, were awarded to Robert Stewart. The Monteiths originated in a part of these estates, Kerse, which centred round modern Grangemouth. Their most infamous deed occurred not long after their arrival in Orkney.

In March 1568, following morning prayers in the Cathedral, one of Robert's servants, John Brown, proceeded to climb the stairs to the triforium but was accosted by the Bishop's guards, who ordered him to leave and threatened to shoot him. Brown went over to the Castle to tell his colleagues what had happened. On hearing his story, a group of Robert's servants, including James and Patrick Monteith, armed themselves and headed for the Cathedral. Seeing John Brown coming towards them, the Bishop's men shot him in the head and killed him, before withdrawing into the Cathedral. Brown's colleagues followed them in and opened fire, killing two of the Bishop's men, Nicol Alexander and James Moir. The other occupants of the Cathedral fled, lowering themselves out of the building on a rope and left Robert's men in possession. This, at any rate, was the story as told by Henryson (26) in a letter to Bellenden of Auchnoull.[195] James Monteith was the likely leader of the attack on the Cathedral and the story involving John Brown was probably a pretext for attacking the building, thus preventing its use as a vantage point for spying on the Castle. In September, James Monteith was pardoned for his part in the Cathedral killings.[196] Later Robert appeared to distance himself from James to keep the peace with Patrick Bellenden, Robert's implacable enemy. James died in 1574 and was buried in the same building where he had carried out the killings.

Patrick Monteith became involved in the administration of the islands and, during the time Earl Robert Stewart was being warded in Edinburgh Castle (1575-1577), power in Orkney appears to have resided in Patrick's hands.[197] In 1577, he, along with twenty-nine followers, was accused of slaying Adam Dickson, but nothing seems to have come of this and, in 1578, he was named sheriff-depute. He became chamberlain of Orkney and Shetland, being responsible for the collection of the earldom rents and revenues, but, after Robert's death, he fell out with the new earl, Patrick Stewart, over dues he was engaged to gather in Shetland. He died in 1597 and his lands passed, firstly to his nephew, James Monteith, and then to James' younger brother, Robert Monteith of Egilsay, who became a firm enemy of Earl Patrick.

29. William Kincaid of Falkirk 1594

Further to the east of the Monteiths, at the east end of the north side of the choir, stands the gravestone of William Kincaid of Falkirk, who was blacksmith to Earl Robert Stewart. The shield with his coat-of-arms consists of a fess ermine between three stars on top and a triple towered castle in base. The shield is surmounted by a crowned hammer showing the tools of his trade. This was the emblem of the trade guild, the Hammermen, which had the right to be described as the 'King of all trades'.[198] (For a description of the Trade Incorporations, see 38). Beneath the shield are the initials 'VK' on either side of tassels coming from the shield. There is no inscription except for 'memento mori' (*remember death*) near the foot of the slab. The top of a skull can be seen at the base, showing that the bottom part of the gravestone is missing. The quality of this stone shows the esteem in which some tradesmen were held in bygone days compared with more recent times.

William Kincaid, along with his brother John, who was also a smith, were from Abbotshaugh near Falkirk and both married sisters, Bessie and Alison Hog (Hossack says Hoy). William had a house and blacksmith workshop on Broad Street.[199] His house was on the site of the old brew house for the Castle (today 17 Broad Street, the shop belonging to Orkney Television Enterprise) and the smithy was between the dwelling house and the Castle.[200]

30. William Maine 1592/Mariore Thomson 1609

This memorial is to be found in a window-like recess on the south side of the nave, near the south transept. The letters 'VM' in monogram along with 'M' and 'T' are above a shield with two coats-of-arms. On dexter, there is a bend with three fleurs-de-lys between a unicorn's head and a pheon with point downwards, whilst on sinister, there is a stag's head erased. Beneath the shield is the text:

> HEIR LYIS VILLIA MAINE BURGDIS
> IN KIRKVAL 1592
> HIS SPOVS
> MARIORE THOMSONE 1609
> AND NYNE OF THAIR CHILDREN

Round the outside in Gothic text is:

> Death nor lyf sal never seperat us fra the faith and love of our saviour and redeemer Jesus Christ.

There are two sources given for the name 'Maine'.[201] The first is from fishermen families in Nairn and its surrounding villages, and derives from the Norse 'Magnus'. The second and more likely source is from the central and southern counties of Scotland, where most of the Scots incomers to Orkney originated at the time of Bothwell and the Stewart Earls.

In 1584, there is a record of William Maine being on an assize, apprising the lands belonging to the Halcros of Brough, Rousay, for arrears of duties.[202] Apprising was a legal process whereby lands were sold to pay debt owed to a creditor. The court proceedings were recorded

William Kincaid was a blacksmith and some of the tools of his trade are hewn into this stone.

William Maine built part of what is now known as Spence's Square, in Victoria Street, Kirkwall, where his initials appear on a putt stone.

by William Bannatyne (36), acting as messenger and sheriff. The proceedings seem to be highly dubious, with the lands being very quickly sold at a knock-down price to Earl Robert Stewart.

William Maine's name also appears as a witness to a conveyance of a tenement in the Midtown of Kirkwall (now Albert Street), dated February 26th, 1590-91, on behalf of Alexander Houston.[203]

William Maine built part of what is now Spence's Square in Victoria Street. There is a putt stone on the north side of 72 Victoria Street with his initials in monogram, similar to those shown on his tombstone in the Cathedral.[204] On the other side of the building is the well known putt stone showing the face of the Reverend William Scott, minister of the Cathedral (1723-1737), complete with Geneva cap and ruff. The Reverend Scott refurbished the house in the early eighteenth century.

As there are very few Maines recorded in Orkney, William Maine's son, perhaps the only surviving member of this large family, is likely to be Thomas Maine, who was a Kirkwall bailie from 1619 to 1638.[205] In turn, his son was also called Thomas Maine, who, in 1657, sold the abovementioned 72 Victoria Street to Oliver Linay (75). A full inventory of the property at the time of this sale, dated 6th January, 1657, has survived.[206]

CHAPTER 7

The Seventeenth Century – 'Thou shalt not make idols'

Many Catholic beliefs were swept away with the Reformation, which saw an insistence on the second commandment. This discouraged displays of art in churches, such as crosses, which were reckoned to promote idolatry amongst the masses.

A memorial to a virtuous life was acceptable as it would inspire meditation and reflection amongst the living. Emblems of mortality, known as vanity motifs, were allowed as they promoted reflection on the transience of earthly life and directed the mind to the hereafter.[207] Vanity motifs were intended to be reminders of mortality and could refer to the funeral, as represented by the coffin or the deid bell, to the future of the corporal body, as represented by the skull and crossbones, and to the passage of earthly life, as shown by the hourglass, sundial, or axe felling a tree.[208] Sometimes, a skilled mason would carve the hour-glass with the sand in the bottom compartment, showing that time had run out for the deceased.

Many of the gravestones within St Magnus Cathedral from this period show the skull in three quarter profile from the left side with an arc incised on the side of the skull. This may well refer to the Orcadian belief that the soul left the body from the left ear. Written evidence for this is sparse but the idea is supported in a 1921 article in *National Geographic* Magazine.[209]

To protect the soul, it was an old superstition that bells had the power to terrify evil spirits. This belief survived the Reformation and it was the custom for a bell to be rung while the coffin was being carried to the grave. This service came at a cost. Many churches had two bells, the great church bell for the wealthy and a little one for the poor. As Walter Traill Dennison comments, "perhaps the evil spirits, to whom the rich were exposed, needed a more powerful charm than those that assailed the poor".[210] For the wealthy burgesses who were buried in the Cathedral, two hand bells preceded the funeral procession and, in addition, the Cathedral bells were rung. Dennison records that the funeral of Earl Robert Stewart required twelve hand bells, as well as all the Cathedral bells. He also states that seven of these bells were borrowed from parish churches, and were never returned by Earl Patrick.[211] Whether this is true is unknown, but it is a good example of the bad reputation that Patrick accrued over the years.

Burials within churches were condemned by Protestant authorities from as early as 1560. In 1579, the General Assembly of the Church of Scotland forbade the practice, on pain of excommunication. The threat of excommunication was certainly not taken seriously in Kirkwall, the nave being screened off at this time from the choir and used as a burial place right up until the nineteenth century, the sale of burial plots within the building being a good source of income.[212] The choir became the place of worship, with pews being installed and galleries and lofts being erected between the arches. Earl Patrick Stewart's first building project in Orkney was to erect a gallery for himself within the Cathedral.[213] Ornate wood carvings and coats-of-arms were installed to identify the pews of the wealthy families. This still did not stop later generations being in dispute over these seats, particularly when they could be bought and sold like any other heritable property.[214] Burial in the choir was only allowed for the very rich, who could afford the expense of removing the stalls.

Post Reformation Bishops of Orkney (30-33)
31. James Law (Bishop of Orkney 1605-1615)

The coat-of-arms of James Law, consisting of a bend sinister between a mullet in chief and a cock in base, is carved above the inside of the north door in the nave.

James Law was born about 1561, son of James Law of Spittal, portioner of Lathrisk, Fife, and Margaret Strang.[215] He was educated at St Andrews University,

This modest memorial to Bishop Law is dwarfed by the one in his memory in Glasgow Cathedral. Bishop Law was once rebuked for playing football on the Sabbath.

The Bishop Law memorial in Glasgow Cathedral. (Picture: Thorfinn Rosie).

gaining an MA in 1581 and becoming minister in Kirkliston in 1585. During this ministry, Law showed himself to be no strict sabbatarian as he was rebuked by the Synod of Lothian for playing football on a Sunday.[216] In July 1587, he married Marion, daughter of James Dundas of Newliston, with whom he had a daughter, Margaret. His second marriage, to Grizell Boswell, produced four sons and two daughters.[217]

By the 1580s, the Church of Scotland had rejected rule by bishops and had, instead, adopted Presbyterian rule by elders. This did not sit well with King James VI's view that Presbyterianism was incompatible with monarchy. He prevented the General Assembly from meeting and made moves to reintroduce the power of bishops. James Law, along with a few other royal supporters, was to play a central role in the King's plans. Having been made a royal chaplain in 1601, Law was appointed titular Bishop of Orkney four years later in the king's newly reconstituted Episcopal Church of Scotland.[218]

With his appointment as Bishop of Orkney, Law was given the task of restoring government rule in the Northern Isles, where Earl Patrick Stewart had fallen out with all the leading families and had become deeply mired in debt owing to his extravagant life style. In 1607, the earl was made to pay Law 4000 merks a year from the revenues of the bishopric estate, which Patrick then controlled. Patrick was also forced to hand over his newly completed Palace of the Yards, known today as the Earl's Palace.[219] As well as his ecclesiastical powers, Law was also King James' Commissioner, Sheriff and Justice-Depute in Orkney.[220] In 1608, Law informed the king of Patrick's oppressive rule in the islands and, by the following year, Patrick was warded in Edinburgh Castle.[221] He would never see freedom again and was later incarcerated in Dumbarton Castle.

In 1610, Law, along with Sir John Arnott, was sent to Orkney with a commission to investigate Patrick's misdeeds in the islands. In March 1611, the Privy Council passed a series of measures designed to rectify the situation in the Northern Isles, which included the abolition of Orkney and Shetland's Norse Laws.

Figure 8 Seal of James Law, Bishop of Orkney, showing his coat-of-arms (from Craven J. B. 1901, *The Blazon of Episcopacy in Orkney 1421-1688*)

While in prison, Patrick appointed his only son, the illegitimate Robert, as his deputy in Orkney with instructions to regain his properties there and collect rents in preparation for his hoped-for restoration to the Earldom.[222] In 1612, Orkney was annexed by the Crown,[223] with administration of the earldom estate being given to Sir James Stewart of Killeath, who in turn appointed his brother-in-law, John Finlayson, to collect the rent and skat. Finlayson was hated in Orkney and, as far as the ordinary people of the islands were concerned, made the restoration of Stewart Earls a better option. Patrick's lavish lifestyle had, at least, recirculated money in the Orkney economy. After Patrick's death, the greater part of rent and skat was taken away from the islands to help pay for the debts of whatever king was in power.

Robert's first attempt to comply with his father's wishes was thwarted by Bishop Law who, after arriving in Orkney in 1612, negotiated with Robert the surrender of the Castle and other fortified places. During this period, Bishop Law held his first sheriff court in St Magnus Cathedral,[224] which sought to restore local government to the islands by appointing bailies and councillors. An equivalent sitting was held for Shetland, at Scalloway Castle. A series of 'country acts' were passed to help regulate the day-to-day management of agriculture. These acts were very likely to have been based on old Norse Laws, which were abolished in 1611.[225] Bailie Courts were set up to implement these regulations.

Back in Dumbarton Castle, Patrick was furious when he heard about the surrender of his properties to Bishop Law and sent his hapless son back to Orkney for a second attempt to regain control in the islands. The rebellion started in June 1614, when Robert took over the Palace at Birsay. By July, the rebels had occupied all the strategic buildings in Kirkwall, including the Cathedral and Castle, and were laying in supplies and ammunition. George Sinclair, Earl of Caithness, showed no hesitation in accepting a commission to suppress the rebellion.[226] Bishop Law was persuaded to join the expedition and, though at first reluctant, seems to have thoroughly enjoyed the experience.[227]

The government forces landed at Carness on 23rd August and took several days to manoeuvre the heavy guns to Kirkwall.[228] The rebels were soon forced out of the Earl's Palace and also lost their main vantage-point, the Cathedral steeple, when some of Robert's followers betrayed his cause and surrendered the building. This left the rebels holed up in the Castle but this proved to be a hard nut to crack. By mid-September, the big cannons had run out of ammunition, the siege being reduced to an exchange of musketry.[229] Evidence of this can still be seen today, with the musket shots peppered along the north side and west end of the Cathedral.

Robert Stewart had little backbone as a leader and negotiations eventually succeeded in securing the surrender of the Castle on September 29th. The immediate consequence, apart from the execution of both Robert and his father, was the order to dismantle Kirkwall Castle. With eleven feet thick walls, this was no easy task. Part of the walls survived up to the end of the nineteenth century when it was finally removed to make way for road widening. St Magnus Cathedral also had a close shave at this time, requiring the intervention of Bishop Law to stop the Earl of Caithness having its roof removed.

Following the rebellion, Bishop Law investigated Earl Patrick's involvement, interviewing many of the rebels. Law also received news that his plans had been approved for the reorganisation of the earldom and bishopric estates, which previously had been jumbled together in a random basis throughout the parishes. While udal land remained in the hands of the udallers, Orkney was to be divided into earldom and bishopric parishes, with the bishop having right to the superior dues of the bishopric and former earldom lands lying in Holm, Orphir, Stromness, Sandwick, Shapinsay, Walls, Hoy and parts of St Ola.[230] The bishop would have supreme authority in both ecclesiastical and civil matters in his parishes, being able to appoint his own sheriffs and hold his own courts.[231] The earldom parishes, in the absence of an earl, were controlled by the king and his tacksmen, who also had rights to the former bishopric lands there.

In 1615, Law was rewarded for his services to the Crown with promotion to Archbishop of Glasgow. He died in 1632 and was survived by his third wife, Marion, daughter of John Boyle of Kelburne, who had a large monument erected in his memory in Glasgow Cathedral, where he was buried.

32. George Graham (Bishop of Orkney 1615-1639)

Bishop Graham's coat-of-arms can be found on a shield above the inside of the west door on the south side. It is quartered, with the first quarter consisting of three escallops in chief, the second and third three roses and the fourth a chess rook.[232]

Figure 9 Seal of George Graham, Bishop of Orkney, showing his coat-of-arms (from Craven J. B. 1901, The Blazon of Episcopacy in Orkney 1421-1688)

George Graham was born in 1565, the second son of George Graham of Inchbraikie (14 miles west of Perth) and Marjorie Rollo. He was well connected, his great grandfather being the first Earl of Montrose. Having been educated at St Andrews University, he gained an MA in 1587. His first ministry was at Clunie before being transferred to Auchtergaven by 1595 and Scone in 1601. It was at Clunie that he met and fell in love with Marion, daughter of the Lord Advocate, Sir Robert Crichton.[233] They married around 1594, after Marion had been kidnapped by many of George's relatives, removing her from the clutches of her mother, who disapproved of the marriage.[234] They had a large family of five sons and at least six daughters. They also adopted two boys. In 1604, Smyth of Braco had died leaving two orphan grandsons (Patrick and Andrew – see 49) in the guardianship of George Graham.[235]

George Graham was promoted Bishop of Dunblane during the period 1603-1606 when James VI was strengthening Episcopacy in Scotland. In 1614, he received a commission along with Henry Drummond of Balloch, father of George Drummond (50), and two other gentlemen, to try two women incarcerated in the Tollbooth of Dunblane on charge of witchcraft.[236] His attitude to this seems to have been sceptical as he was later accused of being 'indifferent to witchcraft'. Another accusation was curling on the ice on a Sunday during a visit to his Perthshire home.[237]

Bishop George Graham had to petition the Privy Council in the 1630s for aid after a famine. It is estimated that one in five Orcadians may have perished.

On August 26th 1615, he was appointed Bishop of Orkney, and was installed by October, living in the Earl's Palace, Kirkwall.[238] While in Orkney, Graham was able to acquire vast estates for his sons, usually with the help of his ward, confidant, son-in-law and business partner, Patrick Smyth of Braco (49). These included Graemshall in Holm, Skaill in Sandwick and Breckness in Outertoun, Stromness. The last of these was given to his youngest son, John. When the older brother, David, moved to Perthshire, his Skaill estate was amalgamated with that of Breckness and John Graham became the first laird of what became known as the Breckness estate.[239]

Among the daughters, Catherine married the Bishop's ward, Patrick Smyth of Braco (49), Marjorie married her cousin, George Drummond of Blair and Balloch (50), and Margaret married William Henryson of Holland in North Ronaldsay, descendant of William Henryson (26).[240]

Bishop Graham oversaw the 1627 Royal Commission into the state of the church in Orkney. This inquiry included an inspection of the state of the school in Kirkwall. It found that it had originally been funded from the Prebend of St Peter, but these lands were then in the hands of Robert Monteith of Egilsay, leaving no provision for the school. An opportunity soon arose to rectify the situation. In 1629, Bishop Graham used the 500 merks Scots, which had been raised in Orkney to support the beleaguered Huguenots of La Rochelle,[241] to re-endow the Grammar School. An additional 1500 merks were raised but, with the demise of Episcopacy and the ensuing civil wars, this endowment was in danger of being lost. In 1649, Bishop Graham's son-in-law, Patrick Smyth of Braco (49), paid the whole 2000 merks to the Earl of Morton in return for a wadset on the land of Isbister in Rendall. Each year the earldom estate was to pay 30 meils of malt to the master of the Grammar School. This became known as 'Isbister Mortification' and continued until 1872. The value of this endowment was worth half of the Prebend of St Peter.[242]

Bishop Graham's later years were neither happy for him nor for Orkney. In 1629, Orkney's trade with Scotland was halted to control the spread of plague introduced from Scandinavia.[243] Famine struck in the early and mid years of the 1630s and Bishop Graham had to petition the Privy Council for help. It is thought that perhaps one in five of Orkney's population died during this period.[244] More Country Acts were instituted to help control the resulting increase in theft and migration. Despite the shortages, the export of grain from the earldom and bishopric estates continued.

Bishop Graham anticipated the demise of Episcopacy and resigned as Bishop in a letter presented by his son, Patrick Graham, to the General Assembly of the Church of Scotland. Accusations against the now former bishop were made, which included his indifference to witchcraft and the aforementioned curling on the Sabbath. In order to avoid excommunication and the resultant forfeiture of much of his personal estate, Graham expressed his contrition in a letter signed at Breckness in February 1639. This was accepted by the Church of Scotland Assembly and he was able to live his remaining years at his retirement home at Myreside in Perthshire, dying in 1643 at the age of 78.[245]

The Mercat Cross 1621

Whilst not a memorial as such, it is worth mentioning the Mercat Cross, which can be found against the wall of the north crossing. The Cross is engraved with the date 1621, implying it was probably erected by Bishop Graham. The original position of the Cross was near the foot of the Strynd, before being moved to the Kirk

Bishop Andrew Honeyman mobilised the folk of Kirkwall to save the Cathedral bells after the spire went on fire.

The original Mercat Cross was moved into the Cathedral to protect it from the elements.

Green in 1762.[246] At some point it had to be mended after being broken when a gale of wind wrecked a tent, which had been attached to the Cross, during a Lammas Fair. The Cross was removed from its site on the Kirk Green in 1954 and replaced with a replica.

In common with other Mercat Crosses throughout Scotland, it would have been used as a meeting place and focal point to hear proclamations, as well as to render contracts binding at a time when written agreements were impossible. It was also used as a place of punishment, the Cross of Kirkwall being provided with the 'jougs', an iron collar in which offenders were placed. Interestingly, this use as a place of punishment is still reflected in Kirkwall to this day, when brides and grooms-to-be are 'blackened', paraded through the town and then cling-filmed to the Cross!

33. Andrew Honeyman
   (Bishop of Orkney 1664-1676)

The arms of Bishop Honeyman can be found inside the west door on the north side. The shield is quartered, with the first quarter showing three mullets on a bend, the second and third a fess counter componee, and the fourth a burning heart encircled by a wreath. Dividing the quarters, there is a fess charged with three crescents, two of which are invected.[247]

Andrew Honeyman was born in 1619 in St Andrews, the son of baker, David Honeyman of Pitairchney, a small hamlet east of the Falkland Hills in Fife. He was educated at the university in that city, gaining MA in 1635.[248] After graduation, he became assistant and then successor to Rev. Samuel Cunningham in a small charge at Ferryport-on-Craig, marrying the minister's daughter in 1642. The couple had nine children, all born in St Andrews. In the same year as his marriage, his abilities were recognised when he was transferred to the prestigious charge of the 'College Kirk' in St Andrews at the youthful age of 23.

Figure 10 The seal of Andrew Honyman, Bishop of Orkney. His coat-of-arms is shown on a shield beneath the figure of St Magnus (from Craven J. B. 1901, *The Blazon of Episcopacy in Orkney 1421-1688*)

Honeyman, carried along with the fervour of the time, signed the 'Solemn League and Covenant', which was, in effect, an agreement between Scottish Covenanters and the English Parliament for the preservation of the reformed church in Scotland and for the reformation of religion in England and Ireland on similar lines. He later changed his views, publishing a pamphlet in 166, urging the acceptance of the English form of religion

This image is thought to be that of Bishop Andrew Honeyman, who survived being shot with a poisoned bullet in an assassination attempt on the man he was accompanying. Orkney Library Photographic Archive

in Scotland.[249] This did his career no harm as he was promoted to Archdeacon of St Andrews and Bishop of Orkney two years later. After a gap of 27 years, Honeyman's arrival in the islands as new bishop, in June 1665, caused quite a stir. His entitlement to residence in the Earl's Palace was, however, denied him for the first seven years of his tenure, the palace being rented by the Earl of Morton.[250] Honeyman was eventually granted a decree against Morton to have his adherents evicted (see 51).[251]

He remained in Orkney for the next three years, administrating his diocese. In 1666, he ordered the recording of all deaths. Taken with the register of baptisms and marriages kept by Thomas Dishington (see 55), these became among the oldest such records in Scotland. After the death of his first wife, Euphan Cunningham, he returned to Edinburgh to write a two volume book called *Survey of Naphtali*, which put the case for royal absolutism.[252] It was during this visit, on the evening of 11th July 1668, that he was in the company of James Sharp, Archbishop of St Andrews. While stepping into a coach at the top of Blackfriars Wynd, Honeyman was shot by James Mitchell with a poisoned bullet, which had been meant for the Archbishop. Although the Bishop survived the assassination attempt, he never fully recovered from the attack, the bullet shattering the bone in his lower arm.

Honeyman was back in Orkney when, on January 9th 1671, the tower of St Magnus Cathedral was struck by lightning, setting the spire on fire. Along with the magistrates, he helped organise the townspeople to pile earth and hides beneath the tower to break the fall of the bells. As a result, only the largest of the three bells sustained damage.

At some time following the death of his first wife, he married Mary Stewart, daughter of Sir James Stewart of Graemsay and descendant of Earl Robert Stewart. Their son, Robert Honeyman, inherited the Graemsay estate and became Stewart and Sheriff-depute of Orkney.[253]

It is very likely that the wound the Bishop received during the attempt on the life of his friend, Archbishop Sharpe, contributed to his early death in 1676.[254] He was buried in St Magnus Cathedral in the south side of the choir, next to Bishop Thomas Tulloch.[255]

34. Murdoch Mackenzie (Bishop of Orkney 1677-1688)

Murdoch Mackenzie was born around 1596, the second son of John Mackenzie of Pluscardy, and was educated at Marischal College, Aberdeen, gaining MA in 1618. He became chaplain to Lord Reay's regiment in the army of Gustavus Adolphus, King of Sweden, during the 30 Years War in Germany. After returning to Scotland in 1636, he became minister of Contin before transferring to Inverness in 1640 and Elgin in 1645. He was consecrated Bishop of Moray in 1662 and then Bishop of Orkney in 1677.

He married Margaret, only daughter of Donald MacLey, a bailie in Fortrose, and had a large family. His wife died in 1676 and was buried in Elgin Cathedral along with her young son, David.[256]

When Murdoch Mackenzie arrived at Scapa in August 1677, it was reputed that he was offered the cup of St Magnus. The cup, which was filled with strong ale, was traditionally offered to newly arrived bishops. If bishops drank the cup, it was considered a good omen. Mackenzie not only drank the cup in one draught, but also asked for more.[257]

Mackenzie spent his episcopate in Orkney and was closely involved in the repair of the Cathedral after the steeple had been struck by lightning. He also helped to

Bishop Murdoch Mackenzie was the last bishop to live in the Earl's Palace and is commemorated in the Cathedral by having his seal on a cupboard door in the custodian's office. Orkney Library Photographic Archive

arrange the dispatch of the 'Great Bell' for repair.²⁵⁸ At Easter 1679, an agreement was reached between Bishop Mackenzie, the Cathedral minister, James Wallace (76), and the Town Council, to "cause repair the ruinous Steeple of the Cathedral Kirk", to lay "the two loftings under the bells", to hang the bells again and to make a platform above the bells.²⁵⁹ The estimated cost was 1000 merks, to be borne by the Bishop, Wallace and the Town Council. Local merchant, Alexander Geddes, was given the task of taking the cracked bell to Holland, with very clear instructions concerning its care. He was instructed to find someone capable of doing the job, to have it weighed prior to recasting and to ensure no inferior metal was added. He also had to ensure that the bell should remain unimpaired in height, breadth, thickness and sound quality. The letters of description and coat-of-arms already on the bell had to be reformed, with the addition of a line stating where and when it had been recast. Geddes completed his mission, having obtained the services of Amsterdam bell caster, Claudius Fremy, to carry out the work. Geddes's ship arrived back in Kirkwall with the recast bell, on 23ʳᵈ August 1682, creating much interest in the community. In addition to the monetary reward Geddes received from the Bishop (500 merks) and the magistrates (800 merks), he and his crew received drink money from a delighted Kirk Session.²⁶⁰

Bishop Mackenzie was the last bishop to reside in the Earl's Palace, where he died in 1688. He was buried in St Magnus Cathedral, in the south transept chapel, and is now commemorated on a cupboard door in the custodian's office by the carving of his coat-of-arms, a stag's head, and the dates 1677-1688.²⁶¹

Figure 11 The Seal of Murdoch Mackenzie, Bishop of Orkney. His coat-of-arms of a stag's head can be seen beneath the figure of St Magnus (from Craven J. B. 1901, *The Blazon of Episcopacy in Orkney 1421-1688*)

35. Tomas Reid 1603

This stone is to be found on the south side of the choir, above that of Lawrence Sinclair (24). It has a shield containing the stag's head of the Reids and the initials,

VR

TR

Underneath is a skull with one bone and the date,

4 MAII 1603

There is a Latin inscription around the perimeter, which, translated, says:

Here lies buried Tomas Reid,
   the flower of whose youth,
Rich in promise,
   was cut down by the sickle of Death.
He died on 4 May 1603 ²⁶²

The first Reid recorded in Orkney was Andrew Reid in 1509,²⁶³ appearing as 'roithman'. ²⁶⁴ Of course, the most famous Reid to have a connection with Orkney was Bishop Robert Reid (18) and the fact this stone shows a coat-of-arms similar to that of the Bishop may indicate a relationship.

The Tomas Reid on the gravestone obviously died when he was young. It is very probable that the initials 'VR' carved above the 'TR' refers to Tomas's father.

This stone to Tomas Reid states he was a youth when "cut down by the sickle of Death".

Clouston mentions a Wat Reid, who had been recorded as a witness at Kirkwall in 1542.[265]

36. Isobel Calcrit 1612/ William Bannatyne of Gairsay

On the north side of the choir stands this red sandstone memorial, which has been trimmed of both its sides, perhaps for use as lintels[266] or to fit a space on the floor of the Cathedral.[267] On top is a shield with arms, a chevron between three water bougets. Below is the text:

> HEIR LYES AN GODLIE AND VERTOUS
> ISOBEL CALCRI(T) SPOUS TO VILLIAM
> BANNATYN OF GARSAY 1612

Under the text is a skull and cross bones, with the skull shown from a frontal view.[268]

The identity of the wife of William Bannatyne has long been a subject of debate, with the surname Calcrit being unknown. Clouston wondered if the lettering here had been re-chiselled and speculated whether the name should have been Gilchrist.[269] There is a charter dating from January 1606 and a sasine from 1608, transferring a tenement in Scalloway, which gives William Bannatyne's spouse as Isobel Pollok and her second son as John Bannatyne.[270] In an unpublished article on William Bannatyne, Hugh Marwick (122) mentioned an inventory of Flett papers lodged in Registry House, in which there is an entry from 1st May 1601 where William Bannatyne's wife is given as Isobel Selkrig (a variable spelling of Selkirk). In this document William's son, Gilbert, is acting as attorney for his mother.[271] Marwick went on to point out that no Selkirks are known to have had the coat-of-arms shown on the gravestone.

William Bannatyne was the son of John Bannatyne, burgess of Lanark.[272] William purchased Gairsay in 1588 and was an important servant to both the Stewart Earls. The surnames Bannatyne, Ballantyne and Bellenden seem to have all been variants of the same name. It is therefore possible that William Bannatyne was related, in some way, to his contemporary, Sir Patrick Bellenden of Evie.

William Bannatyne was becoming a prominant figure in Orkney at the time of Earl Robert Stewart. He helped the Earl acquire the estate of Brough in Rousay from the Halcros by means of a court held by Bannatyne in Kirkwall in 1584.[273] This court apprised these lands, which were then sold to the Earl at a knocked down price. He subsequently became heavily involved in the complex politics of Earl Robert's successor. In 1594, he followed Patrick Monteith (see 28) into the position of chamberlain of Orkney and Shetland, a job with little chance of financial reward as Earl Patrick required his chamberlains to raise huge sums of money to help pay off his ever increasing debts.[274]

William Bannatyne became involved in the conflict Earl Patrick Stewart had with members of his own family over land left by Earl Robert Stewart. After failing to raise the required rents and even trying to raise the money from his own estates, Patrick removed him from office and had him thrown out of Orkney.

Bannatyne's successor as chamberlain, Henry Colville, Parson of Orphir, devised a plan to incriminate the Earl's brother, John Stewart, in a plot to poison Patrick. This involved the torture and imprisonment of one of John Stewart's servants, who implicated Alison Balfour in attempting to murder the Earl by witchcraft.[275] She, along with her family, were tortured in the Castle dungeon by Colville until she made a full confession, which she eventually retracted prior to her execution at the heading-hill (at the top of the Clay Loan in Kirkwall) in December 1594. John Stewart was duly tried for

William Bannatyne was heavily involved with Earl Patrick Stewart. The last recorded mention of Bannatyne is on a jury that condemned to death a "witch".

plotting the murder of Patrick by witchcraft, but was acquitted of the charge. Within a short while after the trial, John Stewart had his revenge, with the murder of Henry Colville in Shetland. Bannatyne sought to curry favour with John Stewart by supplying Colville's killers with supplies at his house on Gairsay before they set off for Shetland.[276] Bannatyne was subsequently tried for being a party to the murder, but he too was acquitted.[277]

During his time as Earl Patrick's chamberlain, Bannatyne was often in Shetland, where he acted as Sheriff-substitute. On 6th July 1595, he obtained the tack of the vicarages of Yell and Fetlar from the vicar, James Lauder. These, in turn, he sub-let and subsequently prosecuted the numerous people who failed to pay the vicarage teinds.[278]

In common with other principal landowners in Orkney and Shetland in 1597, he received a royal letter, charging him to keep the peace. Each person on this General Band, imposed by the Privy Council, was required to pay a security, the size of which depended on that person's relative importance. Earl Patrick and his brother, John, were thus required to find £20,000 and 10,000 merks respectively, while the next tier of landowner, such as Sir Patrick Bellenden of Evie or Malcolm Groat of Tankerness, had to find 5000 merks each. William Bannatyne found himself in the £1000 valuation.

Through the courts, Bannatyne tried to recover the money he had lost in Earl Patrick's service, eventually taking his case to the Court of Session.[279] In 1614, during the siege of Kirkwall Castle, he was part of the assize that tried some of the lesser individuals of the rebellion in the great hall of the Palace of the Yards.[280]

The last record of William Bannatyne was in 1616, when he acted as chancellor or foreman of the jury that condemned to death the alleged witch, Elspeth Reoch, daughter to the deceased Donald Reoch, former piper to the Earl of Caithness.[281]

37. Catherine Craigie 1612/Magnus Pottinger

This stone is to be found on the north side of the nave, near the west end. It consists of a shield with the initials 'MP' above 'KC', together with a round-faced skull. The shield is much worn, but shows three spots ermine, which are associated with Craigie coats-of-arms.

Round the outside is the Latin text, which translated says:

> *Here sleeps the pious and provident*
> *Catherine Craigie formerly wife of*
> *Magnus Pottinger, merchant.*
> *She died in 1612.* [282]

The stone mason must have had a lapse of concentration, with Catherine's initial in the shield spelt with a 'K'.

Magnus, along with his brothers, Edward (see 45) and Gilbert, was the son of John Pottinger of Oback in Deerness (died 1613).[283] The Pottingers were important ship-owners and merchants, whose main property in Kirkwall was on the west side of Victoria Street, just south of property belonging to the Taylors (see 54).

Magnus was murdered by his brother-in-law, Alexander Taylor, who paid blood money for the killing. Hossack quotes the Sheriff Court of 27th February, 1627, which indicates Catherine Craigie was Magnus's first wife and that he subsequently married Elspeth Taylor.[284] This seems to be a complicated tale of family and neighbour intrigue. 500 merks were paid as blood money to Magnus's brother, Edward Pottinger (45), £111 2s 2d to Magnus and Catherine's son, John[285], and £222 4s 4d to Elspeth Taylor and their daughters, Marable and Marion Pottinger. It is not known how Magnus died, but the word "slaughter" is used in the Sheriff Court record.

38. RC 1612 and Kirkwall Incorporated Trades

This stone is found on the south side of the choir and seems to commemorate at least two tradesmen, with the shield bearing the tools of their trade, an axe and a hammer, showing that they belonged to the Trade Incorporation, the Hammermen. Above the shield are the initials 'RC' and below, 'WC', with a date of 1612. The bottom panel contains the words 'Memento Mori' (*remember death*), above the skull and crossbones. This stone was reused in the eighteenth century, with the following being added between the top and bottom panels:

IC MARCH
16 ANNO 1705

Following the Royal Charter granted by King James III in 1486, Kirkwall gained a monopoly of trade within the city bounds. In order to carry out a trade, a licence had to be obtained from the Town Council and the money paid for this privilege was applied to "the common good and weal of our said Burgh and City". The only time the monopoly rights of local merchants and craftsmen were relaxed was during the Lammas Fair, held each year in August. The various trades of Kirkwall were legally empowered to regulate and protect their various interests, with the Town Council acting as a governing legislature, ready to assist them in seeing that the rules were carried out.

Trade Incorporations were set up, each with its own charter; in Kirkwall, there were four Incorporations, the Tailors, the Hammermen, the Shoemakers and the Weavers.[286] Each Trade Incorporation made its own rules and had the powers to set such measures as wages, the duration of apprenticeships, the standard of workmanship and working hours. The Incorporations even had the power to nominate representatives to sit on the Town Council. When funds were available, small pensions were paid to elderly members and widows. The Trade Incorporations were eventually abolished in 1846.

It is likely that the people commemorated on this stone belonged to the family Couper. According to Clouston, a William Couper, carpenter, is mentioned as a householder of Kirkwall in 1561, and as a witness in 1573. In addition, a Robert Couper mortgaged his house in Kirkwall in 1590.[287] The initials 'IC' of 1705 are likely to belong to a descendent of these Coupers.

In Kirkwall there were four Trade Incorporations, powerful organisations that controlled and regulated skilled tradesmen, two of whom are represented on this stone.

39. AB post 1613 – possibly Alexander Banks

This interesting stone lies on the south side of the choir and has two coats-of-arms but no text. The upper shield consists of a fess, between a cushion above and mullet beneath, flanked by the initials 'AB'. The lower shield, which probably belongs to AB's wife, consists of a bend engrailed between two crescents, flanked on the sinister side by the letter 'K'. The dexter side is too worn to identify the letter. This coat-of-arms is unknown, so the identity of the wife remains a mystery.

From the shape of the shields, a date towards the end of the sixteenth or early seventeenth century is estimated.[288] Looking at records from the time, the main possibilities are two members of the Banks family, Alastair and Alexander, who were likely to have been servants of Earl Robert Stewart. In 1591 Robert granted Alastair and his wife, Katherine Good, the tenement which became the Hall of Banks (near the present day Baptist Church in Victoria Street).[289] In his will, Robert owed Alastair £30 for services rendered.[290]

Katherine Good does not fit the initial of the second coat-of-arms, so Alexander may be the brother being commemorated. The coat-of-arms of AB is exactly the same as the arms of Thomas Marjoribanks, an advocate appointed by King James V, so seems to have been a straight steal.

Figure 12 Arms of the current Chief of Clan Marjoribanks (Wikipedia).

Both Alastair and Alexander Banks are mentioned in the *Court Book of Orkney and Shetland 1612-1613* and are described as cordiners (shoemakers) and burgesses of Kirkwall.[291]

40. William Irving of Sebay 1614

This stone, found on the south side of the choir, has a shield with three holly leaves, above which are the initials 'VV'. There is a very crude skull with one bone at the base. The text starts round the perimeter and continues under the shield:

> HEIR LYIS VILLIAM VIRVING SONE TO VMQll VIRVING OF SEBAY BEING SCHOT OUT OF YE CASTEL IN HIS MAJESTIES SV DEPARTIT YE 20 OF SEPTEMBER 1614[292]

This is one of the few gravestones in the Cathedral that gives a cause of death.

As there are two William Irvings mentioned on the gravestone, in the text that follows, the father will be described as 'William Irving senior' and the son as 'the younger William Irving'.

Although Irving is a Scottish name, the Irvings were already a very well established Orkney family by the fifteenth century. In 1425 a complaint, addressed by the community of Orkney, against the rule of David Menzies, was sent to the King of Norway and Denmark, with one of the gudmen signatories being a William Irving.[293] By the sixteenth century, the Irvings of Sebay[294] were among the largest udal landholders. They also possessed a town house situated on the site of the former Flett and Sons in Bridge Street.[295]

William Irving senior's father, James, probably the last Lawman of Orkney[296], must have foreseen how matters would develop and obtained, from King James V, a feudal charter confirming his udal property. About this time he also purchased the land of Horrie in Toab from a woman called Ingagerth. This was one of the earliest transfers of property in Orkney by means of a feu, according to Scottish practice.[297]

The Irvings of Sebay were one of the largest udal landlords and had a town house in Bridge Street, at the present Voluntary Services Orkney offices (formerly Flett and Sons).

William Irving senior was involved in the first recorded case heard by Earl Robert Stewart, acting as Sheriff of Orkney in 1567, when the former sought the removal of one of his tenants, John Aitken, from his lands at Horrie.[298] William senior became a follower of Earl Robert and was installed as tenant of Sebay, after the Earl had dispossessed the Irvings of their land. Robert used his corrupt courts to confiscate property from udal proprietors and install a relative, who was a follower of the Earl. William even prosecuted his own brothers, Magnus, Gilbert and Edward, on behalf of Earl Robert. It was a number of years before they regained their lands.[299]

William senior married Elizabeth Thomson and had two sons, Patrick and William, and four daughters.[300] However, he was granted remission from Earl Robert for adultery with Marjorie Scollay, provided he was answerable to Kirk censure.[301]

William purchased a boat from Earl Robert in 1585 and was later commissioned by the Earl's son, Patrick, to retrieve the artillery from the Spanish Armada ship, *El Gran Grifon*, which had been wrecked off Fair Isle. Patrick had a great interest in artillery weapons and became impatient, when, after two years, William had only recovered six pieces.[302]

In 1610, while Earl Patrick was incarcerated in Edinburgh, Bishop Law was appointed Commissioner of the Peace for Orkney and Shetland and, in turn, appointed William senior as one of his Orkney assistants.[303] Aged about 70, William senior died in July 1614 around the start of the rebellion mounted on behalf of Earl Patrick Stewart.

The younger William Irving of Sebay was on the Government's side during the rebellion and siege of Kirkwall Castle. He was killed by a musket shot from the Castle on September 20th. His death was, however, not lamented by the Earl of Caithness, who called it a judgement, since he was convinced Irving was secretly helping the rebels. Orcadians were considered untrustworthy by Caithness as he had been unable to stop the rebels being supplied with food and drink from the local population.[304]

The Irvings eventually lost their Sebay estate to William Sinclair of Tolhop in the early 1620s.

41. Sir Hew (Hugh) Halcro of that Ilk (Wood Panel) (1644)

This wooden panel can be found on the south side of the communion table in St Rognvald Chapel. The panel has the initials 'HH' above a shield, with the coat-of-arms of three mullets above a lion rampant. These belong to Hew Halcro of that Ilk, son of Henry Halcro and Barbara Stewart, who was the daughter of Lord Adam Stewart (25). 'Of that Ilk' refers to the lands of Halcro in South Ronaldsay.

The use of the lion rampant, usually associated with the royal families of Scotland and Norway, is interesting and stems from the fictitious writing of Van Bassan, who, in the early part of the seventeenth century, linked Halcro of that Ilk as lineally descended from King Sverrir of Norway (1174-1214).[305] Another genealogy traced Halcro descent from a Prince Halcro of Denmark. This gave the Halcros the opportunity to use the lion rampant in their coat-of-arms.

Sir Hew Halcro was married thrice, firstly to Esther Thomson (died 1613), secondly to Jean, daughter of James Stewart of Graemsay (died 1628) and lastly, Isobel Craigie, widow of George Traill.[306] In January 1615, a marriage contract was drawn up between James Stewart of Graemsay, father of his second bride, and Hew Halcro. In this agreement, Hew Halcro promised to give Jean life rent of various lands in Rousay, including Eynhallow.[307] A few years later, part of this contract was renounced in return for a cash settlement on his wife, the deed being signed at the Bu of Hoy in 1619 and being witnessed by, among others, David King of Warbister.[308]

The main estate of the Halcros was in South Ronaldsay, their house being at the Hall of Holland. Hew Halcro also owned the Bu in Hoy, which was originally part of the earldom estate. In 1614, Hoy was transferred to the Bishopric and the lands of the Bu were feued by Bishop Law to Hew Halcro, who built the house about this time and had his initials carved on a putt stone.[309] In 1620, he, along with his wife Jean Stewart, obtained the land of Braebuster in Hoy.[310]

Hew Halcro was an attendant of Earl Patrick Stewart, though he later changed sides. In 1610, along with William Irving of Sebay and others, he was appointed a Commissioner of the Peace for Orkney, assisting Bishop Law and Sir John Arnott in the role.[311] While not siding with the rebellion, Halcro, along with Francis Moodie of Breckness and Henry Stewart, the younger, of Graemsay, actually visited Robert Stewart in Kirkwall Castle during the siege.[312] They were said to have eaten and drunk with the rebel leader.

Clouston described the Halcros as a typical Orkney roithman family.[313] The roithmen or councilmen belonged to the leading families in their districts, who attended the head courts as people in authority, representing their local districts until the early sixteenth century.[314] Sir Hew Halcro continued in this role, being a suitor of court (1617-1626) for both South Ronaldsay and Hoy.[315] He died on 12th May 1644. His granddaughter, Sibilla, is featured at entry 65.

42. Sir William Craigie (1652)/Margaret Halcro (Wooden Panel)

This panel is found on the north end of the communion table in St Rognvald Chapel and was probably carved to commemorate the marriage agreement, in 1620, of William Craigie to Margaret Halcro, daughter of Hew Halcro (previous entry) and Esther Thomson, having the arms of Craigie and Halcro on the shield. The marriage itself only took place in 1624. Originally, this carving and the shield of Sir Hew Halcro were part of one piece of wood making up the pew[316].

This pew was to be the subject of correspondence a hundred years later, when, according to Hossack, Alexander Muat, nearest heir to Hugh Halcro of that Ilk, gave up the Halcro seat to his cousin, James McKenzie, Town Clerk of Kirkwall.[317]

William Craigie's parents were Magnus Craigie, merchant in Kirkwall, and Elizabeth Paplay. Magnus Craigie seems to have been a very successful businessman, whose activities included money lending. Before banks came into being, money lending was often a means for the wealthy to become even wealthier. William continued his father's business, including

Pediment on the front of 45 Bridge Street, commemorating Magnus Craigie and his wife, Elizabeth Paplay, along with their son, William Craigie, and his wife, Margaret Halcro.

money lending, and in 1622 he bought Papdale, to which he brought his wife, Margaret, who had a tocher (dowry) of 2000 merks. Later, in 1640, he acquired the island of Gairsay, where he transformed Langskaill into a mansion house complete with sunken garden.[318] He died in 1652 when his son, Hugh Craigie of Gairsay, along with Arthur Buchanan of Sound, became Members of Cromwell's Scottish Parliament. His other son, David, will be described at 78.

On the front of 25 Bridge Street (currently Sinclair Office Supplies) there is a pediment with the date 1628 above two monograms, formed by the initials 'MC' and 'EP' (for Magnus Craigie and Elizabeth Paplay) and 'WC' and 'MH' (for their son and daughter-in-law, William Craigie and Margaret Halcro).[319]

43. Edward Sinclair of Essonquoy/Ursula Foulzie (Wooden Panel)

This wooden panel is again found in St Rognvald Chapel, next to that of Earl Robert Stewart. It has the initials, 'ES' and 'VF', above and below a shield with arms quartered. In each of the first and fourth quarters there is a galley, the second quarter has three shells and the third has a crown with three mullets. This panel belongs to a descendant of Edward Sinclair of Strome (22), Edward Sinclair of Essonquoy, along with his wife, Ursula Foulzie. Essonquoy was their estate in Tankerness.

Ursula was the daughter of Gilbert Foulzie and Elspeth Kinnaird, whose coats-of-arms can be seen above the arch of Tankerness House. Gilbert Foulzie was Archdeacon and Provost of St Magnus Cathedral and became Kirkwall's first Protestant Minister following the Reformation.

The family commemorated in this memorial suffered financial difficulties which resulted in them selling Tankerness House in Broad Street.

Edward Sinclair's town house was on the east side of Albert Street, next to that of James Adamson (see 57), and he inherited Tankerness House after the death of Gilbert Foulzie around 1595. In 1617, Edward, along with Robert Henryson of Holland, was chosen by the heritors as their representative in Parliament and he became Provost of Kirkwall in 1622, remaining in office until 1636. In 1630, he stood in as Sheriff for John Dick and later became Sheriff in his own right, holding his last court on 15th April 1634.[320] He was involved in adding to the 'Country Acts' or Acts of Bailiary set up for executing justice in Orkney.[321]

He and his son, Gilbert, seem to have developed financial difficulties and the house in Albert Street was sold. In 1633, Edward and Gilbert borrowed money from James Baikie of Tankerness (66) at a ten percent interest rate. This resulted in the sale of Tankerness House to Bishop Graham[322] and eventually, in 1642, it passed to the Baikies of Tankerness. After Edward's death, Ursula was still being sued by James Baikie for the outstanding debt.[323]

44. David MacLellan/M. Groat (Wooden Panel)

This wooden panel from a seventeenth century pew is found on the south side of the seated lectern in St Rognvald Chapel and consists of a shield with the initials 'DMC', above arms of two chevrons impaling three eastern crowns. Below the shield are the initials 'MG'.

'DMC' stands for David MacLellan, who came to Orkney in the service of John Dick, Sheriff of Orkney[324], and acquired the Woodwick estate from the Murrays of Garth (16).[325] Other business interests included a third share in the trading vessel, *Lamb of God*, which he purchased in March 1637.[326]

David MacLellan played a part in preparations for the arrival of the Marquis of Montrose in 1649, but, as with most of the other Orkney gentry, did not take part in the latter's expedition for the Royalist cause.

MacLellan had extensive properties, which, apart from the Woodwick estate, included Wyre, North Ronaldsay, parts of Birsay and lands in Westray.[327] Indeed by 1653, he had accumulated the largest private estate in Orkney, being worth more than £1700 a year in rental. As a comparison, James Baikie of Tankerness (66) acquired estates with an annual rental of just over £1200.[328] These figures are known from the valuation undertaken to fund Cromwell's occupation of the islands, which started in1652.[329] MacLellan later lost much of his Mainland estates when they were apprised in 1662 by Arthur Buchanan of Sound, during the time MacLellan was in prison in Edinburgh (see below). Being a large landowner, he was one of Orkney's Commissioners of Supply, who acted as a form of local government. MacLellan's last meeting with fellow Commissioners was in August 1661, before his incarceration in Edinburgh.

MacLellan represented the congregation of Birsay and Harray in trying to obtain a minister for the parishes. Following Montrose's defeat, most of the ministers of Orkney were deposed or excommunicated by the General Assembly of the Church of Scotland, putting the Church in Orkney into a state of disarray.[330] In May 1654, MacLellan travelled to a meeting of the Edinburgh Presbytery, in which he successfully supported the candidacy of David Kennedy.[331]

David MacLellan, along with Patrick Monteith of Egilsay, was sued by the schoolmaster, John Dishington, who believed that Kirkwall Grammar School was being defrauded of its revenues, which were paid from the Prebend of St Peter. In 1652, Dishington appealed to the Commissioners of the English Parliament, who managed the affairs of Scotland. He obtained letters of horning against MacLellan and Monteith, who had

David MacLellan was a substantial Orkney land owner and in 1653 his entire estate was worth more than £1700 in annual rental, a massive sum for that time.

inherited the lands of the prebendary.[332] Dishington ultimately failed in his action,[333] but he did retain some income from the teinds of Wyre and he was the first to benefit from the Isbister Mortification (refer to 32).[334]

David MacLellan's involvement with the Dicks ended unhappily. He had been appointed chamberlain of the Earldom estate for a seven-year period on 18th August 1648, shortly after the death of the 7th Earl of Morton.[335] Sir Andrew Dick became Sheriff of Orkney in 1643,[336] following the death of his brother, John, whom MacLellan had served. With the 7th Earl of Morton's finances depleted after lending Charles I considerable sums of money,[337] Sir Andrew, in turn, loaned 100,000 merks to Morton. To cover this loan, he obtained security upon Morton's Orkney earldom estate. However, the events of the next few years saw the value of his investment plummet, when the 9th Earl of Morton's rights to the earldom estate were taken away.[338] Sir Andrew continued to try to redeem his money and, in an action against the 9th Earl of Morton, there is a petition to the Court of Session by Sir Andrew, dated 21st November1664, which states that, *"..., and wheras the said David* (MacLellan) *is a prisoner in Edinburgh these thrie years past, and is in great danger of seekness and death whereby his compts* (accounts) *and peapers concerning that compt and reckoning may miscarrie to the great losse and prejudice of all parties"*. Although appointed by the Earl of Morton, MacLellan seems to have been acting as Sir Andrew Dick's chamberlain and was caught up in the legal action taken by Dick to recover his money.[339]

David MacLellan's wife, whose initials were 'MG', was a Groat, whose sinister coat-of-arms on the wooden panel consists of three eastern crowns belonging to that family.[340] Her parents were John Grot of Elsness and Barbara, daughter of James Scollay of Tofts.

45. Edward Pottinger of Howbister c1642

This unusual stone is hidden behind chairs on the south side of the nave, to the east of the Paplay Tomb. About half of the monument is missing, leaving the carvings of a face of a cherub, with four four-pointed stars. The remaining text is in Latin and translated says:

> ....descreet man Edward Pottinger of Howbister who died on 13th A...

In a panel above the cherub, is the Latin vanity, *In life remember death. Time flies.*[341]

Edward Pottinger, brother of Magnus Pottinger (see 37), was a skipper, merchant trader and money lender.[342] He had three marriages, his first wife being Katherine Baikie, who belonged to another important merchant family. Her father was Thomas Baikie, Burgess of Kirkwall, and one of her brothers was James Baikie 1st of Tankerness (66).[343] Edward was in partnership with his other brother-in-law, Magnus Baikie, in the vessel, the *Jonas*, of which Edward was skipper. He bought Howbister (Hobbister, Orphir) in 1633 from Robert Flett.[344]

The Pottingers had built up a prosperous seagoing trading business. The extent of this business is shown by Edward Pottinger's will, which has an extensive list of people who were in his debt or who were owed money by him. Interesting examples were sums owed by Mitchel Scollay in Bergen, Norway (£72 15s Scots), William Manner in Ipswich (£70 Scots) and a great number of the landowners of Orkney along with their wives. Edward would have needed a good accountant to keep up with all these money transactions. Later it would become common for the sons of merchants and lairds to spend some time in a lawyer's office in Edinburgh learning business and estate management. When Edward died in April c1642, he was in the process of building a new ship in the Oyce, for which he owed money to various craftsmen.[345]

Interestingly, the business that the Pottingers had built seems to have been the source of prosperity for at least one branch of the Traills. Patrick Traill probably learnt his sea skills under Edward Pottinger, whose second wife, Elspeth, was Patrick's sister. Traill later went into partnership with Edward's nephew, John (see 37) and married John's daughter in 1654, receiving a third share of the Kirkwall ship, *Nicolas*, as a dowry. Although

Edward Pottinger was a skipper, merchant and money lender with business dealings abroad. He was building a boat at the Oyce at the time of his death.

business was at times risky, it remained prosperous and, in 1667, Patrick was able to purchase the Sanday estate of Elsness from John Grott, brother of David MacLellan's wife (44).[346]

After Elspeth Traill died in 1631, Edward married his third wife, Isobel Stewart, who outlived him.

46. Thomas Sandison 1656/Walter Sandison

On the north side of the nave, next to the transept, is this stone with a blank shield, containing the initials 'TS' above and 'CC' below. Round the border is the text,

> HEIR LYIS THOMAS SANDISON
> SONE TO WALTER SANDISON
> BURGESS OF KIRKVAL
> HE DEPARTED 6 OF MAY 1656[347]

Below is the device MEMENTO MORI (*remember death*) above a skull and cross bones. The skull is shown in frontal view.

The Sandisons lived in what is now Shore Street but

was then known as the Burgh.³⁴⁸ Their house was built by Walter's father, John Sandison, who was a weaver, and consisted of a hall, bedroom ("ane chalmer"), a kitchen, two storerooms ("twa sellars") and a garden ("ye yaird, kaill and ptents").³⁴⁹

It looks as if Thomas Sandison died before his parents but was old enough to have married. The identity of his wife, who had the initials 'CC', is unknown. Walter Sandison's wife was Christian Fea, who, after Walter's death, married a blacksmith, John Irvine. She died in 1670. Her second husband was not allowed to maintain possession of the house as there was no lawful heir from the Sandison line and so the Town Council took possession.³⁵⁰

47. Yenstay - AY/GY 1652 (or 1625)/EY 1663

This very plain stone is found in the north side of the choir and has the initials 'AY' and 'GY' carved at the top. Underneath is a shield, with the initials 'EY' and the date 1663. Beneath the shield is the date 1652, followed by a blank scroll and skull and crossbones.

The surname, 'Yenstay' derives from the lands of Yenstay in the parish of St Andrews.³⁵¹ A genealogy of the Yenstays is given by Clouston in his *Records of the Earldom of Orkney*.³⁵²

According to Clouston, in 1625, Elene Yenstay granted two charters for the sale of her lands. In the first charter she is referred to as the only daughter and heir of her father, the deceased Gilbert Yenstay, and in the second as nearest heir of her father's brother, the deceased Andrew Yenstay. With 1625 being the year Elene sold the lands, Clouston considered that the date 1652 on the stone was a mistake for 1625; the sale of the lands was likely to have followed the death of her father and uncle. The second date of 1663 would be the year Elene died.³⁵³

48. George Sinclair of Rapness 1643

This large gravestone is found on the south side of the choir, between two other Sinclairs, Edward (22) and Lawrence (24). The shield at the top is divided into quarters, with the first and fourth a lion rampant, and the second and third a galley. Above the shield in Latin is, MEMORIA IUSTI EST BEATA (*the memory of the just is blessed*). The rest of the text is also in Latin and translated says:

> *Here rests George Sinclair of Rapness who died on 6ᵗʰ April in the year of our Lord 1643 also his grandson James Sinclair eldest son of John Sinclair of Quendale and of Barbareta Sinclair daughter of the aforesaid George. James surrendered his soul to the Lord on 14ᵗʰ October 1661 in the 15ᵗʰ year of his age.*³⁵⁴

The text in the bottom panel is illegible and there are the symbols of a candlestick, flower and hour-glass.

It is interesting to note that the coat-of-arms shown for George Sinclair would seem to indicate a marriage with a Stewart or a Halcro to legitimatise the presence of the lion rampant. According to Roland Saint-Clair,³⁵⁵ George Sinclair of Rapness married Martha, daughter of James Stewart of Graemsay, son of Earl Robert Stewart. This would certainly be convenient in explaining the royal element of the coat-of-arms. It would seem that Martha was George's first wife and that she did not live long as, by 1620, he was married to Helen Alexander, whose tombstone, dated 1676, is in St Mary's Church in Pierowall, Westray. Again, according to Roland Saint-Clair, George's brother, James Sinclair of Quendale (Shetland) and father of the John mentioned on the gravestone, married another daughter of James Stewart of Graemsay. It is worth comparing the arms shown on this stone with those of Earl Robert Stewart.

This grave-stone of George Sinclair incorporates two lion rampants, suggesting a Royal connection.

George Sinclair's father was Malcolm Sinclair of Quendale in Dunrossness, Shetland[356] who, in 1588, hosted the survivors from the Spanish Armada ship, *El Gran Grifon*, which had been wrecked on Fair Isle.

George Sinclair was part of the 1627 Royal Commission to report on the state of the Church in Orkney. He was sworn in as Commissioner for Westray at Kirkwall on 9th June 1627 by Bishop Graham (32).[357] The minister at this time, Mr Allan Hutton, was excused, being aged, blind and infirm. The report noted the number of communicants in Westray as 430 and in Papay as 64. It also noted the minister's stipend, the number of kirks and their state of repair, and the lack of a school.

On 29th May 1633, George was elected by the other principal landowners to represent them in the Scottish Parliament in Edinburgh.[358]

It would appear that John Sinclair of Quendale, son of George's elder brother, James, married his first cousin, Barbareta, George's daughter. John of Quendale was one of the first Commissioners of Supply for Shetland.[359]

49. Marjorie, 1666, and Beatrix Smyths, 1669/Patrick Smyth of Braco

This stone can be found in the south side of the choir next to Edward Sinclair. On the upper part of the slab is a shield, flanked by initials 'PS', 'MS', 'IA' and 'BS'. The shield contains three objects, a burning cup between a chessman and an escallop pendant from a ribbon. These arms belong to Patrick Smyth of Braco, who also had these carved on his pew in the Cathedral. The text on the gravestone reads:

> HEIR RESTS THE BODYES OF MARIORIE
> AND BEATRIX SMYTHS LAWFUL
> DAUGHTERS TO THE DECEASED
> PATRICK SMYTH OF BRACO AND ISOBEL
> ANDERSONE WHOSE MOTHERLY
> AFFECTION REMAINS YET ALYVE EVEN
> TOWARDS THE DEAD
> BY THIS SEPULCHRAL MONUMENT
> ATTESTED THE SAID MARIORIE IN JULY
> 1666 BEING THE 16 YEAR OF HER AGE
> AND BEATRIX IN OCTOBER 1669 BEING
> THE 14 YEAR OF HER AGE AT GODS
> APPOYNTED TYME LEFT THIS VAIN
> WORLD A HOLY LYF A HAPIE END THE
> SOUL TO CHRIST DOTH SEND WHERE
> IT'S BEST TO BE AT REST.

On either side of the shield are the Latin phrases, MORS PATET (*death waits us all*), HORA LATET (*the hour none knows*) and MEMENTO MORI (*remember*

Much is known about Patrick Smyth of Braco, not all good. He came to a sticky end.

death). Also on either side of the shield are the symbols of an hourglass, candlestick and skull and cross bones.[360]

Although little is known about the teenage girls, Marjorie and Beatrix, much is recorded about their father. Patrick Smyth of Braco was not only son-in-law and business partner of George Graham, Bishop of Orkney (32), but also his ward. Patrick's parents and grandfather were dead by 1604, when he and his brother, Andrew, went to live with Bishop Graham, then in Dunblane. The two brothers came north with Bishop Graham when Graham became Bishop of Orkney. Through this close connection with the Bishop, Patrick acquired many lands in Orkney. In 1618, he married Katherine, eldest daughter of Bishop Graham, and they went on to have 14 children. It is little wonder that poor Katherine did not enjoy a long life and she died in 1637.

Smyth's Kirkwall tenement, at the east end of 'the Ramparts', was on the site of the present Kirkwall Hotel. His main estate was in Holm, where he lived at Meall.[361] After the death of Katherine Graham, Smyth married Margaret Stewart, daughter of Henry Stewart[362] and widow of Hew Halcro of that Ilk (probably son of the Halcro featured at 41). His third wife was Isobel Anderson, who is mentioned on the gravestone and who was a daughter of Thomas Anderson of Lundie.[363] With his three wives, Smyth had a total of 23 children and outside wedlock fathered three illegitimate daughters.[364] After Smyth's death, Isobel married skipper, David Moncrieff, who became a Kirkwall Bailie and Dean of Guild after retiring from the sea.[365]

Patrick Smyth was one of the leading men of the county and typified the local gentry's attitude to the Marquis of Montrose in that they toasted him during his stay in Orkney and helped him recruit troops from the local population, but did not themselves accompany his expedition. Along with the Earl of Morton and some other local lairds, Patrick signed a bond for arms and ammunition to the value of £1800 Scots, which had been delivered to Kirkwall by Captain Hall of Leith in September 1649. Hall was to receive payment from the Marquis of Montrose in Hamburg, failing which the signatories of the bond, or their heirs, would pay.[366] Hall was not recompensed and, in 1652, he assigned the bond to an Edinburgh merchant with full right and title.[367] It is unclear if the lairds involved in this bond ever had to pay up but dispute over it rumbled on for some time.[368]

Smyth was drowned in the Stronsay Firth on 28th April 1655. His body was recovered and buried in Papa Stronsay. Following his death, his son and successor, Patrick, sold the Holm property to Patrick Graham, Bishop Graham's son, who renamed it Graemeshall.[369] In his will, Patrick left a 'furnished' bed and 500 merks to most of his children. Even his stepdaughters were not forgotten, with Jean Halcro inheriting her mother's diamond ring and two bracelets, and her sister, Sibillia (65), receiving a 'furnished' bed.[370]

The memory of Patrick Smyth of Braco continued for some time after his death. Writing in the late 19th century, W. R. Mackintosh recorded a couple of stories still recalled by some elderly people in the islands.[371] One story tells how Smyth tricked an old lady into signing over to him her lands in Holm. Another story relates how Smyth met his death. He had gone to collect rents in Stronsay, where, among his tenants lived a poor widow who was unable to pay. Smyth, however, was determined that if he could not get money, he should at least be paid in kind, so he took forcible possession of every animal belonging to the woman and had them put on board his boat. With all the live cattle on board, his boat became unmanageable and sank after being caught in a gale, drowning not only all the cattle, but also the poor widow's persecutor. How much truth is in these stories is difficult to say, but they confirm Hossack's assertion that he was not popular in Orkney.[372]

50. George Drummond 1653 1660 1662

The first stone on the north side of the nave on entry through the west door once marked the resting place of George Drummond and some of his grandchildren. A shield is flanked by his initials, 'GD', and, below, 'PM' and 'MD' in monogram, for Patrick Blair and Mary Drummond. The shield has the two coats-of-arms of Drummonds and Blairs, the dexter consisting of three bars wavy below two crescents for Drummond and sinister consisting of a chevron between three roundels with a crescent for Blair. Above the shield, in fairly illegible script, is the Latin motto of the Blairs, VIRTUTE TUTUS (*protected by courage*). Below the shield are the dates 1653, 1660 and 1662. 1653 was the date of the death of George Drummond and presumably 1660 and 1662 were the dates of his grandchildren's deaths.[373] The text says:

HERE RESTS GEORGE DRUMMOND
OF BALLOUGHE AND BLAIR. PATRIK,
GIRSILL AND BARBARA BLAIRS HIS
GRANDCHILDREN BY PATRIK BLAIR OF
LITTLE BLAIR AND MARY DRUMMOND
HIS DAUGHTER.

THEY DID LYE DOUN WITH SIGHS
AND CRYES TO JOY AND BLISSE
THEY SHALL ARISE.

Also in Latin are the words:

The whole earth is a homeland to the brave.
The aforesaid Mary, lamenting and mourning
very greatly, put up this stone.

George Drummond was the 6th Laird of Balloch and a nephew of Bishop Graham (32), his mother being Beatrix Graham, the Bishop's sister. Balloch is seven miles from Inchbraikie, from where Bishop Graham originated.[374] On 21st June 1620, George Drummond was in Kirkwall acting as a witness, along with Patrick Smyth of Braco, to the conveyance of some udal land in Stromness. He is described as "apparent of Baloche".[375] This visit occurred very shortly before he married Agnes Napier, the daughter of the "famous John Napier of Merchiston" (see next entry). Their son, John, took an active part in the Marquis of Montrose's campaigns on behalf of King Charles I, eventually escaping to Norway in 1646 with his leader.[376] The

George Drummond was the 4th Laird of Blair and would later become Provost of Kirkwall.

other children of George and Agnes were Henry (8th of Balloch), Robert (9th of Balloch), Mary (see next entry), Agnes and Katherine.

George Drummond became the 4th Laird of Blair, a title to which he became heir through his great grandfather, George Drummond of Lidcrieff, on June 16th 1630.[377] After the death of his first wife, George Drummond married his cousin, Marjory, daughter of Bishop Graham, on 17th August 1633. Among the children of George and Marjory were David, George, Archibald, William, Margaret and Jean.[378] David Drummond became a Bailie of the Town Council and married Christane Graham, daughter of Patrick Graham of Rothiesholme.[379] Margaret became the second wife of Patrick Monteith of Egilsay, while George was apprenticed in 1643 in Edinburgh but later joined the Royalist cause (see below).

George Drummond was very prominent in Orkney, becoming Provost of Kirkwall from 1648 to 1650.[380] He seems, however, to have been on bad terms with the Earl of Morton and was conveniently out of Orkney at the time of the arrival in Kirkwall, in September 1649, of George Hay, 3rd Earl of Kinnoul, who came with some Danish mercenaries to pave the way for the Marquis of Montrose. Montrose's intention was to use the islands as a springboard for an invasion of Scotland on behalf of King Charles II. After being apprenticed in Edinburgh, Drummond's son, George, had joined the Royalist cause and had received a commission that angered the Earl of Morton.[381] In a letter to the Marquis of Montrose, Kinnoull wrote, *"I shall humbly intreat your Lords: to send my Lord (Morton) ane absolute commissione for these Islandes, and that you wold recalle such Commissiones as hes Lords: conseaves to be his prejudice, as George Drummondes, whose father is my Lords ennimie, and is gone to the south to shunne ingaging in this business."*[382] Shortly after this letter was sent, Royalist affairs in Orkney fell into confusion when both Kinnoul and his uncle, the 8th Earl of Morton, died within days of one another.

Unlike his father, young George Drummond took a prominent part in Royalist affairs in Orkney,[383] including the signing of an order note for arms from local merchant, John Pottinger.[384] *"Mister potenger delifer al the Shabers (sabres) you haue to this berer and get a reset (receipt) from him lykuais 2 hag botes* (hagbuts) *of found"* (cast metal).[385] Young George's part in the Royalist cause came to a sad end following Montrose's defeat at Carbisdale, which resulted in the death or capture of most of the Orcadians who made up a large part of his army. Young George was captured by supporters of the Covenanters in Westray and was held in Noltland Castle until Parliamentarian troops, under Captain Cullace, arrived in Orkney to subdue the islands.[386] Young George made several escape attempts, which resulted in his transportation to Caithness, where he was tied to a post and shot.[387]

Too late to prevent his son's execution, George Drummond senior was given a commission by the Committee of the Estates, which governed Scotland at this time, to restore order in Orkney and Shetland. In a letter dated 2nd October 1650, Drummond wrote to Mr Robert Douglas, minister in Edinburgh, concerning this commission and his requirement to raise a regiment. He lamented the state of affairs in Orkney, where all the ministers had been deposed except two.[388] Drummond appealed for a warrant to allow the remaining ministers to marry two of his daughters (one to Patrick Monteith and the other to Patrick Blair). He finished by saying he was about to set sail from Orkney to Shetland to fulfil his orders.[389]

All this worry and turmoil took its toll on Drummond. In a letter dated 29th January 1653, from Marjory's brother to Patrick Smyth of Braco (49), David Graham of Gorthie wrote that he *"expects every moment to hear of Balloch's death and that his sister is a widow"*.[390] His gravestone suggests he died soon after this.

51. Mary Drummond 1664/Patrick Blair of Little Blair

Associated with George Drummond's gravestone is the memorial to his daughter, Mary, which can be found on the north side of the choir, just beyond the Royal Oak memorial. Originally, the two stones are likely to have lain side by side, with the text continuing from one to the other. The text is all in Latin and translated says:

> Here likewise rest the said Mary
> Drummond whose virtues
> accorded with her fair lineage
> for on her mother's side she was
> the granddaughter of the famous
> John Napier of Merchiston.
> Her zeal for Christ sprang from her
> knowledge of Him. She was an obedient
> child, a very loving and compliant
> wife, a kind and untiring mother
> and a most faithful and loyal
> friend. On Feb 8 1664 God rewarded
> her with the death of the righteous,
> as he now rewards her with the
> never ending enjoyment of her Saviour.
> Here too lies Marjorie Blair, who
> died on the 6th August 1670
> at the age of 18
>
> She left surviving offspring,
> Marjorie, Anne and
> Margaret Blair
> to her husband Patrick Blair,
> who very sorrowfully gave
> orders for the erection of
> this monument.[391]

Mary Drummond was the granddaughter of the inventor of logarithms, John Napier.

There is nothing like a bit of name-dropping to get one up on your fellow Kirkwallians! John Napier of Merchiston (1550-1617) was certainly famous, being the Scottish mathematician who invented logarithms and whose name is still remembered today in Edinburgh's Napier University. John Napier's father, Alexander Napier, was married to Janet Bothwell, sister of Adam Bothwell, Bishop of Orkney. Adam Bothwell corresponded with his brother-in-law during his period in Orkney and these letters have been preserved.[392] The Orkney Bishop encouraged Alexander Napier to send his son to school in either France or Flanders and, after attending St Andrews University at the age of 13, John Napier did indeed study in Europe, mainly in Paris. Napier's first wife was Elizabeth Striveling (or Stirling), by whom he had two children, Archibald and Joan. Elizabeth died in 1579 and he married Agnes Chisholm, by whom he had ten children, John, Robert, Alexander, William, Adam, Margaret, Jean, Elizabeth, Agnes and Helen. Agnes married George Drummond in 1620 (see previous entry) and one of their offspring was Mary, the subject of the gravestone.[393]

Mary's husband, Patrick Blair, was the trusted servant of the Earls of Morton, acting as Sheriff-depute in Orkney during the Cromwell years and beyond, and was Provost of Kirkwall 1654-58.[394] Sheriff Blair was given the task of sorting out the affairs of the 7th and 8th Earls of Morton, who had died in Orkney in 1648 and 1649 respectively. An investigation was carried out into the Earls' rentals, arrears, houses and contents, with inventories of the contents of the Palaces of Birsay and Kirkwall being drawn up.[395] His investigations also involved the loan given by Sir Andrew Dick in 1647 to the 7th Earl of Morton (see 44).

Blair was one of the principal heritors of Orkney and, in 1662, was appointed by the Commissioners of Excise to audit all their business. Following the death, in 1663, of Hugh Craigie (see 42), Orkney's representative in Parliament, William Douglas, 9th Earl of Morton, wrote to Orkney's heritors, recommending Sheriff Blair as Craigie's successor. The heritors duly obliged and Blair, with £30 sterling allowed for his expenses, was given a set of instructions, which included trying to recover £2920 paid to the City of Edinburgh during the time of Cromwell's occupation. He was again asked to represent Orkney at Parliament in 1669, when he was instructed to plead for a new valuation of the county to procure an Act in favour of Udallers in Orkney and Shetland, and to procure a warrant for putting "Witches and Incestuous persons to a triall". With the consequences of the upheavals of the previous two decades, he was also instructed to seek an exemption if more demands were made on Orkney. He was to highlight the fact that much support had been given to the Marquis of Montrose in 1649 and 1650, and also that Orkney had recently sent 100 men north to help garrison the fort at Lerwick against attack from the Dutch.[396]

During the height of the war with the Dutch, Patrick Blair had to ensure that people were prepared for any invasion.[397] The justices in the three eastern parishes of St Andrews, Deerness and Holm were particularly singled out and asked to have the beacons ready for firing to bring warning of attack.[398] In 1667, he was given specific intelligence that enemy warships were gathered in Bergen, Norway, ready for an attack on Shetland. He was to give warning to the Governor in Shetland and be on his guard in Orkney. A public proclamation was issued on February 28th at the Mercat Cross in Kirkwall, commanding the inhabitants to make ready all their weapons and gather at the Ball-Ley (area of land on the south side of Papdale) a week later. Instructions were given to the Justices of the Peace in the East Mainland parishes to light their beacons when they saw the beacon on Wideford Hill on fire.[399] The Dutch did attempt an attack on Shetland but turned back on reaching Noss, where they were duped into thinking that the fort in Lerwick had 1000 men and 40 guns.[400]

It was about this time that Sheriff Blair became involved in an affair that led to the downfall of the 9th Earl of Morton. In December 1664, the richly laden Dutch East India merchant ship, *Kennermerland*, was sailing round the north of Britain to avoid English naval activity in the Channel. On its way to Batavia (now Jakarta) in the Dutch East Indies, it struck the Stoura Rock in Out Skerries, Shetland, and quickly disintegrated. Only three men survived, but the local population had rich pickings, reputedly being drunk for "three weeks and a day" on the many barrels of wine and spirits which came ashore.[401] Once word got out, the Earl of Morton claimed possession of the wreck by virtue of his position as Vice-Admiral of Orkney and Shetland, and sent his agents to gather what they could. Some cannons and general cargo were recovered, along with some money chests, whose contents were counted out in Scalloway Castle. Sheriff Blair was asked to investigate but, by this stage, could only make some minor finds and reported that nothing else could be recovered. One of the agents sent by the Earl of Morton was Patrick Traill of Elsness (referred to at 45). His ship was captured by the Dutch in Bressay Sound and he had to pay a ransom, which he borrowed from Patrick Blair.[402] Meanwhile, at the instigation of Charles II, the Exchequer in Edinburgh disputed possession of the wreck and Morton was not only deprived of the goods but was also suspected of withholding some of the loot. After a lengthy investigation, Morton fell into disgrace, having been deemed to owe the King a considerable sum of money and, in 1669, his Orkney and Shetland property was annexed by the Crown.[403]

For a while, Patrick Blair stayed in the Earl's Palace, but, in 1672, he and his family were evicted to make way for Bishop Honeyman.[404] Blair's spouse at that time was Barbara Graham, daughter of Patrick Graham of Graemeshall.[405]

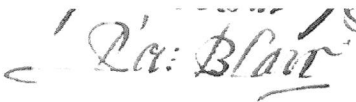

Signature of Patrick Blair from a letter to the Earl of Morton, dated 1665 (OA GD150(D38)2542/10).

52. Blair/Buchanan

Up in the triforium is a seventeenth century triangular gravestone pediment containing a crudely carved human face, together with emblems of mortality and a shield with the coats-of-arms of the Blairs and Buchanans. The dexter consists of a chevron between three roundels and a crescent, representing Blair. Above the shield is the Blair motto, VIRTUTE TUTUS (*protected by courage*). The sinister has the lion rampant of the Scottish Royal Arms, with fleur-de-lys both inside and outside the shield (the correct terminology is double tressure flory counterflory). Beneath the shield is the Buchanan motto NOBILIS EST IRA LEONIS (*the wrath of the lion is noble*).[406] On either side of the shield are the initials, 'PB' and 'IB', indicating a husband and wife. Unfortunately the identity of the couple being commemorated is unknown, except that the husband is a Blair and the wife a Buchanan.

The Buchanans' involvement in Orkney began in the early part of the seventeenth century, after the wife of

Sir John Buchanan of Scotscraig, Margaret Hartsyde, was accused of stealing jewels from her mistress, Queen Anne, wife of James VI. The couple had been in service at the court of King James and, although Sir John was cleared of any wrongdoing, he accompanied his wife into exile in Orkney, where her father was a Kirkwall merchant.[407] While in Orkney, the couple prospered, obtaining much land in Eday and Shapinsay. By 1622, their fortunes had been restored, with John having been knighted and a sub-tack of the Orkney Earldom awarded to him. Sir John acted as manager or rent collector in the islands for other tacksmen, including Sir George Hay of Kinfauns.[408] Sir John sold his estate of Sound, in Shapinsay, to his nephew, Arthur Buchanan, who represented Orkney, along with Hugh Craigie of Gairsay, in Cromwell's Scottish Parliament.

The use of the lion rampant in the family crest was adopted around 1420, when Sir Walter Buchanan married Isobel Stewart, daughter of Murdoch Stewart, Duke of Albany and Regent of Scotland. After Murdoch had been executed by James I, Buchanan's claim to the throne was lost and the colour of the lion was changed to black. The double tressure flory and counter flory were reputedly added after King Charles VII of France rewarded Walter's brother, Sir Alexander Buchanan, for his role in the victory over the English at the Battle of Bauge (1421).

53. John Cuthbert 1651 1668 1669/ Margaret Chalmaer

This large renaissance-style mural monument, with pedestal base and columns supporting an entablature, can be found at the west end of the nave on the north side. Text:

> In hope of a blessed resurrection
> here rests the corps of John Cuthbert
> Merd Burgess of Kirkwall
> Margaret Chalmaer his spouse &
> Margaret Cuthbert their daughter
> spouse to Andrew Mitchell
> Merchand there
> Obierant Anno Domi 1650
> 1651 1668 & 1669

Also in Latin:

> *A citizen of Edinburgh after many years*
> *thankfully gives the honour of a tomb*
> *to the buried ashes of his ancestors.*
> *John Mitchell, a merchant of Edinburgh,*
> *the only surviving son of Andrew Mitchell and*
> *the said Margaret Cuthbert had (this stone erected).*

There are a number of symbols on this monument, with a rose cherub and honeysuckle cherub above the pillars flanking a cherub floral. On the pedestal, from left to right, there is the hourglass, crossed spade and turfing iron, skull, crossbones and crossed staves.[409]

John Cuthbert and his wife, Margaret Chalmaer, had the house next to the Girnell, in Harbour Street. According to Hossack,[410] John Cuthbert was Girnell-keeper to Sir William Dick of Braid, who received an eight year tack of the islands in 1629. William Dick was a descendant of a pre-Reformation provost of the Cathedral, who, through banking and shipping interests, had become one of Scotland's richest men. He eventually impoverished himself, lending money for the Covenanter cause, and died in an English prison.[411]

The Girnell was a most important institution in the county, being the storehouse for bere, oats, malt and meal, paid in kind as rental and skat to the Earldom

John and Margaret Cuthbert lived next door to the Girnell, a very important institution in the county. He was the Girnell-keeper.

estate. The Girnell-keeper's house, which Cuthbert had built around 1647, stood gable-end to the sea. On the opposite side of the road is the Corn Slip, which was used to land and ship the goods to and from the Girnell.

Andrew Mitchell was Dean of Guild on the Town Council and it is known from the Minutes of the Town Council that he was dead by January 1669, which certainly agrees with the date on the memorial.[412]

54. Thomas Taylor 1666/Jennet Pottinger

On the north side of the choir, just past the transept, is this stone with shield and two much worn coats-of-arms. A Pottinger pelican (see next entry) could at one time be made out on the sinister side. On the outside border is the text:

> HEIR LYES ANE HONEST MAN THOMAS TAYLEOR MERCHANT BURGESS IN KIRKWAL SPOUS TO JENNET POTENGER WHO DEPARTED THE 1 OF MARCH 1666

Beneath the shield is:

> CORPS REST IN PEACE
> INTO THIS WORMIE CLAY
> TIL CHRIST SAL RAISE THEE
> TO A GLORIOUS DAY.

In Latin, POST FUNERA VIRTUS, *virtue triumphs o'er the grave*. Finally there is the MEMENTO MORI above the skull and crossbones.[413]

Hossack describes the Taylors as hereditary weavers.[414] Their property was on the west side of Victoria Street, opposite the former Lobban's butcher shop and was a few doors to the north of the home of the Pottingers (36). Thomas and Jennet's son, Magnus, developed the property by building houses on to the back of the building, which he endowed to his children and grandchildren. After Thomas Taylor's death, his widow, Jennet (or Jean), married James Murray of Clerdane[415] and is found living in the Upper Laverock (present day Main Street).[416] She was the daughter of Edward Pottinger (45) and Elspeth Traill, and was born about 1631.[417]

55. Marjorie Pottinger 1669/Thomas Dishington

This large stone is found in the north side of the choir and has a shield at the top, with three mullets above three pelicans vulned, flanked by initials 'MP'. The text says:

> HEIR RESTS MARIORIE POTINGER
> SPOUS TO THOMAS DISHINGTOUNE
> PRAECENTOR AND BURGES IN KIRKWAL
> OBIIT 23 FEBr 1669.[418]

The Taylors were "hereditary weavers" and lived in Victoria Street.

Although not native to Orkney, the Pottingers were well established in the islands by the early 1520s, with Alexander Pottinger of Deerness and his brother Thomas being described as roithmen and therefore one of the most prominent Orkney families. As has been seen, the Pottingers of Kirkwall in the seventeenth century were an important merchant family, with Marjorie being the youngest daughter of John Pottinger and Nicola Craigie.[419] Her sister, Elspeth, married Patrick Traill of Elsness and, just to keep it in the family, her other sister, Katherine, married their cousin, Robert Pottinger of Howbuster (son of Edward at 45).

The Pottinger surname appeared first in England and is associated with an occupation, deriving from the French word 'potagier', meaning a maker of pottage, a thick soup or stew.[420]

Marjorie's worn gravestone shows 'three pelicans in their piety'.[421] The pelicans are shown in the act of

Gravestone of Marjorie Pottinger with the Pottinger coat-of-arms showing "three pelicans in their piety".

wounding their breast in order to feed their young, a symbol of self-sacrifice. This coat-of-arms is also found on the arms belonging to a branch of the family which moved to Ulster in the seventeenth century. This branch seems to have been started by Edward's son, Thomas, who continued in the merchant trading business in Ballymacarrett. His family prospered and, by the middle of the eighteenth century, the country mansion known as Mountpottinger, on the County Down shore of Belfast Lough, had been acquired.

Marjorie's husband, Thomas Dishington, was a significant figure in seventeenth century Kirkwall. His parents were Elizabeth Tulloch and Andrew Dishington, minister in Stromness in 1599, Rousay and Egilsay in 1601 and Hoy c1614.[422] His grandfather was John Dishington, Sheriff of Orkney and Chamberlain to Earl Robert Stewart. Thomas is described as precentor (the person who leads the singing in a church) and session-clerk at Kirkwall.

As session-clerk, Thomas Dishington kept a record of deaths, including which bells, great or small, were to be rung for the deceased. In January 1657, he started a new register of baptisms and marriages. He also read the prayers when there was no minister.[423] This was during Cromwell's time, when most of the ministers had been deposed, following their allegiance to the Marquis of Montrose.

For the defence of the burgh, small arms were freely distributed among the townsmen and, in time of war, a special tax was imposed for buying ammunition. In 1666, during war with the Dutch, Thomas was responsible for collecting this tax in the area 'doon' the street from the Castle.[424]

Thomas's second marriage was to Margaret Elphinstone and the couple had several children, including Andrew, Thomas and James".[425]

In 1677, Thomas Dishington had a house at the back of Tounigar (next to the present-day oil tanks on Shore Street), called Gockhall.[426] The year before, he had brought a complaint to the Town Council that his peats had for years been prey to thieves. Consequently the Town Council issued a decree that his peats be protected.[427] Whether this had the desired effect is not known.

Thomas taught pupils in a private capacity and, in 1681, the Town Council installed him as assistant master in the Grammar School where John Shilps was the recently appointed master.[428] For many years prior to his instalment, Thomas's brother, John Dishington, had been master of the Grammar School until his death in early 1681.[429]

Thomas Dishington died at the start of 1682 and it was noted in the Kirk Session, "there was no Session, because God hath removed Thomas Dishington out of this lyfe to a better".[430] The funeral took place on 6th January and he was interred in St Magnus Cathedral.[431]

56. Patrick Prince 1673/Margaret Groat

This visually explicit stone, with a chequered border, is on the south side of the nave near the west end. At the top of the stone are the initials, 'PP' and 'MG'. The centre panel has a depiction of Death piercing a two-handled urn with a dart, while a cherub blows a call to life on a long trumpet, which projects obliquely downwards. There are also symbols of a coffin, turfing iron, hour-glass, sundial and spade. Above and below is the text, which reads:

> HEIR RESTS THE CORPS
> OF PATRICK PRINCE MERCHAND
> IN KIRKWALL
> SOMETIME ESPOUSED TO
> MARGARET GROTT WHO
> LEFT WITH HER EDWARD
> HARIE MAGNUS HELEN
> AND CATHARINE PRINCES
> TEMPUS ERIT (*the time will come*)
> THIS MONUMENT
> DOTH HEIR PRESENT
> A SUBJECT TO YOUR EYE
> FOR PATRIK PRINCE
> IS NOW GONE HENCE
> AND SO ABOVE DID FLYE
> HE LEFT BEHIND
> 5 CHILDREN KYNDE
> WITH ALL A MOTHER DEARE

Patrick Prince, as a successful businessman, would have gone to the Cathedral nave every September 29 to elect the town's councillors.

> TO HIM AND THEM
> IT WELL BECAME
> A MOTHER AND A PHEARE (*comrade*)
> OBIIT 9 MARCH 1673
> AETATIS 31 [432] (*aged 31*)

Patrick Prince was the son of Kirkwall bailie, Harie (Henrie) Prince, and Elisabeth, natural daughter to Patrick Smyth of Braco (49). According to Hossack,[433] Patrick Prince and his brother, Magnus, were successful merchants in Kirkwall, with Patrick holding much property in the burgh, including a building in Albert Street called 'Hell' (on the site of the former Woolworths).[434] Patrick's house was just south of the present Royal Bank of Scotland, in Victoria Street.[435]

In 1669, following King Charles II's renewal of Kirkwall's ancient liberties and privileges, there was a large intake of new members to the Council, which included a youthful Patrick Prince, as well as James Black (60), David Forbes (72), Robert Richan (61) and Robert Pottinger of Howbister (45).[436] Only a few propertied men were eligible to vote and traditionally they gathered in the nave of the Cathedral each September 29th to elect their Councillors. This date was a throwback to medieval times when saints' days were celebrated. Councillors were regarded as the guardian angels of the town and were elected on the feast day of the archangel, St Michael (Michaelmas).[437]

Patrick's wife was Margaret Groat, eldest daughter of Edward, son of Malcolm Groat of Tankerness.[438] After her husband's death, Margaret built a house on Broad Street, on the northern part of the site of the Provostrie, which had been demolished shortly before 1677. Its replacement had an oriel window, which made it a striking feature on Broad Street until 1884, when it, in turn, was demolished to make way for the current Town Hall. Margaret carried on her husband's business, with much success. In 1677, she was the third highest ratepayer in Kirkwall.[439] According to Hossack, she eventually moved south after marrying Edinburgh merchant, John Baird, on 7th December 1676.[440] This is at variance with Town Council minutes, which indicate that the couple remained in Orkney, with John Baird being, for a while, a member of Kirkwall Town Council.[441]

Shortly before Margaret died, she had given over the care of her children to her second husband. Two of the children, Edward and Catherine, were, however, in the custody of their aunt, Helen Fea, whose first husband was Edward Groat. She was very unwilling to give them up and offered to take on all the children, with the approval and advice of their uncle, Magnus Prince.[442] After coming of age, Edward married Elizabeth, the daughter of Mitchell Rendall of Breck and Barbara Irving (71), and Catherine married the Rev. James Heart, minister of Westray on 28th January 1685.[443] Of the other Prince children, Magnus sold 'Hell' in 1707 to William Fea[444] and Helen married Mr Legate, Sheriff-depute of Orkney.

57. John Sinclair 1676/James Adamson 1682

Next to the north door of the nave is this stone, which has two separate panels. The first panel has the initials 'IS' and 'MC' on either side of a heart. The text reads:

> IN HOPE OF A BLESd
> RESURECTION HERE
> RESTS THE BODYS OF JOHN SIN
> CLAIR MERd OBIIT 7 DE 16(7?)6
> AETA 87 & OF MARJORY CAR
> MICHAL HIS SPOUSE OB (7?) MAY
> 1647 AET 64 & (ALSO?) THER
> CHILDREN 1(671?)

Broad Street, before the building of the Town Hall, showing the Tolbooth in the foreground, on the Kirk Green. The house on the right with the oriel window was built by Margaret Groat, wife of Patrick Prince (56).

Orkney Library Photographic Archive

The second panel reads:

> ALSO BEFOR THIS
> MONUMENT RESTS
> THE BODYS OF JAMES
> ADAMSON MASON BURGES
> OF KIRKl OBIIT 23 APRIL
> 1682 AETA (74 & O)F ISOBEL
> SINCLAIR HIS SPOUSE OB 7 OC
> 1670 AETA 53 & LEFT ALYVE
> PATRICK ADAMSON WHO
> CARVED THIS IN MARCH 1689
> & ANDREW HIS BROYr THER CHILDREN
> VIVIT POST FUNERA VIRTUS
> (*virtue triumphs o'er the grave*)

Between the upper and lower panels on the dexter side can be seen the engrailed cross of Sinclair and on the sinister side a cross-crosslet.[445]

Prior to 1682, many of the gravestones in the Cathedral were likely to have been carved by James Adamson, whose house was on the east side of Albert Street. Adamson was succeeded in his business by his son Patrick, who obtained his freedom to carry out his trade as a mason in 1675.[446] The Adamsons performed much work for the Kirk Session, including an order for a couple of sundials for the Cathedral, when the town clock's reliability was questionable.[447] This first Cathedral clock, possibly dating from 1669, was a fairly crude instrument with only one hand and required daily winding.[448] The town's people felt more comfortable using the sundial.

In 1676, Adamson was chosen to be part of a group carrying out a valuation of all property in the town in order to alleviate the debt burden under which the burgh found itself following the fight to preserve Kirkwall's privileges. It was agreed that all the houses within the burgh, great and small, should be assessed according to their rent valuation. A part of this valuation would then be paid into the town's coffers. [449]

Hossack tells an interesting story regarding this gravestone.[450] James Adamson had received permission to raise a stone on the north wall of the nave for his wife, Isobel, and her parents, John Sinclair and Marjory Carmichal. Eventually James was buried below the stone and, after a few years, his son, Patrick, removed the stone and sold it, "having hewn off the letters". The Kirk Session heard about this and ordered Patrick to restore the stone. This Patrick did and, as can be seen from the text on the stone, took all the credit!

Patrick Adamson was married to Ursula, daughter of Robert Nicolson, the subject of the next memorial.

This memorial was once removed by a family member but the Kirk Session ordered that it be returned. The culprit took full credit for re-carving the stone.

58. Mort Brod - Robert Nicolson

The Mort Brod, perhaps the most easily remembered Cathedral memorial. It is the oldest mortuary board in Scotland and is in memory of Robert Nicolson.

'The Castle' in Main Street, owned by Robert Nicolson, who is remembered on the Mort Brod. Only the remnants of this building can be seen today.

This unique and iconic memorial is found hanging in the north side of the nave. It is a lozenge shaped, wooden hatchment, with a moulded frame, measuring 2 feet 4½ inches square, and is the oldest remaining mortuary board in Scotland.[451] On one face is painted the inscription:

>BELOW DOETH LYE
>IF YE WOLD TRYE
>COME READ UPON THIS BROD
>THE CORPS OF ONE
>ROBERT NICOLSONE
>WHO'S SOUL'S ABOVE WITH GOD
>HE BEING 70 YEARS OF AGE
>ENDED THIS MORTAL LIFE
>& 50 OF THAT HE WAS MARRIED TO
>IEANE DAVIDSON HIS WIFE
>BETWIXT THEM 2
>12 CHILDREN HAD
>WHEREOF 5 LEFT BEHIND
>THE OTHER 7
>WITH HIM'S IN HEAVEN
>WHO'S JOY'S SHALL NEVER END.

A scripture has been painted on the frame,

> "He shall return no more
> To his house neither shall
> His place know him any more". Job VII-X.

The other side is painted with a representation of Death sitting with his right arm resting on a sand glass and carrying a spade over his left shoulder. On the dexter flank is a bell and, on the sinister, the initials of husband and wife in monogram. In the top corner, two angels support a heart on crossed darts and hold a scroll with the admonition, MEMENTO MORI. Around the moulding is another scriptural quotation,

> "Wherefore he saith awake thou that
> sleepest and arise from the dead and
> Christ shall give thee light". Eph V & X1111[452]

Robert Nicolson, glazier, owned the house in Main Street called the 'Castle', the remains of which can still be seen today.[453] He also rented out property on the corner of the east end of Shore Street, where St Catherine's Place begins.[454] Robert had a nasty temper, being fined £50 Scots for he did, "in a sad and cruell manner, with his hands and ane drawn sword, in the night tyme, upon the street of Kirkwall, near or about the tolbuith (then situated at the bottom of the Strynd) of the said Burgh, beat blood, bruise, wound and abuse the said John Adome, complainer, in the back, head, hands and several other parts of his body, to the effusion of his blood in large and great quantities". On another occasion he beat up Patrick Hay, who was a pewterar.[455]

Robert Nicolson's son, James, painted the aforementioned troublesome town clock and the two sundials, provided by Patrick Adamson (57). He placed the clock on the west side of the steeple on 29th June 1683.[456] It is very likely that the Mort Brod was also a product of his artistic talent.

Two daughters are mentioned in the diary of Thomas Brown. Jean Nicolson married William Farquhar, glover, in February 1677 and Ursula married Patrick Adamson, mason, on 22nd November 1683. A son, also called Robert Nicolson, who inherited his father's business, was married on 10th November 1684 to Marie Maich, the daughter of an Englishman,[457] possibly one of Cromwell's garrison.

59. Robert Irving 1679/Barbara Williamson

This stone is found on the north side of the choir, towards the east end. The upper panel has a shield with helm and mantling, together with the initials CRI. The coat-of-arms on the shield has three sheaves of holly, each with three leaves. The first part of the text, on the perimeter of the stone, is much worn, but we can assume the following:

> (HERE RESTS IN THE HOPE) OF
> A BLISSED RESURECTION ANE PIOUS
> AND W(ORTHY GENTLE)MAN
> (ROBERT IRVING) OBIIT (*died*)
> (H)E WAS MARRIED WITH BARB(A)R(A)
> WILLIAMSON THE 10 OF JUN
> (1)652 & LEFT WITH HIR A(LI?)
> (S?)ON MARGARET & MARY
> (I)RVINGS THEIR CHILDREIN
> (VIV)IT POST FUNERA VIRTUS
> (*virtue triumphs over the grave*)
> (M)EMENTO MORI (*remember death*)

The panel at the bottom contains a turfing iron, coffin, hand with candlestick, cherub, hourglass and spade, all above a skull and crossbones.[458]

Clouston interpreted the initials 'CRI' as standing for Captain Robert Irving. From the Orkney Commissariat records, Clouston found that he died in February 1679, but was unable to find any relationship to any of the Orkney Irvings.[459]

Captain Robert Irving was appointed clerk to the Commissioners of Excise in 1661, a position with an annual salary of £100 Scots, to be taken out of his first collections.[460] The total proportion of excise for Orkney in that year was £1550 Scots. Irving was also collector of His Majesty's Cess from c1664-1679,[461] cess being a land tax imposed on landowners to pay for the stationing of troops in peacetime. In 1677, Irving opposed a petition to the Privy Council, drawn up by some local landowners, against the level of cess being imposed.[462]

Irving was often found working in conjunction with Sheriff Patrick Blair (51), who was given the task of sorting out the deceased Earl of Morton's affairs in

Captain Robert Irving received an annual salary of £100 Scots for being the clerk to the Commissioners of Excise. In 1661 the total excise tax raised in the county was £1550 Scots.

Orkney.[463] In November 1653, Irving, along with Captain Andrew Young, assisted in carrying out inventories of Morton's possessions from the Palace of Birsay. This was at a time when the Palace was requisitioned by Cromwell's troops.

Robert Irving was also clerk to the Justices of the Peace in Orkney. In 1665, he signed a document giving free passage to eight marooned mariners, who had been left behind in Shetland after King Charles II's fleet "of eighty sailles" had sailed from Bressay Sound to look for the Dutch fleet commanded by De Ruyter. Free passage to Caithness was given to the mariners after the Justices of the Peace were satisfied that the seamen wished to return to their ships. The Justices of the Peace were also careful to ascertain if there had been any plague in the fleet. With no money to maintain them, the mariners were given a document signed by

Robert Irving, asking other Justices of the Peace and Magistrates of Burghs to assist them in their passage to England to rejoin their ships.[464] It is very likely the authorities in Orkney were only too keen to be rid of this problem and one wonders if these seamen ever did return to their ships.

As the gravestone narrates, Irving married Barbara Williamson in 1652, with whom he had three daughters, Alison, Margaret and Mary, who were all alive when their father died.

60. James Black 1675/Helen Richan

Situated on the north side of the nave, this stone has the following text in two panels:

> HEIR RESTS THE CORPS OF
> JAMES BLACK SOMETYME
> MERCHANT BURGESS IN KIRKWALL
> WHO LEFT SURVIVING
> HELEN RICHEN HIS SPOWS
> JOHN JAMES ROBERT ISABELl
> MARGt AND JEAN BLACKS Yr
> LAWFULL CHILDREN
> OBIIT 20 JUNII 1675
> ANNO AETATIS 35".
> CORPS REST IN PEACE WITHI(N)
> THIS GROUND UNTILL ARC(HANGEL'S)
> TRUMPET SOUN(D)
> SOUL JOY ABOVE
> TIL THY CREATORS MIGHT
> BOTH REUNITE
> TO REIGNE WITH SAINTS IN LIGHT.

In the bottom panel is Greek text, translated as *behold the end of life*, and the symbols of a bell, candlestick, hand with bell, along with another bell above a skull and crossbones. Only the tops of the crossbones are visible, showing the bottom part of the stone is missing.[465]

Blacks had been in Orkney from the time of the Stewart Earls, when William Black had been a servant of Earl Robert Stewart.[466] Henry Black was captain of Kirkwall Castle in Earl Patrick's time[467] and Thomas Black was a former chamberlain of Orkney, who was persuaded to join the rebellion of 1614 and was one of the rebels captured in the Cathedral.[468]

James Black was a prominent Kirkwall merchant whose house was in present-day Main Street, next to the business premises of Robert Richan (61).[469] Like Patrick Prince (56), James Black became a member of Kirkwall Town Council in 1669.[470]

This tombstone was erected by John Richan (see next entry) on behalf of his sister, Helen, James Black's wife. Hossack incorrectly claimed this was the only monument in the Cathedral to have a Greek inscription (see 62 & 63).[471]

Of James Black's children, John ran the family merchant business until his death on 2nd July 1688.[472] Isabel, the oldest daughter, married a skipper, Patrick Linklater, son of the merchant, William Linklater, on 26th November 1685. She died on 14th October 1689.[473] Jean was married twice, firstly to William Orem, notary, in December 1691 and secondly to Charles Steuart, Stewart Clerk of Orkney.[474]

61. Robert Richan 1679/Isabella Bellenden

This richly decorated stone is to be found in the north side of the nave. Surmounted by a crown helm and mantling, the shield is quartered, with the first quarter a stag's head, and the second, third and fourth quarters cross-crosslets with double cross arms. This coat-of-arms is a variation of the Bellendens of Stenness, the Richans having no known arms.[475] Above the shield are the initials 'RR' and 'IB' between three stars. Around the perimeter of the stone is the text:

> HEIR RESTS THE CORPS
> OF ROBERT RICHAN OF LINCLATER
> MERCHAN AND BURGES OF KIRKWAL
> WHO DEPARTED THIS LYFE 1 DECr 1679

The text beneath the shield is in Latin and translated says:

> *He lived 61 years and on the*
> *1st of January 1660 married*
> *Isabella Bellenden*
> *who bore James,*
> *Arthur, George,*
> *Thomas and Margaret*
> *Richen, but James, Arthur*
> *and Thomas died before*
> *their father.*

This stone is in memory of the Richan family, who were exposed to potential scandal in 1677, when a John Drummond claimed to have had carnal knowledge of a daughter.

On either side of the shield are represented an hourglass with spade and turfing iron while below is a large skull and crossbones.[476]

The surname Richan appears to be a purely Orkney name, with Richans owning odal land in Orphir as early as the fifteenth century.[477] Robert was the younger son of Robert Richan, tacksman of Caldale, and was born at Caldale around 1618.[478]

He learned his trade of litster, being apprenticed to Thomas Warwick.[479] A litster was a dyer of cloth and this presumably formed the basis of his business, in which he was very successful. He acquired a considerable amount of property in the Clay Loan area and, in 1667, bought Linklater in Sandwick from Andrew Linklater.

Robert Richan served on the Town Council, being elected in January 1669, following the renewal of Kirkwall's privileges by King Charles II. He very quickly fell out with his fellow councillors, especially Provost Patrick Craigie, whom Richan described as "base and unfamous".[480] Craigie, in turn, warned him about his behaviour, telling him that he risked losing respect as a burgess of the burgh.[481] Robert's poor relationship with the Town Council continued when, in 1675, he was censured for not renewing his burgess ticket. His wife, Isobel, seems to have resolved that issue and paid up.[482]

Isobel Bellenden was Robert's second wife, his first wife being Mary Rowsay, with whom he had a son, Robert, and two daughters, Katherine and Jean. Isobel's parents were Adam Bellenden of Stenness and Agnes, daughter of Bishop George Graham (32). The Bellendens had come to Orkney in the wake of Bishop Adam Bothwell, whose mother was Katherine Bellenden, and through this connection they acquired a great deal of land from the Orkney Bishopric, mainly in Stenness and Evie. Interestingly, Isobel's sister, Ann, was married to Provost Patrick Craigie, who was on bad terms with Isobel's husband.[483]

In 1677, a family crisis was sparked in the Richan household. It was customary at that time for apprentices to live with the family of their employers. After a drinking bout, one of the apprentices, John Drummond, claimed to have had carnal knowledge of Margaret, the only daughter of Robert Richan's second marriage. Drummond was quickly summoned before the Kirk Session, having been reported by Richan's wife, Isobel, whose preference was that the claims be investigated quietly. Drummond confessed he had made up the story and was severely dealt with by the Session.[484] The affair did not seem to damage the reputation of the daughter as, a few years later, she married James Kaa (see 63).[485]

Three generations of the Richan family, from America, pictured beside a memorial stone of their ancestors (61). They came to Orkney in 2011 for a family reunion and are, left to right, Amie Richan, her father, Willard "Will", and his grandson, Henry Tippens-Richan.

Robert Richan's surviving son, George, was married firstly to Elspeth Mudie (George was factor and trustee for the Moodies of Melsetter), secondly to Isobel Dick and thirdly to Anne Ritchie, who survived him.[486] He acquired a site from Robert Nicolson, glazier, of Mort Brod fame (see 58), in the vicinity of the end of Main Street and Hornersquoy, on which he built a house in 1716, which showed above the back door his and his then wife's initials as well as his parents (see line drawing below).[487] In the same year, George

had to obtain a certificate of loyalty from the Kirkwall Presbytery to allow him to travel south, a requirement that followed the failed Jacobite Rebellion.[488] He seems to have inherited some of his father's adversarial characteristics. A few years earlier, in 1710, he had an altercation with the Dean-of-Guild, Andrew Young of Castleyards (79). Richan had insulted Young to such an extent that a fight broke out. Both men were fined, with Richan's penalty being later reduced due to the services he had rendered to the burgh.[489] George died in 1727 and left considerable property in his will.[490]

62. John Richan 1679/Janet Loutit

This stone can be found on the north side of the nave. Within a chequered border are the initials 'IR' and 'IL' between two stars and either side of a heart. Beneath is the text,

HEIR RESTS THE CORPS
OF ANE PIOUS AND VERTOUS
MAN JOHN RICHEN MERCHANT
BURGES OF KIRKWAL WHO WES
MARRIED WITH JANET LOUTIT
AND HAD WITH HIR 8 CHILDREN
VIZ JOHN ROBERT MARGERET
ISABEL CATHARIN AND JEAN
RICHANS BUT WILLIAM
AND JAMES RICHENS WENT
BEFOR THER FATHER TO EN
JOY COELESTIAL GLORE".
DUXIT UXOREM 2 JAN 1666
(*He was married on 2 Jan 1666*)
OBIIT 6 FEBRii AC 1679
(*He died 6 Feb 1679*)
ANNO AETATIS 35. (*Aged 35*)

Around the bottom panel in Greek is, "there remaineth therefore a rest for the people of God" (Heb IV. 9). The symbols in the bottom panel, in order, are a bell with canon, hand with bell and another bell with canon, above a skull and crossbones.[491]

John Richan came from a wealthy family of litsters, his parents being Robert Richan of Ovir Howbister in Orphir and Marion Reid.[492] This Robert Richan is possibly a half-brother of the Robert Richan in the previous entry, making John a nephew of Robert of Linklater. John also became a litster. It was the job of the litster to cleanse and prepare wool for household use. The tailor could then convert it into garments. Litsters also converted flax into cloth.[493]

In 1670, John was threatened by the Town Council for not declaring the trade he was practising. One of the functions of Royal Burghs was to regulate trade by the granting of licences to all classes of traffickers. This function lay in the hands of the Merchant Guild, led by the Dean of Guild. These licences varied from the basic Chapman's ticket, to the full Burgess and Guild Brother's ticket, which gave full trading rights. The cost of the licences varied according to the type of licence granted and the means of the applicant. Richan was ordered to pay £40 Scots and was given until Lammas to clarify his trading position.[494]

John was an elder in the Kirk and was commissioned to purchase a new mortcloth, which was used to cover the coffin in its carriage from the deceased's house to the grave. The new velvet cloth cost £169 18s Scots and a hire charge of two crowns within the town and four outside the town was set.[495] In 1677, he was chosen by the Kirk Session to investigate the rather sensitive case involving the daughter of his relative, Robert Richan of Linklater (see previous entry).

John Richan's house was on Victoria Street, on part of the site of the present day Orkney Hotel. A lintel can still be seen on the building with the initials 'IR' and 'IL' for John Richan and Janet Loutit, on either side of a heart and the date 1670. Richan was succeeded by

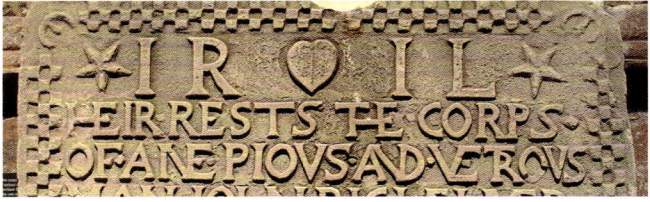
John Richan. A prominent lintel commemorating Richan and his wife, Janet, can be seen on the Orkney Hotel building.

his eldest son, John, who married Margaret Stewart in 1698.[496] The eldest daughter, Margaret Richan, married John Rendall, carpenter, on 13th December 1683.[497]

63. John Kaa 1679/Agnes Loutit

This stone is found on the north side of the nave, beneath that of General Burroughs (100). Under the initials 'IK' and 'AL' with loveheart is the text:

> HEIR RESTS THE CORPS
> OF ANE PIOUS AND HONEST
> MAN JOHN KAA SOMTYM
> BAILY OF KIRKWAL OBIIT
> 28 NOr 1679 AN AET 50
> HE WES MARRIED WITH
> AGNES LOUTIT UPON
> THE 2d JANr 1655
> AGNES 9 CHILDREN BOOR
> UNTO HIR MATE 6 DIED BE
> FOR THER SIR BY CRUEL
> FATE ROB MARGARET
> BARBARA WILLIAM THO
> MAS ELSPET BUT
> JAMES AND GEORGE WITH
> THER DEIR SISTER MARGARET
> SURVIVE FOR COMFORTING
> THE RELICT SAD
> AS SHE'S HAD GRIEF ITS HOPT
> THEY'L MAK HIR GLAD.

In Greek, there is the text, *There remaineth therefore a rest for the people of God* (Hebrews IV. 9) and in Latin, *Remember death* (Memento mori). In the bottom panel are the symbols of a turfing iron, a candlestick, a hand with bell, a clock, a crown and a spade all around the skull and crossbones.[498]

George Black, in his *Surnames of Scotland* gives one possible source of the surname Kaa, as originating from Mackay, with Mac dropped. Lamb, on the other hand, suggests Kaa is an alternative name for Skea, but this seems unlikely.[499]

John Kaa was the son of the notary public, Robert Kaa.[500] He became a Kirkwall merchant and part owner of a trading vessel. Along with Thomas Dishington (55), Kaa was tasked, in 1666, to collect the ammunition tax up the street from the Castle.[501] He built a double tenement on the south side of Albert Street in 1655, the same year as his marriage to Agnes Loutit, who was the daughter of Thomas Loutit of Lyking (67).[502] He became a Bailie (6th October 1674[503]) and was Dean of Guild on the Town Council towards the end of his life.[504]

In December 1674, it was decided that the four Bailies of Kirkwall would lead a purge of the town to rid it of "vagabonds and idle, unprovided persons coming and resorting to this town, and do greatly prejudice and wrong those who are civil persons and steal their peats and kaill". John Kaa was one of the Bailies who led the search up the street from the Strynd to the head of the town, including all the back lanes off the main streets. James Black (60) was part of his search party, while his father-in-law, Thomas Loutit of Lyking (67), was among the party that searched from the Strynd to the Shore. The minutes of the next Town Council meeting reported that the Bailies and Councillors had done due diligence to "the last dayis ordinance" and gave a list of such defective persons, many of whom were evicted from the town.[505] Four years later, John Kaa took part in the Riding of the Marches, in which Kirkwall Councillors checked on the Burgh lands.

Each year, town councillors and other prominent citizens took it in turns to lead the town guard during the annual Lammas Market. In 1676, John Kaa was chosen as Captain for the lower part of the town.

An opportunity was taken in April 1676 to augment the town's diminishing food supplies, when John Kaa and Thomas Loutit (67) were sent out to Wyre Sound to try and buy some sacks of meal from an Irish ship, which was anchored there. The trip seems to have been unsuccessful and a few days later they returned the 50 shillings Sterling given to them by the Town Council to buy the meal, minus the cost of the hire of a boat to get them out to Wyre Sound.[506]

Of the surviving offspring, James Kaa married Margaret, daughter to Robert Richan of Linklater and Isobel Bellenden (61). He served many years on the Town Council, becoming a Bailie like his father.[507] The "deir sister", Margaret, mentioned on the gravestone, married Kirkwall merchant, David Covingtrie (77) on Thursday October 10th 1689.[508]

64. Thomas Baikie 1665

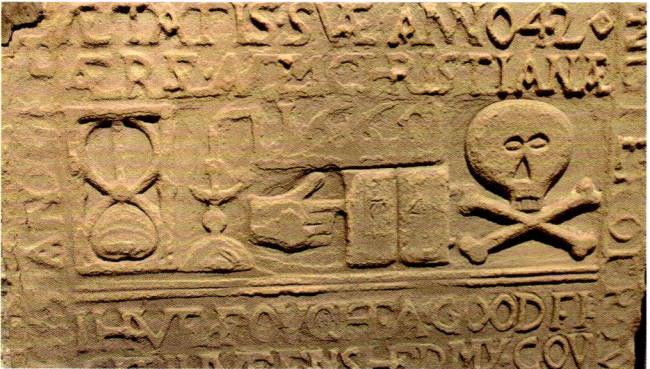

Thomas Baikie was described as "disorderly and unhanesome" by Kirkwall Presbytery.

This stone is on the south side of the nave, next to the Paplay tomb. The text is all in Latin and translated reads:

*In this tomb, calmly waiting
until Christ, Who is without sin
shall come for a second time,
to bring salvation, is laid away
the body of Mr Thomas Baikie,
a highly talented young man,
a very dear friend, a most
eloquent preacher, a most discerning
philosopher, a most
learned theologian, and also
the greatly revered and very
wise and devoted minister of
Egilsay, whom cruel death
forced to leave this life on
the 14th of April in the 42nd
42 year of his age and the year
1665 of the Christian era.*

The symbols of an hourglass, candlestick, hand with finger pointing to an open book and skull (showing front view) and crossbones are carved below, followed by more text,

I HAVE FOUGHT A GOOD FIGHT
I HAVE FINISHED MY COURSE
I HAVE KEPT THE FAITH
HENCEFORTH IS LAID UP FOR ME
A CROWNE OF RIGHTEOUSNESS

Round the perimeter is the text, "Here rests the corps of Mr Thomas Baikie Minister of Rowsay and Egilsha the 14 of April anno 1665 and of his age the 42 yeir".[509]

Thomas, who was a member of the Baikie family of Tankerness, assisted at the Cathedral in 1658. The previous minister, James Douglas, along with most other Orkney ministers, had been deposed for their loyal address to the Marquis of Montrose. The Kirkwall Presbytery did not take to him, describing his 'entry' as 'disorderly and unhanesome', for which Baikie apologised. He consequently gave up preaching in the Cathedral but became minister of Rousay and Egilsay in October 1659. He was described as very learned and a lover of literature, being one of the few native ministers at that time. He married Margaret Stewart.[510]

65. James Baikie of Burness 1679/Sibilla Halcro

This gravestone is located on the south side of the nave. The stone has the initials 'IB' and 'SH' either side of a heart. The text reads:

James Baikie of Burness became senior Bailie on the Town Council. He took part in the Riding of the Marches in 1678 and identified serious encroachments on common land.

HEER IS INTERRED
JAMES BAIKIE OF
BURNESS LATE BAILY
OF KIRKWALL OBIIT
22 MAI 1679 & HEW
JOHN THO ARTHUR
MARGARET BAIKIES
HIS CHILDREN PROC
REAT BETUIXT HIM
& SIBILLA HALCRO
HIS SPOUS DAUGHTER
TO HEW HALCRO OF
THAT ILK AND AN AETATIS 50

The sunken panel below the text shows a crown and sceptre above clouds, beneath which is a bearded figure with folded arms, wearing a loin cloth and flanked by two angels pointing heavenwards. The figure is standing on the skull and crossbones. Also on this panel are the Latin sayings running up from the skull and crossbones to heaven,

AD HOC *to this immortality*
AB HOC *from this life*
PER HOC *through this death*[511]

James Baikie of Burness was nephew of James Baikie 1st of Tankerness (see next entry). Baikie of Burness's town house was on the east side of Albert Street, just beyond the Long Gutter (the part which is now Laing Street). This mansion formed three sides of a square and had an arched gateway. In 1667, James purchased Burness, in Firth, from John Sclaitter.[512]

Baikie was elected Bailie in October 1675[513] and was senior Bailie of the Council by the time he took part in Riding the Marches in May 1678. This annual custom, still re-enacted today, was originally to check on the land owned in common by the burgh. A number of encroachments were identified, the worst being carried out by the owners of Carness and Work, who had built dykes on the common land.[514]

Baikie's wife, Sibilla Halcro, was granddaughter of Hew Halcro of that Ilk (41) and, after Baikie of Burness's death, she married John Sinclair of Braebister.[515] Along with her sister, Jean, Sibilla owned the island of Eynhallow, inherited from the Halcro estate.[516]

Baikie's son, Hew, succeeded him and he purchased from David Craigie of Oversanday (78) the house on Broad Street next to Tankerness House that had been the residence of the Cathedral Treasurer in pre-Reformation times. In 1700 he sold this house to his brother, Thomas (Tho on the gravestone), who was minister of the Cathedral.[517]

This Thomas Baikie was baptised on 1st July 1672 and went to St Andrews University, where he gained an MA. In 1693, when still a student, Thomas was entrusted by the Town Council to carry the taxes to Edinburgh. He must have been deemed reliable and trustworthy by the Kirkwall City Fathers, who, knowing he was due to leave for the Capital, handed him 1000 merks Scots to take to the Receiver-General. He was paid twelve pounds Scots for his troubles.[518]

After the disestablishment of Episcopacy, in 1689, Orkney was without a Presbytery for a while. Thomas, therefore, had to travel to Aberdeen to be confirmed as minister of the Cathedral, being ordained at Cullen.[519] Thomas was an implacable opponent of Episcopacy and suffered for his views, becoming the butt of scurrilous and "reproachful rhyms" (as he called them in a later complaint to the Commission of Assembly). These were circulated by the schoolmaster at Kirkwall Grammar School, Thomas Fullerton, who later became minister of Westray. A famous story tells of how, on a Sunday, early in January 1703, Thomas was ill in bed with no-one available to take his place in the pulpit. He and his wife, Elizabeth Fea, were dismayed to hear the Cathedral bells being rung and, on seeing the congregation make its way into the building, his wife hastily helped her husband to dress. They hurried to the Cathedral, where they found his Episcopalian rival, John Wilson, officiating. Mrs Baikie mounted the pulpit and dragged Wilson out, while Thomas, still with night cap on his head, dismissed the congregation and had the doors locked. David Slater, the Beadle, was dismissed for having rung the bells without Baikie's approval.

It is interesting that it was Thomas Baikie's own relatives, the Baikies of Tankerness, who provided John Wilson and the Episcopalians with a meeting place on Broad Street, following Wilson's removal, in 1694, as minister of the Cathedral. In 1712, after Parliament passed the Act of Toleration allowing Episcopalians freedom of separate worship, Thomas denounced them from the pulpit in a frenzy of intemperate language, calling them "Baal-worshippers".[520]

Thomas Baikie married thrice, all of his wives having the first name Elizabeth.[521] He had ten children with his first wife, the above-mentioned Elizabeth, daughter of James Fea of Whitehall. His second wife was Elizabeth, daughter of John Nisbet of Swannay, with whom he had three children. His third wife was Elizabeth, daughter of David Traill of Sebay, and their daughter, Christina, married Rev. John Yule, who also became minister of the Cathedral and was followed by his son, the Rev. Robert Yule (87). Thus members of the one family occupied the pulpit of St Magnus for some 125 years.[522] Thomas Baikie died in 1740 at the age of 68, and in the 44th year of his ministry.

66. Captain Peter Winchester 1677/Jean Baikie 1674

This memorial of Renaissance style is built into the wall of the south side of the nave. On each side is a pilaster entwined with vine-scrolls, supporting an entablature on which is a triangular pediment. The frieze below the moulded cornice bears two bunches of grapes with stalks crossed and above each pilaster there is a glyph carved with a cherub. The pediment is capped by a bold finial of three thistle heads and on each rake, a dove. Within the pediment and below an hour-glass are the initials 'PW' and 'IB' in monogram flanked by the date 1675. The main text reads:

THIS IS THE BURIAL PLACE OF CAPTAIN
PETER WINCHESTER WHERE LYE
INTERED THE BODIES OF HIS VERTOUS
WIFE JEANE BAKIE DAUGHTER
TO JAMES BAKIE OF TANKERNESS
& OF THEIR 3 CHILDREN ALEXr PETER
& ARTHUR

HIC ABREPTA VIRO TRIPLICI
Here torn from her husband and

Chapter 7 - The Seventeenth Century - 'Thou shalt not make idols'

Captain Peter Winchester was witness in a court case involving one of his sailors. The result was that the crewman's wife was placed on the stool of repentance.

CIRCUNDATA PROLE
surrounded by her three children,

FOEMINEI SEXUS GLO
lies a great glory of the female sex.

RIA MAGNA IACET
She is dead but her virtue is still

OCCIDIT AT REDOLET FRAGRANS
fragrant after death.

POST FUNERA VIRTU
Virtue triumphs o'er the grave

CHARA IOANNA SOLO
Jean was right dear on earth;

CLARA IOANNA POLO
Jean is bright clear in Heaven

1674

Below the text and above the gravestone symbols, in an arch, is the Latin saying, MORS ULTIMA LINEA RERUM, *death is the end of all things.* The symbols consist of a rose, bell, candlestick, hand with bell inverted, tree and axe, rose, bell with skull and crossbones, beneath all of which is the turfing iron and spade crossed.[523]

Captain Peter Winchester was a very prominent figure in Orkney in his day, being an important merchant trader. In the Orkney Archives, there are a large number of his inventories, vouchers, bonds, trading and voyage accounts, and business letters, which show he frequently sailed to Leith and Amsterdam.[524] In 1666, he brought in ammunition for the defence of Kirkwall during one of the wars with the Dutch.[525] He was at least part owner of the armed frigate, *St Peter of Kirkwall*[526] and possibly the *Morton,* as well as the frigate, *Sound,*[527] which, in November 1670, was used to transport the renders (taxes in kind) raised in Orkney to the Exchequer in Edinburgh.[528]

From the surname, it can be deduced that Peter Winchester was not local. Hossack says his family, originally English, came from the Elgin area and that he was probably the son of Peter Winchester, who, in 1638, was Collector of Excise in Kirkwall.

Hossack relates a couple of amusing stories about the Captain, which are worth repeating. When Peter first came to Orkney, he was the subject of a 'wind-up'. He was told that, when he accepted hospitality from an Orcadian, he must eat all that was offered or fight his host, as refusal of food or drink would be an insult. Needless to say, the situation arose when he found himself being hosted by a kindly family in Stromness. He continued to eat all that was put in front of him and the hosts, being surprised by his appetite, kept supplying him with victuals. At last he could take no more and alarmed his hosts with an angry shout, "Oh damn it, no more; I must fight him!"[529] Another story recounts how, on returning from a long voyage, he was summoned before the Kirk Session as a witness. One of his sailors, Patrick Stewart, was surprised to find his wife nursing a young child, a year having passed since he had left Kirkwall. The wife assured her husband that everything was in order, which satisfied the naïve sailor until a friend suggested he look for the father of the child. The sailor was outraged at the friend and had him summoned before the Kirk Session. Captain Winchester was called as a witness and had to confirm the time of their departure from Elwick Bay, which was 31st March 1668. As the baby was born on 9th March 1669, the sailor was fined for leaving home too soon and the wife was placed on the stool of repentance![530]

The dumping of ballast in and around the Oyce, which ultimately led to the filling in of much of the bay, was contrary to King Charles II's laws concerning the clearing and cleaning of 'all ports, crieks, harbours and landing places'. Kirkwall Town Council was responsible for enforcing these rules in the Kirkwall Harbour area. In 1676, Patrick Traill of Elsness (mentioned at 45) was reported for repeatedly carrying out this misdemeanour.

Along with some others, Captain Winchester was asked to view the area where Traill was accused of dumping his ballast and to submit a report to the Town Council. Traill was eventually fined £6 Scots.[531]

Captain Winchester was twice married, his first wife being Jean, the daughter of James Baikie of Tankerness. The date, 1674, on the gravestone probably relates to her death. In March 1676, he married Helen, daughter of Walter Stewart, minister of South Ronaldsay and Burray, and they had a daughter Sibillia. In September 1677, Winchester was tragically drowned off Fraserburgh, along with Richard Dennison, skipper, and fourteen others. Helen Stewart subsequently married John Traill of Elsness, whose town house was in Victoria Street and their richly carved lintel can still be seen on the front of the Orkney Hotel, with the initials 'IT' and 'HS' (John Traill and Helen Stewart) in monogram, along with the year of their marriage, 1679.[532]

James Baikie of Tankerness belonged to an old Orkney family, members of which had been burgesses of Kirkwall since the mid-sixteenth century. Magnus Baikie had acquired land in the toonship of Isbister in Birsay and his son, Thomas, had become a burgess. Each generation had prospered and, by the time Thomas's great grandson was 26, the above-mentioned James was involved in money lending, using the borrower's estate as security. In 1630, James bought land in Tankerness, which included the Hall of Tankerness (originally built in the mid-sixteenth century for the Groats), to add to the land of Grind in St Andrews. It was also through money lending that he eventually acquired his town house in Kirkwall (Tankerness House).

67. Elizabeth Elphinstone 1680/Thomas Loutit

This stone is found on the east side of the north door of the nave and has a border ornamented with floral paterae of two types. The initials 'TL' and 'EE', flanking a heart, are found above the text which reads:

HEIR RESTS THE CORPS
OF ANE VERTEOUS & PIOUS
WOMAN ELIZABETH
ELPHINSTON SPOUS TO
THOMAS LOUTIT OF
LYKING ONE OF THE BAILIES
OF KIRKWAL OBIT 21
MAY 1680 ANO AETATIS
36 THEY WER MARRIED
THE 29 DECEMBER 1668
BETVIXT WHOM WER
PROCREAT JOHN MAG
EDW THO JEAN CLARA ROB
AGNES & DAV LOWTITS

ONLY 2AR ALYVE & 7 LYES
HEIR INTERD WITH HER.

In Latin,

*Oh death how harsh, how grievous
are thy laws!
If there were no death, how
happy everyone would be!
Death waits us all; the hour none
knows, remember death.*

The symbols below are, from left to right, a turfing iron, coffin, candlestick, hand with bell, hourglass and spade, all above a skull and crossbones.[533]

Elizabeth Elphinstone was the daughter of John Elphinstone of Lopness.[534] Her brother was the autocratic Colonel Robert Elphinstone, who came to Kirkwall in 1690 and lived in the Earl's Palace, Kirkwall, after obtaining the tack of both the Earldom and Bishopric estates.[535] Tacksmen, such as Elphinstone and his successor, Sir Alexander Brand, did their best to extract as much as they could out of Orkney, despite a run of bad harvests and widespread famine.

After the death of Elizabeth, Thomas Loutit did not remain a widower for long and, on Thursday 2nd March 1682, he married Marjorie Traill, daughter of James Traill of Westove, at Westness in Rousay.[536] Thomas served on Kirkwall Town Council for many years, starting in July 1670, becoming treasurer in November 1676[537] and Bailie in September 1679.[538] He often worked in conjunction with John Kaa (63) and took part in riding the marches in May 1678. He was a captain of the Town Guard for the Lammas Market of the same year and the one following.

The lands of Lyking in Sandwick had been in the possession of the Loutits since before 1600.[539] The north part of the double tenement at the entrance to Victoria Street, which belonged to Patrick Prince (56), was let to Loutit of Lyking. One of Thomas Loutit's surviving children, Thomas, mentioned on the gravestone, bought the whole property in 1692. This Thomas Loutit was, like his father, a Bailie of the town and became Provost of Kirkwall for a brief time in 1694.

68. Elizabeth Irving 1681/George Traill

Just beyond the south transept, on the south side of the nave, is this gravestone, which has a heart flanked by the initials 'GT' and 'EI'. The text has first, in Latin, MEMORIA JUSTI BEATA, *the memory of the just is blessed*, followed by:

HEIR RESTS THE CORPS
OF ELIZABETH IRVING
SPOUSE TO GEORGE TRAIL

The bottom panel has the symbols of a turfing iron, coffin with bearers, candlestick, hourglass, hand with dart of death, axe hewing down a tree and shovel, all around the skull and crossbones.⁵⁴⁰

Elizabeth Irving, along with her sister, Barbara (71), was the daughter of William Irving of Kirbuster (sometimes described as of Gairstay), 'baillie of Shapinsay' who, as one of the Commissioners in 1627, reported on the state of the island.⁵⁴¹ A younger son of Henry Irving of Elwick,⁵⁴² he was a self-made man who married well, first into the Moodie family, then to Elizabeth Baikie, sister of James Baikie, 1st of Tankerness (66).⁵⁴³ Elizabeth Irving herself married into another well-off Orkney family. In her 1673 marriage contract to George Traill, her father-in-law, James Traill of Westove, gave the couple 3000 merks, with her mother, Elizabeth Baikie, donating 2000 merks.⁵⁴⁴ Incidentally, a descendant of her great uncle was the famous American writer, Washington Irving.⁵⁴⁵

Elizabeth's husband, George Traill of Quandale (Rousay), was Provost of Kirkwall from 1688 to 1691 and again from 1695 to 1698. His first spell as Provost was during the turbulent end of the reign of Catholic King James VII and the subsequent "Glorious Revolution" of William of Orange.⁵⁴⁶

The role of Kirkwall Magistrates included administering the law in the Burgh. In March 1698, Provost George Traill and Bailie James Kaa (63) heard the case of

George Traill was a Kirkwall Magistrate whose sentences – one of which is detailed in this book - sometimes took little account of poor harvests and starvation among the poor.

OF QUANDAL MERCHANT
BURGES OF KIRKWALL
OBIIT 26 JULY 1681 AN
NO AETATIS 42 THEY
WER MARRIED1o JANr
1674 BETWIXT WHOM
WER PROCREAT JEAN
JAMES & ELIZABETH TRAILS
SERIUS AUT CITIUS SED
Whether sooner or later
EM PROPERAMUS AD UNAM
we hasten to one place
TENDIMUS HUC OMNES
Hither are we all bound
HAEC EST DOMUS ULTIMA
This is the last home
FATI OMNIA MORS AEQUAT
of fate. Death levels all.
MEMENTO MORI
Remember death.

Selling fish at 'The Brig'. The house to the rear was built by George Traill around 1682 and was demolished to make way for, what was recently, Stevenson's the newsagents.

Jean Seatter, who was accused of stealing some cuts of beef, a pair of stockings and some bere. She was also accused of hiding them in the house of Ursula Nicolson (58), who was charged with reset. Ursula was cleared of her charge, but Jean Seatter was found guilty and sentenced to be taken to "the rampart of the bridge tomorrow about 11 of the clock, and there to be stripped of her clothes above the belt, and to receive from the Lockman three stryps with a cord or tow about her shoulders at the said place". The punishment was to be repeated at the Mercat Cross and at the head of the town. Banishment from the town was to follow.[547] This justice was meted out at a time of failed harvests and general starvation amongst the poor.

In May 1689, George Traill, as commissioner, attended a meeting of the Estates of Scotland, called by Prince William of Orange in order to gain acceptance as king north of the border. George Traill reported to the Town Council on his attendance at the meeting, explaining that he had returned home after the convention had been dissolved and a parliament called. George Traill did not find himself sufficiently warranted to attend this parliament.[548] The situation in Scotland took some time to resolve and it was a year later before William was offered the crown.[549] As a result of the political unrest, there was much nervousness in Kirkwall, with four canons being placed on carriages near the Corn Slip next to the Girnel.[550]

George Traill appears to have fallen out with his fellow Magistrates and Councillors, as he left town in 1698 in what Hossack describes as a 'huff' and a new Provost had to be elected.[551] The Town Council wrote to him, asking him to return to Kirkwall and "behave as Provost".[552]

George Traill's first wife, Elizabeth Irving, died in 1681 and was buried in the Cathedral.[553] Traill then married Anna, second daughter of James Baikie of Burness (65),[554] on 9th March 1682,[555] and built a house in Bridge Street near the brig (present day Stevenson's stationer shop).[556] The red sandstone lintel, with their initials 'GT' and 'AB', can still be seen today on the east side of the building.

Regarding the children mentioned on the gravestone, Jean was baptized on July 20th 1676 and James on March 9th 1678. This James must have died young as George Traill, with his second wife, Anna Baikie, had another James, who was baptised on August 18th 1684. Elizabeth (written as 'Baffe' on the baptismal record – 'f' representing the cursive 's') was baptized on June 17th 1679.[557] She went on to marry Thomas Jamieson, shipmaster of Queensferry.[558]

69. George Liddell of Hammer 1681

This stone is the most westerly on the south side of the nave and is one of the best preserved gravestones in the Cathedral. It has a shield with helm and mantling, a wreath and the arms of Liddell and Traill. The dexter arms on the shield consist of a bend with three mullets between a bird's head erased in chief and a boar's head in base, being the arms of the laird of Hammer. The sinister arms consist of a chevron between two muscles in chief and a trefoil in base, representing his wife's family. Round the perimeter, the text is:

HEIR LYIS IN HOPE OF A
BLESSED RESSURRECTION A WORTHIE
GENTLEMAN
GEORGE LIDDELL OF
HAMMER WHO DIED THE 27 OF OCTOr
1681 AETAIS 48

In the middle is text in Latin, which translated says:

*Death hastens; no flight avails
to pay the tribute of mortality.
Man is bound by nature's law.
All things go back to whence
they came and seek their mother
and what has been returns
again to nothingness.
But more I lament the loss
of time. Material damage everyone
can make good. None can make
good the loss of time. Remember death.*

The panel at the bottom contains the symbols of a turfing iron, coffin, candlestick, hand with bell inverted, hour-glass and spade over skull and crossbones.[559] Two faces are also to be seen on the gravestone. The one on the left is shown with two small wings, representing Liddell's soul being carried to heaven. The face on the right has a hat with neck band showing that Mrs Liddell was still alive at the time the stone was carved.

George Liddell was for a time Chamberlain to the Stewartry of Orkney and had lands at Hammer in Birsay. He married Elizabeth, daughter of Thomas Traill of Holland, in 1661. They had several children, including William, Andrew (1671-c1730), Patrick (baptized on November 6th 1677 by James Wallace) and a daughter, Catharin, who died very young.[560]

In 1679, George Liddell pursued Patrick Craigie through the courts for debts, which resulted in the former Provost being jailed. Craigie had successfully defended Kirkwall's municipal rights, procuring a new confirmation of these ancient privileges.[561] Although he was successful, Craigie had not only accrued a bill

George Liddell's dogged pursuit of a debt resulted in a former Kirkwall Provost being jailed. The Provost, Patrick Craigie, had previously defended the town's privileges to his own personal cost.

of £7000 Scots for the burgh of Kirkwall, but also had squandered his own fortune and that of his wife. Liddell took advantage of Craigie's predicament, seeing the opportunity to acquire much of his property, which included lands in Sandwick and Holm together with a house in the Laverock (Victoria Street).[562] Patrick Craigie died in the Tolbooth in Kirkwall in 1682.

George Liddell predeceased Patrick Craigie, the diary of Thomas Brown not only giving the time of his death, around 4 am on Thursday 27th October 1681, but also the place where this happened, in 'Mags Paplay's tenement'.[563] This is likely to have been the tenement in Bridge Street, near the present day Torvhaug Inn, belonging to Magnus Paplay, weaver.[564] George's second son, William, inherited the estate.

70. John Edmondstone 1682/Elizabeth Mowbray

This stone can be found on the south side of the nave. Round the perimeter, the text reads:

> HEER LYIS ANE HONEST GENTLEMAN
> JOHN EDMONDSTONE BAYLIE OF
> KIRKWALL OBIIT 26 JAri 1682
> AETA 81 & ELI(Zt) (MO)WBRAY HIS
> SPOUS AETATIS SUAE 60

In the middle:

> HEER ALSO LYIS ANE DISCREIT
> WOMAN ANNA EDMONSTONE
> (note the missing 'd' in Edmonstone)
> HIS DAUGHTER
> & SPOUS TO ARTHUR
> MURRAY MERd BURGES
> OF KIRKWALL & GEORGE
> JOn PAT MATH ARTH ALEX
> ELIZt & ANNA MURRAYES
> THEIR CHILDREN.
> SERO GALLICANTU
> *At even, and at the cock crowing*
> NOCTIS MEDIO ET MANE
> *at midnight and in the morning*
> PULSAT DOMINUS DOMUS
> *the master of the house knocks*
> NAM
> *for*
> INFANTES PUBERES
> *Death, who spares none, has but*
> GRANDAEVOS SEMISENESQUE
> *lately carried off from one and*
> UNA EX AEDE TULUT NUPER
> *the same house, young people,*
> MORS NEMINI PARCENS
> *people advanced in years and*
> *people of middle age.*

The panel at the bottom has the symbols of hour glass, skull and crossbones and coffin.[565]

John Edmondstone succeeded his father-in-law, Matthew Mowbray, as Chamberlain-depute of Orkney and was in office in 1653.[566] Mowbray was also a Bailie of Kirkwall, being elected in 1621-22, 1629-31 and 1638-41.[567] Mowbray resided in South Ronaldsay in the mansion house of Newark, which was built in the 16th century, but little of which remains today. Mowbray died in 1648 and was buried in St Peter's Kirkyard, South Ronaldsay.[568]

Edmondstone and his son-in-law, Arthur Murray, inherited, from Matthew Mowbray, a property on the west side of Victoria Street, which became known as 'Arthur Murray's Great Lodging'. This house had stone carvings from the Bishop's Palace inserted into the walls. It was also used as a convenient stopping point for the administration of the 'cat', when convicted criminals were being whipped through the town.[569] The prisoners were led to the Ramparts at the Shore, stripped to the waist and whipped by the hangman. Surrounded by the officers of the Burgh, with the drummers in front, the offenders were led to various stages in the town where further flogging was administered.[570] One of these stages was in front of Arthur Murray's tenement in Victoria Street. For good measure, victims could then be banished from Kirkwall for life. Much of Murray's Lodging was eventually demolished in 1900.[571]

John Edmondstone was Bailie of Kirkwall in the period leading up to the arrival of the Marquis of Montrose. With no Town Council in the years 1651-1654, he resumed his duties after this period, when Patrick Blair (51) was Provost.[572] Following the Restoration, he was one of the Kirkwall councillors to be declared a rebel on grounds of disloyalty, charges brought by the 9th Earl of Morton, who also mounted an attack on Kirkwall's privileges.

Arthur Murray was brother to Patrick Murray (75) and descended from the Murrays of Garth (16).[573] Hossack describes Arthur as unscrupulous in acquiring wealth and property, having to be censured by Kirkwall Magistrates.[574] He was accused, among other things, of treating the Magistrates with contempt and using ungentlemanly language. He forcibly acquired a property and then boasted threateningly that, if he was put out of the property, he would "ryve off the roof". On another occasion, he was taken to court for applying an "ell-wand" (a measuring rod an ell or arm in length) to one of his customers with enough force to draw blood.

Anna Edmondstone, Arthur Murray's wife, died on 27th August 1685.[575] Arthur Murray survived into old age and, in 1702, after the birth of an illegitimate child, promised to pay £200 to the Session of Kirkwall to avoid retribution for his third act of sin in relation to fornication.[576] At this time, moral delinquents were dealt with severely. In 1677, the authorities passed an act requiring all adulterers and adulteresses to stand at the great Church door, in habits of sackcloth, from the second bell to the third and thereafter proceed to the public place of repentance, where they stood until the blessing was said. Murray would certainly want to avoid this ignominy and he had the financial means to do so.

The money he paid to the Kirk Session was to go toward the building of a new guardhouse on the Kirk Green. This was a pressing issue for the Kirk as the town guard, based in the nave during each Lammas market, caused all sorts of mayhem in the Cathedral. These included lighting fires, drinking, fiddling, piping, cursing, firing off guns and, worst of all, pursuing ministers with muskets and halberds whenever they entered on church business.[577] Presumably their officers, most of whom were members of the Town Council, did not stay with their men to provide the discipline required to curb such behaviour. The scorch marks on the pillars of the Cathedral nave could still be seen at the beginning of the twentieth century, prior to the major restoration provided by the Thoms bequest (99).

Arthur Murray's daughter, Isobel, who was married to Robert Pottinger, Bailie, sued her father for the residue of her mother's estate, which had been handed down from her grandfather, John Edmondstone.[578]

71. Barbara Irving 1682/Mitchell Rendall

This stone is on the south side of the nave and has a border of architectural ornamentation called patarae, with the initials 'MR' and 'BI' on either side of a heart. The text reads:

> HEIR RESTIS THE CORPS
> OF ANE PIOUS AND
> VIRTUOUS WOMAN
> BARBARA IRVING
> SPOUSE TO MITCHEL
> RENDAL OF BREK
> WHO DEPARTED THIS
> MORTAL LYF THE 16
> OF DEr 1682 & OF HER
> AGE THE 45 YEAR WHO
> HADE BETWIXT THEM
> WILLIAM ARTHUR
> ELIZABETH MERIORI
> MARGARET ELIZABETH
> JEAN AND ELSPETH
> RENDALS THEIR CHILDREN
> MEMENTO MORI

The panel below contains the symbols of a turfing iron, coffin and bearers, candlestick, hourglass, hand with dart of death, axe hewing down a tree and shovel, all around a skull and crossbones.[579]

The *Diary of Thomas Brown* records that Barbara Irving, spouse to Mitchell Rendall of Breck, departed this life about three in the morning of Saturday 9th of December 1682.[580] She was the daughter of William Irving of Kirbuster (or Gairstay) and Elizabeth Baikie. Barbara's sister was Elizabeth Irving, wife of George Traill of Quandale (68). In 1667, Barbara was given life rent of lands in Westray by her husband, Mitchell Rendall,[581] who belonged to an important local family.[582]

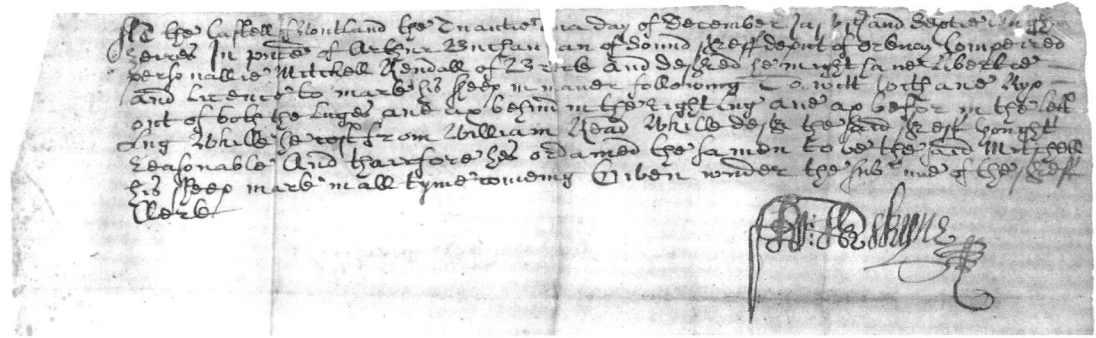

Figure 13 Extract by Arthur Buchanan of Sound, Sheriff Depute of Orkney, registering a sheep mark for Mitchell Rendall of Breck, 1668 (OA D2/4/13).[585]

Mitchell Rendall of Breck, in Rendall, was a prominent merchant and town councillor in his day. Sheep seem to have been an important part of his estate as, in 1668, he registered a sheep mark with the Sheriff-depute of Orkney, Arthur Buchanan of Sound. Lug marks were important in distinguishing sheep from different owners, especially when the animals roamed common land. The Bailie Courts kept a register of these marks and strict regulation was required to avoid disputes.[583] These types of marks were still being used in North Ronaldsay until well into the twentieth century.[584]

Mitchell owned Tounigar in Shore Street, which is one of Kirkwall's oldest surviving houses, currently forming part of the Shore Street oil depot. He bought this house in 1665, but later built another residence slightly to the east, called the "Great Lodging".[586] It was to this house that Mitchell brought his second wife, Margaret Moncrieff, in 1686. Any trace of his 'Lodging' has long gone, as the area was cleared to make way for the oil tanks.

Mitchell obtained his freedom from Kirkwall Town Council and was admitted as a merchant and guild brother in April 1674 after paying the 100 merks fee.[587] He became a member of the Council in 1677.[588] At a meeting in June 1679, which Mitchell Rendall attended along with David Craigie of Oversanday (78), the perilous state of the country was discussed. There was a real fear of invasion, caused by the second Covenanter rebellion, and it was thought expedient for the Council, with the help of the Stewart of Orkney and the Bishop, to organise the inhabitants of the parishes and isles in "ane sufficient poustor of defence against the common enemy in providing themselves with armor & am'onition". It was also agreed to issue a proclamation through the town by tuck of drum ordering all the men of the burgh between 16 and 60 to gather all the weapons, armour and ammunition they could find and muster on Broad Street the following Tuesday so that the strength of the town be evaluated. Those that did not heed this order to muster were threatened with losing their liberty to carry out their trade within the burgh.[589]

On 22nd June (1679), however, the Covenanter rebels were defeated at the Battle of Bothwell Bridge by a government army under the Duke of Monmouth.[590] In December of the same year, over 200 of the prisoners were drowned when the ship *Crown* that was transporting them to the American plantations foundered in a storm off Deerness. The tragedy is commemorated by a nineteenth century monument erected on the cliffs near where the ship sank.

Mitchell Rendall continued on the Council for a number of years and was still a Councillor in 1689. In November 1686, he collected the stent and cess for the burgh below the Castle, along with David Covingtrie (77).[591]

Of the children of Mitchell Rendall and Barbara Irving, Marjorie (Meriori) married Edward Scollay, skipper, and lived further down the close from the 'Great Lodging'.[592] William Rendall inherited Breck and, in January 1686, married firstly Anna, the daughter of David Craigie of Oversanday and Jean Graham (78),[593] and secondly Ann Pottinger. William became a Town Councillor in 1698.[594] Margaret Rendall was contracted to marry David Sutherland of Windbreck on 2nd February 1688.[595] Elizabeth married Edward Prince in 1690.

The Rendalls of Breck had their own coat-of-arms. Part of the arms was found attached to a letter from William Rendall of Breck. It shows a shield with the upper half broken off; the lower part shows the profile of a seal with its tail curved downward.[596]

72. Margaret Hendersone 1683/David Forbes

This stone can be found on the north side of the nave beneath the Mort Brod. Within a vinescroll border is the following text:

> HEIR RESTS THE
> CORPS OF A PIOUS
> & VIRTUOUS WOMAN
> MARGARET HENDERSONE
> SPOUS TO DAVID
> FORBES NOTAR PUBLICK
> & COMMON CLERK
> OF THIS BURGH
> OBIIT 3 Jul II 1683
> AETATIS SUAE 54
> THEY WERE MARIED 29
> NOr 1655 & HAD BETWIXT
> THEM ROBERT
> THO ARTH BARBARA
> & ELIZABETH FORBESES
> WHEROF ELIZABETH
> SURVIVED HER MOTHER.
> MEMENTO MORI

The bottom panel contains the symbols of a coffin, hourglass and another coffin, all above a skull and crossbones.[597]

Little information is available on Margaret Hendersone but her husband, David Forbes, held important positions in the town, such as Town Clerk and Church Treasurer. The Forbes' house was on the west side of Albert Street. The surviving daughter of the Forbes, Elizabeth (sometimes referred to as Elspet), married James

Young, the keeper of the King's girnel[598] (chamberlain of the Earldom estate), who became a Bailie of the town in 1681.[599] He was a brother of Mary Young, who is described at 79.

In 1672, David Forbes played an important role in the inauguration ceremony of James Wallace (76) as minister of the Cathedral. This was a grand occasion and the formal documents (Bishop's presentation, Collation and Institution) were read by David Forbes in front of Bishop Honeyman, the Magistrates, Councillors and the Presbytery elders and brethren.[600]

Following his death on Sunday 30th November 1684, Forbes was given a free burial for his faithfulness and diligence as Church Treasurer. He was replaced as Town Clerk by Thomas Brown, of diarist fame.[601]

73. Robert Leigh 1683/Hugh Leigh

Following the nineteenth century restoration of the Cathedral, no wall space was found for this gravestone, so it was deposited in the triforium. It has a shield with helm and mantling, the latter wreathed with a dove for a crest, surmounted by a label inscribed "INNOCENS" (*innocent*), which is held between two angels blowing a trumpet. There are three martlets on the shield. The Latin inscription says:

> *Here lies Robert Leigh, the son of*
> *Master Hugh Leigh, the minister of*
> *Bressay in Shetland, a boy of out-*
> *standing character and the ornament*
> *of his age, who, while attending*
> *school, died of scarlet fever on*
> *October 8th AD1683, aged 8 years.*

Below the text is a sunken panel, with the symbols of an hourglass, a skull and crossbones together with a spade and a turfing iron crossed.[602] This is one of only two gravestones in the Cathedral to indicate the cause of death, in this case being scarlet fever.

Hugh Leigh was a native of Moray and was educated at King's College, Aberdeen, gaining an MA on 19th July 1666. In 1670, he was admitted to the Shetland parishes of Bressay, Burra and Quarff, which had been united in the sixteenth century. In 1684, he wrote a publication, *A Geographical Description of the Island of Bressay*.[603] He is recorded in the minutes of Kirkwall Town Council as obtaining a burgess ticket in October 1677.[604]

He married his first wife, Marjorie, daughter of Robert Gifford of Burra, on 28th September 1670. They had a son, Robert, commemorated on the gravestone, who was attending school in Kirkwall when he contracted scarlet fever, then a major cause of death, especially in children. The couple also had another son, called John.

Leigh's second wife was Elizabeth, daughter of Lawrence Williamson, shipmaster in Bressay. They had a daughter, Elizabeth, who married Robert Craigie, merchant in Lerwick.[605]

Hugh Leigh transferred his allegiance to Presbyterianism in 1698, petitioning the General Assembly that he might be received into Presbyterian communion. He was suspended in 1702 for beating his second wife but was restored by a committee of the Synod in August 1704. He died in January 1714, aged about 68.

74. David Monroe 1684/Jean Richan

This stone is found in the north side of the choir and has a shield with helm and mantling and contains an eagle's head erased. The text, which starts round the perimeter, reads:

> HEER RESTS THE CORPS
> OF A VIRTUOUS AND HONEST MAN
> DAVID MONROE
> DYER AND BURGES IN KIRKWALL
> WHO LEFT SURVIVING
> JEAN RICHEN HIS
> SPOUS AND JOHN AND
> ELIZABETH MONROES
> THEIR CHILDREN THEY
> WER MARRIED 21 DEr
> 1675 OBIIT 21 SEPT 1684
> AETATIS SUAE 34
> VIVE MORI MUNDO
> *live to die to the world*
> MEMENTO MORI
> *remember death*

The bottom panel contains the symbols of an hourglass, skull and crossbones and coffin.[606]

David Monroe made a living as a litster, a dyer of cloth.

According to Thomas Brown, David Monroe, litster, departed this life about two in the morning of 8th October 1684.[607] Jean did not remain a widow very long, marrying Hugh Clouston in October 1685, who was also a litster by trade. In January 1689, Clouston paid Kirkwall Town Council the sum of £50 Scots for his freedom as litster and merchant guild brother.[608]

David Monroe's wife, Jean, is very likely to have been connected to the Richans mentioned previously (61 and 62).

75. Patrick Murray 1687/Anna Linay

This stone is found in the south side of the choir and has a shield with helm and mantling. The coat-of-arms on the shield consists of a mullet beneath a chevron and a crescent with two mullets above. The text says:

The Linay family lived in a house at the foot of the Strynd and the surname is now known as Lennie.

> HERE RESTS THE BODIES
> OF PATRICK MURRAY
> NOTAR PUBLICK
> & STEWART CLERK OF
> ORKNAY OBIIT 30 JUNI
> 1687 & OF ANNA LINAY
> HIS SPOUSE DIED 27 NOr
> 1686 & OF THRE OF THER
> CHILDREN WHO LEFT
> ALYVE FRAN ALEXr &
> ELZt MURRAYES THER
> CHILDREN
> PATRICIUS VERE FUERAT
> *He was truly a gentleman*
> LEGISQUE PERITUS
> *and skilled in law*
> SCRIBA FIDELIS ERAT
> *He was a faithful clerk*
> VIR ET HONESTUS OBIT
> *and died an honest man.*
> MEMENTO MORI
> *Remember death*

The symbol of a skull and crossbones is found at the base. There is a cherub capital on top, which does not belong to this slab. The Latin inscription on this capital is:

> AD MANDATA DEI FIDI CHELERESQ
> MINISTRI
>
> *Faithful and swift messengers at God's command.*[609]

Patrick Murray was a brother of Arthur Murray (70)[610] and was descended from the Murrays of Garth (15). He was Stewart Clerk of Orkney for many years following King Charles II's decision in 1669 to annex the earldom and make it into a Stewartry, effectively making Orkney and Shetland a Crown Dependency.

The surname, Linay, is now known as Lennie, but comes from the old place name Linay, found in Grimeston in Harray and in North Ronaldsay.[611] The Linays owned the house at the foot of the Strynd called Ridgeland and it passed to Anna Linay, forming part of the dowry to her husband, Patrick Murray. The Town Council rented it from the Murrays for use as a Town Hall and Prison. It did duty as the Tolbooth for nearly a century. In 1683, the Murrays acquired the property in Victoria Street to the north of present day William Shearer & Sons. This property passed to their son, Francis, who was born on 23rd May 1678.[612] In 1709, the Town Council purchased the property of Ridgeland from Marion Ritchie, widow of Francis Murray.[613] Patrick Murray and his wife also seem to have inherited 72 Victoria Street from Anna's father, Oliver Linay, who had purchased this part of what is now called Spence's Square from Thomas Maine (see 30).

Patrick and Anna's son, Alexander Murray, was baptized on September 15th 1683 by James Wallace, with Sir Alexander Mackenzie of Broomhill, Alexander Dick, Alexander Geddes (of Cathedral bell fame), and Sibilla Halcro (65) being among the witnesses.[614] As all the male witnesses were called Alexander, the choice of name for the baby seems academic. The couple also had another boy, called Patrick, born on 7th August 1681, who must have died young.[615]

76. Elizabeth Cuthbert 1685/James Wallace 1688

This well-preserved gravestone is on the south side of the nave. The stone is flanked by two long, thin columns, each surmounted by a finial. The upper part of the stone is spanned by an arch, on which a crescent moon and galaxy of stars represent the firmament. The arch supports a third finial, at either side of which

James Wallace, Cathedral minister, was one of Orkney's first published historians, saga writers aside.

is a cherub. In each spandrel is incised a heart with a chevron. The figure of a woman, clothed in a robe and with hair hanging loose, kneels in prayer with eyes uplifted. An arm issues from among clouds, holding in the hand a crown and, opposite the arm, is a rose. In front of the woman is an hourglass with skull and crossbones. The text below reads:

> IN HOPE OF A BLESSED RESURRECTION
> THER LYE INTERRED BEFORE THIS
> MONUMENT THE BODIES OF ELIZABETH
> CUTHBERT SPOUS TO MR JAMES
> WALLACE MINISTER OF KIRKWALL
> & SO(ME OF THER) CHILDREN. [616]

James Wallace was born in Banffshire in 1642 and was educated at King's College, Aberdeen. He became schoolmaster at Fortrose, before being presented to Lady Parish in Sanday by Bishop Honeyman in November 1668, for which David Forbes (72) drew up the notarial certificate.[617] While in Sanday, he wrote to David Forbes, asking him to "send me with the first boat a pair of shoes for my sister; she desires they may be prettie big".[618]

Rights of presentation of ministers to the Cathedral were sometimes disputed between the Bishops and Town Council. In May 1672, Bishop Honeyman indulged in a spot of nepotism by proposing to appoint his brother, George, as Cathedral minister. This was not popular in the town and the magistrates, led by Provost Patrick Craigie, reminded the bishop that the Town Council had the right of patronage.[619] Both parties then supported the appointment of James Wallace as minister of the first charge of St Magnus Cathedral. He was to be the last Episcopal minister of the Cathedral to die in office.[620]

In 1673, James Wallace and his wife, Elizabeth Cuthbert, who may have been a daughter of John Cuthbert (53), bought a house just off Albert Street, which formed three sides of a square and was distinguished by a quaint, porch-like doorway, above which were the words "Welcome Welcome" and a double heart. One visitor in December 1681, Edward Rynd, was not at all welcome, as he assaulted the minister in his own home. Things could have gone very badly for James Wallace had it not been for the intervention of some neighbours. Rynd, who was a weaver, had been under church discipline for what Craven describes as the "grossest indecency". He had obviously felt aggrieved and had told Bishop Mackenzie he would rather be hanged or shot than carry out his penance. Rynd was placed in the irons at the Tolbooth on the orders of Bailie David Moncrieff and was subsequently banished from Orkney.[621] Rynd was a troublesome character and is mentioned in the minutes of Kirkwall Town Council in previous years for various misdemeanours.[622]

James Wallace was one of Orkney's first historians, saga writers precluded, writing his *Description of the Isles of Orkney* at the instance of Sir Robert Sibbald, Geographer Royal for Scotland, with whom he kept up a constant correspondence.[623]

James Wallace's wife, Elizabeth, died in 1685 and was buried in the Cathedral next to some of their children who had died young. Wallace, himself, succumbed to a fever in 1688 and was buried next to his wife. He left money for the Cathedral and the Kirk Session purchased two communion cups on which Wallace's name was engraved. His *Description* was published after his death by his eldest surviving son.

77. Nicola Traill 1688/David Covingtrie

This elaborately sculptured gravestone is on the south side of the nave, just to the east of the Paplay Tomb. There are two figures. The first, a woman, in contemporary costume and with her hair hanging loose, stands on a globe, across which runs the word VANITAS, meaning emptiness or worthlessness. With her left arm uplifted in invocation, she gazes upwards through a pointed arch to a figure of the Saviour, who stands on clouds. From her mouth issues a scroll, inscribed with AD TE QUACUN VOCAS DULCISSIME IESU, *to thee, Sweetest Jesus, by whatever path Thou callest*. Above the figure of Jesus is an arch with the words, HEAVEN OPENED, carved in relief on either side. A cherub is found on either side of the arch, which is supported on each side by a debased ionic pilaster. The figure of Christ is robed, and has a glory round the head. In the right hand is a standard bearing a St George's Cross, which hangs from a staff shaped like a Latin cross. The left hand holds a crown, showing him to be the King of Kings. The text, to the right of the female figure, has the initials in monogram of 'DC' and 'NT' and says:

IN HOPE OF A BLESSED RESURRECTION
HEER RESTS NICOLA TRAIL
SPOUSE TO DAVID COVINGTRIE
MERd & BURGESS OF KIRKWAL
OBIIT 23 JULII 1688
AETATIS SUAE 33
& OF SOME OF THER CHILDREN
MEMENTO MORI.

Beneath the text are the skull and crossbones.[624]

Nicola Traill was the sister of George Traill of Quendale (68) and daughter of James Traill of Westove and Jean Cok (daughter of Rev. Thomas Cok). She died in the morning of 23rd July 1688.[625]

David Covingtrie was rent collector to Bishop Mackenzie, acting as his chamberlain. His parents were John Covingtrie and Jane Kirkness. The Covingtries had arrived in Orkney in the early seventeenth century and had started Kirkwall's first baking (baxter) business in Baxter's Close (now Tankerness Lane).[626]

As well as being Bishop Mackenzie's Chamberlain, David Covingtrie was a merchant with some shipping interest. For the freedom of being a burgess and guild brother, Covingtrie was ordered by the Town Council to pay 100 merks or else be stopped from trading. He was admitted as burgess and guild brother on 6th November 1674, but did not pay the fees until February the following year.[627] In 1676, David Covingtrie was part of a commission appointed by the Town Council to review the rents of all lodgings and houses in Kirkwall, in an attempt to raise more money to alleviate the debt in which the burgh found itself. He was a regular collector of the cess and stent for the burgh and was also a member of the Town Council, becoming a Bailie in 1691. After the death of his first wife, he married on 10th of October 1689, Margaret Kaa, only daughter of deceased John Kaa (63) and

Nicola Traill and David Covingtrie are remembered by this highly elaborate and decorative stone. David Covingtrie's family started the town's first baking business.

Annas (Agnes) Loutit.[628] His third marriage was to Mary Elphinstone in 1693.[629]

78. Jean Grahame 1694/David Craigie of Oversanday

This very tall stone is found on the south side of the nave. Above a shield is the motto, SORS OMNIA VERSAT, *chance changes everything*. The shield, with helm and mantling and a boar passant for a crest, has the coats-of-arms of Craigie impaling Graham. On the dexter side is an ermine boar's head erased between two crescents and a mullet. On the sinister side are three escallopes and a lion rampant between three roses. The initials 'DC' and 'JG' are either side of a heart. The text starts round the perimeter:

HERE RESTS A VIRTUOUS
GENTLEWOMAN (J)EAN GRAHAME
SP(OUSE) TO DAVID (CRAIGIE)
OF OVE(R SANDAY)
SHE DEPARTED THIS LYF THE

Being the granddaughter of a Bishop did not deter Jean Graham from having a public spat with another woman and giving her a "cuff".

<pre>
2 DAY OF NOr 1694 AND IN THE
     50 YEAR OF HER AGE
      THER CHILDREN WER
      BARBARA MARGARET
       BURIED AT HOLME
   ANNA SPOUSE TO WILLIAM
     RENDEL YOr OF BREK
    MARGARET AND WILLIAM
       CRAIGIES BURIED
        IN THIS CHURCH
       ANNA HER CHILDREN
         MITCHIL DAVID
      JEANE AND WILLIAM
        RENDELS WHOM
       THE LORD PRESEVE.
</pre>

Above the symbol panel are found the words, AUSPICE DEO MEMENTO MORI, *under the guidance of God, remember death*. The symbols are an hourglass, skull and crossbones, and coffin.[630]

Jean Graham was the daughter of Patrick Graham of Rothiesholme and Graemeshall and granddaughter of Bishop Graham (32). She married David Craigie in 1665. Jean seems to have been a bit of a busybody as, in 1673, she reported Elspet Bellenden to the Kirk Session for loose morals in spending the night with widower, George Ritchie, Chamberlain to Bishop Honeyman. The two women had a verbal exchange, which ended in Jean giving Elspet a "cuff". The incident was witnessed by Isobel Anderson (49) and her husband David Moncrieff, who both backed Jean Graham, saying Elspet had abused Jean with "base words". The Kirk Session investigated and Elspet was soon hounded out of Orkney.[631]

David Craigie was the son of William Craigie of Gairsay and Margaret Halcro (42), and was a very prominent political figure in Orkney in the latter half of the seventeenth century. His brother, Hugh, who was for a while Orkney's representative in Parliament, sold him the Thesaurerie on Broad Street, which had been the Cathedral treasurer's residence. David also procured from his brother the udal land at Oversanday (Deerness). Later, he and his wife, Jean, went to live at Papdale and the Thesaurerie was sold to Hew (Hugh) Baikie of Burness (65).[632]

As one of the leading heritors or landowners of his time, David Craigie was a Commissioner of Excise, Justice of the Peace and represented Kirkwall in Parliament (1681-82 and 1685-1688).[633] In 1665, he was nominated by his fellow Commissioners to persuade the Lords of the Privy Council to release Orkney and Shetland from paying dues that should have been collected in 1649-50, the period Montrose's forces had occupied Orkney.[634] David Craigie was also active on the Town Council for a lengthy period, being Dean of Guild in 1669 (taking over from Andrew Mitchell, 53) and becoming Provost of Kirkwall ten years later.[635]

During the second Dutch war, David Craigie, along with the Earl of Caithness and others, agreed to fit out a privateer called the *Jonet of Zetland*, under the command of Captain Ronald Murray. The ship succeeded in obtaining at least one prize when the *Peter of Rotterdam* was brought into Kirkwall Bay in April 1667.[636]

As Provost, Craigie had to defend Kirkwall's rights against the Stewart Principals (or Sheriff Principals) of Orkney and Shetland, who claimed the superior duties from the lands of Mudisquoy, Soulisquoy and later Pickaquoy.[637] This involved a number of trips to Edinburgh, one of the first being in February 1681, when he and David Drummond (son of 50) travelled to the capital to hear the complaint of Captain Andrew Dick,[638] which subsequently cost the Council £15 sterling.[639]

In 1687, Craigie was ordered to appear before the Privy Council, along with Bailie Robert Arskyne, on charges of insolent behaviour toward Bishop Mackenzie and his son, Sir Alexander Mackenzie, who was Sheriff of the Bishopric. The dispute seems to have arisen over the release of a prisoner in the Tolbooth of Kirkwall, who had been convicted of theft by Sheriff Mackenzie.[640] Craigie was made to crave pardon for any wrong or injury he had done to the Bishop or his Sheriff.[641]

In the same year, Craigie was voted out of office as Provost, but the election result was set aside on the instruction of King James VII, who had issued decrees suspending elections in Royal Burghs in 1686 and 1687.[642] The letter from the Privy Council arrived too late to stop the election of 1687 but the previous office bearers continued in post after receipt of the letter. Craigie was eventually replaced by George Traill (68) as Provost, in 1688, again by order of King James VII.[643]

Barbara and Margaret, the daughters of David Craigie and Jean Graham died young and, as the gravestone says, were buried in Holm. Their other daughter, Anna, married William Rendall of Breck (see 71) in February 1686, the couple producing four children. Sadly, Anna died a few years later, in Papdale, during the morning of 1st July 1691.[644]

CHAPTER 8

The Eighteenth Century – An Acrid Smell

With the 9th Earl of Morton having been discharged from all he was alleged to have taken from the *Kennermerland*,[645] and the 10th Earl having been rewarded with a place on the Privy Council for supporting William of Orange,[646] the Earls of Morton had seen a revival in their fortunes towards the end of the previous century. In 1707, the Earldom of Orkney and Lordship of Shetland were granted by the Crown to the Earl of Morton, reward, perhaps, for his support for the Union of Parliaments.[647] The grant was made irredeemable in 1742. Protracted litigation, however, with the Orkney lairds, particularly over accusations that the Earls and their factors had falsified Orkney's ancient system of weights and measures to exact a greater value of produce collected as rent and skat,[648] convinced James Douglas, the 14th Earl, to accept an attractive financial offer for his Orkney and Shetland estates from Sir Lawrence Dundas, who had made his fortune as an arms supplier.[649] The Earldom estates, though now much reduced in size, remain in the hands of the Dundas family today.

Freemasonry became popular in the eighteenth century among the leading citizens of Kirkwall, with the founding of a Lodge in 1736. Meetings were held in houses belonging to the Lodge brethren, in rotation, until 1750, when an agreement was reached with the Town Council for the use of the upper room of the new Tolbooth on the Kirk Green.[650]

The Jacobite rebellion of 1745 produced little real support from Orkney. Any Jacobite sympathisers in the islands, however, were dealt with severely after the defeat at Culloden. Retribution in Orkney was led by Benjamin Moodie of Melsetter, who was promoted to Captain and given a commission to root out rebels in the islands.[651] Moodie relished the prospect of revenge for the murder of his father and the recent looting of his home at Melsetter by a Highland detachment sent to raise money and recruits for the Jacobite cause.[652]

Oats and bere continued to be the staple crops grown, with potatoes and turnips gradually appearing about the middle of the century. While agricultural improvement was slow to develop, the kelp industry took off in Orkney in the eighteenth century to such an extent that Orkney became one of the main sources for the kelp ash that was produced from the burning of dried seaweed. This ash was needed for the production of soap and glass in the expanding factories in the south. For the Orkney lairds, it was an industry that needed little capital outlay and required a great deal of labour, of which they had a plentiful supply in their tenants.

The eighteenth century saw an expansion in transatlantic trade, with ships from the Hudson Bay Company regularly anchoring at Stromness for supplies and recruits. Whalers and merchant vessels bound for the Americas also called in and the town grew rapidly. Kirkwall, as a royal burgh, still had a monopoly of foreign trade and passed on some of its taxation to the "unfree traders" of Stromness, who were paying no tax on their activities.[653] In 1742, a group of Stromness merchants, led by Alexander Graham, a descendant of Bishop Graham (32), challenged Kirkwall's authority over them, and 16 years of legal wrangling through the local courts, the Court of Session and finally the House of Lords followed. Kirkwall eventually lost the case but the legal representatives for Stromness failed to get costs.[654] Graham was financially ruined and unsuccessfully sued his fellow Stromnessians in an attempt to recover the money he had spent on the case.

79. Mary Young 1750

This yellow sandstone gravestone is an obvious copy of the stone to Elizabeth Cuthbert (see 76), with the figure of a woman kneeling in prayer, her eyes uplifted. The text says:

> Augt. 1750
> Here was interrd the corps of
> Mary Young spouse to John
> Riddoch then one of the Magistrates
> of Kirkwall and afterwards Provost
> of said Burgh.
> She lived regarded
> and dyed regretted.

Mary Young belonged to a very prominent Kirkwall family. Her father was Andrew Young of Castleyards, who was girnell-keeper and rent collector for, among others, Sir Alexander Brand.[655] He was also clerk and collector of cess for the Commissioners of Supply and a member of Kirkwall Town Council, being Dean of Guild and then Provost in 1710-12. It was this Andrew Young who had been involved in the altercation with George Richan of Linklater (see 61). Young was married twice, his first wife being Jean Moncrieff. After she died, he married Margaret Mackenzie, daughter of William Mackenzie, Commissary of Orkney, and granddaughter of Bishop Mackenzie (34). They had a large family, with their eldest daughter being Mary Young. Mary had three brothers and four sisters, including Sybilla, who married James Gordon of Cairston. Margaret Mackenzie outlived her eldest daughter, Mary, by a decade.[656]

John Riddoch was the eldest son of George Riddoch of Bleroch and was a writer (lawyer) in Edinburgh. He came to Kirkwall in 1732 as Sheriff-Clerk, on a commission from George, 13th Earl of Morton. He also acted as Sheriff-substitute and Comptroller of Customs. John and Mary married in 1734 and built a house at 5 Broad Street, on the site of the South Block House of the Castle.[657] This house is now the business premises of Lows Orkney. Riddoch acquired Cairston in Stromness through loaning money to James Gordon younger, who was married to Mary Young's niece (daughter of Mary's brother, Andrew). Gordon's business enterprises went disastrously wrong and the estate was put up for sale. By this stage, Riddoch held bonds over Cairston and, to prevent losing his money, decided to purchase the estate outright.[658]

Being Sheriff-substitute at this time had its dangers. In 1739, Riddoch was part of a group investigating oppressions in South Ronaldsay, allegedly being perpetrated by Sir James Stewart of Burray. The party was led by James Douglas, 14th Earl of Morton, who was acting as Stewart and Sheriff of Orkney. On their return journey through Burray, they took into protective custody a servant of Sir James Stewart. On discovering what had happened, Sir James Stewart gave chase with a large retinue of followers, accosting Morton and his party at Graemeshall in Holm. Morton and Stewart grappled with one another and, in the general mêlée that followed, Riddoch was shot in the leg. Stewart and his men were successfully prosecuted by the Earl of Morton for the affray and part of their fine was put towards the building of a new Tolbooth in Kirkwall.[659]

Some years later, Riddoch was again wounded, this time as a result of the Kelp riots. The period 1739-42 had seen a series of bad harvests. Many people blamed the acrid smoke from the burning of tang for causing the poor crops and a scarcity of fish. There had been dissension on the Orkney Mainland, but the worst trouble happened in Stronsay, where the industry in Orkney had first started. In 1742, the Stewart-depute, Andrew Ross, sent Riddoch to Stronsay with a warrant for the arrest of rioters, who were led by Peter (or Patrick) Fea of Dunatoun. With the memory of his experience in Burray still fresh, Riddoch swore in about a dozen Kirkwall tradesmen and armed them with swords and pistols. He timed his raid for maximum surprise, arriving at Peter Fea's house at midnight. The raiders broke into the house and dragged Fea out of bed but had to leave empty handed after Fea's wife became hysterical. Riddoch allowed Fea to remain in the house with his wife provided he surrendered when ordered. Riddoch and his party went on to other houses on the island, making in total four arrests. While on their way to arrest Peter Fea's brother, John, they were confronted by a large crowd of about 60 people led by John Fea himself. Riddoch ordered them to disperse in the King's name. At this point, Peter Fea arrived with a similar crowd and made straight for Riddoch. In the ensuing mêlée, Riddoch's hat and wig were knocked off and he suffered a large cut on his head. Bleeding profusely, Riddoch and his men had to beat a hasty retreat and returned to Kirkwall without any prisoners. The Stewart-depute was appalled by the anarchy, particularly when it began to spread to other parts of Orkney, and dispatched an urgent request for troops to be brought from south as soon as possible.

In 1744, Riddoch, as Sheriff-substitute, tried the case brought against some of the Orkney lairds who had withheld superior dues as a result of their complaints against the Earl of Morton concerning the alleged manipulation of the weights and measures. There were complaints that the Earl's officials were acting as both pursuers and judges.[660] The case eventually went to the Court of Session where Morton won his case over unpaid rents, but it was another 15 years before the dispute over the weights and measures was resolved, again in favour of Morton.

Following the Jacobite defeat at Culloden, Riddoch was on the look out for Orkney rebels returning to their island estates. As agent for the Earl of Morton, he had been in conflict with many of these rebel lairds and was determined to see them punished. He passed on intelligence to the navy that twelve persons, disguised, masked and dressed as sailors, had passed over from the Orkney Mainland to Shapinsay.[661] This information led to the burning of James Fea of Clestrain's house of Sound. Following this episode, the government sent Captain Benjamin Moodie of Melsetter to Orkney with a detachment of marines to capture the rebels.

After having been on the Council since 1733, Riddoch became Provost of Kirkwall in 1764 and remained in post for twenty years.[662] One of his final acts as Provost was a step into national politics and exemplified the corruption of the British political system at the time. In 1784, after a brief spell in power, Charles James Fox, one of the outstanding Whig politicians of his era, was looking for a safe seat, following legal challenges to the vote in his Westminster seat. Sir Thomas Dundas, Riddoch's new feudal superior, was very willing to help Fox, who was soon made a burgess of Kirkwall, thus qualifying him to stand for the Northern Burghs of Kirkwall, Wick, Dornoch, Dingwall and Tain. It was Kirkwall's turn to act as presiding burgh, but first had to choose its candidate. The representatives of the working classes, the Deacons of the Trade Incorporations, supported Sir John Sinclair of Ulbster. With the representative of the tailors excluded from the meeting, owing to a previous dispute, Riddoch objected to the legality of the votes of the other Deacons, saying they were neither burgesses of Kirkwall nor freemen. The Council agreed to deprive the Deacons of their vote and supported Riddoch in putting Fox's name forward. At the meeting of the Northern Burghs, Wick and Dornoch supported Sir John Sinclair as their parliamentary candidate, but Riddoch won the day with support from the delegates from Tain and Dingwall. Fox was so grateful he sent Kirkwall Town Council a portrait of himself. He soon returned to his Westminster constituency, however, once the legal wrangling there had been sorted.[663] Meanwhile, Sir John Sinclair had hedged his bets by buying an English rotten burgh in case of defeat.[664]

80. James Spence 1781/Janet Spence 1802

This plain, sandstone gravestone can be found on the south side of the choir. The text is as follows,

    WAITING their SAVIOUR's call
    to JUDGEMENT
    Here LIE the BODIES of Mr JAMES
    SPENCE many years TOWN Clerk of
    this BOROUGH and of Mrs JANET
    SPENCE his WIFE: eldest Daughter
    of the Revnd. Mr BLAW late Minister of
    the GOSPEL in the island of WESTRA:
    he died in the year 1781 Aged 70 years
    and she Died on the 11th day of April 1802
    Aged nearly 93 years
    Their Grave is 19 feet North from this
    Stone Being the Burying Ground of his
    Ancestors the Spences of Scapa
    A Tribute of filial Duty by
    their Youngest Son
    Graeme Spence
    1802

The Spences of Scapa were long associated with Kirkwall Town Council, with George Spence being a Bailie of the Town and Town Clerk in 1706. He was succeeded as Town Clerk by his son, William.[665]

James Spence came from Westray, where his father, also called George Spence, was schoolmaster. His mother was Margaret Buchanan.[666] James trained as a writer (lawyer) in the town and himself became Town Clerk of Kirkwall in 1747, taking over from the previously mentioned, William Spence. In 1757, he gave evidence in the Pundlar case, being called to exhibit the town records.[667] His age at that time was given as 42, which indicates a birth year of 1715, as opposed to that shown on the gravestone of around 1711.

James kept up the Westray connection by marrying Janet Blaw in 1740. Her father, William, who is mentioned on the gravestone, was born in 1673, the son or grandson of Edward Blaw, notary public in Kirkwall. William was ordained in 1699, becoming minister in Westray. He married Mary, daughter of George Traill of Holland (Papa Westray) and had one son and four daughters. He seems to have been a strict sabbatarian; there is a tradition which holds that he hanged his cat for killing a mouse on the Sabbath.[668] Blaw had endless trouble with his in-laws. His brother-in-law, Thomas Traill of Holland, took an extreme dislike to him after the Kirk Session tried to rebuke Traill for "flagrant and repeated sins".[669] Blaw complained that the laird did not attend church, took money collected for the poor, forced his servants to work on Sundays and refused to pay his tithes. He also criticised the laird for not paying his father's fine concerning the sin of fornication. Traill, in turn, called his brother-in-law a "knave", a "witless villain", "a coal-stealer", along with many other derogatory descriptions, and refused to allow Blaw to set foot on his land. When coming over to Papay, the minister had to moor his boat at "the Minister's Flag" and walk the two miles to St Boniface Church by the shore.[670]

The Spences' youngest son, Graeme,[671] who was responsible for this memorial, was born on 24th February 1758 and became a maritime surveyor for the Admiralty, assisting his cousin, Murdoch Mackenzie (nephew of the famous mapmaker of the same name and son of Janet's sister, Elizabeth Blaw). Murdoch Mackenzie said of Graeme, "No person excels him in skill, assiduity and integrity in surveying".[672] The cousins had surveyed large parts of the English Channel and, after succeeding Mackenzie, Graeme Spence carried out a survey of the Isles of Scilly, completing his work in 1792. In 1801, he acted as pilot to Lord Nelson on HMS *Medusa*, when Nelson was in charge of defending the English Channel against invasion by Napoleon's army in Boulogne. Spence invented many instruments related to surveying, several of which were used by the Royal Navy. He is perhaps best remembered, at least in Orkney, for promoting Scapa Flow as a naval base. In 1812, his *Proposals for Establishing a Temporary Rendezvous for Line of Battle Ships in a National Roadstead called Scapa Flow, formed by the South Isles of Orkney* were posthumously submitted to the Admiralty.[673] It took another century before his suggestion was taken up and became much more than a "temporary rendezvous".

81. The Groat Memorial

This mural tablet of white marble is found on the south side of the nave near the west end and has an anchor with the motto, "Anchor Fast" above a text, which says:

The Groat Memorial.

In Memory of
Malcolm Groat, of Wards, Esq;
His Relative
Donald Groat, of Newhall, Esq;
Chamberlain of the bishopric of Orkney;
And The Latter's Son;
Robert Groat, of Newhall, Esq, Sen; MD
And
William Groat, Esq;
Chamberlain of the bishopric of Orkney.
They, All, Died
During the Eighteenth Century.

Malcolm Groat was actually "of Warse" in Caithness and was a writer, whose legal business took him to Orkney. In 1741, he sold the ferry house and other property in Duncansby to William Sinclair of Freswick.[674] Malcolm was business adviser to Benjamin Moodie of Melsetter, son of Captain James Moodie, who had been shot in Broad Street. From 1746, Malcolm acted as resident factor of Moodie's estate in Walls. He arrived at Melsetter shortly after it had been looted by a party of Highlanders. Led by Alexander Mackenzie of Ardloch, the Highlanders had invaded Orkney to raise money and recruits for the Jacobite cause.[675] Malcolm wrote to Moodie informing him of the damage done, blaming Sir James Stewart of Burray for his encouragement of the rebels.[676]

In 1767, Malcolm advanced money to Alexander Graham, who was in great financial difficulty after successfully fighting the monopoly of Kirkwall through the courts.[677] Malcolm died in 1772.[678] From evidence given in the Pundlar Process, which states that his age in November 1757 was 40, it can be surmised he was born in 1717.[679]

Donald Groat of Newhall was a cousin of the above-mentioned Malcolm and was an important merchant in Kirkwall. In his evidence in the Pundlar Case (November 1757), he gave his age as 65 and stated he had been a member of Kirkwall Town Council since 1733, acting either as a Councillor, Bailie or Dean-of-Guild.[680] He went on to say that he had resided in Orkney for 48 years and, in that time, the "Punders and Bysmars" were made and adjusted by the Deacon of Wrights in Kirkwall.[681] He had been for several years Chamberlain of the Bishopric of Orkney as well as factor for various local lairds, and in this capacity he frequently exported bere and meal to Norway. He described himself as a considerable dealer in the commodities of Orkney and thereby regularly used the "Punders and Bysmers". He denied ever saying that standard weights in Orkney had been greatly increased.[682] Needless to say, his evidence was for the defence.

In March 1726, in his capacity as Chamberlain of the Bishopric, Donald Groat wrote a description of the state of the Bishop's Palace. He lamented that it was "wholly ruinous, being without roof, loftings and loft, except lofts in the hall which seem to be rotten and spoyld". He insisted that he was not responsible for its lamentable condition.

From 1733, Donald Groat became involved in the production of kelp, beginning at Carness and Quanterness.[683] In 1741, he was caught up in the kelp riots when, at Rennibister, he lost a good quantity of newly cut ware and freshly burnt kelp, along with cutting tools. The rioters proceeded to his shores at Quanterness, where they did similar damage. As a result, 14 men were brought to court on charges of rioting.[684] Together with James Baikie of Tankerness,[685] for whom he acted as factor, he also had contracts and tacks for the cutting and burning of kelp along the shores of Westray, Rousay, Egilsay and Eday.[686]

Donald Groat acquired land in Deerness, including Halley, Creya, Yeldabreck, Nether Stove and Cornsquoy,[687] and, along with his first wife, Margaret Cobb (died in 1729), owned property in Kirkwall.[688] The Deerness lands were passed on to his eldest son, Dr Robert Groat.

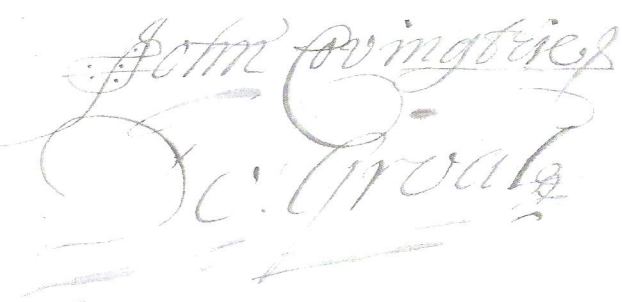

Signatures of John Covingtrie of Newark (77) and Donald Groat on an agreement between the two dated 1740 (OA D2/36/10).

Robert Groat, son of Donald Groat and Margaret Cobb, is first described in 1757 as "an apothecary living in Jermyn Street, St James's, London". By the time he came back to Orkney, around 1762, he was practising as a physician. He married a daughter of Thomas Baikie of Burness and became a well-known and respected local figure. For Dr Groat's services, some wealthy individuals, such as the Graemes of Graemeshall, who were related to Groat's wife, paid an annual subscription plus the price of any treatment, such as 2s 6d for a 'bleeding'.[689] There seems to have been a sliding scale of charges, depending on ability to pay. Thus, for the preparation of a dose, described, perhaps appropriately, as 'a vomit', a charge of 1s was made to a well-off person, while a manservant or maidservant was charged 6d and a child 4d. He also treated horses with such substances as elixir of myrrh and aloes, spirit of turpentine and blue vitriol. Some people, such as Cecila Steuart (1721-1792), wife of Rev Alexander Riddoch of Kirkwall, complained of his high fees and, to ease the 'extraordinary charges', she started paying an annual subscription of one guinea.[690] Dr Groat died in 1782 and was succeeded in his medical business by his son, also called Robert.[691]

William Groat, another son of Donald Groat, took over his father's merchant business and, as well as being Chamberlain of the Bishopric Estate, was a prominent member of Kirkwall Town Council, becoming a Bailie of the town.

William continued his father's involvement in kelp-making and his father's association with James Baikie of Tankerness, obtaining a nine-year tack of the shores of Baikie's estate for the annual rent of £120 sterling.[692] He later fell out with some of the trustees of the Baikie estate, appointed after James Baikie had died in 1764. These included Baikie's wife, Janet Douglas, his brother, John Baikie, landwaiter of the customs,[693] and John Riddoch (79). In 1772, William hoped to obtain a two-year extension to his tack, but that tack had been given to one of the trustees, John Baikie. Workers employed by Groat were instructed to cease operations and those that refused were subject to intimidation by the Sheriff-depute, John Riddoch. As a result, William Groat put in a claim of £100 sterling against the three trustees, in compensation for breach of contract, as well as a claim for the value of the kelp he was prevented from manufacturing. The claim was hotly disputed by the trustees.[694]

82. Traills of Westness & Woodwick

"Traills up the toon,
Traills doon the toon,
Traills in the middle;
De'il tak the Traills guts
For strings to his fiddle".

This little rhyme is not part of any memorial in the Cathedral but reflects how widespread the family had become in Orkney, after arriving in the islands in the service of the Stewart Earls. By the eighteenth century there were seven or eight branches of the family in Orkney, owning estates at Westness and Frotoft in Rousay, Tirlet in Westray, Holland in Papa Westray, Elsness, Westove and Hobbister all in Sanday, Woodwick in Evie and Sebay in Toab.[695]

The Traills commemorated in this imposing neo-classical style marble memorial, which is found on the north wall of the choir just passed the north transept, belong to the Westness and Woodwick branches and cover some 200 years in time. It shows two coats-of-arms, the first belonging to the Traills, with their motto, DISCRIMINE SALLUS (*judge carefully*), above a beacon set in the sea. On the shield is a chevron between two lozenges (mascles) in chief and a trefoil in base. The second coat-of-arm belongs to the Balfours and will be described under John Traill of Westness. The text below the coats-of-arms reads:

This commemorates the marriage of John Traill and Helen Stewart. It is situated on the front of the Orkney Hotel. The Traill family memorial in the Cathedral memorial covers more than 200 years and over a dozen individuals. They were significant land owners and the memorial represents the Westness and Woodwick branches.

JOHN TRAILL of Westness
heir to JAMES TRAILL of
Woodwick, his uncle, was
married to MARY BALFOUR
October 1745
She was also interred here,
19th August 1794

WILLIAM HENRY TRAILL
of Woodwick J.P., D.L. of Orkney
Born June 13th 1861, Died August 23rd 1924
interred in North Ronaldsay

His only Son
WILLIAM DOUGLAS TRAILL
Born January 14th 1895, Died March 8th 1911
interred at Atherington, Devon.

And His Daughters
KATE JOAN (ROBERTSON)
Born November 28th 1897 Died 7th May 1931

NORAH VALENTINE (THOMSON GLOVER)
Born February 14th 1900 Died August 18th 1984 and
her husband

JOHN WILLIAM THOMSON GLOVER C.B.E.
Born July 30th 1887 Died January 11th 1943

JAMES TRAILL of Woodwick
Provost of Kirkwall, was
Interred here 10th February 1733.

MARGARET TRAILL, his Wife
was also interred here,
January 1763

JOHN TRAILL of Woodwick
Died February 1805

JOHN TRAILL Born March 24th 1822
Died July 17th 1822

WILLIAM TRAILL of Westness & Woodwick
Born 31st Jan 1797 Died 19th May 1858
Interred at Rousay.

WILLIAM TRAILL of Woodwick
M.D., J.P. & D.L. of Orkney
Born 8th Sept 1818 Died 10th Dec 1886
Interred at St Andrews, Fife.

JOHN TRAILL of Woodwick
J.P. for Orkney Civil Engineer Madras
Born 22nd Sept 1851 Died 5th Sept 1898
Interred in churchyard here.

James Traill of Woodwick 1733

The son of William Traill of Westness and Barbara, eldest daughter of George Balfour of Pharay, James Traill was born in 1683 and became a writer (lawyer) in Edinburgh.[696] As well as his professional work, James Traill was an excellent business man, being involved in the merchant trading business and engaging in commercial dealings on the Continent, especially with Norway and Holland. Many of his business letters to his brother-in-law and partner, David Traill of Elsness, have been preserved and were published by Hugh Marwick (122).[697] James's success enabled him to purchase Woodwick and North Ronaldsay, as well as the town house in Bridge Street, known as the Gallery, which he rebuilt. Sadly, Traill's house has not survived. After serving the Traills as a town house for more than a century, the Gallery was converted into a hotel. In 1890, it was bought by Mr Robert Garden (see 102), who turned it into a shop and business premises. A disastrous fire in 1938 razed it to the ground, leaving the open parking area found today.

The doorway of The Gallery, in Bridge Street, installed during renovations in 1763.

One building left by James Traill, however, has partially survived. At the back of his house, he set out a large garden and planted many trees, among which he built a summer house. This was made from the ballast stones from Pirate Gow's ship, *Revenge*, which had run aground on the Calf of Eday in 1725. Gow and his crew had been captured by Traill's friend, James Fea of Clestrain, and sent to London for trial.[698] With Fea's permission, Traill had recovered some of the stones, which had been dumped on the beach at the Calf of Eday when Gow's ship was refloated. The building was later decorated with sea shells (see 102), with the result that it became known locally as the Groatie Hoose ('groatie buckie' being the local name for a cowrie shell).

In 1730, James retired from business, settled in Kirkwall and entered the Council, being made Provost in his first year. There were no fewer than five Traills on the Council at that time. As Provost, James Traill was faced with a crisis during the annual Lammas Fair of 1732, when around forty Highlanders, armed with swords and pistols, defied the Town Guard and mocked the Magistrates. Invariably poorly equipped and often subject to ridicule from the local population,[699] the Town Guard was certainly in no position to disarm such a well-equipped group. The carrying of weapons by strangers coming to market was banned by municipal law and townspeople were prohibited from lodging a stranger until he had first handed over his weapon. Traill moved quickly to rectify the situation and convened an evening meeting of the Town Council, in which it was agreed to command the inhabitants of Kirkwall to provide a full list of lodgers and to confiscate the belongings of the Highlanders, to be returned if they were of good behaviour. It was also agreed to seize the oars and rudders of the boats of strangers and to prohibit the ferries from carrying the rioters out of the islands.[700] It is not known how the whole episode ended, but it evokes comparisons with the Wild West.

Margaret Traill 1763

Margaret Traill was the daughter of John Traill of Elsness in Sanday and his first wife, Helen Stewart, who was the widow of Captain Peter Winchester (see 66). The lintel of her parents' town house can still be seen on the front of 40 Victoria Street (the Orkney Hotel). Interestingly, it was Margaret Traill's grandfather, Patrick Traill of Elsness, who had entered the merchant trading business of the Pottingers (see 45).

Margaret kept a recipe book, which has survived and can be found in Orkney Archives (D14/7/1). The recipes contain a surprisingly wide variety of ingredients and require considerable effort to prepare. It includes cod's head dressed the Scots way, ragar of breast of veal, pickled pigeons, pancakes without butter, carrot cake, tansey pudding and, unusually for this time, an orange pudding.

Margaret married James Traill in October 1712 and they had nine children, none of whom survived childhood. This was obviously a source of great sadness for the couple.[701] James Traill died in 1733 and, with no surviving children, his estate passed to his nephew, John Traill of Westness (see below). Following her husband's death, Margaret was pursued by William Liddell of Hammer (son of 69) for the sum of £131 Scots, being given only a few months to pay up. When no payment was forthcoming, Liddell, in keeping with his father's tenacity, employed a lawyer to conclude the matter.[702] Margaret remarried, this time to Hugh Baillie, Collector of Customs, on 6th March 1736.[703] She lived to a good age and was interred with her first husband in 1763.

John Traill of Westness 1795/ Mary Balfour 1794

John Traill of Westness was the son of George Traill of Westness (brother to the previously mentioned James Traill) and Margaret, sister of William Bellenden of Stenness. He inherited the Woodwick estate, the island of North Ronaldsay and the town house in Kirkwall from his uncle. He married Mary, the daughter of John Balfour of Trenaby, in October 1745. The second coat-of-arms on the monument belongs to Balfour of Trenaby, with the motto, 'fordward' above an erect arm in armour, with the hand grasping a baton. Beneath is a shield with the coat-of-arms of three mullets in chief, a chevron with otter's head erased and an X in base. John Traill and his wife Mary made considerable changes to his uncle's town house in Bridge Street, with a lintel above the door recording their names and the date of these alterations, 1763.[704] This was at a time when his fortunes had recovered following the collapse of the Jacobite rebellion.

In 1746, government forces intercepted a letter sent by some of the Orkney lairds, including John Traill, declaring support for Prince Charles. As a result, Benjamin Moodie was given a commission to apprehend these lairds as well as Sir James Stewart of Burray.[705] With little chance of surviving in a Hanoverian prison, John Traill of Westness, together with William Balfour of Trenaby, Archibald Stewart of Brugh and John Traill of Elsness, went into hiding. After capturing Sir James Stewart, who was transported to London and died on a prison hulk, Moodie turned his attention to the four lairds in the North Isles. With the help of some of their loyal servants, they managed to avoid capture, although they suffered much hardship and mental strain, having to resort to caves in the cliffs of Westray when troops were sighted or were expected. Moodie issued an ultimatum, instructing them to appear in Kirkwall by a given date or have their houses destroyed and goods seized.[706] The mother of John Traill, Margaret, Lady Westness, appealed to Moodie to respect her interest in Westness as liferentrix. The day after the ultimatum expired, Moodie arrived at Westness with his detachment of marines, who plundered the house and burnt everything, including the outhouses and barns. Lady Westness and family had to shelter in a stable. Four of the ablest men on the estate were taken prisoner. From Rousay, Moodie and his men sailed to Eday where they carried off prisoners and cattle from the estate of another wanted Jacobite supporter, James Fea of Clestrain. Westray was next, where Trenaby was looted and burnt, followed by Cleat, belonging to Archibald Stewart, with more prisoners being taken. Moodie moved on to John Traill's property in North Ronaldsay where all the young men on the island were seized. In Sanday, Elsness was put to the torch. After a fleeting visit to Stronsay, Moodie took his plunder and prisoners to Kirkwall. The loot was sold by public roup and the prisoners were held in captivity until they agreed to join the army. Those that refused the army were sent to the navy. The tragedy of this affair was not the burning and looting of the lairds' houses, but the imprisonment and forcible pressing into the armed services of the innocent young tenants of the island estates, who had nothing to do with the Jacobite uprising. Moodie continued to harass the North Isles, but failed to capture the missing rebels.[707]

Early in 1747, the discomfort of their time in hiding became too much and the group split up. While Stewart, the eldest of the four, stayed on in the North Isles, John Traill and the others made for Caithness, to the estate of William Sinclair of Freswick, where they stayed until the Act of Indemnity was passed in June 1747. This allowed them to return to Kirkwall, where they were welcomed by their relatives. The sudden appearance of the erstwhile fugitives angered the supporters of the Earl of Morton and a warrant was soon issued for their arrest. The three lairds were, however, released after a couple of days' confinement.

John Traill gradually regained his prosperity and became a burgess of Kirkwall in 1765. He was a large man, even by today's standards, being 6ft 6ins in height, but in later life was bent with rheumatism, which he blamed on his time hiding in caves.[708] In 1791, he gave the mansion house of Westness, along with other properties and lands in Rousay, Firth and South Ronaldsay, to his grandnephew, George Craigie, whose wife, Mary Balfour, was a niece of John's wife and had been named after her aunt. It was Craigie who rebuilt the mansion house in 1792, replacing the old house destroyed in 1746.[709] John Traill died in Kirkwall at the end of April 1795 and, with no children, the Woodwick and North Ronaldsay estate passed to a cousin's son, Lieutenant John (Jack) Traill. Westness House remained the property of George Craigie, but with his sudden death in 1796, his wife was given life rent of the house until it passed to the heirs of Jack Traill.[710] It is thought Craigie hanged himself from a beam in the north-east attic of his new house.[711]

John Traill of Woodwick 1805

Known as Jack, John Traill was the son of Lieutenant William Traill of the Royal Navy, a cousin of John Traill of Westness, from whom he inherited the Woodwick and Westness estates. Jack was born at Saltash in Cornwall. With the patronage of his relation, John Traill of Westness, he obtained a commission in the army, joining the 76th Regiment of Foot, known as Macdonald's Highlanders, where, starting as an ensign, he rose to the rank of captain. Jack served with some distinction in the American War of Independence during the period 1779 to 1782.[712] The regiment was captured following the surrender of Lord Cornwallis' army at Yorktown, the last land battle in the American War of Independence. Despite attempts to persuade them to join the rebel cause, the regiment remained loyal to King George and was released following the signing of the Treaty of Paris in 1783.[713]

On his return to Scotland, Jack had a relationship with an East Lothian girl called Jean Hume, and a son, John, was born in 1784. On 16th March 1790, Jack married Sibilla, daughter of the late Rev. Hugh Sutherland, minister of Harray and Birsay, and his wife, Margaret Traill, another daughter of a Traill of Elsness. Their first child was named James at the special request of John Traill of Westness, in recognition of the beneficial influence of his uncle, James Traill of Woodwick. Unfortunately, both James and the next son, Gilbert, died young and only the youngest son, William, outlived his father, being eight years old when his father died.[714]

John Traill 1822

John Traill was the infant son of William Traill below.

William Traill of Westness and Woodwick 1797-1858

William Traill was the youngest son of Jack Traill of Woodwick and was only eight when his father died. The tutors and curators appointed by his father were Lord Armadale (Sir William Honeyman of Graemsay), Admiral Graeme (6th of Graemeshall), Malcolm Laing of Papdale (85) and Gilbert Laing (later Laing-Meason). It appears that Gilbert Laing was prominent in William Traill's upbringing. A portrait of Gilbert Laing, thought to have been painted by Sir Henry Raeburn, in the possession of the Traill family, has an inscription on the back describing Gilbert as William Traill's guardian.[715]

William married firstly Harriet Sarle on 9th June 1817 in Lisbon. Harriet's father, Charles Sarle, was a member of the Royal Factory of British Merchants in the Portuguese capital. Sometime after the death of Mary Balfour (wife of George Craigie) in 1818, William and Harriet moved to Westness House and had nine children, including the infant John mentioned on the gravestone. Harriet died at Westness in 1841 and William married Henrietta Moodie Heddle of Melsetter on 7th February 1843. They went on to have another eight children.

William Traill's large physical presence proved invaluable in protecting the Sheriff-substitute, Charles Shireff, during the 1832-1833 Parliamentary election, which saw the popular (in Orkney) Samuel Laing (89) take on the sitting candidate, George Traill of Ratter and Hobbister. Laing had convincingly won the Orkney vote but the arrival of the Shetland votes had been delayed owing to the weather. Laing's supporters had become boisterous and, when the Shetland votes eventually arrived, revealing an overall win for his opponent, there was a riot in Kirkwall in which one of Traill's supporters lost his life. With his jacket torn up the back, the Sheriff had great difficulty in declaring the result and it was only through the actions of William Traill in defending him from the mob that he was able to do so. The Sheriff was too frightened to leave his house for a fortnight, holding the County Courts in his living room.[716]

Following William's death in 1858, his eldest son, Dr William Traill, resigned from his post in India and applied to be made the guardian of his many half brothers and sisters. Westness House was sold after the death of Henrietta in 1863.

William Traill of Woodwick MD 1818-1886

William Traill of Woodwick was the eldest son of William Traill and Hariet Sarle. His father's private museum, which included a collection of shells, stimulated an interest in natural history, which he maintained throughout his life. He was educated at Kirkwall Grammar School and then Edinburgh University, where he graduated MD in 1841, under the tutelage of Dr Thomas Traill, second husband of Christian Robertson (see 83). His first medical appointment was at Madras, in the service of the East India Company.

William served in Hong Kong and Singapore before going to Malacca from 1850 to 1852. He married his cousin, Emma Harvey, in Singapore on 4th February 1847. She was the daughter of James Harvey and Patience Sarle of Bath. They had seven children,

Dr Thomas Traill was professor of Medical Jurisprudence at the University of Edinburgh and editor of the Encyclopaedia Britannica. He was the second husband of Christian Robertson, whose character attracted vastly differing opinions from the opposite sex – see James Watson (83).
Orkney Library Photographic Archive

including the John Traill and William Henry Traill mentioned on the stone.

After inheriting Westness and Woodwick, he spent more time in Orkney, becoming involved in archaeology and writing papers on Skara Brae and the Broch of Burrian. He took an interest in local plants and grew specimens sent by his brother in New Zealand. New Zealand flax can still be seen at Holland House in North Ronaldsay. In 1883, he published *A Genealogical Account of the Traills of Orkney*.

Dr Traill died at 19 North Street in St Andrews, Fife. His property passed to his son, John Traill.

John Traill of Woodwick 1851-1898

John Traill was born in Malacca and became a civil engineer in Madras. He died in Orkney at a relatively young age and was buried in St Magnus Cathedral churchyard.

William Henry Traill of Woodwick 1861-1924

William Henry Traill was the youngest son of Dr William Traill and Emma Harvey. He was educated at St Andrews University and in Switzerland, being a good rugby player in his day. He started work with the

London, Brighton and South Coast Railway Company before going to India, where he played a prominent role in the development of the railway network in that country, reaching the position of Traffic Superintendent of the Great Indian Peninsular Railways. On the death of his brother, John, in 1898, he succeeded to the estates of Woodwick and North Ronaldsay. Fifteen years later, he returned from India to live permanently in Orkney. He represented North Ronaldsay on Orkney County Council, was Chairman of the North Isles District Committee and was Deputy Lieutenant of Orkney. In addition, he was Chairman of the Kitchener Memorial Committee, the voluntary body of Orcadians who organised the construction of the Kitchener Memorial. He did not live long enough, however, to see it unveiled at Marwick Head as he died in a shooting accident in North Ronaldsay while hunting rabbits near his home. He fell while crossing a dyke, causing the gun he was carrying to discharge, killing him instantly. His burial took place in the kirkyard of North Ronaldsay. He was survived by his widow, Norah, a daughter of General Gaye of Devon, and two daughters, Kate and Val.

William Douglas Traill 1895-1911

William Douglas Traill was the only son of William Henry Traill and died young while attending Clifton College. When Traill senior died, *The Orcadian* reported his death as the end of an era. "By the death of Mr Traill, the last surviving landed branch of an old Orkney family becomes extinct on the male side, though collateral still remain outside the islands". By the time of his death most of the Woodwick estate had been sold off to the tenants.

Of the daughters of William Henry Traill and Norah Gaye, Kate Joan Traill married Hamish Neil Robertson in 1920. He was a son of Duncan J. Robertson (107) and grandson of James Robertson (92). Hamish was the holder of the Military Cross and the Croix de Guère. Norah Valentine Traill married Colonel John William Thomson-Glover, an Indian Army officer in the 35th Sikhs, who was appointed British consul-general in Sinkiang Province (NW China) in 1932.[717]

CHAPTER 9

The Nineteenth Century – Cathedral Ownership Questioned

The early decades of the nineteenth century raised questions regarding the adequacy of the Cathedral as a place of worship. The labyrinth of pews and galleries in the choir meant that many people in the congregation had to sit where they could neither see nor hear the minister properly. With the building leaking like a sieve and lacking any system of heating, attendance at a church service in the Cathedral was described as 'highly prejudicial to health'.[718] Separated from the choir by a partition, the nave continued to be used as a graveyard and, between 1769 and 1808, no fewer than 138 burials took place. This led to the floor level being raised to such an extent that steps were required from the west doors into the nave and many of the square bases of the columns were concealed.[719] Wooden lattice doors were installed, so that in summer the main doors could be opened, allowing plenty of air to circulate, minimising the smell and also keeping dogs out. Extensive burials in the churchyard had also resulted in a build up of earth on the south side of the building, well above the level of the floor within.

In 1825, the Bishopric estate was taken over by the Crown, who entrusted its management to the Barons of the Exchequer. Control was transferred, in 1833, to the Commissioners of Woods and Forest, who assumed ownership of the Cathedral, thinking it part of the Bishopric estate. They were encouraged in this by, among others, Alexander Peterkin, Sheriff-substitute for Orkney and Shetland (1814-1823), who strongly argued that the burgh had never exercised any act of ownership over the building.[720]

In 1847, the Commissioners began a major restoration, the chief aim of which was to make the building wind and watertight. To improve the interior, all the gravestones were dug up, the best preserved being retained and placed round the side walls. The bodies were removed and reburied in a communal grave in the kirkyard, on the north side of the nave.[721] There is no lack of irony in the fact that Kirkwall's elite ended up like paupers in a communal, unmarked grave. The stench caused by the process of exhuming bodies caused the congregation to vacate the building in August 1847 and move to a temporary newly built church, just to the east of the Cathedral (see 91). The Government intervention was arguably essential to the survival of the Cathedral and provided the foundation for future restoration work. The Town Council did not have the resources to carry out a major renovation and it is very doubtful if its members would have countenanced the digging up of their ancestors.[722]

Kirkwall Town Council was slow to defend its rights over the Cathedral, perhaps deliberately waiting until the Government had spent a considerable amount of money on the building. It was not until May 1850 that a petition was sent to the Commissioners of Woods and Forests, claiming ownership of the building.[723] The Town Council was under pressure from Kirkwall Presbytery to restore the seating in the Cathedral and provide a suitable and permanent place of worship for the parishioners of Kirkwall and St Ola. Government plans to reseat the Cathedral fell far short of Presbyterry demands for the accommodation of 876 people, the Commissioners being opposed to the building of galleries.[724]

The Town Council was unsure of its rights and sought legal advice, which declared that the magistrates and inhabitants of the Burgh were the only legal owners of the Cathedral and consequently could provide seating in any manner they chose.[725] With the Government ignoring the Council's claims over the building,[726] the Town Council, along with the heritors, offered to give up ownership of the Cathedral in return for funding towards the building of a new church, fear of litigation by the Presbyterry being the driving force behind this move.[727]

By October 1851, having examined the evidence presented by Kirkwall Town Council and probably having weighed up the costs of maintaining St Magnus Cathedral, the Commissioners decided to give up any claim to the building, thus precluding them from having to contribute toward another new church. Resolution of the whole issue was, however, still a long way off and there followed a period of strife between the Presbytery on the one hand and the Town Council and heritors on the other. The former wanted a new parish church, after receiving a report that the Cathedral pillars were not strong enough to hold up the galleries required to house the congregation. Having successfully regained control of the building, the Town Council quickly declared the Cathedral as the legal Parochial Church of the parish of Kirkwall and St Ola and, to try and placate Kirkwall Presbytery, appointed Edinburgh architect, David Bryce, to draw up plans for seating.[728] It would take another four years of haggling before work was completed to the satisfaction of both parties. With new seating in place, the congregation was able to return to the building in 1856.

The temporary church was sold to a building contractor, who demolished it and used the materials to construct a range of buildings on Ayre Road, where the former church's arched doorway can still be seen today. Thankfully, the Town Council's record in looking after the Cathedral improved and the public ownership of the building has since then been largely a cause of great civic pride.[729]

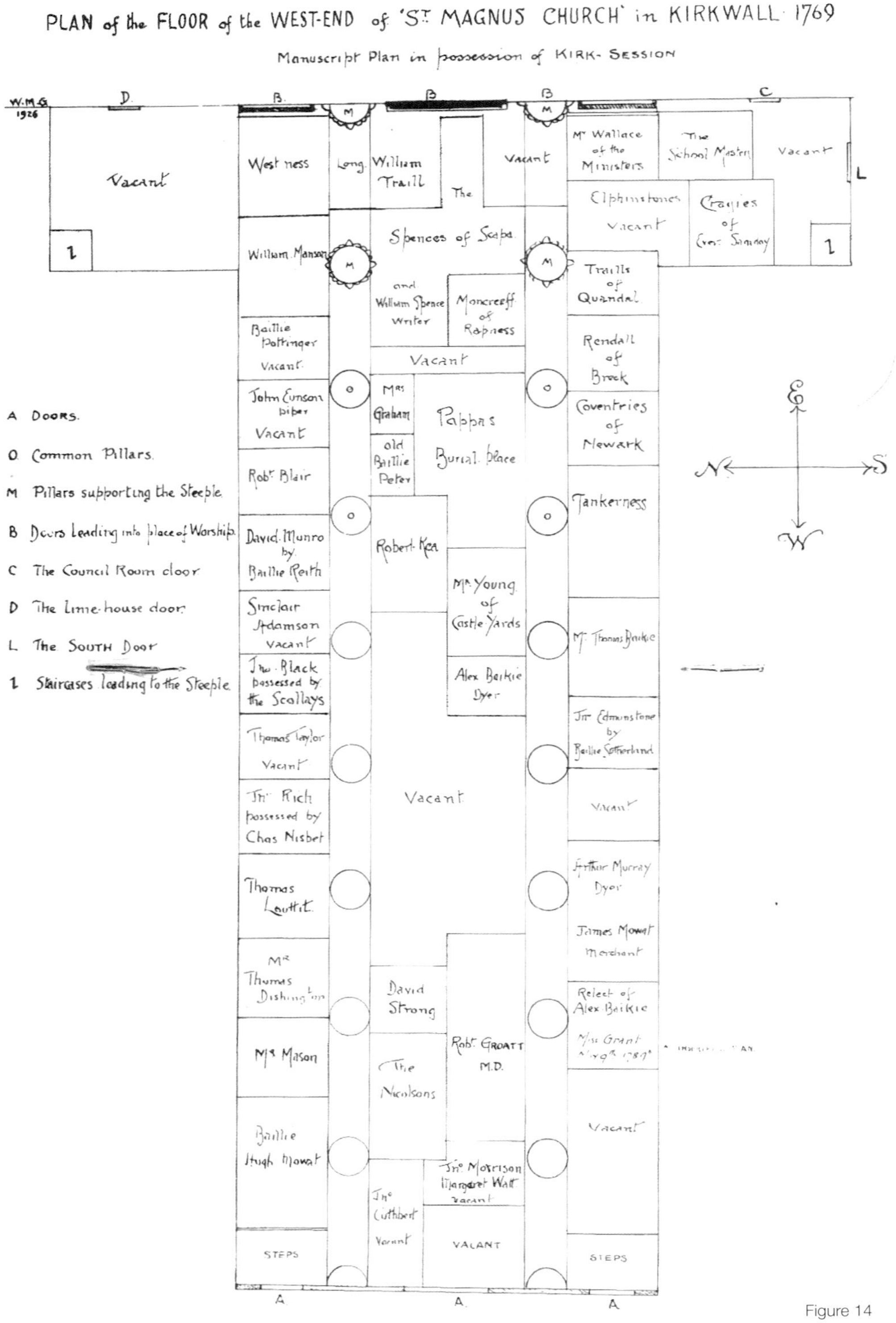

PLAN of the FLOOR of the WEST-END of 'ST MAGNUS CHURCH' in KIRKWALL 1769

Manuscript Plan in possession of KIRK-SESSION

A Doors.
O Common Pillars.
M Pillars supporting the Steeple.
B Doors leading into place of Worship.
C The Council Room door.
D The Lime-house door.
L The South Door
1 Staircases leading to the Steeple.

Figure 14

Chapter 9 - The Nineteenth Century - Cathedral Ownership Questioned

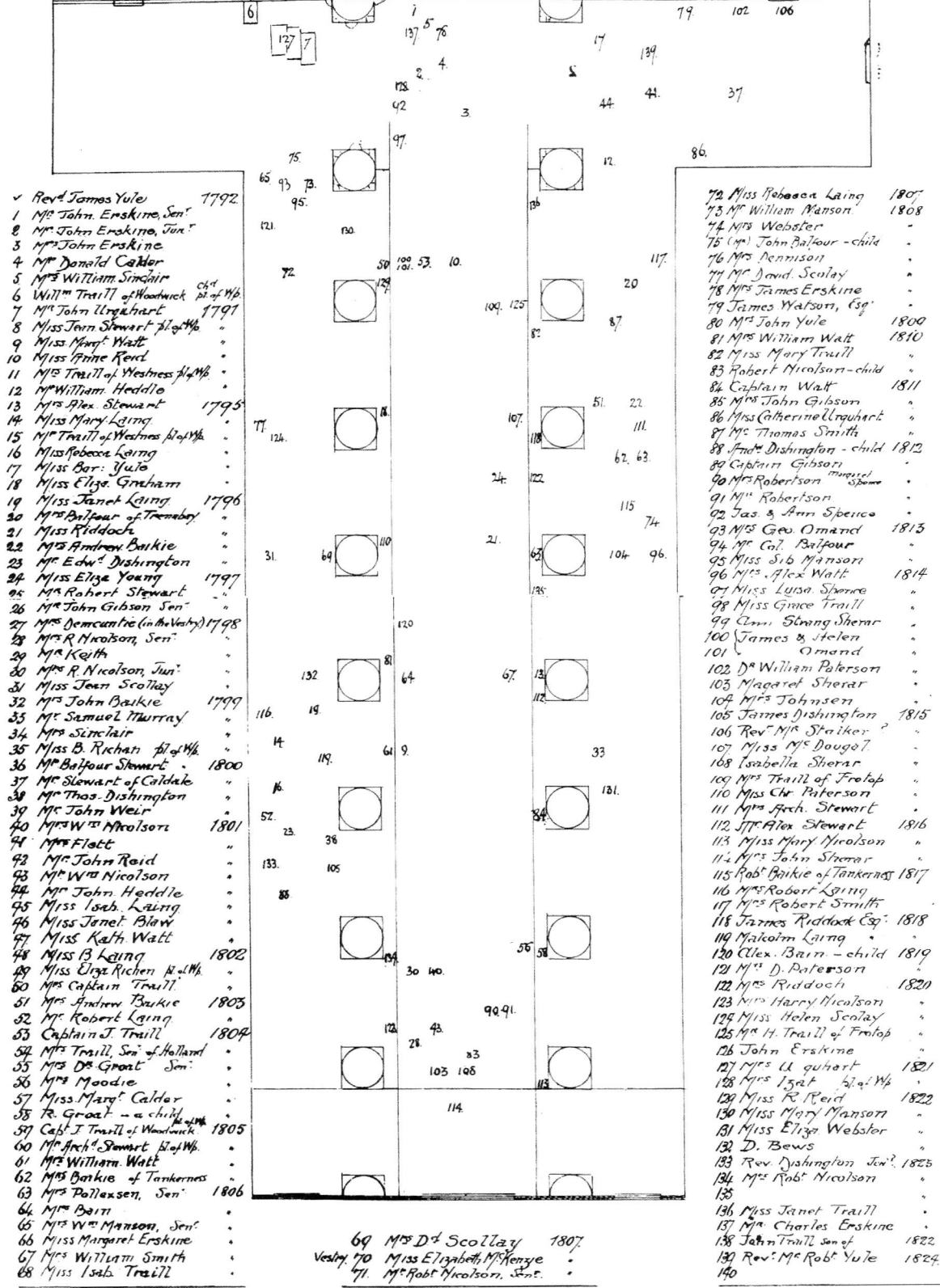

Figure 15 Floor plan of nave showing burials 1792-1824

83. James Watson 1770-1808

This memorial tablet is found on the east wall of the south transept. The inscription says:

> Sacred
> to the Memory of
> A Beloved Husband
> James Watson
> born 26th of March 1770 at Dumfries
> died 27th of March 1808 at Crantit.

Prior to arriving in Orkney, James Watson was in partnership in a drapery and haberdashery business in Dumfries, along with George Duncan, writer. They traded under the firm of Duncan and Watson.[730]

Watson came to Orkney in 1799 to act as Chamberlain of the Earldom estate for Lord Dundas. He was much less overbearing than his predecessor, Captain James Sutherland (later Lord Duffus), but was accused of being "motivated by blundering self interest" and described as "a broken down pedlar of Dumfries" in a printed circular of the time.[731] His efficiency in stopping Orcadians plundering shipwrecks made Watson unpopular in Orkney and he incurred the wrath of Kirkwall's Town Councillors by interfering with their jurisdiction as Admirals of the Port of Kirkwall. Acting as Vice-Admiral Depute of Orkney (Lord Dundas being the Vice-Admiral), Watson authorised the sale of some damaged flax from the *Carolina*, which had gone aground within Kirkwall's port area. The Council was prepared to take the matter to court, if necessary.[732] The Vice-Admiral at that time, however, was the acknowledged Receiver of Wreck for both Orkney and Shetland and was the judge of all things maritime.[733]

Watson, as Vice-Admiral Depute, therefore, dealt with numerous wrecks at the time and again came up against the Kirkwall magistrates after the brig, *Confederacy*, went ashore in Stronsay in 1804. As the vessel was lying in an exposed position, it was sold to Thomas Traill, the Provost of Kirkwall, for a low figure. The vessel was patched and eventually taken to Aberdeen to complete the repairs. The Provost, however, was taken to the Vice-Admiral's Court by two of the ship's crew (both from Westray) for non payment of wages. Following the case of the *Carolina*, Watson seems to have been only too glad to have the Provost brought to his court. The Provost on the other hand was furious, arguing that the four Bailies of Kirkwall should deal with the case and that Watson had no jurisdiction within the bounds of the Port of Kirkwall. This did not impress the Vice-Admiral Depute and in 1806 he issued an arrestment warrant on the *Confederacy*, then lying in Kirkwall harbour. The Provost was forced to submit to the Vice-Admiral Depute and the two Westray seamen won their case.[734]

During the invasion scare of 1804, when a small squadron of Franco-Dutch ships was threatening the north of Scotland, James Moodie of Melsetter was called upon to raise a volunteer force to defend Orkney. He made commissions for his friends, with James Watson becoming his second-in-command.[735] Problems soon arose, however, with the Stromness volunteers unwilling to co-operate with a Kirkwall-led force. Watson made further attempts to form a volunteer regiment, in 1805 and 1806, but, with invasion looking less likely after Nelson's victory at Trafalgar and the bickering between Kirkwall and Stromness continuing unabated, apathy prevailed.[736]

The grounding of the Dutch frigate, *Utrecht*, on Sanday, with over 400 Dutch soldiers and sailors, highlighted the need for a local volunteer force. Troops had to be sent from Caithness and James Watson, acting as Vice-Admiral Depute, accompanied a platoon to Sanday to recover plunder from the wreck. As it turned out, the Dutch were in too pitiful a state after the shipwreck to provide much of a threat, over 50 of them having drowned. The Sanday folk, meanwhile, had great pickings from the wreck and, despite the presence of Watson, along with a platoon of Caithness Volunteers, were in no mood to hand over their booty.[737] Watson was unequivocal on the matter, writing on 14th April 1807, that the wreck was *"completely plundered by the inhabitants who as soon as they discovered the ship had taken possession of it and seized & carried off everything of value belonging to it that they could possibly remove and secrete. They were even barbarous enough to rob the unfortunate officers & crew of their Private Property and in some instances their clothes. A few of the islanders with the most shocking inhumanity refused to give shelter in their houses to some of the crew, whom they turned out, and who in consequence Perished in the night and were found dead next morning"*.[738] Following Watson's death at the end of 1808, his wife continued to try to obtain the share of the salvage due her deceased husband.[739]

James Watson's wife was Christian Robertson, born 30th December 1780, daughter of the Reverend Harry Robertson, Minister of Kiltearn, Ross-shire. They married at Kiltearn in June 1800 and made their home at Crantit, near Kirkwall.[740] She made her house a regular meeting place for the young people of the town and enjoyed bringing couples together. Samuel Laing (89) described her as "gay, agreeable and lively, and of a very hospitable turn".[741] Laing, however, strongly disapproved of her match making and never forgave her for encouraging his sister, May, to enter into an unhappy marriage with a Captain Shaw. After the death of her husband, Christian married an old school friend of Laing's, Dr Thomas Stewart Traill (1781-1862), who became Professor of Medical Jurisprudence at Edinburgh University and later oversaw the production of the eighth edition of *Encyclopaedia Britannica*. Laing's final epitaph on Christian, now Mrs Traill, was, "a vulgar woman; will always keep him down in society".[742] Dr Traill certainly did not agree and regarded his wife as a remarkable woman, writing a 429 page biography of her after she died. His uncle, the Reverend Robert Yule (87), described her as "the best and most delightful woman I ever knew".[743]

84. Thomas Smith c1778-1811

This polished black limestone plaque is found in the south side of the nave, above the gravestone of Nicola Traill (77). The inscription says:

> To The Memory
> of
> THOMAS SMITH
> Landwaiter of the
> Customs,
> who died 12th Sept. 1811
> aged 33 years
> He lived beloved,
> and died regretted.

A Landwaiter was a customs officer, whose duty was to wait or attend on landed goods from ships. An important part of his duty was to ensure that the locals did not pilfer from the many ships that came ashore in the winter storms. During the lifetime of Thomas Smith, more than 200 ships were wrecked or lost in Orkney waters. A large percentage of them came ashore on the low lying islands of North Ronaldsay and Sanday, with approximately 22 vessels coming ashore in the vicinity of Start Point on Sanday between 1789 and 1811.[744]

It is very likely Thomas Smith became employed as a landwaiter through his father, Thomas M. Smith, who was also a landwaiter. The employment of customs officers tended to run in families.[745] During the dispute between the Smiths' superiors (see 86), James Riddoch (the Collector of Customs) and William Manson (Comptroller of Customs), Thomas senior was witness to some shady dealing. His report to the Comptroller, dated 7th March 1796, described how, the previous June, he had witnessed a large chest, thought to contain wine, being landed out of the brigantine, *Pallas*. Smith was surprised at this as her cargo had previously been offloaded and checked by Riddoch along with fellow landwaiter, Andrew Baikie (grandfather of the explorer). Smith followed the chest to Baikie's home, where it was deposited by the crew. He reported this to Riddoch's assistant but it appears nothing was done.[746]

Young Thomas Smith took the oath of office on 26th October 1803, being sworn in before William Manson, Comptroller. The oath said, *"I do solemnly swear that I will to the best of my skill and knowledge perform and fulfil the employment committed to my charge and inspection as an officer of His Majesty's Customs in the Port of Kirkwall in Orkney and that I will not directly or indirectly be guilty of or connived at any fraud to the hurt of His Majesty's Revenue and that I will not take or receive any reward or gratification other than my salary, and what is or shall be allowed from the Crown, or the regular Fees established by Law for any service done or to be done in the execution of my Employment in the Customs upon any account whatever So help me God".*[747]

On 26th October 1808, Thomas attended the wreck of the brig, *Sir Sydney Smith,* bound from Sweden to Liverpool with a cargo of iron and deals. After the ship had been driven ashore at Widewall Bay, the crew was rescued. The ship was deemed beyond repair, the cargo was landed and Custom duty of £213 5s 9d was paid. For his part in overseeing the landing of the cargo, Smith received £3 8s 6d.[748]

Thomas Smith died at a relatively young age and was buried near his plaque.

85. George Omond c1760-1813

This mural tablet is found on the north wall of the nave next to the north transept. The inscription says:

> Sacred
> to the memory
> of GEORGE OMOND of Fair Isle,
> who departed this life the 1st of Feb. 1813
> aged 53 years.
> Likewise his two daughters
> JANE OMOND   HELEN OMOND
> aged 8 years   aged 6 years
> who both died in July 1811

George Omond was born around 1760 in Fair Isle. His maternal grandfather was the Reverend George Reid, who was master of Kirkwall Grammar School from 1727 to 1734, but was dismissed by the Town Council for excessive discipline of his pupils. He subsequently moved to Fair Isle as a missionary, before being called, in 1752, to be minister of Nesting in Shetland.[749] While in Fair Isle, one of his daughters, Helen, married a local islander with the surname Omond. Their son, George, came to Kirkwall to be with his uncle, John Reid, who was a prosperous Kirkwall merchant and who had no son. John Reid took the young George under his wing, bringing him into partnership with his firm.

In June 1789, George travelled to Liverpool on business and kept a diary of his visit, which has been preserved.[750] He was in a hurry to meet a vessel belonging to the firm, which was expected to arrive in Liverpool from Sweden. The ship was the *Resolution*, which had been built at Kirkwall in 1787 and was of 111 registered tons. George went by sea from St Margaret's Hope to Peterhead and from there travelled by post horse along the coast road through Aberdeen, Stonehaven, Montrose and Dundee to Edinburgh, crossing the Firths of Tay and Forth by ferry. He then took a coach to Carlisle, Lancaster and Preston, before catching a post chaise[751] to Liverpool. The whole journey took 10 days. One of George's first business contacts in Liverpool was with John Gladstone, father of future PM, William Ewart Gladstone. George sailed back to Orkney on the *Resolution*.

In 1801, his uncle died and George became sole partner of John Reid & Co., general merchants and shipowners. In 1803, he married Jean McKinlay, niece of another Kirkwall merchant, and they had the two daughters mentioned on the plaque, who sadly died young. They also had three sons, who survived childhood. When George died in 1813, he had over £6000 in his Edinburgh bank account, a considerable sum of money at that time. He also owned much property, including a farm and a building in Albert Street on the site of the present Bank of Scotland in Kirkwall. Furthermore, he was the part owner of four sailing vessels.

His widow settled in Edinburgh and all three sons graduated from Edinburgh University.

86. James Riddoch c1746-1818

This white marble tablet, framed in black marble, is found in the south side of the nave near the Paplay Tomb. The inscription says:

> Sacred
> To The Memory Of
> JAMES RIDDOCH, ESQr
> Of Cairston,
> Late Provost Of Kirkwall,
> Who Departed This Life
> 16th Feb. 1818, Aged 72 Years
> Also Of
> JANET YOUNG,
> His Spouse,
> Who Died 30th Dec. 1819,
> Aged 77 Years.

James Riddoch was the only son of John Riddoch and Mary Young (79). In 1763, James was appointed Sheriff-clerk, working alongside his father[752] and, in 1788, he succeeded his father as Collector of Customs in Kirkwall.[753] He was also Collector of Stamp Duties, being responsible for issuing liquor licences, but appears to have turned a blind eye to those who operated without any licence. In Kirkwall, in 1789, there were fifty-five unlicensed retailers of ale, spirits and wine (Stromness had forty-two). The Sheriff-Clerk at the time, James Sinclair, wrote to Edinburgh to complain about this situation, but Riddoch was still unwilling to act. A Supervisor of Excise was sent north to investigate.[754]

As Collector of Customs, Riddoch firstly worked under George Ross and secondly under William Manson, who was appointed the Comptroller of Customs in 1790.[755] Riddoch and his clerk, William Spence, did most of the work, such as supervising the subordinate customs officers and carrying out the book keeping. It was a lucrative position with many opportunities for making additional income. Riddoch and Manson, for example, shared the money gained from herring bounty fees,[756] took two-thirds of customs fees and kept all the profits arising from holding bonds lodged as security at the customs house. As owner of Cairston, Riddoch found it convenient to superintend the customs generated by the growing harbour in Stromness.

Riddoch and Manson were prominent freemasons, with Manson being elected Master in 1791 and Riddoch a year later. Riddoch had previously been elected in the years 1773 and 1783.[757] Both men, however, fell out in 1794, with Manson accusing Riddoch and others, notably the Magistrates and Town Council of Kirkwall, of conniving to smuggle. Manson even accused Riddoch of threatening to shoot him.[758] It is worth quoting some of the allegations of corruption he presented to the Board of Customs in Edinburgh,

"It is well known to every Person of Observation or knowledge of the affairs of this Country that for many years past up to the present time, the Magistrates & Town Council of Kirkwall have for the past been made up of persons notorious for their smuggling and who by their great luck in that line, some of them have made independent fortunes……The Collector of Customs (Riddoch) has long been a Member of that Council, and generally takes the lead of them in most of their political & antiministerial deliberations, whither it be for the election of a Member of Parliament, or delegate to the returning Borough, or for Members of their own Incorporation, into which body it is difficult for any Inhabitant to get admission………It has been the practice here, upon the arrival of all decent strangers, who come to this place, either upon business or pleasure, that the Collector, with the Provost & some

of the Magistrates, usually wait upon them and present them with the Freedom of the Borough; this leads to other civilities, feasting and conviviality commences between the strangers and the people above mentioned and generally continues until their departure. This puts a stop to the knowledge of their practices and stifles every information which would be brought against them and their unlawful traffick." In addition, Manson criticised Riddoch for not keeping the customs boat in the North Isles, where it would be more useful and accused him of being lax in the execution of his duties.

Riddoch countered that Manson did not know his job, was often absent and did little work.[759] As well as giving a detailed rebuttal of Manson's accusations, he posed a number of questions concerning Manson's ability to carry out his duties.[760] The Comptroller of Customs in Inverness, Thomas Gilzean, was sent to investigate. His report, dated 30th May 1796, cleared Riddoch of any wrong doing. While the members of the Board were critical of Manson's lack of knowledge of the customs service, they were careful not to upset his Balfour relations. The report stated, *"...the Board being hopeful that the differences between him and the Collector may subside, and that both of them from a sense of duty and interest may still be led to co-operate for the good of the service".*[761] Things did settle down and, towards the end of William Manson's life (he died in 1808), the two were still working together in their respective positions and jointly signing letters.[762]

After the death, in 1803, of his cousin, the Landwaiter Andrew Baikie, Riddoch became benefactor and guardian to Baikie's son, John, then serving with the Royal Navy, and daughter, Janet. A third sibling, Mary Margaret Baikie, had been adopted by Mrs Craigie of Westness, after the Baikies' mother died in 1796.[763] A number of Riddoch's letters to John Baikie, written while John was in naval service, have been preserved in the Orkney Archives.[764] He wrote concerning John's career, financial affairs, family and local news, and moral advice to a young man as to the behaviour befitting an officer.

After being a member of Kirkwall Town Council for many years, James Riddoch became Provost of Kirkwall in 1814, and was in post for four years until his death. It was during Riddoch's spell as Provost that Kirkwall Town Council fell out with the Trustees of Sir William Honeyman's estate, whose factor was John Rae (father of the explorer). The dispute possibly stemmed from Rae's resentment against Riddoch for removing him from the customs, a position Riddoch considered incompatible with the office of a factor.[765]

Riddoch objected to Stromness becoming a burgh of Barony, which would allow for the election of a Town Council and give it the ability to attract trade by holding a weekly market and an annual fair. Kirkwall strongly objected to the fair being held in August, the same month as the Kirkwall Lammas Fair. James Riddoch, the only heritor to object to his property being included in the new burgh, did not want to be subject to the privileges and jurisdictions that would accrue from Stromness becoming a burgh of Barony. When the Stromness petitioners, led by Alexander Davidson, achieved their goal in 1817, James Riddoch's lands in Cairston were excluded from the burgh boundary.[766] The weekly market and annual fair was moved to the first week of September.

James Riddoch married his cousin, Janet Young, whose parents were Andrew Young (brother of James' mother) and Barbara Baikie.[767] This was her second marriage, the first having been to Captain Allen.[768] Janet's sister, Margaret, who was known as 'Miss Peggy', was the wife of James Gordon of Cairston, whose business failure led to the sale of Cairston to James Riddoch's father (see 79).[769] James died without issue and Cairston passed to the Pollexfens (see 88).

87. Rev. Robert Yule 1763-1824

This memorial tablet is found on the south side of the nave, just passed the south transept. The inscription reads:

To The Memory Of

THE REVEREND ROBERT YULE

Born 21st July 1763, Died 7th June 1824,

After Having Been 32 Years,
First Minister Of Kirkwall

A Few Of His Personal Friends
Have Erected This Tablet

In Grateful And Respectful Memorial
Of Talents Which They Venerated
And Worth Which They Loved

MDCCCXXV

Robert Yule was the son of the Reverend John Yule, the previous minister of the first charge of St Magnus Cathedral. His mother, Barbara, daughter of Thomas Traill of Hobbister, was John Yule's second wife, his first being Christina, youngest daughter of Thomas Baikie (65), previous minister of the Cathedral. Robert Yule gained his MA at Marischal College, Aberdeen in 1779. He was presented by the Magistrates and Town Council of Kirkwall in 1788 and ordained in July 1789. He started his career in Kirkwall as assistant to his father and, following the latter's death in 1792, took

The Rev Robert Yule was responsible for many repairs to the building and the windows he installed – some of which still exist – are unique in shape and are unknown in any other cathedral or church.

over as minister of the first charge. Robert married Anne, daughter of Thomas Traill of Tirlet (Westray) and Marjorie Blaw, on Christmas Eve, 1788.[770]

Prior to being ordained as assistant minister of the Cathedral, Yule acted as tutor to the two sons of Thomas Balfour of Elwick in Shapinsay.[771] He and his wife also looked after Anne's nephew, the previously mentioned Thomas Stewart Traill. When the minister of Shapinsay died, Thomas Balfour was keen to have his friend take over as minister of the island. The stipend of £90 was slightly more than that of St Magnus Cathedral and the work much less onerous. However, patronage of the country parishes of Orkney lay with the Dundases, who had bought the earldom from the 14th Earl of Morton. Kirkwall differed from the country parishes in that the burgh's ancient charter gave the right of patronage to the Magistrates. Sir Thomas Dundas chose Yule's brother-in-law, Rev. George Barry, to be minister of Shapinsay. Barry was married to Yule's sister, Sibella, and was Second Minister of the Cathedral.

During the war with Revolutionary France at the end of the eighteenth century, Thomas Balfour set up the Orkney and Shetland Fencible Regiment for home defence. The regiment was in existence from 1793 to 1799. Rev. Yule acted as chaplain and was paid a small allowance for his services.[772]

Rev. Yule became a freemason in 1811 and, in 1817, oversaw the arrangements for the first Church attendance by the Kirkwall Lodge.[773]

Rev. Yule had many repairs carried out to the fabric of the Cathedral, re-glazing most of the windows by 1822, with the exception of those, especially in the nave, which had been built up with stone or wood. The windows installed were made in the style of ash leaves, being symbolic of the tree of life. These leaf windows were unique, with no other cathedral or church being fitted with windows of the same pattern.[774] While most of these windows were replaced by stained glass during the early twentieth century renovation, a few survived and can still be seen today, especially through a tour of the upper levels.

Robert Yule stayed in the Old Manse, adjoining the south end of the Bishop's Palace, which ultimately proved detrimental to his health. In 1793, shortly after the death of his father, who had also lived in this manse, Robert asked the heritors to repair the manse, which they readily agreed to do. However, only limited repairs were carried out and the manse remained in a poor state. Dampness would seem to have been a problem and Robert was compelled to keep a fire lit in the house 24 hours a day. He ultimately developed a chronic disease of the lungs, which prevented him from carrying out his duties as minister in his latter years.[775]

88. Margaret Riddoch c1740-1825

This black marble plaque is found in the south side of the nave above the gravestone of James Baikie of Burness (65) and has the following inscription:

> Sacred
> To The Memory Of
> MARGARET RIDDOCH
> Relict Of
> Henry Pollexfen
> Who Died 31st July 1825
> Aged 85 Years

Margaret Riddoch was the daughter of Provost John Riddoch (79) and sister of James Riddoch (86). Her sister, Mary, had married Henry Pollexfen, who had arrived in Stromness in the service of the Hudson Bay Company. He was then a widower and a trip through to Kirkwall so impressed him that he stayed, rather than sail over to Canada. Henry's son from his first marriage, also called Henry, came to visit his father and similarly found life in Kirkwall to his taste, particularly after meeting Margaret Riddoch, whom he eventually married. Father and son had therefore married sisters. Margaret and Henry went on to have a large family, with the ninth child inheriting Cairston.[776] This was Thomas Pollexfen, who became a keen agricultural improver, introducing improved varieties of turnip and grass seed, and pioneering the export of live cattle.[777]

89. Malcolm Laing c1763-1818/ Samuel Laing 1780-1868

Above the gravestone of Elizabeth Elphinstone (67) in the north side of the nave is a white marble tablet, framed in sandstone, with the following inscription, the first part being in Latin:

> Here lies
> *Malcolm Laing*
> who described the history of
> of his native land with great skill,
> set out in pure and
> clear speech.
> He was born on the 15th of the Kalends of Feb.
> AD 1763.
> He died on the 17th of the Kalends of Dec.
> AD 1818.
> His wife surviving
> she took care to place this marble,
> a monument of love and longing.[778]

SAMUEL LAING OF PAPDALE 1780-1868
NOTABLE PROVOST OF KIRKWALL
TRAVELLER, AUTHOR,
TRANSLATOR OF HEIMSKRINGLA.

The marble tablet to Malcolm Laing was first erected in 1834,[779] while the tribute to Samuel Laing was added in 2004, being the last memorial, to date, to be placed in St Magnus Cathedral. There appear to be discrepancies in the information given on the memorial stone for Malcolm Laing. Most sources give 1762 as the year of his birth, as opposed to 1763 on the memorial stone. Also, Samuel Laing, in his autobiography, says Malcolm died on the evening of 16th November 1818.[780] The discrepancies can partly be explained by how one interprets the Roman calendar.[781]

Malcolm, the eldest of 18 siblings, was born in the double tenement in Albert Street, bought by his merchant father, Robert Laing, in 1760. The house is behind the present day shop of Starlings (57 Albert Street). His mother, Barbara Blaw, was a granddaughter of Rev William Blaw (80).

Malcolm was educated at Kirkwall Grammar School, then still at the south-east end of Broad Street. After attending Edinburgh University, he qualified as a lawyer, being called to the bar in 1785, and became close friends of eminent people such as Lord Cockburn, Sir Walter Scott and Charles James Fox.

As a young barrister in Edinburgh, he shared a house in George Street with Adam Gillies (later Lord Gillies, 1766-1842), where mutual friends would gather to discuss the politics and literature of the day. After dining at half past four in the afternoon, copious quantities of claret would be drunk until four, five or

Malcolm Laing died in 1818 and was buried in the Cathedral. His brother, Samuel, was added in 2004, the last memorial to be placed in the Cathedral.

six in the morning.[782] Malcolm, along with many of his contemporaries, was enthusiastic about the principals of the French Revolution. He defended Joseph Gerrald, one of the 'Scottish Martyrs', who had been encouraged by events in France to seek political reform in Britain. Despite a highly regarded, eloquent speech by Laing, Gerrald was sentenced to transportation to Botany Bay for 14 years.[783]

Historical research was much more to Malcolm's liking than legal work, and he wrote a number of historical works, the most prominent being his *History of Scotland from the Union of Crowns to the Union of the Kingdoms*. He also made a critical study of the

Gaelic poems allegedly written by the ancient Gaelic poet named Ossian and in 1805 Malcolm brought out a two-volume edition of *Ossian*, showing the poems' true source as the poetical works of James Macpherson.

Having made his fortune in shipping and the kelp trade, Malcolm's father had bought Papdale in 1783 to add to the extensive lands he owned in Shapinsay, Stronsay, Eday and Sanday. After his father died in 1803, Malcolm sold the town house and moved to Papdale, where he built the Georgian mansion of Papdale House.[784] He took a considerable interest in agricultural improvement, bringing a flock of Merino sheep to Stove, in Sanday. In 1805, Malcolm married Margaret Dempster Carnegie, daughter of Thomas Carnegie and Mary Gardyne. She lived to a good age (born 1780, died 1864) and was buried in Greyfriars Cemetery, Edinburgh.[785]

Malcolm Laing was Convener of Orkney's Commissioners of Supply in 1805 and became MP for Orkney and Shetland in 1807, representing the counties until 1812. In 1808, he spearheaded plans to build a pier at Kirkwall. Subscriptions were sought and Malcolm headed the list with a £100 donation. In a letter to Watt of Breckness, seeking a contribution for the new pier, he described it as "the only public work that has been attempted in the County since the Cathedral was erected".[786] Work began on the Thomas Telford design in April 1809 and was completed in 1811, at a cost of around £4000,[787] with an additional west pier being added in 1813 to give extra shelter.

By 1814, when Sir Walter Scott paid him a visit at Papdale, Malcolm was in a poor state of health. Scott reported that, *"Our old acquaintance, though an invalid, received us kindly. He looks very poorly and cannot walk without assistance, but seems to retain all the quick, earnest, and vivacious intelligence of his character and manner"*.

It was while at dinner on Christmas Day 1814 that Malcolm heard news of the destruction of the Odin Stone and some other standing stones in Stenness. An incomer, by the name of Captain Mackay, who leased the land on which the stones stood, was irritated by the large number of people who regularly visited the site, resulting in damage to the fields. Lovers, for example, regularly plighted their troth by holding hands through the hole in the Odin Stone. Mackay was insensitive to local traditions and had the stones removed. Malcolm Laing was horrified at the destruction of these antiquities and immediately petitioned his fellow diner, the Sheriff-substitute for Orkney, Alexander Peterkin. He advised that Laing and the Provost of Kirkwall, James Riddoch (86), who was also present, should, as Justices of the Peace, apply to the Procurator Fiscal to execute a 'Sist and Suspension' against Captain Mackay. This was duly carried out and the remaining stones were thankfully saved. Laing suspected that the Factor, John Rae (father of the explorer), had actively colluded with Mackay in this act of vandalism. Laing was convinced that Rae's resentment against Riddoch (see 86) was at the root of the problem.[788]

Malcolm Laing died in 1818 at the age of 56, was buried in the Cathedral and left his estate to his brother, Samuel, who was the youngest of the Laing brothers. His other surviving brothers, James and Gilbert were already well provided for and Samuel was in the best position to continue the management of the Laing estate.

Samuel Laing was born in the same house as his elder brother and educated in Kirkwall (one of his fellow pupils being Thomas Stewart Traill[789]), before being sent to Liverpool, to gain knowledge of business in the counting house of Robert Gladstone (uncle of the future

Malcolm Laing was an MP for Orkney and Shetland and led the campaign to build a harbour at Kirkwall. Designs drawn up by the famous Scottish engineer, Thomas Telford, were accepted and construction completed in 1811. This portrait was painted by his brother, Samuel, who shares his brother's memorial.
Orkney Library Photographic Archive

Prime Minister).[790] To complete his mercantile education and learn German, he spent a couple of enjoyable years (1799-1801) in north Germany, being based at Kiel in Holstein (then part of Denmark). After returning to Scotland and a brief trip home to Orkney, he was sent to the London counting house of William Gillies, brother of Malcolm's barrister friend, to continue his business education.[791] This was not to his liking and a spell as a clerk in a mercantile business in Rotterdam followed during the Peace of Amiens.[792] He stayed on after the resumption of hostilities, despite Holland being then under French control and soon got caught up in the momentous events of the time. He helped two escaped British naval officers and a midshipman avoid the French and got them back to England. With French activity increasing along the Channel ports for a possible invasion of England, Samuel realised it was time to leave Holland and he escaped to England on a neutral ship, disguised as a German seaman.

With these adventures behind him, he received a commission in the Royal Staff Corps, which undertook scouting, surveys and fieldwork. It was in the winter of 1805, while stationed at Hythe in Kent, that he met his future wife, Agnes Kelly, the daughter of the Barrack Master, Captain Kelly. In 1808, he was posted to Gibraltar and then served in the Peninsular War, seeing action at Rolica, Vimeiro, where his horse was shot dead from under him, and later at Corunna.

Samuel gave up his military career after his return from Corunna. His father's old business partner, Gilbert Meason, had died and his brother, Gilbert, had succeeded to his property, becoming Gilbert Laing Meason. His brother had offered him the position of manager of the lead mines at Wanlockhead in Dumfriesshire, part of old Gilbert Meason's property portfolio. This would give Samuel a handsome salary of £800 per year and allow him to marry his sweetheart, Agnes Kelly. They married in March 1809, settled at St Andrew's Square in Edinburgh and spent summers at the mines at Wanlockhead.[793] This was the happiest period in Samuel's life. The couple had two children, Elizabeth born in December 1809 and Samuel in 1811. Their idyll unfortunately did not last as Agnes took ill and died in the autumn of 1812. After burying Agnes in the Canongate Churchyard, he took his children to England, to be brought up by their maternal grandmother and aunts.[794] More woes followed when the business venture into which he entered collapsed in 1816 and he had to be bailed out by his brother, Gilbert. The income from the lead mines also dried up with the collapse of the price of minerals. His other brother, James, who had made a fortune in Jamaica, suggested starting a herring fishery in Orkney to feed the slaves on his plantations. Samuel set to work, procured six Fife boats and chose Malcolm Laing's property at Whitehall in Stronsay as an ideal site for a fishing station. After an initial failure to find fish, the boats soon returned heavily laden. The following year, 400 Orkney boats were fitted out and the Stronsay fishery soon grew to huge proportions despite the loss of the West Indian contract.[795]

Samuel's success soon led him to be elected to Kirkwall Town Council (October 1816), becoming a Bailie in the following year. He also represented Kirkwall at the annual Convention of Royal Burghs from June 1813 to May 1817.[796]

Samuel had been toying with the idea of emigrating to America, but the death of his brother, Malcolm, changed everything. He brought his children and sister-in-law, Mary Kelly, to Papdale and threw himself into running the estate. There were still financial problems to deal with, including debts amounting to £7700, accrued by Malcolm for his various agricultural improvements, and there was also the remainder of the money which he owed to Gilbert. To raise funds, he had to run the estate more efficiently and obtain more income from rents. He removed cottars from Stove and resettled them on self-contained crofts adjacent to the farm. This gave him rent income, allowed him to grow new crops and enabled him to introduce new breeds of cattle and sheep on the main farm.

Samuel was generous to Kirkwall in the gifting of land for building schools and churches. His popularity in the town soon led him to become Provost in 1822, a post he held for the next 12 years. He often represented the burgh and the county in dealings with the authorities in the south. As has been mentioned previously (82), Samuel stood for Parliament in his home islands and narrowly lost, causing a riot in the streets of Kirkwall.

With the loss of the election and his financial prospects looking grim, following a collapse in kelp prices, Samuel decided to cut his ties with Orkney, where he would have a much diminished position if he remained. He put the estate into the hands of trustees in return for an annual allowance and, in July 1834, settled in Norway, where he began a new career as a travel writer. His first book extolled the virtues of Norway, arguing that Britain could learn a lot from Norse history and particularly Norway's modern democracy.[797] More books followed, including a very critical account of Sweden and he became very popular, especially among politicians, diplomats and economists, keen to learn more about the countries he described.

In 1841, after returning to Britain, Laing started on his greatest work, the first English translation of Snorri

Sturluson's *Heimskringla*, which was eventually published in three volumes in 1844 and included a 'preliminary dissertation' developing themes from his book on Norway.[798] This publication had a huge impact on Victorian Britain and his translation has the distinction of being one of the longest surviving books in print next to the Bible and Shakespeare.[799]

Further publications followed, his last in 1851 concerning the Danish Duchies of Slesvig and Holstein in which he condemned German nationalism and criticised Britain's lack of support for Denmark.[800] Following his son's election to Parliament in 1852 as Liberal MP for Northern (Wick) Burghs (which included Kirkwall), Samuel stopped writing and retired to Idvies House, near Forfar, living with his daughter and family. In 1864, he suffered a stroke, which diminished him intellectually and physically. He was cared for at his daughter's Edinburgh house at Lynedoch Place, where he died in 1868 and was buried in the Dean cemetery.[801]

Today there is still a living link to the two distinguished brothers. In his autobiography, Samuel Laing wrote, *"We lived in that house in Kirkwall a little below the broad street which is distinguished by two or three middling sized Plane Trees, which were planted by my father and are almost the only trees in the country"*. After Malcolm Laing sold their town house, it eventually came into the hands of Kirkwall chemist, Thomas Sclater. By this stage there was a large 18 feet wall around the garden, which held three mature sycamore trees. To help pay for his commercial speculation, Mr Sclater divided the house into flats, chopped two of the mature trees down and removed the high garden wall to make room for a row of one-storey lean-to shops. There seems to have been general disapproval of his actions as, to stop litigation, he sold his rights concerning the third tree to the Town Council, provided the Council undertook to keep it pruned.[802] This tree became affectionately known as the Big Tree, which, though a decrepit shadow of its heyday, still stands proudly in Albert Street.

90. George William Traill 1792-1847

On the east wall of the North Transept there is a large white marble tablet on a black base, which says:

Sacred
to the memory of
GEORGE WILLIAM TRAILL ESQUIRE
of Viera and Rousay
and of the Bengal Civil Service
Born 2 Oct. 1792, Died 20 Nov. 1847

He was for many years commissioner
of the Province of Kumoan, one of the
North-Western Provinces of India,
where his memory is still cherished
as a wise and beneficient ruler.

George William Traill was the son of William Traill, one of the Westness Traills, and Mary Colebrooke, who had married in 1789. Mary was the daughter of Sir George Colebrooke, Baronet, English merchant banker, Chairman of the East India Company and MP, who bankrupted himself in unwise speculations. Mary's first husband was Count Adrien de Peyron and together they had a son, Charles Adolphe Maria de Peyron. He died relatively young, but left an illegitimate daughter in India, who was the mother of Frederick Burroughs (100).[803]

George William Traill was educated at the East India Company College of Haileybury in Hertfordshire, entering it in 1808.[804] This college was designed to produce administrators for the Company's interests in India and places at Haileybury were much sought after. Traill's family connection made his entry a foregone conclusion. Having gained a good grounding in law, mathematics, economics, botany and oriental languages, Traill arrived in India in 1810 and, after five years' service, was appointed assistant to E. Gardner, the political officer of an expedition sent up to Nepal, which resulted in Nepal ceding the mountainous province of Kumaon to the East India Company. With the province being absorbed into the rest of British India, Gardner assumed the roles of Commissioner for Affairs of Kumaon and Agent to the Governor-General of India. While Gardner remained busy with his military and political duties in Nepal, the burden of running the province fell to his assistant and Traill officially took over the role in 1816. He resisted any centralising tendency and ruled with the attitude that a frontier administrator knew what was good for his territory better than any distant authority. Being able to speak and write the local language, his administration was looked upon as just, wise and progressive.[805] Traill conducted a major survey of Kamaon, which still continues today to form the basic document for determining village boundaries.[806] He also managed to reorganise and simplify the region's complex taxation system.[807]

Traill retired from the India service in 1836, assumed the guardianship of his distant young relative, Frederick Burroughs, and used his wealth to buy up property in Rousay whenever any appeared on the market. By 1845, he had acquired Frotoft, Wyre, Quandale, parts of Wasbister and the land of Westness (but not Westness House, which still belonged to William Traill

George William Traill had a successful career in India and later bought up property in Orkney. Initially regarded as a good landlord, he later ruthlessly cleared crofters from their homes; the only 'Highland-style' clearance in the county.

of Westness and Woodwick). Traill may have been well regarded in India, but in Orkney he is remembered as the tyrannical laird who undertook the only clearance in the county on the scale of those carried out in the Highlands, clearing the township of Quandale on the west side of Rousay. To begin with, Traill undertook some improvements, which gave the people of Quandale some hope for the future. His plans changed, however, following the purchase of the lands at Westness.

Traill was an absentee landlord, visiting Orkney only during the summer and staying at Viera Lodge in Rousay. His factor was the hard but very competent Robert Scarth, one of the prime movers of agricultural reform in Orkney. Scarth acted as factor for a number of estates, including that of William Traill of Westness and Woodwick (82). Following the kelp collapse of 1831, he oversaw the demise of run rig in North Ronaldsay with the division of much of the land into small farms. The rent increases resulting from this reorganisation saw 32 families being forced to leave the island. The purchase of the lands of Westness opened up the possibilities of being rid of the unprofitable crofting township at Quandale and of creating a sheep pasture, utilising cheap government loans for draining and re-seeding. Traill readily approved Scarth's plans, with the result that, after the harvest of 1845, eviction notices were issued to the crofters of Quandale.[808] The evictions took a number of years to complete and met with some opposition, especially from the Free Church minister, Rev. George Ritchie. Traill insisted that the land was his and he had a right to do with it as he pleased.

Described as a "quiet, liverless East Indian and millionaire, as dark and hard as mahogany,"[809] George Traill died suddenly in the toilet of his London club in November 1847. An autopsy revealed a heart condition of long standing.[810] Being unmarried and childless, his estate passed to Frederick Burroughs, who, at the request of his guardian, changed his name to Traill-Burroughs. George Traill had been referred to as 'uncle' by his young protégé.

91. Rev William Logie 1786-1856

This large, rather ugly, granite memorial is found on the east wall of the south transept. The inscription says:

> Erected
> In Memory Of
> The Reverend William Logie D D
> Minister Of The First Charge of
> Kirkwall and St Ola
> By Members of his Congregation
> In Affectionate Remembrance
> Of His Faithful Ministrations
> Among Them For 32 Years
> And In Testimony Of Their Admiration
> Of His Talents And Respect For
> His High Character, Piety And Worth.
> Dr Logie
> Was Born 23rd February 1786
> Ordained 25th April 1811
> Died 5th September 1856

William Logie was the son of merchant Alexander Logie, whose business was in Bridge Street.[811] William's father also had the estate of Isbister in Rendall. Growing up, William was to experience the deaths of seven siblings and would later have to suffer the loss of a number of his own children. As well as his elementary education at Kirkwall Grammar School, he received private tuition, which included classical studies, under the supervision of Rev. Robert Yule (87).[812] He had no interest in following his father into business, his ambition lying with the Christian ministry. At Edinburgh University he combined the studies of medicine and divinity, while also maintaining a keen interest in chemistry and French. After qualifying as a minister, he was licensed to preach the Gospel by Kirkwall Presbytery in September 1809, delivering his first sermon in Shapinsay and subsequently in various parishes throughout Orkney. In November 1810, he was presented to Lady Parish in Sanday by Sir Thomas Dundas. After being ordained the following year,

The Rev William Logie was instrumental in having a new church in Kirkwall built, St Peter's Chapel, on the site of the present St Magnus Centre.

William served in that parish until the death of Robert Yule in 1824, when he was presented to the first charge of St Magnus Cathedral by the Magistrates and Town Council. In 1814, he married Elizabeth, daughter of Kirkwall merchant, James Scarth.[813] They had a large family, which included Dr James Logie (110).

When the Logies moved to Kirkwall, they stayed in the Old Manse, which adjoined the Bishop's Palace, the same manse that was so detrimental to Robert Yule. The Logies also found it very unsuitable and, in 1825, petitioned the heritors to have it repaired. They had not been in their new abode very long, when, perhaps fortuitously, it caught fire and they had to seek alternative accommodation.[814] Prior to the fire, William's only surviving sister, Isabella, and her husband, shipmaster Henry Leask, had conveyed to him their property in Bridge Street before moving to Portobello.[815] In compensation for losing his manse, the heritors gave him an annual sum of money as rent for a house. By 1832, the family was living at Daisybank, at the junction of what is now East Road and Berstane Road.

Along with the minister of the second charge, Peter Petrie, Logie wrote an appeal to the heritors of the Parish of St Ola and to the Magistrates of Kirkwall regarding the appalling state of the Cathedral as a place of worship and requesting a new building.[816] The two men, however, disagreed on what should happen after a new church was built. William Logie wanted the whole congregation to transfer to the new church, while Mr Petrie preferred that the two charges separated. By private subscription and a grant from the Church of Scotland's extension fund, a new church, which became known as St Peter's Chapel, was eventually built in 1841, on the site of the present St Magnus Centre. With Logie and his congregation continuing worship in the Cathedral, Petrie moved his congregation to this new church. Both ministers were present in Edinburgh at the infamous General Assembly of 1843. Petrie was one of the many ministers to walk out of the Assembly and join the Free Church. William Logie remained in the hall and stayed loyal to the Church of Scotland.[817]

Petrie and his congregation, who followed him into the Free Church, continued to use St Peter's Chapel until the members were eventually evicted from the building to make way for Rev Logie and his congregation, who had been forced to leave the Cathedral, owing to the restoration work being carried out by the Government.

In 1841, William Logie was involved in what is regarded as the first modern UK census. Each household was required to complete a census schedule, which contained the household address, the name, age, sex, occupation, and place of birth of each person living at the address. The information was collected by enumerators, who also helped record details in households where no-one could write. It was William Logie's duty to confirm that the information had been collected according to the rules of the census.[818]

On 25th March 1854, near the end of his life, William Logie was awarded the degree of Doctor of Divinity from Edinburgh University.[819] He died on 5th September 1856 and was buried in St Magnus Cathedral Cemetery, not having lived long enough to witness his congregation move back into the building.

92. James Robertson 1799-1876

This bronze plaque is found on the south wall of the choir and says:

To the Glory of God and in Memory of

JAMES ROBERTSON, Sheriff-Substitute of Orkney

Born in Atholl 1st December 1799

Died at Kirkwall 12th January 1876

For thirty years a worshipper and office bearer in this Cathedral

This memorial is placed here by his Widow and Family

James Robertson 1799 - 1876

James Robertson, Sheriff-substitute of Orkney for nearly 30 years kept a daily journal, starting on 15th November 1842 and continuing, almost without fail, until November 1875. His journal has survived and consists of five leather bound volumes. The first ten years were transcribed and annotated by the late Dr J. B. Loudon and can be found on the internet.[820] His journal arose out of a need to keep a record of the letters he wrote, these forming an important element of the text. He always started his daily entry with a brief summary of the weather, which makes his journal of particular interest to those interested in historical meteorology. By the very nature of diaries, much of his journal is fairly repetitive, but it does provide a unique insight into his life in Orkney in the middle of the 19th century.[821]

James Robertson, or *JR* as he referred to himself, was born in 1799, the son of tenant farmer Duncan Robertson of Milton of Invervack, in Blair Atholl, Perthshire. His mother was Margaret Robertson from Kindrocht, a few miles north of Invervack. He trained as a lawyer in Edinburgh, starting as a clerk in John Young's offices in Castle Street before becoming a partner in a law practice with William Forbes Skene (1809-1892) until 1841. He thoroughly enjoyed his time in Edinburgh and expressed a wish to retire there. In July 1841, he became Sheriff-substitute in Stornoway, before moving to Tobermory in Mull, to take up the position of Sheriff-substitute of North Argyll. Being a Gaelic speaker was a great advantage, but he did not enjoy his time in Mull, finding the mild, damp winters in the Western Highlands depressing. He jumped at the chance of a transfer to Orkney, moving up in March 1846. He rented a house in Albert Street (known now as the Custom House) from the Balfours of Balfour and Trenaby.[822] Later he became the first tenant of Buttquoy House, renting it from Dr Robert Baikie of Tankerness.[823] *JR* quickly established himself in Orkney society, becoming firm friends of the Balfours, and was regularly invited to Cliffdale in Shapinsay, soon to become Balfour Castle.

JR read avidly, wrote letters on an almost daily basis, especially giving endless advice to members of his family in Atholl, and enjoyed receiving the London papers to keep up to date with national events. He

Sheriff James Robertson pictured with his wife, Harriet. His bachelor days ended when he was aged 59, but he still went on to have a sizeable family, left to right, Duncan, Bess, Barbara, Emily and Margaret. Pictured at his home, Buttquoy House. *Orkney Library Photographic Archive*

was, however, continually frustrated by the constant interruption to the post caused by the weather and wrote frequent letters of complaint to the Post Office in Edinburgh.[824]

As Sheriff-substitute, it was his job to organise meetings of the Commissioners of Supply and, in January 1849, that body adopted his petition to convert the Earl's Palace into a county hall, court house and jail. The court house and jail at that time were situated on the Kirk Green and were considered to be spoiling the view of the Cathedral. *JR* was a strong advocate of this proposal and was still pursuing the issue with the Government more than a decade later.[825]

At the age of 47 he was five feet nine inches tall and weighed eleven and a half stones.[826] He kept trim by regular walking, his favourite walks being to the top of Wideford Hill and to 'Sir Hugh's Seat'at Gaitnip.[827] While laudably keeping an eye on his weight and girth, *JR* had hypochondriac tendencies, often giving himself unnecessary and painful treatments.[828]

JR served as Sheriff-substitute under Charles Neaves, William Aytoun, Adam Gifford and finally George Thoms (99), the last of whom he described as "a nice, jolly fellow".[829] *JR's* annual salary in 1852 was £385 and, with the low cost of living in Kirkwall together with what he described as 'easy work', he considered himself very well off. He was able to employ a housemaid, a cook and later, when children came along, a nursemaid. As well as in Kirkwall, *JR* held court in Stromness, Sanday (its district court was discontinued in March 1848) and South Ronaldsay.

At times his trips to the isles could be quite an adventure. On one occasion, he had a nightmarish journey back from St Margaret's Hope after setting out at eight o'clock on a beautiful calm morning in a dog cart for Holm.[830] By nine o'clock the wind was starting to get up, but he reached St Margaret's Hope before 11 without getting wet. Court business did not take long and he was able to leave for Holm by midday. The normal ferry had been away at the herring fishing and the catch still had to be unloaded, so a small boat was used instead. She was skippered by a man called Laughton and crewed by a boy of 12 or 13 along with an elderly man called William Oddie. They rowed into Water Sound and sailed round to Hunda. Kemp, the gig driver, had joined *JR* on the journey and was very sick as the wind rose severely from the north east, accompanied by heavy rain. Matters worsened when they passed Hunda, where the boat began to fill up with water. Oddie used one of his shoes to bail water and *JR* helped him using the other one. With Oddie continuing to bail and the boy taking the helm, Laughton and *JR* took to the oars. Kemp was still vomiting. The boy was soon unable to steer and *JR* made Kemp take an oar, while he took over the helm. After a struggle, they made the lee shore of Glimps Holm at half past two. Laughton and Oddie walked to the high point of the island and saw that no boat could make it to Holm in such a storm. They hauled up their craft, removed the cork to empty the water and sailed back across to Burray, where they spent the night at the Ferry House. Kemp and *JR* were given the ben end of the house and were fed potatoes, herring, bread, cheese and butter, all fortified with a glass of whisky. The gale moderated at the turn of the tide next evening and they reached Holm safely at 7 o' clock. *JR* was very happy to get to the comfort of his own home that night.

In addition to holding court, *JR*'s duties were varied. They included the investigation of unusual deaths (there was no police at this time), the organisation of elections to parliament, including the maintenance of civil order during an election, the gathering and distribution of money for the poor, the division of the commons, decisions regarding lunatics and the identification of potato blight. *JR* was also responsible for organising Orkney's 1851 census. *JR* had numerous meetings regarding the poor with the various clergy, particularly the Cathedral Minister, Rev. William Logie, with whom he had a normally good relationship, and the Minister of the United Presbyterians, Rev. Paterson, who was described by *JR* as a "disagreeable fellow", after having had an altercation with him on the street.[831] *JR* had a prudish side, thoroughly disapproving of the Orcadian habit of 'bundling' (courting in bed). He accosted Rev. Paterson on the subject, who assured him that his own congregation were "pure and innocent as lambs". *JR* told Paterson he considered them no better than black sheep as far as this mode of courtship went and he was left "malcontent and dolorous" after their meeting.[832]

JR's first mention of Kirkwall's annual Ba' game was on 12th January 1849, when he wrote approvingly in his journal, *"Old new year's day, and football play on the street, but I did not observe Mr Mitchell or any of the better classes of inhabitants among the players."* *JR* would have been aware of his predecessor's attempts at curbing this practice. Sheriff-substitute C. Gordon Robertson had suggested improvements to the Kirk Green, which included planting trees and flowers. The Town Council readily agreed and, as the success of this scheme would be endangered by the street football, the sheriff issued an edict banning the Ba'. In defiance, January 1846 saw an even larger crowd gather for the New Year's Day game. The sheriff was in a fury and threatened some of the participants with imprisonment. The aforementioned John Mitchell, the Town Clerk, overheard this threat and shouted, "You'll need to put us all in jail", as he plunged into the scrum, later emerging with only one tail to his coat.[833]

With an interest in antiquities, *JR* enjoyed visiting archaeological sites, taking measurements and writing a description of the Ring of Brodgar.[834] He also opposed pulling down any part of the remains of Kirkwall Castle.[835] A close contemporary and friend was George Petrie, the amateur archaeologist who excavated Skara Brae and to whom he gave authority, in 1858, to recover the largest hoard of Viking silver ever found in Scotland, from the people who made the discovery, near the shore of the Bay of Skaill. *JR* delivered the artefacts himself to the authorities in Edinburgh, where the treasure trove remains. Sir Henry Dryden, the antiquarian and archaeologist, was a frequent visitor to *JR*'s house during his summer visits to study the Cathedral, a building in which *JR* had a particular interest. During the Government renovations, *JR* was a frequent visitor, even on occasion assisting with some manual labour and hurting his knee in the process. After William Bissett, the first Superintendent of Works, died (31st December 1848), *JR* composed an inscription for his gravestone, which can be seen in the Cathedral churchyard, complete with Masonic marks.[836] On 31st December 1851, he handed the keys of the Cathedral to Rev. Logie, after the Government conceded ownership of the building to the Magistrates and Town Council of Kirkwall.

Any visiting dignitary would call on *JR* to receive a tour of the Cathedral and Earl's Palace. The Home Secretary, Sir George Grey, for example, appeared on

JR's doorstep in August 1851.[837] Two years earlier, *JR* showed the historic buildings to Jane Griffin, Lady Franklin, and her constant companion, Sophie Cracroft, a niece of her husband. *JR* was to entertain the two ladies on a number of occasions over the next few years. Lady Franklin came to Orkney to seek news, from returning whalers, of her husband, Sir John Franklin, who had left Stromness some four years previously, to seek the fabled Northwest Passage.[838] *JR* described Lady Franklin as *"decidedly like a Gentlewoman, pleasing in manners, has evidently seen much society; is about sixty years of age or under; English, little and with a red mark on the left eye-lid. She is a pleasant mannered woman, but she is extremely restless"*.[839]

Although *JR* was a member of the St Magnus Cathedral congregation, he was an Episcopalian at heart, even seeking access for Episcopalian worship in St Magnus Cathedral.[840] *JR* was an active Freemason and was instrumental in arranging for the members of Kirkwall Lodge to resume their meetings in the Town Hall, after losing their place to the Prison Board.[841] *JR*'s intervention ensured the Masons were able to use the Assembly Rooms of the old Town Hall on the Kirk Green until 1887, when they moved to their present building in Castle Street.

In 1859, at the age of fifty-nine, *JR*, the long-term bachelor, married the daughter of his deceased friend, Rev. William Logie (91). Harriet Logie, whom he had known since his arrival in Orkney in 1846, was nearly half his age. The couple went on to have a son, Duncan (107), and four daughters, Elizabeth, Margaret, Barbara and Emily Harriet.[842]

JR died at Buttquoy House on 12th January 1876 and was buried in the north east side of St Magnus Cathedral Cemetery. His wife and daughters were all buried alongside him.

93. Rev. James Stuart 1834-1883

On the baptismal font at the west end of the nave is a small plaque, with the following inscription:

<blockquote>
To the memory
Of the
Rev. James Stuart
For fifteen years minister of the Free Church
Kirkwall
Born 1834, ordained 1868, died 1883
A friend of the poor
A giver of hospitality

Presented
By the
Rev Alexander Goodfellow
South Ronaldshay
</blockquote>

The Rev James Stuart was a diplomat who smoothed out disagreements in his congregation. He also recognised the plight of the poor, once donating his boots to a tinker.
Orkney Library Photographic Archive

James Stuart was born in the parish of Kirkmichael, Banffshire, in 1834 and went on to study at Aberdeen University.[843] He became the minister of the Kirkwall Free Church, which was then on the site of the present East Church in King Street.

The Kirkwall Free Church arose out of the Disruption of 1843, in which 474 ministers left the Church of Scotland, including Rev. Petrie, former minister of the second charge of the Cathedral. For a number of years after the Disruption, the breakaway congregation met in St Peter's Chapel, in spite of repeated calls to quit. This had been built by the Established Church as an additional place of worship for the Cathedral congregation. The Free Church was eventually forced to relinquish control of the building in August 1847 and quickly built a new church in King Street, which opened in June 1848.

The minister of the Free Church congregation at this time was William Sinclair, formerly of Grange, Aberdeenshire. The later years of Rev. Sinclair's ministry saw increasing friction between himself and a

The font in memory of Rev Stuart was presented by another minister, Alexander Goodfellow, who led the United Free congregation in South Ronaldsay for almost 50 years and was a staunch supporter of crofters' rights.
Orkney Library Photographic Archive

section of the congregation and, with failing health, he applied for an assistant who would become his successor. As a result, probationer, James Stuart, was ordained in July 1868 as his assistant, succeeding to the post on the death of Rev. Sinclair, in 1874. Unfortunately the appointment of Rev. Stuart as assistant did not bring immediate peace to the congregation and those who were set against Rev. Sinclair campaigned for the rights of the new minister. There were numerous disputes regarding payments to the two men and an attempt was made to evict Rev. Sinclair from the Manse in King Street.

James Stuart, who was described as a most amiable man, eventually brought harmony to the congregation and was very popular in the town during his nine years as minister. He was known for his generosity, on one occasion arriving at the pulpit in his slippers, having given away his last pair of boots to a tinker, who had come begging at the Manse door. Rev Stuart died very suddenly on 22nd April 1883 and was followed in post by Alexander Isdale.[844]

Alexander Goodfellow, who presented the font, was born at Lochee, Dundee, on 5th June 1852. He was brought up in the Free Church, being educated at Lochee Free Church School before becoming an apprentice baker.[845] The arrival in Britain, in 1873, of the American evangelists, Moody and Sankey, set him on a religious path. He enrolled at the University of Edinburgh and later at the Free Church College. He was an assistant at Inch Free Church before being licensed by the Free Presbytery of Wigtown and Stranraer. He became minister of the South Ronaldsay Free Church in July 1878, a position he retained for the rest of his life. He married Barbara Dunnet Sutherland in Wick on 13th September 1883.[846]

Like many of his fellow Free Church ministers, Goodfellow was a supporter of the crofters and was well known for his ultra-radical views. He invited James Leonard to preach after Leonard had been evicted from his Rousay croft by General Burroughs (100) for giving evidence to the Napier Commission.[847]

Rev Goodfellow, founder of the Orkney Colportage Society, was a keen antiquarian and wrote a number of books related to church history in Orkney, such as *Sanday Church History*, *Birsay Church History*, *Dr Paterson* and *Two Orkney Pulpit Worthies*. He was a member of the editorial committee for the *Orkney and Shetland Old-lore*, which had its first issue in 1907. In September 1910, he was among a party that accompanied the philologist, Dr. Jakob Jakobsen, to Swona. Dr Jakobsen was in Orkney to collect information on dialect and place names.[848]

Goodfellow died on 26th September 1927, after nearly half a century's service to the South Ronaldsay community. He was buried in St Mary's Churchyard at Burwick.

94. William Balfour Baikie 1825-1864

The first of the two most impressive memorials in the Cathedral is found beneath the great East Windows on the north side. This cenotaph, in memory of William Balfour Baikie, was designed by Shetland architect, James T. Irvine,[849] who incorporated Shetland serpentine into the memorial. The cenotaph was originally placed in the north aisle of the nave between two pillars and was relocated to its present location in the east end following the early twentieth century renovations. Six shields decorate the monument, each having a coat-of-arms, except the one on the east side, which is blank. The coat-of-arms of the Baikies, consisting of three flames of fire either side of a chevron containing a lion rampant and two mullets, can be seen on the middle shield on both the north and south side of the monument.

On the north side, the Baikie shield is flanked to the east by the coat-of-arms of his mother's family, the Huttons, consisting of three annulets gules, and, to the west, by that of the Traills, consisting of a chevron between two mascles above and a trefoil in base. The remaining arms belong to that of England, Scotland and Orkney. The text on the south side of the memorial says:

WILLIAM BALFOUR BAIKIE
M.D.R.N., F.R.G.S., (Scot)

Born at Kirkwall 27th August 1825

The explorer of the Niger and Tchadda, the translator of the Bible into the languages of Central Africa and the pioneer of Education, Commerce and Progress, among its many nations. He devoted life, means and talent to make the heathen savage and slave, a free and Christian man. For Africa, he opened new paths to light, wealth and liberty - for Europe, new fields of science, enterprize and beneficence. He won for Britain new honour and influence, and for himself the respect, affection, and confidence of the chiefs and people. He earned the love of those whom he commanded, and the thanks of those whom he served, and left to all a brave example of humanity, perseverance, and self-sacrifice to duty. But the climate, from which his care, skill, and kindness, shielded so many, was fatal to himself and when, relieved at last though too late, he sought to restore his failing health by rest and home, he found them both only in the grave. He died at Sierra Leone 12th December 1864.

The north side of the memorial shows the crest of the Baikies, with the motto, 'Commodum Non Damnum' (meaning profit not loss), and the following text,

This cenotaph was raised by his countrymen in token of their respect for his character, talents and virtues, their admiration of his useful life, and sorrow for their own loss in his early death.

The people that sat in darkness have seen a great light. Beautiful are the feet of him that bringeth good things.
'Well done good and faithful servant'.
They that turn many to righteousness shall shine as the stars for ever and ever.[850]

William Balfour Baikie was the son of Lieutenant (later Captain) John Baikie, R.N. and Isobella Hutton. His father saw active service in the navy during the Napoleonic Wars and became agent of the National Bank of Scotland, Kirkwall's first bank. His half brother was Samuel Baikie, the Master Builder, who built some of Kirkwall's most prominent buildings, such as the Town Hall, the Commercial Bank (8 Albert

William Balfour Baikie. The explorer's memorial is appropriately opposite that of John Rae's, in St Rognvald Chapel, under the East Window.

Street), the King Street Church, St Magnus Hall and large parts of Dundas Crescent and East Road. He also built the National Bank in Stromness, Cleaton House in Westray and the Covenanters Memorial in Deerness.[851]

William was educated at Kirkwall Grammar School and also at a private school in Kirkwall, along with his Balfour cousins[852] and some others, including James Logie (110), where they were taught by Mr Gardiner. At 16, Baikie went to Edinburgh University to study medicine, where one of his tutors, Dr. T. S. Traill (then Professor of Medical Jurisprudence), probably stimulated an interest in natural history. In 1846, Baikie, along with his friend, Robert Heddle, and Kirkwall bookseller, W. Reid, formed the Antiquarian and Natural History Society. Two years later, Baikie and Heddle published part 1 of *Historia Naturalis Orcadensis*, being a catalogue of birds and mammals. An intended second volume on flora never appeared as the two men started out on their respective careers.[853]

Baikie was a keen Freemason and, in 1844, was elected as an office bearer in the Kirkwall Kilwinning Lodge. His father had been one of the last Masters in 1819; William, himself, became Master in 1846.

In the same year as his publication, Baikie qualified as a surgeon and followed in his father's footsteps by joining the Royal Navy as an assistant surgeon. After serving on several ships, he became assistant surgeon in the naval hospital at Gosport between 1851 and 1854. While at sea, Baikie had cruised along the coast of Africa and had become fascinated by that Continent. His opportunity to explore parts of it came in 1854 when he was appointed medical officer and naturalist to an expedition travelling up the River Niger to try and locate the explorer Heinrich Barth, using a specially-

William Balfour Baikie was an explorer in Africa but, in an Orkney context, his adventures are perhaps over-shadowed by John Rae's. Baikie achieved enormous success in the Niger area of the continent, where a tribe still refers to white people as 'Ndi baykay' after the Orcadian.

Orkney Library Photographic Archive

built steamer, called the *Pleiad*. Command of the expedition quickly passed to Baikie when the leader of the expedition, John Beacroft, died before exploration had begun. The *Pleiad* set off with 12 Europeans and 54 Africans[854] and explored 700 miles of river. They ascended the Benue, the eastern branch of the Niger, 250 miles beyond the point where previous explorers had turned back. Baikie filled many notebooks with linguistic, ethnological and general information, and gave names to a variety of geographical features, such as Mount Traill and Mount Trenabie.[855] While Baikie failed to find any sign of Barth, the expedition became Britain's most successful expedition so far in this part of Africa, with everyone involved surviving. For the first time, Europeans spent months on the river with no loss of life, due to Baikie's use of quinine to ward off malaria. Baikie's expedition was also the first such expedition to make a profit, opening up the prospect of trade in this part of Africa.[856]

Following a brief visit home to Kirkwall, in March 1857, Baikie embarked on a second expedition to the Niger. His instructions were to set up trading posts on the river. He was given command of the small steamer, *Dayspring*, and he established one trading post on the Niger delta, which he called Lairdsport, and another, Lairdstown, on the Benue confluence, where the River Benue and Niger meet. Disaster, however, struck in October 1857 when, after travelling 300 miles further up the Niger and visiting the Emir of Nupe at Bida, his boat foundered on a hidden rock. Baikie and some of his crew were stranded for a year with few provisions. When a relief vessel finally arrived, Baikie refused to embark until he had paid his debts to the natives who had given assistance to his stranded party. He followed the relief vessel in a canoe, which was laden with gifts from the local people.

After being denied by slavers the establishment of a Consular Agency at Rabbah, not far from where he had been marooned,[857] Baikie returned to Lairdstown, the trading post he had set up on the Benue confluence where the Emir of Nupe had allowed him to settle. Baikie moved his base to a more convenient site across the river and renamed it Lokoja. It was here he stayed for the next five years and founded Britain's first permanent settlement in the interior of West Africa. His only other European companion was his zoological assistant, John Dalton, who eventually had to leave in 1862, after falling ill. Far from trying to transplant British ways into Africa, as his successors would do, Baikie went native, wearing sandals and the long cotton shirt called a tobe. He lived in a mud hut with a thatched roof and took a native mistress, with whom he had several children. His little settlement, lying in an area where slavery was a way of life, became a refuge for many natives fleeing from this barbaric trade. This made Baikie an enemy of the slave traders and he often had to sleep with a sword and alarm bell by his side. Things improved when he made friends with Masaba, the Emir of Nupe, who realised that this stubborn white man, with the ability to keep the peace among the neighbouring loose-knit states, was determined to stay. He allowed Baikie to continue in his role as ruler of the little enclave. Baikie even became known as the King of Lokoja.[858] Within the trading post, he started a market to which native produce was brought for sale or barter. He did impose his Christian views and the market he started was always closed on Sundays. He collected vocabularies of nearly 50 African dialects and translated parts of the Bible and the Prayer Book into the local language, Hausa. After four years, his tiny colony had grown to some 200 natives, most of whom had either been redeemed from slavery by Baikie or had put themselves under his protection. His reputation and influence had by now spread far and wide.[859]

By 1864, his health was poor and Baikie decided to return to Britain. He was taken to the coast by paddle steamer and then to Sierra Leone, where he stayed at the home of an old Orcadian friend, Charles Heddle.[860] Instead of immediately catching the mail steamer back to England, Baikie remained an extra month to sort out his manuscripts and natural history collections. He fell ill, however, succumbing to malaria, and was buried in Freemantle.

Queen Victoria wrote a personal letter to the Emir of Nupe, informing him of Baikie's death and urging the Emir to put a stop to the slave trade, knowing that this was an issue close to Baikie's heart.[861]

Today, Lokoja is the capital city of Kogi State in central Nigeria and has a population of around 200,000. When Nigeria gained its independence in 1960, a special issue of *Nigeria Magazine* declared that Baikie stood out as "one of the foremost explorers of the Nigerian hinterland".[862] The Igbo tribe still use the expressions, 'Ndi baykay' for white people and 'Ani baykay' for Europe.[863]

95. Dr. John Rae 1813-1893

On the opposite side from the cenotaph to William Balfour Baikie is the magnificent Portland stone sculpture of a sleeping John Rae with an open book and musket by his side. This monument, sculpted by Joseph Whitehead of London[864] and financed by public subscription, was first unveiled in the Cathedral nave, next to the Paplay tomb, in December 1895. It was relocated to its present site during the early twentieth century renovations. The statue of Rae sits on top of a granite plinth, which has the following inscription:

JOHN RAE M.D., L.L.D., F.R.S., F.R.C.S.,

ARCTIC EXPLORER

INTREPID DISCOVERER OF THE FATE OF
SIR JOHN FRANKLIN'S LAST EXPEDITION

BORN - 1813   DIED - 1893

EXPEDITIONS 1846-7, 1848-9, 1851-2, 1853-4

At the back of the monument are the words,

Erected by public subscription, 1895.

John Rae was born in the Hall of Clestrain, in Orphir, on September 30th 1813. He was the sixth child and fourth son of John Rae senior, who came from Lanarkshire, and Margaret Campbell, from Argyll. Rae's father was the factor to Sir William Honeyman's Orkney estate and a year after Rae's birth, his father played host to Sir Walter Scott. It was later said that Scott modelled two characters, Brenda and Minna, from his novel, *The Pirate*, on Rae's two older sisters.[865]

Dr John Rae and his wife, Kate. Rae's trekking and mapping exploits in northern Canada are legendary but he incurred the wrath of the Establishment when alleging cannibalism by Royal Navy seamen on the Franklin Expedition. He was subsequently proved correct but, sadly, after he died.

Orkney Library Photographic Archive

John Rae was educated at home by a series of live-in tutors, but enjoyed an active outdoor life while growing up in Orkney. He revelled in sailing, climbing, trekking, hunting and shooting, all essential skills for his future career. At the age of 16, he left Orkney to study medicine at Edinburgh University, but soon switched to the Royal College of Surgeons, where he could obtain his diploma more quickly.

After qualifying in 1833, Rae looked to widen his horizons and seek some adventure. Since 1819, his father had been the chief representative of the Hudson Bay Company (HBC) in Orkney. He had secured clerical posts in Canada for two of Rae's older brothers and now Rae himself signed up to become surgeon on the HBC ship, *Prince of Wales*, which left Stromness in June 1833. With him went 31 other Orcadians, employed by the HBC.[866] Rae intended to serve only one season, but, after spending a winter on Charlton Island in James Bay, he soon realised that the lifestyle in the HBC service suited him well and he accepted the post of surgeon at Moose Factory, at the southern end

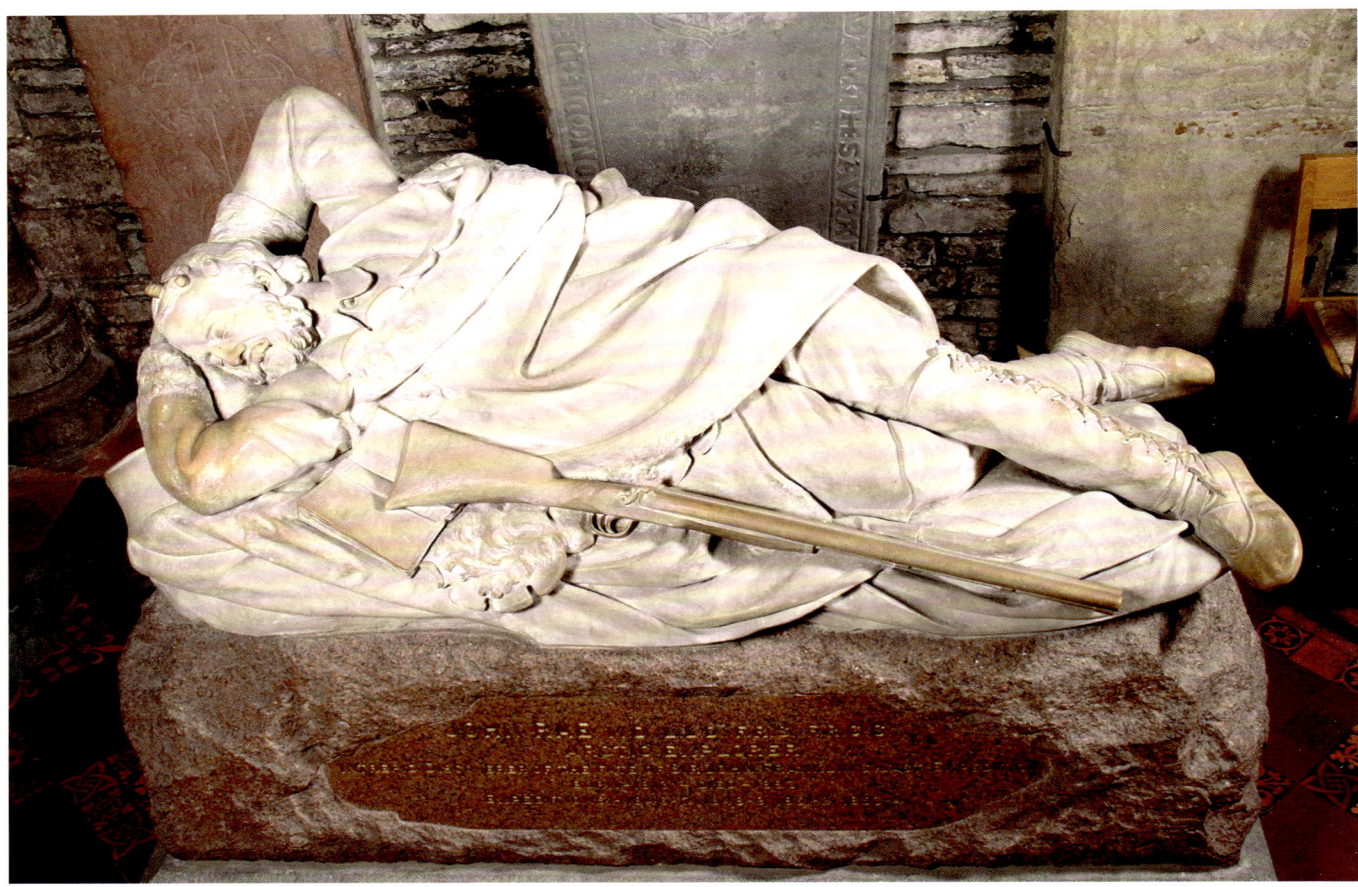

John Rae, the explorer. Arguably the most dramatic and eye-catching memorial in the Cathedral.

of James Bay. He held this post for the next ten years, learning survival techniques from the native peoples and acquiring a great respect for their culture, traditions and skills. He became the foremost expert in the use of snow shoes, regularly covering long distances to make house calls on the native population. On one occasion he covered 105 miles in less than two days without suffering any resulting aches and pains.[867] He earned the nickname, "Aglooka" - "he who takes long strides"- from the Eskimos.

The Hudson Bay Company was founded in 1670 and known as 'the Governor and Company of Adventurers of England trading into Hudson Bay'. For several centuries, it controlled the fur trade in much of British controlled North America. Part of its remit was to map the north coast of North America and, in particular, to seek the final link in the Northwest Passage. This was the Holy Grail of Victorian exploration and British merchants could only dream of the riches such a waterway would bring. John Rae's survival skills soon brought him to the attention of the Governor of the HBC, Sir George Simpson, who recognised Rae as the best person to complete the Arctic survey. Rae received training in surveying and soon hatched a plan for his first expedition into the frozen north. His expedition was to be the first time Europeans had wintered in the High Arctic, while living off the land.[868] With him he took four Orcadians (among them John Corrigal and George Flett), one Shetlander, one Scot, two French-Canadians, a half-breed Metis and a Cree Indian. Later he recruited two Inuit hunters to join the party. When they set off, few people thought they would be seen again. The 1846-47 expedition was, however, a huge success, with some 655 miles of unexplored coastline being traced. After an absence of 15 months, Rae brought his men back safely and in good health, much to the astonishment of many back at the HBC base at York Factory.

Rae's subsequent expeditions were caught up in the search for the Franklin expedition. The British Government had, in 1845, financed a major expedition to find and navigate the last unknown section of the Northwest Passage. Two ships, *Erebus* and *Terror*, were kitted out with the most advanced technology of the day, as well as libraries containing more than 1000 books, and three years worth of food supplies. The expedition called in at Stromness, where its leader, Sir John Franklin, dined with members of Rae's family and stayed overnight at the home of Rae's sister, Marion, and her husband, Dr. John Hamilton.[869] The ships sailed in May 1845, with every expectation of complete success. By 1848, however, no word had been received from or about Franklin and, with public concern mounting, the Admiralty sent out three expeditions, two of these by sea and a third overland, to be led by Sir John Richardson. He chose John Rae as his second-in-command. This proved to be Rae's least successful expedition, finding no trace of Franklin. It was also the only venture in which he lost a member of his party. After being promoted to Chief Factor of the Mackenzie River District, based at Fort Simpson, Rae embarked on a third expedition (1850-51), but it was not until his final expedition (1853-1854) that he solved the two great Arctic mysteries.

While mapping the west coast of Boothia Peninsula, he discovered a navigable channel between Boothia and King William Island that, although frozen over with "young ice", was free of the pack ice that made sea travel impossible. He was convinced that this channel, which became known as Rae Strait, was the final link in the Northwest Passage. It would be another half century before Rae was proved right, when the Norwegian explorer, Roald Amundsen, became the first to navigate the Northwest Passage in 1903-04, using Rae's discovery.[870]

It was on his return journey from his discovery of Rae Strait that Rae met Eskimo hunters, who were able to relate the story of the last survivors of the Franklin expedition, showing that the 128 officers and men from *Erebus* and *Terror* had all perished. With numerous relics from the Franklin expedition now in his possession, Rae hastened back to England to pass on the bad news and reduce the possibility of more lives being put at risk in needless searches. While the news of the demise of the Franklin expedition was, by this time, not unexpected, the story he brought back was completely unpalatable to Victorian society. Much against his intentions, the full report to the Admiralty was published in *The Times*. It included the horrific statement that the remnants of the expedition had been driven to the last resource – cannibalism. Rae was faced by a campaign of vilification, led by the formidable Lady Jane Franklin, who was determined to glorify her dead husband as the true discoverer of the Northwest Passage. She enlisted the help of Charles Dickens, who condemned Rae for believing "the word of a savage". Rae steadfastly defended the Inuit and consequently paid the penalty; he was the only major British explorer of the age not to receive a knighthood.[871] He did, nevertheless, receive a substantial reward from the Admiralty for ascertaining the fate of the Franklin expedition, which allowed him to retire from the HBC.

His exploration days were not over, but affairs of the heart took precedence and, in 1860, he married Catherine Jane Alicia (Kate) Thompson in Toronto. Her father, an Irish major, had initially opposed the marriage of his 21 year-old daughter to the much older explorer, who had famously 'gone native' and who, he thought, more than likely had taken some Indian wives. After the marriage, the couple headed back to Britain.[872]

Later that year, Rae was employed by the Atlantic Telegraph Company to conduct the land portion of a survey to install a telegraph cable from Britain to North America by linking northern Scotland, Orkney, Shetland, Faroe, Iceland, Greenland and Labrador. He surveyed in the Faroe Islands, crossed Iceland on horseback and reconnoitred the southern coast of Greenland, meeting some of the local Inuit. In 1864, Rae proved again that he was the most outstanding rough-country traveller of his age. The HBC employed him to survey a route for a telegraph line from Red River, Winnipeg, to the Pacific. The distance of some 2000 miles, which included a crossing of the Rocky Mountains, was completed by Rae with no serious mishaps or accidents.[873] During his travels, Rae continued to collect native Indian artefacts, many of which are preserved in the National Museum in Edinburgh. Exhibited along with these are some of his personal possessions and the artefacts from the Franklin expedition he obtained from the Inuit.

John Rae never forgot his roots. He regularly returned to Orkney to enjoy some sailing, visit family and shoot on his 160 acres at Westhill in Rendall. In 1865, he and his wife settled at Berstane House, just outside Kirkwall. Kate did not take to island life and, after two years, the couple moved back to London. Here Rae could mingle with others who had a passion for the Arctic and attend meetings of the Royal Geographical Society, which later awarded him a fellowship.

Rae had joined the Orkney Artillery Volunteers in 1860 and later transferred to the London Scottish Regiment when he made London his permanent home. He refused a commission and became the oldest private in the volunteer force. At the age of 74, he was still able to walk 20 or 25 miles a day, carry out drill and teach the youngsters shooting.[874] He resigned from the London Scottish Regiment in 1890.

In a letter to her Canadian niece, Kate wrote a very moving account concerning her husband's last days.[875] One of his last requests to his wife was to send off his subscription to Kirkwall Sailing Club. Rae died on July 22nd 1893 of an aneurysm and Kate, along with her sister, Emily, transported his body to Orkney for burial. The town came to a standstill, flags were flown at half mast and the Cathedral bells tolled for the passing of one of Orkney's most famous sons. His body was taken to St Magnus Cathedral, with some of Kirkwall's leading citizens acting as pall-bearers and accompanied by the members of Kirkwall Kilwinning Lodge in full regalia.[876] Rae was buried in the Cathedral Kirkyard, near the wall next to Copland's Lane.

This country has a tendency to celebrate failures, Robert Falcon Scott and Sir John Franklin being cases in point. It is regrettable therefore that, for nearly a century, the exploits of John Rae, the most successful Arctic explorer of his day, were largely forgotten. Thankfully, in recent years, there has been a renewed interest in his many achievements, leading to the unveiling of a blue plaque on his Kensington home in June 2011, of a statue on Stromness Pier Head in September 2013 and of a small plaque in Westminster Abbey in September 2014.

96. Rev. Charles Clouston 1800-1884

The most easterly window of the north aisle of the nave is dedicated to the Reverend Charles Clouston. The window, designed and produced by Messrs Ballantine and Son, Edinburgh, was installed in 1887, at a time when there were no stained glass windows in the Cathedral. It depicts a scene from I Kings, Chapter 18:44, when tidings are brought to the Prophet Elijah that a small cloud has at last appeared on the horizon thus answering his prayers for rain. This depiction was meant to symbolise Clouston's scientific achievements, particularly his study of meteorology.[877] At the base of the widow is a brass plate, gifted by the parishioners of Sandwick, which reads:

The Rev Dr Charles Clouston had a fraught time when Christian churches splintered during the Disruption, in the mid 1800s, but he had other talents and was regarded a father of Scottish meteorology, later contributing to the Encyclopaedia Britannica. *Orkney Library Photographic Archive*

To The Memory Of
The Revd Charles Clouston LLD LRCS
For 58 Years Minister of Sandwick
Physician, Naturalist, Meteorologist
Born 1800 Died 1884

Charles Clouston's father, William, was the minister in Sanday and North Ronaldsay for 21 years followed by then Sandwick and Stromness for another 38. William was one of the Orkney Ministers who contributed to the Statistical Account of Scotland, his observations being among the best accounts produced anywhere in the country.[878]

Charles was born in Sandwick and educated at Edinburgh University, where, as well as qualifying for the Ministry, he studied meteorology and botany. He also obtained a degree in medicine. He was licensed by the Presbytery of Cairston in 1821, before becoming the assistant to his father in 1826, and then succeeding him, in 1832, as minister for Sandwick. With the union between Stromness and Sandwick dissolved, a new manse was needed for the Sandwick minister, to be paid for by the heritors or landowners in proportion to their respective holdings. Work began in March 1833 but was still incomplete in November 1835, when Clouston complained that the heritors were slow in meeting their funding obligations. More conflict arose over the need for a new church for Sandwick. The heritors accepted the need for a new building, but there was disagreement over where it should be built. Clouston wanted a more central location in the parish, which would be nearer his manse. The principal heritor, William Watt of Breckness, preferred the church to be rebuilt on its existing site. Eventually the latter option was agreed and the building found today on the north end of the Bay of Skaill was completed in 1837.[879]

Charles Clouston remained loyal to the established church, but faced stiff competition from compatriots, who 'came out' in 1843 to join the Free Kirk. John Garson had just finished his studies in Edinburgh and had returned home to become an assistant in Birsay and

Harray. When news of the Disruption reached Orkney, Garson immediately joined the Free Kirk and, as a result, was excluded from preaching by the Presbytery. Charles Clouston was brought in to preach in the Harray Kirk on the following Sunday, but was outdone by the young Garson, who had a larger congregation outside the Kirk. There was then a race on horseback between the two rival ministers to get to the Birsay Kirk, cheered on by their respective congregations.[880]

Charles Clouston's services to his flock were more than spiritual. In a submission to the 1843 Poor Law Commission for Scotland, he said, "We do not provide a doctor for the poor from the poor funds. I myself, however, studied medicine, and obtained a diploma, and I am in the habit of prescribing for the poor and supplying them with medicines gratuitously". After the 1858 Medical Act, he was registered as a medical practitioner. The letters LRCS after his name stand for Licentiate of the Royal College of Surgeons of Edinburgh, which he first obtained in 1819.[881]

Clouston continued his interest in the subjects he studied at university, making a detailed study of Orkney's weather and becoming regarded as the father of Scottish Meteorology.[882] He identified several new plant species in Orkney and gave lectures on subjects such as geology. Visiting scientists to Orkney would invariably call at his door. The famous geologist, Hugh Miller, wrote about such a visit in the late 1840s.[883] Charles was the first President of the Orkney Natural History Society, formed in 1837, and contributed to *Encyclopaedia Britannica* on the subject of weather. Later, Clouston wrote a description of Orkney in Anderson's 1850 *Guide to the Highlands and Islands of Scotland* and, like his father before him, wrote the Sandwick section of the *New Statistical Account*. For his services to science, the University of St Andrews conferred on him the degree of LL.D in 1868.

He married Margaret, the daughter of his cousin, Edward Clouston of Smoogro, in 1837 and they had seven children.[884] His youngest son, Robert Stewart Clouston, became the foremost Orcadian artist of his generation[885] and his granddaughter became the wife of Orkney's foremost historian, J. Storer Clouston (120).

97. Thomas Peace 1832-1892

On the base of a window on the south side of the nave, to the east of the window dedicated to B. H. Hossack (98), is a memorial to Thomas Peace. It says:

In Memoriam Thomas Peace

Provost of Kirkwall Died June 26 1892

Thomas Peace was born in Kirkwall in July 1832. He was educated at Kirkwall Grammar School before being apprenticed to banker and merchant, James Spence. At the age of 20 he went to Edinburgh, entering the drapery business of Duncan Maclaren MP.[886] It was here that he met his future business partner, Charles Low, and, in 1854, the two young men left Edinburgh to set up business in Kirkwall as 'Peace and Low' on the site of the present Clydesdale Bank, at 3 Broad Street. The wholesale and retail business flourished and they established themselves as leading merchants of the town, selling a variety of goods, such as drapery products, hats, bonnets, carpets, dresses and sports equipment. In 1881, they employed nine men, eleven girls and five boys.[887] The shop was later destroyed by a fire in 1932.[888]

Thomas Peace was among the first to join the Volunteer Movement in Orkney. In 1859, the Government authorised the setting up of Volunteer Corps to provide defence units throughout the country.[889] The Orkney Corps was set up in 1860 as an artillery unit and by the following year a battery of two canons, christened *St Magnus* and *St Ola*, was situated at the Mount on Cromwell Road. Kirkwall was the first unit to be formed, followed by other units in the country areas and islands. The corps made up its own rules, with the introduction of a system of fines to punish those who disobeyed orders or who did not attend regularly. The volunteers elected their own NCOs, among whom was Thomas Peace, being made a sergeant[890] and serving in the Volunteers for 17 years.[891]

Thomas Peace had a long involvement in local politics, becoming a member of Kirkwall Town Council at a relatively young age and rising up through ranks before becoming Provost during the last five years of his life. He was also on the Harbour Commission and became a member of Orkney County Council upon its inception in 1890. Thomas Peace was also an active Freemason, becoming Master of the Kirkwall Lodge. It was through the Masons that he formed a friendship with Sheriff Thoms (99), who was a frequent visitor to his house.[892]

The highlight of his public service came in September 1883, when, as senior Bailie, he had to stand in for the Provost, Samuel Reid, and make a speech in honour of two of the most famous men in Britain. The Prime Minister, W. E. Gladstone, and the Poet Laureate, Alfred Lord Tennyson, were on a cruise up the west coast of Scotland. When it was discovered that Kirkwall was to be a stopping point, a meeting of the Town Council was hastily convened to decide what to do with the illustrious visitors. Bailie Peace was late for this meeting as he was entertaining another famous politician, Joseph Chamberlain.[893] When Peace arrived, he urged his fellow councillors to offer Gladstone the Freedom of Kirkwall.

After Gladstone's ship anchored in Kirkwall Bay, Thomas Peace, along with some of his fellow councillors and the Town Clerk, went out to the ship to see if the honour would be accepted. Gladstone agreed, provided that the Poet Laureate was offered the same honour. The following morning, a party, including Gladstone, his wife and some of their daughters along with Tennyson, landed at Kirkwall and were taken to the Cathedral by Peace, who also took them to the Earl's Palace and Maeshowe. They lunched near the cairn, where Gladstone proposed a toast to his host and to Kirkwall, saying, "prosperity to the town and trade of Kirkwall". The visitors returned to Kirkwall and were taken to the Paterson Church, the only venue big enough for the crowd wishing to witness the presentation ceremony. The building was packed with around 1500 people, the afternoon having been declared a holiday. Thomas Peace addressed both men individually before presenting them with their honorary burgess tickets. Tennyson had asked that there should neither be a speech in his honour nor one from him in return. Thomas Peace did, however, give him a short address. Gladstone replied on behalf of both men with a speech that described the achievements of his half century in politics and that was fulsome in his praise for St Magnus Cathedral. He also praised Orkney for raising 600 artillery volunteers for the defence of the country and thanked Bailie Peace for the way he had discharged his duties as chair. Before departing for their ship, Gladstone and some other members of the party dropped past Peace's house, which was in Broad Street, next door to his business and had been built by John Riddoch (79).

Thomas Peace married Elizabeth Lees, who was born in Walls. The 1871 census shows her mother, Susannah Lees, originally from Dunnet in Caithness, living with them, along with their domestic servant, Helen Flett, who is shown in the 1881 census as still working in the Peace household. Although the Peaces had no children of their own, they had a special interest in the family of their business partner, Charles Low. His sons were Thomas Peace Low and John Lees Low, who later became lawyers and started the business of T. P. & J. L. Low in the Peaces' house.

Thomas Peace did not enjoy good health and, for the last twenty years of his life, suffered from what was described as "an affection of the heart".[894] This condition caused him a lot of pain and many sleepless nights, which he concealed from the public. One of his last visitors was Dr Logie (110), who took him out for a drive a few days before he died. The Town Council attended his funeral in their corporate capacity, as well as his fellow Freemasons in their regalia.

CHAPTER 10

The Twentieth Century – Cathedral Future Secured

Worries about the future of St Magnus Cathedral were to the fore at the start of the century. The announcement of Sheriff Thoms' large legacy for the restoration and repair of the Cathedral came as a huge relief, until a legal challenge was submitted from the Sheriff's nephews, who were not at all happy about missing out on such a vast sum of money. Fortunately, the case was dismissed and Kirkwall Town Council was able to secure the generous legacy.[895]

Tenders were sought and three architects submitted competitive plans. There were concerns expressed regarding over-restoring the building, with the result that the less elaborate, but still extensive plans of Edinburgh architect, George Mackie Watson, were eventually chosen. Work began in 1913 and took another 17 years to complete. The main external change was the construction of a tall copper spire to replace the small pyramid roof of the bell tower. The plain windows were replaced with stained glass (see Appendix), the floor was tiled and the choir screen, galleries and pews were removed. Worship transferred from the choir to the nave. One criticism was the loss, again, of the long view from the nave to the east window, due to the positioning of the organ screen. Extensive excavations, required for the installation of a new heating system, caused more exhumation of human bones, including those reburied following various nineteenth century renovations. These were all deposited in a pit in the churchyard on the north side of the nave, near the area where those removed from the Cathedral in 1848 had been re-interred.[896]

Kirkwall's rights over St Magnus Cathedral were once again challenged when the Church of Scotland claimed ownership over the building, after the Government passed the Church of Scotland (Property and Endowments) Act in 1925. As the Cathedral was used as a parish church, the general trustees of the Church of Scotland assumed they now had ownership of the building. The case went to court in 1928, but an out-of-court settlement was reached, where ownership was acknowledged to lie with Kirkwall Town Council, who would hold it in trust for the community and nation, and make it available as a Church of Scotland parish church.[897]

The occasion of the 800th anniversary of the founding of St Magnus Cathedral was celebrated in style, with the staging of a pageant on St Olaf's Day, 29th July 1937, the scale of which is difficult to see ever being surpassed in Orkney. With a script written by Eric Linklater (125) and Joseph Storer Clouston (120), eight scenes told the story of events leading to the building of the Cathedral. Orcadians literally went to town to celebrate this event, with a cast of more than 600 and a total audience of nearly 7000.[898]

The 1970s saw a major threat to the future of St Magnus Cathedral, when it was discovered that the west end of the building was in danger of collapse, due to subsidence. A major public appeal, led by the Society of the Friends of St Magnus Cathedral, was launched and £300,000 was soon raised, which allowed the installation of substantial steel girders to shore up the vaulted roof of the nave. Since then, much repair work has been carried out, aided by the employment of a cathedral mason. By the end of the century, the Cathedral boasted a brand new, copper spire.

98. Buckham Hugh Hossack 1832-1902

On the base of a window on the south side of the nave, above the wall memorial to Captain Peter Winchester (66) is a dedication to Kirkwall's historian, B. H. Hossack, which reads:

In loving memory of

BUCKHAM HUGH HOSSACK

Born 20th June 1832 Died 4th Jan 1902

Buckham Hugh Hossack was born in Stronsay, the son of Hugh Hossack of Hunton and his spouse, Elizabeth Davidson. Hossack's father was originally from Caithness, while his wife was born in Jedburgh in 1802. The couple moved to Stronsay in the 1820s.[899] Hossack was educated at Kirkwall and then Edinburgh, where the family moved, when Hossack was still quite young. In his younger days, Hossack enjoyed long expeditions on foot. During one summer holiday, he walked from Kirkwall to Holm, caught the boat to Burray, crossed that island on foot, took the boat to South Ronaldsay, walked to the South Parish and crossed the Pentland Firth in a small boat. He then proceeded to walk all the way to Edinburgh.[900]

Hossack became a teacher and was for many years English master at the Edinburgh Institute, Dr Oliphaunt's

B.H. Hossack wrote Kirkwall in the Orkneys which remains the definitive book on the town's history. *Courtesy of Lodge Kirkwall Kilwinning No 38²*

School and various private schools. During his vacations he travelled extensively, not only throughout Britain, but also on the Continent and America. He published, anonymously, a little book entitled, *A Vacation Trip to Greece and Back in the Summer of 1862*.

He gave up teaching about 1880 and returned to Orkney to live. He had married Sybla R. Monteith, the daughter of a wealthy Indian Army contractor, in 1875. According to some notes Ernest Marwick made concerning B. H. Hossack, Stanley Cursiter (126) had said that Hossack's wife was a girl of some wealth and good family, and that he eloped with her to Orkney. This, according to Cursiter, was the reason for his giving up teaching and moving home.[901]

The couple initially rented Smoogro House, in Orphir, before buying land at Craigiefield, near Kirkwall, and building the mansion house which can still be seen today. Hossack soon took an active interest in local affairs and was elected on to the first Orkney County Council, representing St Ola without a break until the end of 1901. He was a Justice of the Peace for the county and represented the County Council on the Harbour Commission. With his educational background, he was elected to the School Board of Kirkwall (Landward) and St Ola and became a member of the County Committee on Secondary Education. He was certainly not afraid to make his views known, for example, criticising Kirkwall Town Council for imposing a charge on local organisations using the Cathedral vestry (south transept chapel) as a meeting place.[902]

Hossack was an active Freemason, becoming Master of the Kirkwall Kilwinning Lodge and, at the time of his death, was Depute Provincial Grand Master. He was an enthusiastic golfer, being one of the original members of the local golf club, who played at Pickaquoy at this time. He was also a member of the Orkney Club and Kirkwall Sailing Club, and was one of the vice-presidents of Kirkwall Swimming Club. He officiated for many years at annual events of the latter two clubs.[903]

Politically, he was a supporter of the Liberal Party and campaigned for Sir Leonard Lyell[904] at all the elections from 1885 until 1900, when ill health forced him to take a back seat. Ecclesiastically, he was a member of the Established Church.

Hossack is most remembered now for his labour of love, which was researching and writing a historical and descriptive account of Kirkwall. Rather than providing a chronological history of the town, he traced the history of each building in the town and wrote about all the inhabitants down through the years. The result of his researches was encyclopaedic in scope and the publication, with its many illustrations, was lavish in production, making *Kirkwall in the Orkneys* the most sought after Orkney book on the market. Over the years, its second-hand value grew to such an extent that it became unavailable to most collectors. In 1986, for the 500th anniversary of the granting of the Royal Charter to Kirkwall by King James III of Scotland, *The Orcadian* republished it. This was much to the delight of many not fortunate enough to have a copy and to the anger of those who did, owing to the decrease in value of their investment. While *Kirkwall in the Orkneys* contains many factual errors, it still remains one of the most consulted books on Kirkwall and Orkney history.

Hossack lived to see his labour of love published in 1900. He died on the 4th January 1902 and was buried with full Masonic honours in St Magnus Churchyard.

99. Sheriff G. H. M. Thoms 1831-1903

The main East Window, consisting of a rose window above four lancet lights, was installed in 1918 in memory of Sheriff Thoms, whose legacy saved the

The magnificent East Window is dedicated to Sheriff Thoms, whose legacy saved the Cathedral.

While his father was a leading Free Church man in Dundee, George Thoms joined the Established Church and attended St Giles Cathedral during his time in Edinburgh. He took a great interest in the restoration of St Giles by Sir William Chambers and always hinted he would like to see St Magnus Cathedral similarly restored. His other interests included being a member of the Royal and Geographic Societies of Scotland, a Fellow of the Scottish Society of Antiquaries and a Commissioner of Northern Lighthouses.[905] He was also an enthusiastic Freemason and became Provincial Grand Master of Caithness, Orkney and Shetland.

Thoms maintained a great affection for his home town of Dundee, where he owned a house and the estate of Aberlemno. He gifted a 500-acre piece of ground in 1896 for the foundation of the Morgan Hospital[906] and he placed in St Mary's Parish Church a memorial window dedicated to those in his family who had served the city in a public capacity.

Thoms was one of life's great eccentrics. He imposed a printed set of rules in his house and fined his domestic servants for any infraction of these rules. Being fair minded, he also fined himself and even his cat, 'Sambo', if it disturbed the peace of the house. He kept what he referred to as his 'laughing waistcoat', with elastic sides, which he wore on occasion when he went out to dinner.[907] One of his legal documents stated that he should be buried "in a wicker basket or other slight coffin, so as to have a chance to begin early at the general scramble at the resurrection". He adopted the second middle name of MacThomas, after claiming to be Chief of Clan MacThomas of Glenshee. He referred to himself as "Ye MacComish" and even designed a clan tartan.[908]

The honorary rank of Vice Admiral was a source of great delight to the sheriff, with his friends calling him "Admiral of the Pentland Firth". He purchased for himself a full Vice Admiral's uniform, including naval sword and telescope, but he had little knowledge of naval etiquette.[909]

It is easy to dwell on Sheriff Thoms' eccentricity, but there was much more to his character. He had a genuine affection for the people of his sheriffdom and, for example, did much to encourage Shetland knitwear, including paying the costs of having island knitters display their skills at the Edinburgh International Exhibition of 1886.[910] He also encouraged the selling of Orkney chairs on a commercial basis.

He continued as Sheriff of Caithness, Orkney and Shetland until poor health forced him to resign in July 1899, when he retired to Edinburgh. He suffered badly from gout and spent much of the last few years of his

building for future generations. The wording, chosen at his behest, at the base of the window reads:

> To the Glory of God and in Memory of George Hunter MacThomas Thoms, Sheriff and Vice Admiral of Orkney and Shetland, and Sheriff of Caithness, Orkney and Shetland 1870-1899.

St Magnus Cathedral would have been in danger of becoming a crumbling ruin, were it not for the intervention of this highly eccentric sheriff, whose last act was to leave an enormous legacy to fund a complete restoration. This transformed the building into the magnificent edifice we see today.

George Hunter Thoms was born in Dundee in 1831, the son of Patrick Hunter Thoms, who was Provost of Dundee from 1847 to 1853. He was educated at Dundee, qualifying as an advocate and being called to the bar in 1855. He was appointed Advocate-Depute by Lord Advocate Young and was author of '*A Treatise on Judicial Factors*', which was published in 1859. In 1870, he took over from Adam Gifford as Sheriff of Caithness, Orkney and Shetland.

Sheriff George Thoms probably saved St Magnus Cathedral by leaving a fortune from his estate to the Town Council to facilitate urgent repairs. His legacy was unsuccessfully challenged in a celebrated court and the majestic East Window is dedicated to him.
Orkney Library Photographic Archive

life in a wheelchair, looked after by his man-servant, Adam Melrose. His eccentricity shone through in his will. For example, he left the brass knocker from his Edinburgh house at 26 Cluny Drive to the Society of Scottish Antiquaries. He also left money to St Giles Cathedral, but the residue of his estate, including his properties in Dundee and Edinburgh, was left to restore and repair St Magnus Cathedral. This bequest was worth many millions of pounds in today's prices and came with the condition that stained glass, depicting the Crucifixion, be placed in the great east window of the Cathedral. If possible, this was to be in three lights, and be marked with the memorial text now shown at the base of the window.[911] His relatives, particularly his nephew, Alfred, who had stood to inherit the bulk of his estate, were understandably disappointed at losing out on such a fortune and decided to contest the will, arguing that Thoms was of unsound mind.[912]

The case was heard in the Court of Session and produced some shocking and salacious evidence for the time. There were, for example, allegations that Sheriff Thoms had fallen under the spell of his man-servant, Adam Melrose, who had turned the sheriff against his own family and friends, and that Melrose had often been under the influence of drink while in charge of his disabled master. Medical evidence showed that, about six or seven years before his death, running sores broke out on Sheriff Thoms' head and body, with a discharge from his nose and mouth, all caused by syphilis.[913] The jury, however, took only half an hour to find that the late Sheriff Thoms had been of sound mind and that his bequest would indeed go to restoring St Magnus Cathedral.

100. Lt. General Sir Frederick Traill Burroughs 1831-1905

Above the gravestone of John Kaa (59), on the north side of the nave, is the memorial to General Burroughs, which says:

IN LOVING MEMORY
of
SIR FREDERICK W. TRAIL BURROUGHS
K. C. B.
OF ROUSAY AND VEIRA
COLONEL OF THE
ARGYLL AND SUTHERLAND HIGHLANDERS
IN THE 2nd BATTn OF WHICH (THE 93rd)
HE SERVED THROUGHOUT THE CRIMEAN WAR,
THE INDIAN MUTINY WAR
AND THE UMBEYLA CAMPAIGN.
VICE LT. OF ORKNEY
DIED IN LONDON 9th APRIL 1905 AGED 74
ALSO TO THE MEMORY OF
HIS WIFE
LADY ELIZA DOYLY TRAILL BURROUGHS
HIS FAITHFUL COMPANION
THROUGH STORM AND SUNSHINE
DIED 1st FEBRUARY 1908 AGED 58
ERECTED BY HER DEVOTED NIECE
LADY SINCLAIR OF DUNBEATH.

Frederick William Traill Burroughs had no blood connection whatsoever with Orkney, but, at the age of 16, was to inherit one of its biggest estates and, later, a reputation as the worst of Orkney lairds. He was born in India in 1831, the eldest son of General F. W. Burroughs and Caroline de Peyron. His maternal great grandmother, Mary Colebrooke, had remarried after the death of his great grandfather, Charles Adrian de Peyron, who had been killed in a duel. Mary Colebrooke's second marriage was to William Traill and it was from their son, George William Traill (90), that the young

Rousay's "Little General", Frederick Burroughs, and his wife, Eliza. His reputation for ill-treating crofters on the island is curiously defended in an 'In Memoriam' notice placed in The Orcadian every year, suggesting 'a different story'.

Orkney Library Photographic Archive

Frederick inherited the Rousay estate. G. W. Traill had taken on the role of guardian and had organised young Burrough's schooling, first at Blackheath in London and later at Hofwyl in Switzerland, hoping that the mountain air would help the young lad to grow.[914] George William Traill might have been generous financially, but he did nothing for his young protégé's self esteem, especially regarding his height. Frederick only grew to a little over five feet and he remained very conscious of his small stature throughout his life.

Shortly before joining the army, Burroughs was in Orkney to visit his new inheritance and paid a brief visit to Shapinsay to see David Balfour's new house. Here he was introduced to Sheriff-substitute James Robertson (92),[915] who, a few weeks later, had to loan the young laird some money.[916] After Traill's death, while Burroughs was still under the age of 21, the estate was run by members of a trust, which included Sir Edward Colebrooke, who was now Burroughs' guardian. Sir Edward insisted Burroughs be kept short of money.[917]

Burroughs went to Fort George to join the 93rd Battalion of the Sutherland Highlanders as an ensign. After a relatively easy spell in this country, which included being part of an honour guard for Queen Victoria's first visit to Balmoral, Burroughs was posted with his regiment to Crimea, where he fought at the Battle of Alma and commanded a company at Balaclava.

In 1857, following the outbreak of the Indian Mutiny, Burroughs found himself part of a column of some 4,000 troops, led by Sir Colin Campbell, sent to relieve Lucknow. Here a small British force, along with many women and children, was holding out in the Residency against a rebel force estimated between 30,000 and 60,000 strong. During the attack at Lucknow, Burroughs was wounded by a sword blow to the head and was cited for the Victoria Cross, being first through one of the breaches in the defences. Sir Colin Campbell's small force successfully broke into the Residency, but was too weak to hold out, resulting in a swift evacuation under the cover of darkness. Over the next few months, the British built up their forces before advancing again on Lucknow. It was during this advance that Burroughs received the bitter news that he would not be awarded a Victoria Cross.

Though still well outnumbered by the rebels, Lucknow soon fell to the British. Burroughs was wounded again, when the house he was reconnoitring was blown up. He received compound fractures in his right leg. He was lucky not to lose his leg and it was some eight weeks later before he could take his first steps on crutches. He returned to Britain to recuperate and it was during this period of sick leave, while on a visit to his Rousay estate in the summer of 1859, that he was granted the Freedom of Kirkwall.

His next posting back in India was to Peshawar, near the Khyber Pass. Cholera was a major problem and Burroughs soon found himself in command of the regiment, after two senior officers died of the disease. In 1864, after being promoted to lieutenant-colonel, he commanded the regiment during the Umbeyla Campaign.

In 1870, the regiment returned to Britain and Burroughs was, for a while, in command at Edinburgh Castle. He finally retired from the army in 1873, while the regiment was stationed at Aldershot. Nicknamed 'Wee Frenchie' by the men of the 93rd, he was given a great send-off by his regiment. His exploits are still celebrated in the Argyll and Sutherland Highlander's Museum at Stirling Castle, where some of his personal effects are on display.

His new life involved spending much of his time on Rousay, enjoying shooting, fishing, running his estate, going on trips abroad in the summer and living part of the winter in Edinburgh or London. His involvement in his estate increased after the retirement, in 1873, of his long-term factor, Robert Scarth, who had always warned against burdening the estate with debt. In 1853, shortly after coming of age, Burroughs had bought property in the districts of Sourin and Wasbister from the Earl of Zetland, making him owner of practically the whole island.[918] Ten years later, he purchased Westness House after it came on the market, following the death of William Traill's wife, Henrietta (82).[919] Burroughs married in 1870, but, despite renovating the house, his new young bride found it too cramped and old-fashioned. As a result, he set about building the mansion house of Trumland, to a design by the architect, David Bryce. All this cost money and, while Burroughs had inherited a large estate, this did not include his 'uncle's' Indian fortune. He had always been advised to live within the limits provided by his estate rents and army pay, but, increasingly, his grandiose schemes were funded by borrowing.

This state of affairs was workable while agriculture remained buoyant and, for a while, relations with his tenants remained cordial. Burroughs even took an active interest in the welfare of the island. From 1870 until 1883, he was involved in many improvements to the social life of the island, such as the building of Trumland Pier in 1871. He was also instrumental in starting the first steamship service to the island (1879), the first ploughing match (1874), the first Agricultural Show (1874), the annual school picnic and the beginnings of a postal service to the island.[920] However, after Burroughs took control of the estate, following Robert Scarth's retirement, rents rose very quickly at a time when agriculture was beginning to slide into a depression. Tenants found it increasingly difficult to pay and rent arrears rose rapidly. Events came to a head when the Napier Commission, set up to look into the condition of crofters and cottars, arrived in Orkney in 1883 to take evidence.

The Rousay crofters organised themselves, aided by the Free Kirk Minister, and prepared a strong case to present to the members of the Napier Commission. This so astounded and angered Burroughs that he evicted the ringleaders, the first time crofters had been evicted as a direct result of giving evidence to the Commission.[921]

The Crofter's Act was passed in 1886 and actually went further than the recommendations of the Napier Commission, giving all crofters security of tenure and setting them 'fair rents' to be decided by a Crofters Commission. Burroughs looked for loopholes in the Act and was condemned in the Press, as well as by the Crofters Commission itself.

Not all aspects of Burroughs' character were negative. He was courteous and well liked by his household servants. At a time when it was considered improper for a master to recognise a servant girl on the street, Burroughs would always doff his hat whenever he met one in town, much to the girl's embarrassment.[922] He took a great interest in the welfare of former soldiers, advocating better pensions and the provision of asylums where required.[923] When old comrades of the 93rd fell on hard times, he would often help them financially. Locally, he was touched by the heroism shown by men from Hoy and South Ronaldsay, who, in two separate incidents, had risked their lives to save people in distress in the Pentland Firth.[924]

Burroughs would have happily left Rousay in 1889 if he had been successful in selling his estate. Due to a combination of depressed agricultural conditions and the bad publicity regarding his relationship with his tenants, a sale was not forthcoming. His standing in the community improved somewhat in his later years. He was returned unopposed as Rousay's first County Councillor and was re-elected a few years later, in 1892, on a low poll.[925] In 1904, he received a knighthood, which he regarded as compensation for missing out on a Victoria Cross. He was a popular figure at regimental dinners and was made honorary colonel. Shortly before being due to chair a regimental dinner to mark the 50th anniversary of Balaclava, he took ill and died in London a few months later. He was buried in Brompton Cemetery.

Curiously, a sense of injustice on behalf of Burroughs finds voice every year in the 'In Memoriam' section of *The Orcadian*. In 2012, for example, the following dedication appeared, "Frederick (Fred) W. T. Burroughs. Died 9th April, 1905. A brave soldier and dutiful proprietor. You may have heard a different story – but there are always two sides to every story".[926] Frederick Burroughs' wife is similarly remembered on the anniversary of her death.

Eliza D'Oley Geddes, came from a similar Indian army background as her husband. She was the youngest daughter of Colonel William Geddes of the Bengal Horse, who, as a young officer, had served with George William Traill (90) during the 1815 Nepalese campaign. As a competent artist, a number of her watercolours of the Rousay landscape were hung in Trumland House. She started a local branch of the Scottish Girls' Friendly Society, becoming county president of that organisation. It was aimed at servant girls and combined religion and good advice with a bit of entertainment.[927] In common with her husband, Eliza was an Episcopalian, regularly taking communion in St Olaf's when she was in Kirkwall with her husband.[928] While in Rousay, the couple had to make do with worshipping in the Established Church, where Eliza played the harmonium until her husband fell out with the minister. The couple then transferred to the United Presbyterians. Mrs Burroughs did not long survive her husband, dying at her home at 70 Warwick Square in London in 1908.

101. James David Marwick 1826-1908

On the base of a window on the north side of the nave next to the window dedication to Rev Charles Clouston (see 96), is a memorial to James Marwick, which reads:

"To the Glory of God and in loving

memory of James David Marwick 1826-1908"

James Marwick had the distinction of being the leading local government official in Scotland's two largest cities and was involved in raising Glasgow to become the second most important in the Empire. He was born in Leith, the eldest son of William Marwick and Margaret Garrioch, both from Kirkwall. When still very young, his father was struck with a serious illness, resulting in James being adopted by his paternal grandfather, also called James Marwick, and being brought up in Kirkwall. He went to the Secession School and later attended Kirkwall Grammar School. In 1842, he went to Edinburgh with the intention of studying medicine, but instead began an apprenticeship in the solicitor's office of James B. Watt and attended classes at Edinburgh University. After qualifying, he became a Procurator at Dundee for a number of years before returning to the capital, in 1854, to join the son of his former employer, John H. Watt, in forming the legal firm of Watt and Marwick. He married his partner's sister, Jane Watt, in 1855 and had two sons and two daughters.[929]

He became involved in local politics, being elected to Edinburgh Town Council in 1856 and representing the Stockbridge ward. He later took up the position of Town Clerk of Edinburgh. While in post, he published a number of handbooks on the conduct of municipal business. He was also Clerk to the Convention of Royal Burghs from 1861 to 1876. In 1872, however, his health broke down from overwork and, on medical advice, he accompanied official delegations to exhibitions in Copenhagen and Moscow.

After returning, he was poached by the Lord Provost of Glasgow, Sir James Watson, who persuaded him to take the town clerkship of Glasgow. At first he was reluctant to accept this post owing to the loss of his legal practice which would entail, but the salary of £2500, the highest for any local government official in Britain, helped change his mind. Once in place, he set about reorganising the office of the Town Clerk, creating deputies and establishing a clear chain of command. During his time in Glasgow, he oversaw many major projects, such as the introduction of a municipal tramway system, the development of Glasgow's water supply and the establishment of an electricity department. He also expanded Glasgow city's boundaries, eventually raising the city to the status of a county. Having built up a reputation as the leading authority on municipal law in Scotland, he wrote many books on the subject and edited a number of volumes of local government records. He was elected a Fellow of the Royal Society of Edinburgh in 1864, received a degree of LL.D from Glasgow University in 1878, had the Freedom of Kirkwall conferred and, in 1888, was honoured with a knighthood by Queen Victoria, the first time such an honour had been given to a municipal officer in Scotland. Marwick was reputedly very handsome, which had been noted by the Queen, when she had seen him on civic deputations to Buckingham Palace.[930]

Interestingly, a son, also called James, became an accountant and went on to found one of the predecessor companies of the global financial firm, KPMG.[931]

102. Robert Garden 1846-1912

In St Rognvald Chapel there are three chairs beneath the statues of Kol, Rognvald and Bishop William. They were designed by Stanley Cursiter and were presented in 1968 by Dora Garden in memory of her husband, Rev. William Barclay (see 116) and her parents, Robert Garden and Margaret Jolly.[932] The chair on the north side has the initials, RG, for Robert Garden, while that on the south side has MJ for Margaret Jolly.

Robert Garden was born in 1846, in Rayne, Aberdeenshire, the illegitimate son of John Garden and Barbara Allan.[933] After starting work as a 'herdie' boy and then an apprentice shoemaker, he became a Master Slater, working in Aberdeenshire and the North of England. Whilst contemplating emigration, a chance meeting with an Orcadian in Newcastle, saw him head northwards instead. He had been told that the merchants of Orkney did not send out vans amongst the farms.[934] Having commercial ambitions, he saw his opportunity and arrived in Orkney in 1873, starting out with a horse-drawn van and a small stock of groceries.[935] He toured some of the Mainland parishes, paying good prices for the farmers' eggs and selling his goods at low prices. This succeeded well and more vans followed, covering the whole of the Orkney Mainland. Eventually these became motorised, Robert Garden being among the first to bring mechanised transport to Orkney. The islands were not forgotten and he began trading with shop boats, firstly in sailing ships, then using small

Robert Garden and his wife, Margaret Jolly, with their daughter, standing in front of the newly re-built Groatie House.

steamers. These ships included *Endeavour, Gleaner, Zoona, Klydon, Thankful, Lizzie Bain, Star of Hope* and *Cormorant*. Islands with no piers, such as Swona, Stroma or Fara, were served using a small rowing boat to ferry customers out to the shop. Even Rackwick, in Hoy, received a visit in the summer. One ship, *Lizzie Bain*, was sadly lost, along with her three crew, in November 1888, when she was in a collision with the much larger steamer *Queen*, which was on her way from Aberdeen to Stromness.[936] Robert Garden's floating shops also ranged further afield, circumnavigating Shetland and travelling down to the Kyle of Tongue and Loch Eribol in the north of Sutherland. His ships even sailed down the west coast as far as Ullapool, establishing branches in many of the small ports they used.[937] The ships took merchandise from Kirkwall to sell and brought back a variety of Highland produce to be re-shipped to markets in the south of Scotland.[938] The last sea shop belonging to Messrs R. Garden was the *Gleaner* and was sold to a Caithness business in 1932.[939]

Robert Garden's business empire was centred at the back of his house on Bridge Street (formerly owned by James Traill (82)) and, to make way for warehouses, Traill's little summerhouse, made using ballast from Pirate Gow's ship, had to be taken down. When members of the public began removing some of the ballast stones as mementos of Pirate Gow, Robert Garden had the little summerhouse rebuilt in its present form to prevent more being lost. Local dressed stone was used for its base and the remaining ballast stones for the spire, on top of which he placed a weathervane with replicas of four of his shop boats.[940] Decorated with sea shells, the little summerhouse became known as the *Groatie Hoose*.[941]

To house the growing number of workers he required, he built several blocks of tenements close by his business premises. These houses were much needed in Kirkwall at the time, and the area is still known as Garden Street. His retail and wholesale business involved the buying and selling of everything from farm seeds and fertiliser to groceries, crockery, hardware and drapery. The business also included a bakery, a mineral water factory and a weaving business. He produced an annual manure and seed pamphlet, containing advice for farmers on the growing and manuring of crops. This pamphlet received much praise from agricultural publications outwith Orkney. Robert Garden was not blind to the effects his successful business was having, and, in 1892, he paid surety of the rent for a competitor at Papdale Mill. The tenant, William Meil, was losing trade following Robert Garden's success with the Ayre Mill and was having difficulty in paying his rent.[942]

Robert Garden took an active part in public life, being a prominent member of Kirkwall Town Council for seventeen years and rising to become Bailie of the town. He was a member of the Harbour Commission and latterly an Orkney County Councillor. He took a keen interest in the restoration of St Magnus Cathedral, of which congregation he was an elder, and was one of the Thoms' Trustees. Prior to Sheriff Thoms' bequest, he suggested the restoration of the spire in a style similar to that which was eventually adopted. He was also heavily involved in trying to obtain a clean water supply for Kirkwall, which caused him no end of controversy and criticism. He was a supporter of bore holes and, in 1905, took a sample of water from the Grainbank bore, sending it south for analysis at his own expense, after opponents had expressed concern about the water quality.[943] He also offered to pay for the drilling of further holes, but fell out with Kirkwall Town Council over the issue.[944] Much of the opposition he faced probably stemmed from jealousy over his business success.

Robert Garden had a fascination for the travels of some of the Norse Earls of Orkney who had ventured as far as Jerusalem. In 1909, he decided to do his own epic trip across Europe to the Holy Land, sending back reports to be published in *The Orcadian*. He died less than three years after returning from his extensive travels, passing away on 4th September 1912. He was buried in St Magnus Cathedral cemetery.

103. Margaret Jolly (wife of Robert Garden) 1856-1938

Margaret Jolly was born at Westhill, Shapinsay, on 22nd April 1856, the daughter of William Jolly and Margaret Dennison. During her early years, the family moved into Kirkwall, where her parents ran a grocer shop in Albert Street. While she was still in her teens, she met Robert Garden, who had come to Orkney to try his hand at starting a business. They married on 16th September 1874 and went on to have a family of seven daughters and two sons. She assisted him in building one of Orkney's largest and most successful businesses.

After the death of her husband, Margaret formed a partnership with her younger son, William, to run the family business. This continued until 1916, when she retired and her place was taken by Gilbert Archer, managing director of Tod and Sons of Leith. The business was formed into a private limited liability company, with Gilbert Archer as chairman and William Garden as managing director.[945]

Margaret enjoyed travel and, after her husband died, she made further trips to the Continent, accompanied by members of her family. This included a return visit to Norway, which was a favourite destination.

Margaret was a Justice of the Peace for Orkney, a member of Kirkwall Parish Council, a member of the St Magnus Cathedral congregation for fully sixty years and Vice president of St Magnus Women's Guild. She also served on a number of charitable societies, but is most remembered for providing the funds to build a much needed new hospital. The original Balfour Hospital, which today is the West End Hotel in Main Street, was insufficient for the ever increasing number of patients and was not capable of being equipped to meet more modern requirements. The Trustees of the hospital, however, had no funds for a major construction project. Following the death of her husband, Margaret offered to provide a modern hospital building as a memorial to her late husband. Those plans were delayed by the outbreak of war, the resources being unavailable to commence such a scheme, and it was not until 1927 that the Garden Memorial Building was ready for opening at a new site at Hornersquoy.[946] Despite the new building being named after Robert Garden, the hospital continued to be named the Balfour Hospital, after its original benefactors.

Shortly before her death, Margaret received the

Margaret Jolly was married to Robert Garden (102) and together they built one of Orkney's largest and most successful businesses. After her husband's death she went on to become prominent in Orkney society, led charitable causes and funded the building of a new hospital, the Garden Memorial Building.
Orkney Library Photographic Archive

upsetting news that her old family home in Bridge Street had been destroyed by fire. This historic house was at that time being used as Garden's main shop, housing the company's retail grocery, drapery, footwear and china departments. The fire was one of the worst in Kirkwall's history, with the heat so intense that it damaged the fronts of the shops opposite.[947] There was concern that the fire would spread to the nearby, recently completed oil depot, which had just taken delivery of its first oil barely a fortnight before.[948]

Margaret stayed at Ayre House and died there on 18th May 1938 at the age of 82.

104. Pat Shearer 1914

On the wall of the south transept, just next to the nave is a brass plaque, which says:

> To the memory of
> PAT SHEARER
> Chief Officer of the steamer "Hangchow"
> who lost his life at sea on Nov 11th 1914
> while endeavouring to save a man
> who had fallen overboard.

Erected by his brother officers
of the Chinese Coast Officers Guild.

Peter, or Pat as he was known, was born around 1880, the second son of Kirkwall coal merchant, Peter Shearer, and his wife, Charlotte Johnston. The couple had a large family of 11 surviving children and lived at 17 East Road.[949] Pat's father was the sole partner in the coal merchant company of William Johnston and Co, which was sequestrated in 1913.[950]

Pat Shearer died after jumping into the sea to save a Chinese sailor, who had fallen overboard from the *Hangchow* off the coast of China.[951] His fellow officers, who were all British, were astounded by the fact that he had bothered trying to save the life of a Chinaman. According to a relative, Pat, being an Orcadian, valued all human life equally and his family was very proud of his selfless action.[952] At the time of Pat's death, his family were living at Mounthoolie in Kirkwall.[953]

The SS *Hangchow* was built by Scott's of Greenock in 1885 as a cargo vessel for the China Steam Navigation Company of London. She was nearly 260 feet long, weighed 1572 tons (GRT) and could steam at 10 knots, using 18 tons of coal per day. With British officers and a Chinese crew, she was mainly used for the Chinese coastal trade, but also made voyages to New Zealand.[954]

The Chinese Coast Officers Guild, which paid for the plaque in the Cathedral, represented a majority of British officers working for the China Steam Navigation Company and the Indo-China Navigation Company. In 1916, the Guild called its members out on strike for more pay, demanding a 25% increase in salary for masters and 15% for officers.[955] The Guild was criticised for being unpatriotic by going on strike and disrupting British commerce during a time of conflict.

105. Benjamin David Craigie Bell 1859-1915

This plaque is found on the south side of the choir near the east end. The text says:

To the Glory of God
and sacred to the memory
of BENJAMIN DAVID
CRAIGIE BELL L.R.C.P. & S.Ed.
J.P. Born July 26th 1859
Died March 31st 1915
30 years Practitioner in
Kirkwall. Beloved
And respected by all who
knew him.
"Greater love hath no man than this: that a man
Lay down his life for his friends."

Benjamin David Craigie Bell was born in Shetland, being the son of Robert Bell, Sheriff-substitute of Zetland, and Robina Hunter of Lunna. He had numerous siblings, most of whom died young, with two brothers and a sister surviving to adulthood. His mother, Robina, died in 1863 of scarlet fever at the young age of 34. Sheriff Bell subsequently married Agnes McCrae Bruce of the Symbister family and the children of the first marriage always looked upon her as mother.[956] As a young man, Benjamin Bell enjoyed spending his holidays in Shetland. He studied medicine at Edinburgh and became a Licentiate of the Royal College of Physicians and Surgeons. After qualifying, he came to Kirkwall as assistant to Dr Logie (110), eventually taking over the whole practice when the latter retired.

Dr Bell held a number of public positions, succeeding Dr Logie as Medical Officer of Health for the Burgh of Kirkwall and working to improve the sanitary conditions of the town. In 1903, he warned Orcadians from the rural areas that seeking the bright lights of Kirkwall might be damaging to their health. He contended that country people moving into Kirkwall were more likely to contract infectious diseases, such as tuberculosis, than those brought up in the town.[957] In his 1913 report on the health of Kirkwall, he warned against the dangers of bottle feeding babies and stressed the fact that breast fed babies always had a better start in life. He strongly advocated state aid to help those on low wages obtain extra rooms for sleeping. He held that the crowded rooms of the poor, with the old and the young sleeping in the same room, were a breeding ground for disease.

Other positions he held included Joint Medical Officer of the Parish Council of Kirkwall and St Ola, as well as some of the rural Parish Councils. He was also Medical Officer for the Orkney Combination Poorhouse, which was built in 1883 at a cost of £3000 to house up to 50 inmates.[958] The building was situated to the south of Kirkwall on what is now Old Scapa Road and, after 1930, it became the Orkney County Home. As Medical Officer of the Northern Lighthouse Commissioners, he regularly visited some of the lighthouses round Orkney and in Fair Isle. He held a similar position for Kirkwall Post Office and Kirkwall Prison and was Medical Examiner under the Factories and Workshop Acts. He was also a Justice of the Peace for Orkney.

Dr Bell married Edith Campbell Christison in 1896 and the couple, who had no children, lived at 65 Albert Street. Edith was a daughter of Sir Alexander Christison, who had served as a surgeon in India and was President of the Royal Victoria Hospital in Edinburgh. Her grandfather was the famous Edinburgh toxicologist and physician,

Sir Robert Christison, who had been one of Dr Logie's lecturers at Edinburgh University (see 110).

Dr Bell took an interest in the Big Tree. In 1910, with signs of decay beginning to show, he called for something to be done to preserve the famous tree; otherwise action would have to be taken to cut it down. After two years of prevaricating, a railing was eventually raised around the tree by Kirkwall Town Council to give it some protection. For more than a century now, the Big Tree has been 'dying', but each spring still manages to produce a fresh crown.

With the outbreak of war, there was a reduction in the number of men practising medicine in Orkney, with the consequent increased pressure on those who remained. This took its toll on Dr Bell and, after catching influenza, other complications set in, from which he never recovered. He was only 55 when he died, and, judging by the tributes in both local papers, was much missed. His funeral was held in St Magnus Cathedral and he was buried in the new cemetery at Orquil (started in 1913).[959]

106. Sir Thomas Smith Clouston 1840-1915

The brass plaque to Sir Thomas Clouston is found on the east side of the north transept. It is decorated by a border of Celtic-style knot work, with brooch designs in each corner. Within the border are a Norse longship and a shield with the Clouston coat-of-arms, consisting of three stags. The plaque certainly reflects a strong attachment to Orkney. The text reads:

In Memory of
SIR THOMAS S. CLOUSTON Knt.
M.D., LL.D., F.R.C.P.E., F.R.S. Edin., J.P.
OF SMOOGRO AND HOLODYKE
For 35 years physician superintendant, Royal Edinburgh Asylum. Lecturer on mental diseases, University of Edinburgh. President Royal College of Physicians. A pioneer in the treatment of mental affections. A physician, author and teacher of world wide reputation.
A loyal Orcadian and
Freeman of Kirkwall.
Born 22nd April 1840. Died 19th April 1915.

Thomas Smith Clouston was the younger son of Robert Clouston of Nisthouse in Harray. After initial education at the local Harray Parish School, he went to West End Academy in Aberdeen, before entering Edinburgh University at the early age of 15. He graduated MD in 1861, receiving a gold medal for his thesis on the nervous system of the lobster. He took an interest in the study and treatment of mental illness, working as an assistant at the Edinburgh Royal Asylum for four

Sir Thomas Clouston was an Orcadian who became an internationally recognised expert in mental health and science. Though based in Edinburgh, he was proud of his island heritage and built a holiday home at Holodyke in Harray, which he used often. He is pictured here with his wife, Harriet, son Storer, daughter-in-law Winifred, and grandchildren.
Orkney Library Photographic Archive

years under its superintendent, Dr David Skae. At the young age of 23, Clouston was appointed medical superintendent of the Cumberland and Westmorland Asylum at Carlisle, where he worked until 1873, when he took over from his former chief at the Edinburgh Asylum. He quickly made changes, leading to improved methods of treatment. He sought to renovate and reconstruct the institution, which culminated in the opening of Craig House in 1900.[960] On its completion, Clouston said that, "nothing we can do for the comfort of our patients is too much to atone for the cruelty of the past years".[961] This was renamed the Thomas Clouston Clinic in 1972 and now forms part of Napier University.

Clouston became a popular and acclaimed teacher of mental diseases and, in 1879, he was appointed the first lecturer on the subject at the University of Edinburgh. He published a number of works, starting, in 1883, with '*Clinical Lectures on Mental Diseases*', which went to five editions in this country and saw two editions published in the United States.[962] He also edited for many years the '*Journal of Mental Science*'.

His annual asylum reports were widely reported in the national press and he used these to speak directly to the populace at large. He played a prominent part in the creation of a council of public morals in Scotland and wrote on the subject of matrimony. Today, much of his writing is viewed as representing conventional codes of morality expressed in the language of science.[963]

Many honours were conferred on him in later life. He was President of the Royal College of Physicians of Edinburgh and of the Medical Psychological Association of Great Britain and Ireland. Aberdeen University in 1907 and Edinburgh University in 1911 conferred upon him honorary Doctorates of Law, while King George V bestowed a knighthood on him in 1911.

On 27th April 1864, Clouston married a widow, Harriet Segur Williamson, the daughter of William Storer of New Haven, Connecticut.[964] The couple had three children, one of whom was the author and historian, Joseph Storer Clouston (120). Sir Thomas Clouston, an enthusiast of all things Orcadian, maintained his links with Orkney, spending summers along with his family at the holiday home he had built at Holodyke in Harray.[965] He retired in 1908 and was made a freeman of Kirkwall, an award he valued as the highest among the many other honours bestowed on him.[966] He died suddenly of a stroke at his Edinburgh home of 26 Heriot Row just short of his 75th birthday and was buried in the Dean cemetery.[967]

107. Archibald Garden Robertson 1898-1917

This wooden plaque to Archibald Robertson, which has the emblem of the Black Watch, is found on the south wall of the choir, above the memorial to his grandfather, Sheriff-Substitute James Robertson (92), and reads:

> To the glory of God
> and in memory of
> ARCHIBALD GARDEN ROBERTSON
> SECOND LIEUTENANT IN THE
> BLACK WATCH AND ATTACHED
> TO THE ROYAL FLYING CORPS.
> SECOND SON OF DUNCAN JOHN
> ROBERTSON AND MARGARET
> KEIR GARDEN. BORN AT CRANTIT
> St OLA ORKNEY 23RD FEBRUARY 1898.
> KILLED IN ACTION NEAR ROULERS
> BELGIUM 8TH JUNE 1917.

Archie Robertson was born at the family house of Crantit in 1898 and was named after his maternal grandfather, Archibald Garden JP of Bernera Dyke, Forres. Archie was educated in the south, firstly at Pembroke School, followed by Haileybury, which started out as a training college for the East India Company (see 90),

Archibald Robertson was an airman in World War One and was reported missing when flying over Flanders. His father, a well known public figure, opposed his son's name being added to the war memorial when it was revealed that initials would be used, rather than full forenames.

but after 1862 became an independent school. He received his officer training at Sandhurst and obtained his commission in August 1916 in the Black Watch. Thereafter, he transferred to the Royal Flying Corps, which was then a part of the British Army.[968] Archie qualified as a flying officer in January 1917, before being sent to the Front at the end of March. He was soon injured in an accident and was sent back to Britain on a fortnight's sick leave to recover. On June 8th, he was reported missing after his plane went down over Flanders. A short time later he was confirmed dead, aged only 19.[969] He is commemorated on the Arras Flying Services Memorial, Fubourg-d'Amiens Cemetery, Arras, Pas de Calais, France.

Archie's father, Duncan J. Robertson, mentioned on the plaque, was the son of James Robertson (92) and Harriet Logie and had a long, varied and distinguished career. He was born on 14th January 1860 at Buttquoy House in Kirkwall and was educated at Edinburgh Academy and Edinburgh University, where he studied law. His legal apprenticeship was served with the Edinburgh firm of Messrs Scott, Moncrieff and Traill. In 1888, he returned to Kirkwall to set up in private practice as a solicitor. A short time later, James Macrae, then Clerk to the Commissioners of Supply, died and Duncan Robertson took over his legal business, calling it Macrae and Robertson. He succeeded Macrae as the Commissioners' Clerk, the title changing to County Clerk in 1890, with the setting up of County Councils throughout Scotland. These were reconstituted in 1929, with Duncan Robertson being the only Clerk still in place from their original inception. He remained in post for another 11 years, retiring in September 1940. He held positions on many other bodies, but the one on which he spent most time was as Clerk and Treasurer of Balfour Hospital. The success of the 1923 appeal, which saw over £3000 raised for supplying the hospital with x-ray equipment and for securing the services of a resident surgeon, owed much to Robertson.[970]

Duncan Robertson, or *DJR* as he was known,[971] was appointed Vice Consul for Denmark in 1888, for Sweden in 1915 and fulfilled the position for Norway over a long number of years. With Kirkwall being a Contraband Control Base in the 1914-1918 conflict and handling hundreds of ships of neutral and friendly nationalities, he was very busy on consular duties for the Scandinavian countries during this period. For his services, he was knighted by both Denmark and Norway, and awarded an OBE in this country.

DJR was factor of a number of Orkney Estates and was one of three trustees who managed the Breckness Estate for twenty years, following the death of William G. T. Watt in 1909.[972] It was during his time of managing the estate that guardianship of Skara Brae was transferred, in 1924, to HM Commissioners of Work. One of his many legal clients was Frederick Traill-Burroughs (100), whom *DJR* represented during much of Burroughs' acrimonious dealings with his Rousay crofters.

It is difficult to imagine how *DJR* had time for a private life, but he had many outside interests. He was an active Freemason, was on the editorial committee of Orkney and Shetland Old-lore Miscellany and was a founder member of the Orkney Antiquarian Society. Ornithology was a passion and he photographed birds in their natural haunts, particularly on the island of Eynhallow, writing *Notes from a Bird Sanctuary* concerning his observations on that island.[973] He had bought Eynhallow around 1924, made it into a Bird Sanctuary and his trustees sold it to Orkney Islands Council in 1980. As an accomplished poet, his collected verse was published in *Waith and Wrack*.[974] He contributed a number of articles to *The Orkney Book*, published in 1909. This book provided information on a range of subjects on Orkney, and *DJR's* poem, *Sons of the Isles*, appeared in the foreword.

Despite being a public servant, *DJR* was not shy at making his views known. In 1922, he withheld permission for his son's name to be added to the proposed Kirkwall and St Ola War Memorial. In order to have names, ranks and regiments carved on the Memorial in single lines, it was proposed to reduce the names by using initials. *DJR* was strongly of the opinion that the fallen be accorded the honour of having their names in full.[975] The situation was eventually resolved when the contractor, Messrs Garden and Co of Aberdeen, indicated that *DJR's* son's name, rank and regiment could be etched in one line, thus: 2/Lt Archer Garden Robertson, Black Watch.[976] *DJR* also strongly opposed the proposed new organ screen for the Cathedral, describing it as "a desecration of the Cathedral to carry out such a scheme".[977]

Margaret Keir Garden was born in 1869, her parents being Archibald Garden JP of Bernera Dyke, Forres, and Jane Macleod. She married *DJR* in Forres in 1890, the couple going on to have three sons and four daughters.

108. William Baikie Watson 1918

William Baikie Watson was awarded the Military Cross for bravery in World War One.

This bronze plaque is found on the wall of the north side of the choir and says:

To the Glory of God
and in proud and loving memory of
William Baikie Watson.M.C.Lieut.RFA
only surviving son
of the late James Watson Uddington Douglas
Lanarkshire and of Mrs Watson Albert Hotel
who died of wounds in France 29th Sept 1918 aged 25.
Interred in Lowrie British Cemetery Havrincourt.

William Baikie Watson was born in Newmains, Lanarkshire, where his father, James, was a station master. His father died when William was still young and he and his mother, Mary, moved to Kirkwall, where she leased the Albert Hotel in 1905.[978] Mrs Watson was born Mary S. Baikie in Flotta in 1861. Her younger sister, Isabella Hatton Baikie, lived with her in the Albert Hotel and helped run the establishment.[979] Mary and Isabella seem to have come from a very poor background, with their unmarried mother, Catharine Gunn, who came from Stroma, being described as a pauper.[980] Intriguingly, in the 1911 Census, 76 year-old Catharine Gunn is shown as a visitor staying at the Albert Hotel and having private means.[981]

After school, William became a law apprentice.[982] He joined the Royal Garrison Artillery Territorials in

Orkney and, when his period of service expired, he volunteered to serve abroad in the Royal Field Artillery. After receiving his commission as Lieutenant, he was sent to France, where he was in the thick of the action. In September 1917, during the Battle of Passchendaele, he volunteered to go forward and reconnoitre during a fierce German bombardment of the front line. He collected stragglers and formed a line that held against a German attack, earning himself the award of a Military Cross.[983]

In April 1918, he was wounded and treated in hospital in Britain.[984] On recovery, he was sent back to France and died from wounds received in action, on 29th September 1918. His name also appears on the next memorial.

109. Great War Memorial

The Great War Memorial was unveiled by an army captain, from Stronsay, who had lost two brothers in the conflict.

At the west end of the nave, on the north side, is a marble plaque dedicated to the members of the congregation of St Magnus Cathedral killed during the Great War. The plaque was unveiled, appropriately, on 11th November 1923 by Captain Gordon Sutherland of Rothiesholm, Stronsay, who had lost two brothers in the conflict, both of whose names appear on the memorial.

On the St Magnus War Memorial there are 52 people commemorated. Some of the deaths occurred during the many major battles of the Great War. Others who did survive the war succumbed to the 'Spanish Flu', the worst natural disaster in human history. This was an influenza pandemic, which lasted from 1918 to 1920 and killed at least 50 million people world wide. There are also a number of civilians mentioned on the plaque, most of whom died when the little steamship, *Express*, sailing from Leith to Kirkwall with two servicemen gunners on board, was sunk in a collision with the destroyer, HMS *Grenville*, in the Pentland Firth, with the loss of all hands.

The following is the wording of the plaque and a brief description of each person mentioned on the memorial.[985]

TO THE GLORY OF GOD
AND TO THE HONOURED MEMORY
OF THE MEN OF THIS CONGREGATION
WHO GAVE THEIR LIVES
FOR KING AND COUNTRY IN THE
GREAT WAR
1914   1918

Kenneth Alexander: Private in the 8th Battalion, the Seaforth Highlanders. He was killed on 27th August 1917, aged 31, during the Battle of Passchendaele. Kenneth was buried in Brandhoek New Military Cemetery No. 3, Belgium.

Edwin I. Barnett: Private in the 7th Battalion, the Seaforth Highlanders. He was the son of Mrs Barnett of Victoria Street, Kirkwall. After being wounded in action on 8th August 1915, he died the same day. He had enlisted toward the end of 1914 and his battalion had been with the British Expeditionary Force since April.[986] He was buried in Chocques Military Cemetery, Pas de Calais.

Arthur S. (Sanderson) Buchanan: Captain in the Royal Engineers. He was born in Kirkwall in February 1888, the son of bank agent and solicitor, Angus Buchanan, and his wife Jenny Sanderson. Arthur trained as a Civil Engineer and was a Lieutenant in the 10th Battalion, the Seaforth Highlanders, when he married Gertrude McCankie in Edinburgh in April 1916. He died on 15th February 1919, just short of his 31st birthday, during the Spanish Flu pandemic. He was buried in Edinburgh (Dean, or Western) Cemetery, Midlothian.

James Cooper: Private in the Auckland Regiment, New Zealand Expeditionary Force. He was the son of Captain Charles Cooper (of the ketch, *Rose*), School Place, Kirkwall. He enlisted on the outbreak of war and was sent to Egypt with the New Zealand and Australian Forces. After taking part in the Suez Canal Operation he was sent to the Dardenelles. He took part in the Anzac (Australian and New Zealand Army Corps) landing at Gallipoli, but was wounded in the left arm, which was subsequently amputated and he died of complications in Hampshire on 24th June 1915. He was buried in St Magnus Cathedral Cemetery.

James Corse: Corporal in the 2nd Pioneer Infantry of the American Expeditionary Force. He was born in 1890, the son of David Corse, Strynd, Kirkwall, and was educated at the Burgh School before emigrating to the United States in 1911. James became a sheet metal worker, before being drafted into the army in May 1918. After contracting pneumonia (Spanish

Flu) in France, he died on September 21st 1918.[987] He was buried in St Mihiel American Cemetery, in north-eastern France.

Robert Craigie: Fireman on SS *Express*. He lived at 34 St Catherine's Place and died on 9th February 1918, aged 34, when the little steamer was in collision with a destroyer in the Pentland Firth.[988]

John Cutt: Corporal in the 1/5th (the Sutherland and Caithness) Battalion of the Seaforth Highlanders. John was from Holm and was killed on 9th April 1917, during the first day of the Battle of Arras, aged 35. He is commemorated on the Arras Memorial, Bay 8.

Thomas Cutt: Gunner in the 118th Siege Battery, Royal Garrison Artillery. He was killed in action on 5th July 1918, aged 21, as a result of the German Spring Offensive. He was buried at Grootebeek British Cemetery, in Belgium.

James Dunnet: Corporal in the 285th Company, the Royal Engineers. James came from South Ronaldsay and died during the Spanish Flu Pandemic on 25th November 1918, aged 27. He was buried in Montecchio Precalcino Communal Cemetery Extension, in Italy.

George Eccles: Gunner in the Royal Marine Artillery, HMS *Cyclops II*. He lived at 29 Victoria Street, Kirkwall, and was married to Georgina. George died suddenly of heart failure on Rousay on August 10th 1918.[989]

David Finlayson: Mate on SS *Express*. He died of a broken neck on 17th November 1916, aged 54, in a winch accident at Kirkwall. David was buried in St. Magnus Cathedral Cemetery.

George Foulis: Seaman on SS *Express*. He lived in St Catherine's Place and died on 9th February 1918, age 38, when the little steamer was in collision with a destroyer in the Pentland Firth. He was buried in St. Magnus Cathedral Cemetery.

James Fox: Seaman on SS *Express*. He lived in Junction Road, Kirkwall and died on 9th February 1918, age 18, when the little steamer was in collision with a destroyer in the Pentland Firth.

Adam Frisken: Chief Petty Officer on HMS *Swiftsure*.[990] His mother lived at Shore Street, Kirkwall and he had joined the navy as a youth.[991] After dying of dysentery on 10th February 1916, aged 39, at Nasrich Hospital in Cairo, he was buried in Cairo War Memorial Cemetery, Egypt.[992]

William Frisken: Private in the 6th Battalion, King's Own Scottish Borderers. He died of his wounds on 16th February 1917, aged 29 and was buried in Aubigny Communal Cemetery Extension, Pas de Calais, France.

David Gordon: Gunner in 145th Heavy Battery, Royal Garrison Artillery. He was killed on 8th November 1917, aged 29, during the Battle of Passchendaele. David was buried in the Huts Cemetery, in Ieper, Belgium.

Albert Gullion: Lance Corporal in the 1st Battalion, the Seaforth Highlanders. Known as "Abbo" to his family, he died in Kirkwall, on 14th March 1920, aged 20, of tuberculosis, probably as a result of being gassed in the trenches.[993]

Robert Hay: Private in the 1st Battalion, the Seaforth Highlanders, Mesopotamia Expeditionary Force. Mesopotamia covered much of modern day Iraq and was part of the Turkish Ottoman Empire. Robert was killed on 19th July 1916, aged 25, and was buried in Basra War Cemetery, Iraq.

William Hay: Private in 1/6th (Morayshire) Battalion, the Seaforth Highlanders. He was 20 when he died as a prisoner-of-war of wounds received during the German Spring Offensive on 29th April 1918. William was buried in Cologne Southern Cemetery, Germany.

Thomas Harcus: Private in the 1st Cameronians (Scottish Rifles). He died on 3rd April 1918, aged 25, during the German Spring Offensive and is commemorated on the Tyne Cot Memorial (Panel 69), Belgium.

James W. Harrold: Private in the 2nd Battalion, the Seaforth Highlanders. He was the eldest son of George and Eliza Harrold, 6 Long Wynd, Kirkwall. James was killed on 11th April 1917, aged 20, during the Battle of Arras. He was buried at Brown's Copse Cemetery, Pas de Calais, France.

James W. Holland: Private in the 1st Battalion, the Seaforth Highlanders, Mesopotamia Expeditionary Force. He was the son of Mrs Holland, Aim's Place, Kirkwall.[994] Private Holland died of his wounds at the 31st British Stationary Hospital in Mesopotamia, on March 9th 1917, aged 21 years. James was buried in Amara War Cemetery, Iraq.

George M. (Miller) Laird: Private in the 38th Battalion, Canadian Expeditionary Force. He was the son of Captain William Laird, Kirkwall and was killed on 27th October 1916, aged 21, during Battle of the Somme. George is commemorated on the Vimy Memorial, Pas de Calais, France.

James A. Learmonth: Private in the 7th Battalion, the Seaforth Highlanders. He was the son of John Learmonth, Soulisquoy, St Ola and was killed on 11th October 1916, aged 19, during the Battle of the Somme. His body was not found or identified, but he is commemorated in Pier & Face 15C, Thiepval Memorial, France.

Alexander M. Leask: Private in the 9th Battalion, the Seaforth Highlanders. He was killed on 21st March 1918, aged 29, during the German Michael Offensive.[995] The son of Kirkwall carter, William Leask, he had been in France for 18 months before he was killed.[996] He was buried in Fins New British Cemetery, Sorel-le-Grand, France.

David S. Linklater: Private in the 9th Battalion, the Seaforth Highlanders. He was killed on 25th September 1915, aged 31, during the Battle of Loos, when a high explosive shell hit the communication trench in which he was working.[997] David is commemorated on the Loos Memorial (Panel 114), Pas de Calais, France.

James Mackay: Private in the 7th Battalion, the Seaforth Highlanders. He was the youngest son of John and Margaret Mackay, 14 Victoria Road, Kirkwall. Having recovered from his wounds, he was placed in the Reserve Battalion at Cromarty. He died of influenza and pneumonia, aged 21, in the Military Hospital there, on 11th November 1918, the day war ended. James was buried in St. Magnus Cathedral Cemetery.

Hugh Marwick: Saddler in the Royal Army Service Corps. His mother lived in St Catherine's Place and he had two brothers serving in the forces, one in the navy and the other in the Royal Scots.[998] He died of wounds received during the 1918 Allied Offensive on 15th August, aged 38, and was buried in Ligny-St. Flochel British Cemetery, Pas de Calais, France.

Francis (Frank) I. Milne: Canadian Iceland Transport Service. He was the son of George Milne, a baker from Aberdeenshire, and his wife, Betsy Smith from Stenness. Frank's parents lived in Albert Street, Kirkwall and had a total of ten children. Before the war, he moved to Edinburgh with his brother, William (see next entry), working as a grocer's assistant. In April 1912, he emigrated to Wisconsin and was working as a sheet metal worker at the time he registered for the draft in 1917. When Frank died of tuberculosis on 1st November 1920, aged 32, he was staying with his sister, Maggie Mitchell, in Arizona.[999]

William Milne: Private in the Highland Light Infantry. He was a brother of Frank (above). After joining up, he trained at Fort George as a Private in the Highland Light Infantry, before dying of epilepsy and liver disease in the District Asylum at Craig Dunain Hospital in Inverness on 15th June 1916, aged 31.[1000] His name is on his parents' gravestone in St Magnus Cathedral Cemetery, along with his brothers, John and David, the latter dying in Racine, USA, in September 1917.

Andrew Nicholson, junior: Private in the 3rd Battalion, the Seaforth Highlanders. He was the son of Andrew and Margaret Nicholson of Little Corse, Kirkwall. Andrew was working as a postman when he was called up. Andrew died on 4th April 1917, aged 18, in Cromarty Military Hospital of meningitis and was buried in Cromarty Cemetery.

Alfred Osburne: Private in the 7th Battalion, the Seaforth Highlanders. He had served on the Western Front for two years and eleven months, before being killed in France on 11th April 1918, aged 20, during the German Spring Offensive. He was the son of Mrs Osburne, 4 Victoria Road, Kirkwall and had two brothers serving in the war, one in Mesopotamia and the other a seaman on a battleship. He is commemorated on Tyne Cot Memorial (Panel 134), in Belgium.

James Reid: Private in the 7th Battalion, Canadian Expeditionary Force. He was killed on 22nd September 1916, aged 32, during the Battle of the Somme. James is commemorated on Vimy Memorial, Pas de Calais, France.

George Rendall: Royal Navy Reserve Engineman on HM Trawler *Goeland II,* which was used for minesweeping. George was born in Westray, the son of a wool weaver. He drowned on 9th November 1917, aged 39, and was buried in Aberdeen (Trinity) Cemetery.

George I. (Irvine) Rendall: 2nd Engineer on SS *Express*. He lived in Garden Street, Kirkwall and died on 9th February 1918, age 48, when the little steamer was in collision with a destroyer in the Pentland Firth.

John Rendall: Private in the 8th Battalion, the Seaforth Highlanders. He was born in Westray and died on 23rd April 1917 during the Battle of Arras, aged 22. John was buried in Guemappe British Cemetery, Pas de Calais, France.

James Robertson: Gunner in the 253rd Siege Battery, Royal Garrison Artillery. He died on 21st April 1918, aged 36, during the German Spring Offensive. James was buried in Blangy-Tronville Communal Cemetery, Somme, France.

John Rosie: Private in the 6th Battalion, King's Own Scottish Borderers. He was the son of John and Jane Rosie, 10 Warrens Walk, Kirkwall, and was killed in action in France on 22nd March 1918, aged 19 years.[1001] John was buried at Peronne Communal Cemetery Extension, Somme, France.

George Sandison: Private in the 1/6th (Morayshire) Battalion, the Seaforth Highlanders. The second son of William Sandison of Leith, he served an apprenticeship with Northern Ensign in Wick and afterwards worked his trade in Edinburgh. His wife, Katie Taylor, and child lived at 6 Long Wynd, Kirkwall.[1002] George was killed in action in France on 9th April 1917, aged 29, during the first day of the Battle of Arras. He is commemorated on the Arras Memorial (Bay 8) at Pas de Calais, France.

Donald M. Scott: Assistant Paymaster in the Royal Naval Reserve. He was the son of shoemaker, Thomas Scott. Donald died in Kirkwall on 30th October 1920, aged 29.

William J. (John) Sinclair: Lance Corporal in the 1/6th (Morayshire) Battalion, the Seaforth Highlanders. The son of Mr and Mrs W. T. Sinclair, Albert Street, Kirkwall,[1003] he died, aged 20, of wounds received in action during the German Spring Offensive, at a Stationary Hospital on 29th March 1918. He was buried in Wimereux Communal Cemetery at Pas de Calais, France.

George W. Sinclair: Private in the 1st Battalion, the Seaforth Highlanders. He was killed in action at Istabulat in Mesopotamia on 21st April 1917, aged 29, and is commemorated on the Basra Memorial in Iraq.

John W. S. Sinclair: Sapper in the Inland Water Transport, Royal Engineers. He died on 2nd February 1919, aged 21, during the Spanish Flu pandemic. John was buried in Les Baraques Military Cemetery at Pas de Calais, France.

James Simison: Private in the 7th Battalion, the Seaforth Highlanders. He was killed on 12th October 1916, aged 20, during the Battle of the Somme. His body was never identified, but he is commemorated on Thiepval Memorial, Somme, France.

Robert M. Smith: Lance Corporal in the Royal Scots Fusiliers. He was working as a Law Clerk in Kirkwall when he died of heart disease on 6th May 1919, aged 26.

Anderson Sutherland: Acting Major in 51st Battery, 39th Brigade, Royal Field Artillery. He was the third son of George Sutherland, Sherriff-substitute of Orkney. He served at Salonika in Greece, as well as in France. In 1917, while serving as a Lieutenant on the Western Front, he won the Military Cross for extinguishing burning ammunition.[1004] On 1st November 1918, he was wounded in action during the Allied Offensive and died six days later at 61st Casualty Clearing Station in France.[1005] He was buried in Premont British Cemetery at Aisne, France.

Goodwin Sutherland: Second Lieutenant in the Gordon Highlanders. He was the fourth son of George Sutherland and brother of Anderson Sutherland. Another brother, Captain Douglas Sutherland, won the Military Cross and the Distinguished Service Order. Goodwin was killed on the first day of the Battle of Arras, on 9th April 1917, aged 20.[1006] He is commemorated on the Arras Memorial (Bay 8) at Pas de Calais, France.

Anderson Sutherland (on the right) was awarded the Military Cross but was fatally wounded in action in November, 1918.
Orkney Library Photographic Archive

James W. Tulloch: Private in the 1st Battalion, Black Watch. He was the son of W. R. Tullock of the Kirkwall Cycle and Motor Depot.[1007] James was actually born in the United States, where his father had learned his trade, becoming friends with Henry Ford in the process. Holding a US passport, there was no requirement for James to join up. Early in 1915, he wrote to a friend saying, "I am glad to say I am still in good working order, complete with two legs, two arms and a neck, although I have seen a few spare parts looking for owners. Wish this business was over and could manage to get home amongst you all again, for a day or two. Hope the time is not far off when it will be possible."[1008] He was killed on 26th September 1915, aged 22, during the Battle of Loos. He is commemorated on Loos Memorial (Panel 83).

William Baikie Watson: See 108.

J. Duncan Webster: Private in the 1/6th (Morayshire) Battalion, the Seaforth Highlanders. He was the son of Mr and Mrs Webster of the St Ola Hotel, Kirkwall and had only been in France a short while before being killed on 23rd March 1918, aged 19, during the German Spring (Michael) Offensive. Duncan is commemorated on the Arras Memorial (bay 8) at Pas de Calais, France.

John Wick: Private in the 4th Pioneer Battalion, Australian Imperial Force. He was born in Bridge Street, Kirkwall and emigrated, aged 22, to Australia, where he worked as a labourer in Brisbane. After joining the Australian Forces in 1916, he was killed during the German Offensive in April 1918. He was buried in Warloy-Baillon Communal Cemetery, near Derancourt in France.

James Willets: Private in the 1/5th (the Sutherland and Caithness) Battalion, the Seaforth Highlanders. He died of wounds received during the 1918 Allied Offensive on 9th December, aged 24. James was buried in Tourgeville Military Cemetery, Calvados.

110. James Scarth Spence Logie 1820-1920

This granite memorial is found on the east wall of the south transept beneath James Watson (77). It reads:

In Loving Memory Of
JAMES SCARTH SPENCE LOGIE
LRCSE, LRCPE, MDEd, JP
For 65 Years An Elder Of This Church
And For 56 Years A Medical Practitioner
In This Town And Country
Born In Kirkwall 11th May 1820 Died 17th July 1920
"Blessed Is He That Considereth The Poor" Psal 41. 1.
His Beloved Wife BARBARA SINCLAIR SPENCE
Born 6th Oct. 1828 Died 18th Aug 1913.
"In Her Tongue Was The Law Of Kindness."
Prov. 31. 26.

Dr James Logie was born in Kirkwall, in the house in Victoria Street of his maternal grandfather, James Scarth. The son of Rev William Logie (87), he was four when his father became the Cathedral Minister and the family moved into the Old Manse in the Watergate. He received his elementary education at the Grammar School in Kirkwall before setting off to study medicine at Edinburgh University. After qualifying as a Licentiate of the Royal College of Surgeons in 1841, he took his degree of MD at the early age of 22, studying under, amongst others, Sir James Young and Sir Robert Christison.[1009] His favourite teacher was Professor James Syme, described by some as the greatest surgeon Scotland ever produced.[1010] After graduating, he worked as an assistant to doctors in Newcastle and Carlisle, before moving to Paris in 1845 for further study at the university there.[1011]

Towards the end of 1845, he set up his own practice in Kirkwall, which soon covered the whole of Orkney.

Dr James and Barbara Logie. Dr Logie, was highly regarded throughout Orkney as a medical practitioner, risking life and limb to reach patients in atrocious weather conditions. He was one of the first surgeons to use anaesthetic in operations.
Orkney Library Photographic Archive

Outside Kirkwall, there were only two doctors, one in Stromness (Dr Garson[1012]) and one in Sanday, both of whom frequently summoned Dr Logie for consultation. That year also saw the opening of the Balfour Hospital in the present day West End Hotel, with Dr Logie being one of the original medical staff. His early operations were performed without anaesthetic, but soon after Sir James Simpson's discovery of chloroform, Dr Logie was one of the first surgeons in the North of Scotland to make use of the new discovery in his practice. Being a doctor in these days was no easy profession, with house calls having to be made by horseback over rough hill tracks, often snow covered in winter. He later recalled many wild night rides, with numerous narrow escapes from drift and bog, as he travelled to the remote parts of the Mainland. The isles too had to be covered, travelling in a small sailing vessel, often in stormy conditions. He became known as simply 'the doctor', being held in high regard both as a physician and a surgeon.

Dr Logie held a number of public offices, being Medical Officer for Kirkwall Prison and the old Parochial Board of Kirkwall and St Ola, as well as several Mainland Parishes and a few of the North Isles. He was also a Justice of the Peace and a Commissioner of Supply. As a young man, he was fond of hunting and kept a greyhound, which he used for coursing while riding over the countryside. A keen fisherman well into his eighties, he was forced to give up horse riding at the tender age of ninety, owing to failing eyesight.[1013] The Church was also an important part of his life and he became an elder of the St Magnus Cathedral congregation in 1855, remaining in post for an incredible 65 years.

A close acquaintance of Dr Logie was Sheriff Thoms (99), who made a very prophetic statement to the doctor regarding St Magnus Cathedral. In reply to Dr Logie's wish that one day some rich Orcadian might restore the Cathedral, Thoms emphatically said, "The day will come, and the man will come". Dr Logie later said to his wife, "I am sure he has it in his noddle to do it himself".[1014]

Dr Logie married Barbara Sinclair Spence on 20th February 1851. She was the daughter of his cousin, James Spence of Eastbank, agent for the Commercial Bank of Kirkwall. Their first child, a son, called William Alexander, was born on 18th February, 1852. He was followed by three daughters over the next 12 years. The Logies lived at 2 Broad Street, the house that once acted as the Tolbooth and was formerly known as Ridgeland.

As has been seen, Dr Logie had an amazing constitution, only retiring at the age of eighty-one. He outlived his successor, Dr Bell (105), despite being some four decades older, and celebrated his centenary in May 1920. He died two months later and was buried in St Magnus Cathedral Cemetery, in a walled lair near the Palace Road gate.

111. Margaret Manson Graham 1860-1933

At the east end of the choir, near the cenotaph of William Balfour Baikie, is a wooden plaque dedicated to the only woman to have such a memorial within the Cathedral. It says:

> MARGARET MANSON GRAHAM
> Nurse and Missionary: Rescuer of
> Children Abandoned to Die: Devoted
> Her Life to Christian Work in Nigeria
> Born Orphir 1860 Died Arochuki 1933

The plaque was unveiled on 18th October 1964 by Harry S. Mowatt, who worked with Sister Graham and was with her during her last days.[1015]

Margaret Manson Graham was born at Little Twartquoy, near the top of Hobbister Hill in Orphir, the daughter of woollen weaver and crofter, John Graham, and his wife, Isabella.[1016] She had two elder sisters and a younger brother. After attending Orphir School, a couple of miles down the hill from her home, Margaret was appointed school monitor and assisted the sewing mistress in running the school. By 19, she had qualified as a teacher and became a communicant in Orphir Free Church, in which her parents were members.

A few years later she left teaching to become a nurse, completing her training in Glasgow, where she heard of the work done in Nigeria by the Scottish missionary, Mary Slessor. Following a Government request for nurses to serve in Nigeria, Margaret offered her

Nurse Margaret Manson Graham was a brave Orcadian who worked in very dangerous parts of Africa, where she was never far away from murder and witchcraft.

services and, in February 1895, she sailed for Calabar. She had left the cold of a Scottish winter for the stifling heat of West Africa, where she set to nursing the sick crews of British trading vessels, lying at anchor in the Cross River. As William Balfour Baikie (94) had found, tropical diseases were rife and the area was known as "the white man's grave". A colleague who had travelled with Margaret died from typho-malarial fever only two months after arriving in Nigeria.

Towards the end of the nineteenth century, part of Nigeria had become a British protectorate, with its headquarters at Calabar, near the south east coast. A new hospital was built and Margaret was asked to become its first sister in charge. With the majority of patients being critically ill, and with only two nurses to help, nursing in Calabar hospital was hard work.

This part of Africa was a dangerous place, with tribal wars, drunkenness, murders, witchcraft, slave trading and cannibalism everyday occurrences. The chief culprits were thought to belong mainly to one tribe, the Aros, and the British decided to use force against them. Margaret was engaged as a nursing sister to accompany the expedition to pacify the tribe.

At first she was based at the Military Hospital at Itu. Later she moved to Arochuka, the heart of Aro country, and nursed the wounded under canvas and in blistering heat. Finally she saw action at Bende, a remote and unexplored area north of Arochuka. Eventually, after four months of combat, the British surrounded the Aros and destroyed the skull-topped shrine of their supreme deity. For her part in the hostilities, Margaret received the Africa General Service Medal (Aro Expedition) with clasps. She was also decorated with the Order of St John of Jerusalem by King Edward VII at Buckingham Palace, for devotion to duty during a native rising at Aro in north Nigeria.[1017]

Margaret returned to her work at Calabar before retiring from Government service in 1919. She returned home, but soon became restless. Despite her age, she sought active service once more, requesting to return to Arochuka as a missionary nurse. She sailed back to Arochuka and for the next 11 years was based there at the Slessor Memorial Home as the third member of a trio of female nurses. The birth of twins was still looked upon with dread and superstition by the local people and one of her first jobs was to procure a sanctuary for outcast women and babies. She also supervised the building of a dispensary, the equivalent of a modern-day casualty department.

Despite the opposition of the local witch doctor, Margaret would visit the nearby villages, dressed in her white coat and sun helmet, helping the sick, the outcast and the hungry. At her dispensary, she treated tropical ulcers, leopard maulings and native diseases. She especially enjoyed healing children and training women in child welfare. Once, she saved the life of a baby boy who had been left to die after his mother had died in childbirth. She had been called to help the woman, but she arrived too late. When she asked about the baby, she was met with blank looks and had to search for the infant herself. She was about to give up and return to the Mission, when she heard a faint cry in the bush. The baby had pneumonia and Margaret brought him back to the Mission to be cared for. She christened him Okorafo, the Aro word for Tuesday, it being a local custom to name a child according to the day of its birth.

Margaret repeatedly asked for her salary to be used for medicines for the Mission. This was eventually agreed and she became an honorary missionary. For her, it was a great pleasure to be an honorary worker and she described her time with the Aro people as "sheer joy". She was delighted when Orkney Presbytery recognised her as their "special missionary" and helped to maintain her work in Nigeria.

In 1931, Margaret returned to Orkney for a holiday. This was to be her last visit to her native islands. After returning to Africa, she continued to work at her dispensary, even though she became so frail that she had to be carried there. She died at the Slessor Memorial Home among the people she loved, on October 14th 1933. Little Okorafo took his place at the foot of the coffin as it was borne 70 miles down the Cross River. Margaret was laid to rest near to Mary Slessor, on a raised knoll overlooking the Bay of Calabar.[1018]

112. HMS *Royal Oak* 1939

The memorial to HMS *Royal Oak* is found on the north side of the choir. It consists of a plaque above a glass-topped case, which displays a book of remembrance, recording the names of the sailors who lost their lives when the ship was torpedoed in Scapa Bay. The book is left open to display the names of those lost, with one page being turned each week. Should there be a special request to see a particular name, that page is left in view for the remainder of the day, before the normal cycle is resumed. The plaque, which was originally unveiled in 1948, in the nave, reads:

IN MEMORY OF
833 OFFICERS AND MEN OF
HMS "ROYAL OAK"
WHO LOST THEIR LIVES WHEN
THEIR SHIP WAS SUNK IN SCAPA BAY
BY U47 ON 14TH OCTOBER 1939

HMS Royal Oak memorial. One page of the remembrance book is turned every week.

After much cross-checking and research, it is now accepted that 834 lives were lost. Following the recovery of the ship's bell from the seabed near the wreck in the 1970s, a new memorial was created in the choir.

HMS *Royal Oak* was the last battleship to be built at Devonport Dockyard in Plymouth and was completed in time to form part of the British Grand Fleet, which left Scapa Flow at the end of May 1916 for a confrontation with the German High Seas Fleet off Jutland, on the Danish coast. At the ensuing Battle of Jutland, *Royal Oak* was credited with three hits on the battle-cruiser, *Derfflinger*, which knocked out one of her turrets.[1019] At the end of the war, *Royal Oak* was part of the massive allied fleet that oversaw the surrender of the German High Seas Fleet and its internment in Scapa Flow.

Royal Oak belonged to the *Revenge* class of super-dreadnoughts, which survived to see service in the Second World War. Their prime armament comprised eight 15 inch guns, which could hurdle a 17-hundredweight (876 kg) shell up to 18 miles away. Two examples of these guns, taken from a couple of *Royal Oak's* sister ships, can be seen on display outside the Imperial War Museum in London.

Royal Oak's last sortie saw her patrolling, along with a couple of destroyers, to the west of Shetland, where she received some structural damage due to heavy weather. She returned to Scapa on the 11th of October 1939 and anchored at her mooring near Gaitnip, next to the seaplane tender, *Pegasus*. With the Commander in Chief of the Home Fleet suspecting an imminent attack on Scapa Flow by the Luftwaffe, the fleet was dispersed to safer ports. *Royal Oak* was left behind to carry out repairs and provide additional anti-aircraft cover for Scapa Flow.

Meanwhile, the German U boat, *U-47*, under the command of Gunther Prien, managed to break into the naval base by threading its way through the blockships sunk in Kirk Sound, with only the aurora borealis to light the way. Finding a seemingly empty anchorage, ships were eventually sighted to the north and an attack was prepared. The first two attempts were unsuccessful, but two of the third salvo of three torpedoes hit their target, leaving a gaping hole in the side of the ship and causing cordite in a magazine to ignite. *Royal Oak* quickly listed to starboard and sank beneath the waves. The death toll might have been much higher if the skipper of the tender, *Daisy 2*, moored on the port side of the battleship, had not been alert to the situation. Of the 420 crew who survived the sinking, an incredible 386 were rescued by the crew of the tender. The British authorities were slow to realise the cause of the disaster and it was some time after *U-47* had escaped before attempts were made to seal the anchorage.

Surprisingly, it took a considerable time before the wreck of the *Royal Oak* was given protection as an official war grave. In 1957, the Admiralty invited tenders for salvaging the vessel.[1020] This caused an outcry both locally and from relatives of those lost in the sinking. Orkney County Council unanimously agreed to protest in the strongest terms against the proposal to raise the *Royal Oak*[1021]. The Government soon relented and abandoned its plans.

Today, the 620 foot ship lies nearly upside down, having settled deeper under the waters of Scapa Flow. When she first capsized, her 15 inch guns swivelled round, pointing down as she sank. This resulted in the ship being propped up by these guns once she reached the sea bed. In the intervening years, the tops of the turrets have given way and the large guns now lie hidden underneath the wreck. The wreck is marked by a buoy and for many years also occasional sheens of oil from her leaking fuel tanks. These were at last stopped a few years ago when the Ministry of Defence arranged for much of the oil to be removed. Each year, on the 14th October, the anniversary of her sinking, a wreath is cast to the waters above the wreck.

113. Alfred Baikie 1861-1947

Beneath the east window on the north side is a wooden plaque dedicated to Alfred Baikie. It says:

> In Memory of ALFRED BAIKIE
> of Tankerness CB Eleventh Laird
> Born 9th March 1861 Died 21st October 1947
> HM Lieutenant for Orkney & Zetland 1931

Alfred Baikie was prominent in recruiting Orcadians for the new 226th Heavy Anti Aircraft Battery, formed to protect Scapa Flow at the start of World War Two. He was actually born a Cowan but changed his name as a condition of inheriting the Baikie estate and becoming 10th laird. He was appointed Lord Lieutenant and became a prominent and popular public figure.

Orkney Library Photographic Archive

Alfred Baikie was actually born Alfred Cowan, being the son of William Layman Cowan and Deborah Hodgson Dover. His father had taken over the management of the Baikie estate from the 9th laird, Dr Robert Baikie. The latter had found the climate in Orkney not to his liking and had moved to Edinburgh to practise medicine. Both of Alfred's parents, who were second cousins, were connected to the 9th laird. William Cowan was the elder son of Robert Baikie's niece and his mother was a daughter of Robert Baikie's sister, Mary.[1022]

The Cowans lived at Tankerness House and, after the death of Dr Robert Baikie, who had no children,

Alfred's older brother, William, became the 10th laird in 1889. As a condition of inheritance, William changed his name to Baikie.

Alfred became a consultant engineer and spent much of his working life abroad. In 1888, he married Annie Traill Fotheringhame of Lynnfield, Kirkwall, a sister of his brother's wife, and the couple had a son, Robert. Annie died in 1896 and Alfred remarried in 1902, this time to Mary Anne Stewart Traill, the youngest daughter of Thomas Traill of Holland, Papa Westray, the couple producing a daughter, Margaret.[1023] Changing his name to Baikie, Alfred became the 11th laird of Tankerness in 1898, after his brother died at the early age of 48.[1024] As laird, Alfred set about improving the Hall of Tankerness. A skilled craftsman, he performed much of the work himself, such as making windows and wood panelling, as well as plastering walls. By the time the First World War finished, however, large estates had become unprofitable and Alfred began to break up his own landed property. Much of Tankerness House in Kirkwall was divided up and rented out, though Alfred and his wife maintained a small flat in the building.

Alfred was a County Councillor and served as County Convener from 1909 to 1917. In 1929, he was appointed Sheriff-substitute for Caithness, Orkney and Shetland, and was made Lord Lieutenant of Orkney and Shetland in 1930. He chaired the Garden Memorial Building Fund and, in 1927, performed the opening ceremony of the new Garden Memorial Hospital. In 1938, he led the recruiting drive for the new 226th Heavy Anti-Aircraft Battery, in which many Orcadians served during World War Two. He was a keen yachtsman and played the cello in the Kirkwall amateur orchestra, along with his daughter, Margaret, who played the drums.

Alfred was a popular figure in Orkney and news of his death, at the age of 87, was given headlines in *The Orkney Herald*. He died at his home in the Hall of Tankerness and his remains were flown from Hatston Airport to Aberdeen, in an Allied Airways Rapide, for cremation.

114. Caroline Cumming Spence 1879-1924

Following the death of his first wife, Rev. Andrew Campbell paid for the lectern which sits at the crossing. The lectern has a small plaque, which says:

To the Glory of God
And in thankful remembrance of his servant
Caroline Cumming Spence MA (Edin)
A native of this city and royal burgh, wife of
Revd A. J. Campbell MA (Cantab) Minister of
St John's Church, Glasgow
Born 28th Dec 1879 Died in Glasgow 8th Jan 1924

Caroline Cumming Spence, or Carrie as she was affectionately known, was gifted with good looks, intelligence and artistic talent. Her father, Robert Spence, came from Birsay, while her mother, Mary Anne Spence, was born in Evie. Robert started as a counter assistant in the shop of Mr James Cumming in Albert Street. After becoming indispensible to the firm, Mr Cumming gave him a partnership and the business of Cumming and Spence was formed.[1025] The friendship between the two is reflected in Carrie's middle name of Cumming.

Caroline Cumming Spence's father was a Kirkwall businessman. The business Cumming and Spence traded in Albert Street up until about 15 years ago.

Carrie had several brothers and sisters, and the family lived in Broad Street.[1026] She did well at school and, unusually for a woman at this time, went off south to university. It has been said that she was the first woman graduate to come from Orkney.[1027] She came home to work as a teacher. It is very likely she met Andrew James Campbell while she was studying in Edinburgh. He had completed his classics degree at Oxford and was doing his theology training at Edinburgh University, where Caroline was studying. The couple were married in Kirkwall on 3rd September 1902, at a time when Andrew was minister in Lerwick.[1028] Eight years later they moved to Glasgow.

Carrie was an accomplished artist, making drawings of street scenes in Glasgow, Lerwick and, of course, her native Kirkwall. Glasgow Cathedral was a particular source of inspiration. She also painted in watercolours and her still life of wilting flowers once hung in the Scottish National Gallery in Edinburgh.

Sadly, Carrie developed a tumour and was confined to bed for the last few weeks of her life. She died in 1924 at her home in Glasgow at the relatively young age of 45.[1029]

115. Andrew James Campbell 1875-1950

Immediately in front of the organ screen is a carved wooden chair, which carries a small dedication. The small plaque is easily missed as it is covered by a cushion. The wording on the plaque is:

TO THE GLORY OF GOD
AND IN LOVING MEMORY OF
ANDREW JAMES CAMPBELL D.D.
MINISTER OF St COLUMBA CHURCH,
LERWICK, SHETLAND,
ST JOHN'S CHURCH, GLASGOW AND EVIE,
ORKNEY,
CLERK TO THE PRESBYTERRY OF GLASGOW
1929-1936
FREEMAN OF THE CITY OF KIRKWALL 1945
MODERATOR OF THE GENERAL ASSEMBLY 1945
BORN 30TH JUNE 1875
DIED 1ST MAY 1950

Andrew James Campbell was born in Crathie, the son of a Buchan schoolmaster, and was educated at Ardallie Parish School, followed by Fettes College, Edinburgh. Later, he went to St John's College, Cambridge, where he rowed for his college. He graduated as MA in 1897, with Honours in Classics. After graduating, he completed his theology training at the University of Edinburgh. He became an assistant at the East Parish Church of St Nicholas in Aberdeen and two years later, on 21st March 1902, was called to Lerwick Parish Church, where he stayed for eight years, thoroughly enjoying his time in that town.[1030] It was during his first year as minister in Lerwick that he married his first wife, Caroline Cumming Spence (114). In 1910, he transferred to St John's Church in Glasgow.[1031]

With the outbreak of war, Rev. Campbell joined up, becoming chaplain with the 52nd (Lowland) Division

The Very Rev Andrew Campbell married an Orcadian and subsequently became the Evie minister and Moderator of the General Assembly for the Church of Scotland.

and seeing service at Gallipoli, as well as Palestine and Egypt. He wrote a log of his experiences at Gallipoli, which was published in *The Orcadian*.[1032]

After the war, Rev. Campbell returned to his parish church in Glasgow. From 1921 to 1924, he was Hastie Lecturer to Glasgow University. The lectures formed the basis of his book, *Two Centuries of the Church of Scotland 1707-1929*, published in 1930. Owing to his expert knowledge of Church law and procedure, he was appointed Joint-Clerk to the Presbytery of Glasgow in 1929. This was a full-time appointment, requiring his resignation from his Glasgow charge. In 1933, Glasgow University conferred on him an honorary Doctorate of Divinity. By this stage, Rev. Campbell had married Anna Mary Robertson from Shetland, his first wife having died in 1924.

The call of the Northern Isles was strong and Rev. Campbell gave up city life when he decided to return to the work of a parish minister, accepting the call to Evie, Orkney, in 1936. He had a strong interest in the Northern Isles and published *Fifteen Centuries of the Church in Orkney* in 1938. In 1945, he was given the Church of Scotland's highest honour, Moderator of the General Assembly. This was the first time a minister from the Northern Isles had received such an accolade. During his time as Moderator, he made a 2000-mile tour of the British occupied zone of Germany and also made an extensive journey round naval establishments in Britain. 1945 also saw him receive the Freedom of Kirkwall, along with two other recipients, John Mooney (121) and ex Provost John White.

Rev Campbell retired in the early part of 1948 because of failing health. His last visit to Orkney was in September 1949, when he officiated at the wedding of his first wife's niece, Elizabeth Mackintosh, to Robert Miller in the Paterson Church.[1033] Rev. Campbell had made a promise to Elizabeth many years previously that he would carry out her wedding ceremony. Despite failing health, he came north and fulfilled that promise. He died at his Edinburgh home on May 1st 1950 and was survived by his second wife.

116. Rev. William Barclay 1888-1958

In St Rognvald Chapel, there are three chairs beneath the statues of Kol, Rognvald and Bishop William. The middle one contains the carving, "WB 1921 DG" and also a dedication, which says:

> Dora Garden had me made in memory
> of her husband
> the Rev Wm Barclay Minister of this Cathedral
> for 17 years 1919-1936.

The Rev William Barclay was a Cathedral minister who complained about the council's stewardship of the building. He alleged the local authority was allowing behaviour in the Tower stairwell which "was outside the bounds of decency".
Orkney Library Photographic Archive

The other two chairs are dedicated to his parents-in-law, Robert Garden (102) and Margaret Jolly (103).

William Barclay was born in 1888 in Dalserf, Lanarkshire, the only son of John Barclay and Jessie McDougall. He was educated at Dalserf School, Larkhall Academy and Glasgow University, gaining his MA in 1915. He was licensed by the Presbytery of Hamilton in 1917, before serving as a 2nd Lieutenant in the Royal Field Artillery during the remainder of the First World War. After the war, he came to Kirkwall as minister of the second charge of St Magnus Cathedral, before being admitted to the first charge on Christmas Eve 1919. On the retirement of Rev. John Rutherford, William Barclay became sole minister of the united Cathedral congregation. He married Dora, daughter of Robert Garden, Kirkwall Merchant, and Margaret Jolly, in 1921.[1034]

With the increase in visitor numbers to the Cathedral, Rev. Barclay felt compelled to write to the Town Council in 1934 to complain about the vandalism and desecration perpetrated within the building following an excursion day from Caithness. He informed the Council that light fittings had been wrenched off the wall, the Bell Tower was being used as a place of public convenience and that "the behaviour on the stairway leading to the Tower was outside the bounds of decency". He strongly advocated that there should be no admission to the Cathedral Tower except for guided tours, for which a charge would be made.[1035]

Rev. Barclay did much to collect and preserve ecclesiastical documents in Orkney. He suggested using one of the ante-rooms of St Magnus Cathedral as a repository for all official church records. By 1933, a half-ton steel door was placed at the entrance to the old courtroom, situated in the first landing, on the south side. The passage from the court to the dungeon was filled in to complete the sealing of the record room.[1036] As a result of this work in preserving Orkney church records, he was elected a Fellow of the Scottish Society of Antiquaries in 1931.[1037]

Some of the success of the Cathedral octocentenary celebrations was attributed to the enthusiasm and careful planning carried out by Rev. Barclay. Although he had left Orkney before the octocentenary, he returned to help out and preach the Sunday sermon, which was broadcast from Kirkwall by the BBC.[1038]

Rev. Barclay left Orkney in 1936 to take up the ministry of Shawlands Old Church in Glasgow, a position he held until his retirement for health reasons in October 1957. He died on July 9th 1958 in Edinburgh.

Rev. Barclay's son, Robin, trained as a doctor in Edinburgh before practising in New Zealand, where he settled and married a girl from Tauranga.[1039] After Rev. Barclay's death, his widow, Dora, also moved to New Zealand and ended her days in Tauranga.

117. Peter Copeland Flett 1878-1960

On the base of the window, opposite the St Magnus pillar, on the south side of the choir, is a dedication to P. C. Flett. The window shows St Simon, the patron saint of ironmongers, and was chosen by Kirkwall Town Council as an appropriate memorial to P. C. Flett, who was a prominent ironmonger in his day. The dedication says:

Provost P.C. Flett, who regularly gifted trees to the town. He was heavily involved in the 1935 Silver Jubilee commemorative plantation at the Willows.

Peter Copeland Flett OBE
1878-1960
Provost of Kirkwall
1940-1947
A devoted servant of
this City and of the Cathedral.

Kirkwall business man, Peter Copeland Flett was a long-term member of Kirkwall Town Council and Provost of the city during much of the Second World War years. He was a native of Kirkwall, the son of James Ferguson Flett, who founded the ironmongery and seed business that became known as P. C. Flett Ltd. His older brother, Sir John Flett, became a renowned geologist and Director of the Geological Survey of Great Britain.

After attending the Kirkwall Burgh School, P. C. Flett served his apprenticeship with his father before going to Aberdeen in 1897 as an improver and becoming a foreman at Aberdeen ironmongers, Messrs Shirras, Laing & Co Ltd. He soon returned to Kirkwall and took over the management of his father's business, controlling it for the next 60 years.

Outside his business, P. C. Flett was a member of the Orkney Royal Garrison Artillery for 17 years, retiring with the rank of sergeant-major at the age of 34. He was a keen swimmer and his first public office was that of secretary of Kirkwall Swimming Club. He was also involved in the scouts, later becoming President of the Orkney Scout Council for four years.

He was first elected to Kirkwall Town Council in November 1911, at a time when the town was bitterly split over the Burgh water supply. Some people supported bore holes, while others, including P. C. Flett, favoured a Wideford Hill reservoir. He soon rose through the ranks of the Council, becoming Dean of Guild in 1913 and Bailie in 1917. Apart from a four-year spell out of the Council, he served continuously until his retirement in 1947. He was Dean of Guild again between 1935 and 1939, before being elected Provost in 1940. During his wartime term of office as Provost, he was much in contact with the various branches of the Armed Services and co-operated in a number of wartime savings campaigns.

He served on the Kirkwall & St Ola School Board and was twice a member of Orkney County Council. During the First World War, he officiated on the Food Control Committee and, when the war ended, he carried out a five-year plan to provide work for returning servicemen. This plan was aimed at reviving the local white fish industry. He bought three 40-foot boats, which operated out of Kirkwall, Longhope and St Margaret's Hope, giving employment to eight men. He was a member of the committee which organised and financed the erection of Kitchener's Memorial at Marwick Head and also served on Orkney Harbours Commission, being closely associated with the £35,000 extension of Kirkwall Pier, just before the outbreak of World War Two.

A keen Freemason and trout fisherman, as well as an enthusiastic member of the Orkney Club, P. C. Flett had a deep interest in Orkney history and was an authority on St Magnus Cathedral. He was a member of the Thoms' Trust, taking an active interest in the Cathedral's restoration, although himself a member of the Paterson Church congregation. In later years he took a particular interest in astronomical theories regarding the Ring of Brodgar, in Stenness, and carried out a number of personal investigations.

Gifts of trees and flowers were regularly donated to the town by P. C. Flett and he was involved in the plantation of trees at the Willows to mark the Royal Silver Jubilee of 1935. A prominent Unionist, his public services were recognised with the award of an OBE in 1938.[1040]

A bachelor all his life, P. C. Flett lived at 21 Willowburn Road in Kirkwall and died in Eastbank Hospital on 26th January 1960 at the age of 82. He was buried in St Magnus Cathedral churchyard. The firm of P. C. Flett Ltd. carried on in Kirkwall until it was wound up in 1984.[1041]

118. Harald Leslie, Lord Birsay 1905-1982

On the south wall of the choir is a simple plaque to Lord Birsay. Beneath a shield with his coat-of-arms is the following text.

> To the Glory of God
> and in Memory of
> Harald Leslie, Lord Birsay KT
> 1905-1982

Harald Robert Leslie was one of Scotland's foremost lawyers and a very popular figure in Orkney, much in demand to launch an appeal, to speak at a parish sale of work or open a fair, school or hall.[1042] He was actually born in South Shields of Orkney parents, Robert Leslie, a master mariner, and Margaret Mowat Cochrane, both of Stromness. He was educated at Earlston Public School in Berwickshire, Glasgow High School and Glasgow University. After qualifying, he pursued a legal career, becoming a solicitor in 1930 and being called to the Scottish bar in 1937. His early ambition had been to go to sea but he was dissuaded by his widowed mother, his father having died of a heart condition while serving in the merchant navy during the First World War.

His legal career was interrupted by the advent of war, when Harald joined the Royal Scots. When his posting was delayed, he briefly served as a stoker on a small steamer taking military supplies around Scapa Flow.[1043] He had a distinguished war record, being mentioned in dispatches and receiving the MBE (military) in

Lord Birsay, Harald Leslie, was a leading lawyer in the 1950s and subsequently became a Sheriff-Principal in the Borders. His parents were both Orcadian, though he was actually born in South Shields.

1945. At the time of his demob, he had the rank of Lieutenant-Colonel.

Harald returned to his legal career after the war, becoming Advocate-Depute in 1947 and taking silk in 1949. He also dabbled in politics, standing as a Labour candidate for the Orkney and Shetland Constituency in the 1950 General Election.

In the 1950s, Harald became a leading Scottish QC. In 1958, he defended Peter Manuel, one of Scotland's most notorious serial killers, who was accused of eight murders and possibly linked to seven more.

Between 1956 and 1961, Harald was Sheriff-Principal of Roxburgh, Berwick and Selkirk, being particularly proud of the fact that Sir Walter Scott was one of his predecessors on the Bench.[1044] His stint in the Borders was followed by four years as Sheriff-Principal of Orkney, Shetland, Caithness and Sutherland.

In 1965 he was appointed Chairman of the Scottish Land Court, a position he held for 13 years. For this role he was able to take the judicial title of Lord Birsay. He adopted this name through his ownership of Queenafiold, which overlooks the Loch of Boardhouse in that parish. His involvement with the Scottish Land Court saw him dealing with many aspects of agricultural law in disputes between landlord and tenant. He covered some 5000 miles per year settling disputes, with full court sittings being held in virtually all parts of Scotland during his time as Chairman.

Outwith his legal career, Harald was active in a huge number of organisations, such as the Savings Movement, General Medical Services, Boys Clubs, Youth Clubs, the Shipwrecked Fishermen and Mariners' Royal Benevolent Society and was Honourary President of both the Edinburgh and Glasgow Orkney and Shetland associations. Being a lay preacher, he became Lord

High Commissioner to the General Assembly of the Church of Scotland in 1965 and 1966. He served as chairman of a number of national bodies and was very interested in the Scots Language, becoming President of the Scottish National Dictionary Association as well as leading the appeal for a Concise Scots Dictionary.

Harald became a CBE in 1963 and was installed as a Knight of the Thistle in St Giles Cathedral in 1974. This was Scotland's highest order of chivalry, an honour rarely given. In 1966, he was given LLD degrees from Glasgow and Strathclyde Universities, and in the same year was made an Honorary Fellow of the Educational Institute of Scotland for services to education.

In December 1945 Harald married Robina Margaret Marwick (known as Rena), a daughter of Provost J. G. Marwick of Stromness. She qualified as a doctor and was GP in Sanday before joining the war effort. In July 1944, with the rank of Captain, she was landed in Normandy and followed the troops through France, Belgium, Holland and finally Germany, treating injured British soldiers on the way. She witnessed at first hand the horrors of Nazi Germany, when she was part of the British liberation of the German concentration camp of Belsen, the same camp in which Anne Frank had died a few weeks earlier. She spent the next few months treating the survivors and wrote of her experiences in letters home to her father in Stromness.[1045]

The couple settled in Edinburgh and adopted a son and a daughter.[1046] The family spent as much time as they could in Orkney, staying at their cottage of Queenafiold. Harald was interested in all things Orcadian and, in 1968, took an active part in the International Conference held in Orkney to mark the Quincentenary of the Impignoration, which saw Orkney pass from Scandinavian control to the Scottish Crown.[1047] Four years later, he officially launched the very successful appeal to save the west end of St Magnus Cathedral from collapse. In 1979, he became an Honorary Sheriff in Orkney, a position in which he took great pride. He saw it as a completion of his judicial career by being part of the administration of justice in his native islands during his years of retirement.

Harald died of a coronary thrombosis at his home at 27 Queensferry Road in Edinburgh on Saturday November 27th 1982.[1048] Following his death, Harald's wife, Rena, gifted a Steinway piano to St Magnus Cathedral in memory of her husband.

119. Sir R. A. A. S. Macrae 1915-1999

Within St Magnus Cathedral, the Friends of St Magnus have a collection trolley. It is usually found near the crossing and it has the following dedication:

Col Sir Robert Macrae was one of the key organisers of the "Save St Magnus" appeal.

THIS DONATION BOX IS DEDICATED
TO THE MEMORY OF
COL. SIR R. A. A. S. MACRAE
KCVO, KSt, O. O., MBE 1915-1999
WHO WORKED TIRELESSLY FOR
THE PRESERVATION OF ST MAGNUS
CATHEDRAL.

Robert Andrew Alexander Scarth Macrae, or *RAAS* as he was known to his military colleagues, or Bobby to his friends, was born in Purley, Surrey and attended school in Lancing in Sussex, before going on to Sandhurst. His father, also called Robert, who was an Inspector General of Police in India and later Commissioner of the Port of London Authority, had Orkney connections.[1049] The previous mentioned Robert's father, who came to Kirkwall as Procurator Fiscal, had married Agnes, daughter of Robert Scarth of Binscarth.[1050] As a result, the young Robert had many holidays in Orkney. These continued after his father's death when Robert was only 11.[1051]

Robert was commissioned into the Seaforth Highlanders in 1935 and had become Adjutant of the 4th Battalion by the start of the Second World War. He was part of the British Expeditionary Force in France in the first year of the war. His battalion fought a succession of defensive battles against the German advance, thus helping the Dunkirk evacuation. Robert was eventually taken prisoner at St Valery in June 1940 and spent the next five years in German prisoner-of-war camps, which included Dachau.[1052] Before the war, Robert had become engaged to Violet 'Toby' MacLellan from Dumbarton and, within a month of his repatriation, the couple were married.

Robert continued his service in the army after the war and his first posting was back in Germany, followed by a spell in Greece. In 1952 he was appointed second-in-command of the Black Watch, seeing two years action in Korea, and participating in the first and second Battles of the Hook. He was awarded an MBE for his services during this conflict. After Korea, he served with the Black Watch in Kenya during the Mau Mau emergency. In 1956 he was appointed Commanding Officer of the Regimental Training Depot at Fort George before commanding the 11th Seaforths at Dingwall. Having been promoted to the rank of Colonel in 1963, Robert retired from the army in 1968 and returned to the family home of Grindelay in Orphir.

He took on the tenancy of Binscarth Farm after the death of his cousin, Bob Scarth, eventually purchasing the farm in 1978. As well as farming, Robert was very active in the community. He represented North Ronaldsay on Orkney County Council from 1970 until its demise in 1974, followed by a four-year spell on the new Orkney Islands Council. He also served on Orkney Health Board and was appointed a Justice of the Peace and Honorary Sheriff. He became a Deputy Lieutenant of Orkney in 1946 and Vice-Lord Lieutenant from 1967, before being appointed Lord Lieutenant from 1972 to 1990.

Robert was heavily involved in the Longhope disaster appeal after the Longhope lifeboat was lost with all hands in the Pentland Firth in 1969. A short time later, when it was realised that St Magnus Cathedral was in danger of collapse, he was one of the key organisers of the 'Save St Magnus' appeal.

In 1987, Robert was personally decorated by King Olaf of Norway, being made Commander with Star of the Order of St Olaf, the highest award a foreigner can receive. He was made a Freeman of Orkney in 1990 and that year also saw him made Knight Commander of the Royal Victorian Order (KCVO), a personal gift from the Queen, following her visit to Orkney in 1987.

Robert died in the Balfour Hospital on November 15th 1999, with his funeral service taking place in St Magnus Cathedral.

Poets' Corner

At the east end of the Cathedral, near the sleeping figure of John Rae, is a series of plaques in honour of eight twentieth century Orcadian poets, writers, artists and historians, some of whom were nationally and internationally renowned in their day. The term 'Poets' Corner' is usually linked to a part of the south transept of Westminster Abbey, which contains a high number of memorials to poets, playwrights and writers. This part of the east end of St Magnus Cathedral is the Orkney equivalent. The plaques are set up thus:

GEORGE MACKAY BROWN 1921-1996 POET	ROBERT RENDALL 1898-1967 POET AND CONCHOLOGIST	
EDWIN MUIR POET 1887-1959 A FREEMAN OF THIS ROYAL BURGH	JOHN MOONEY 1862-1950 HISTORIAN Historian Author Antiquary	J. STORER CLOUSTON 1870-1944
STANLEY CURSITER 1887-1976 HER MAJESTY'S PAINTER & LIMNER A FREEMAN OF THIS ROYAL BURGH	HUGH MARWICK D. Lit 1881-1965 SCHOLAR AND HISTORIAN	ERIC LINKLATER 1899-1974 AUTHOR

There is one surprising omission from this illustrious group; the name of folklorist, broadcaster and journalist, Ernest Walker Marwick (1915-1977). Without him, this quiet corner of the Cathedral might not have become known as Poets' Corner. This is perhaps a slight exaggeration, but it was Ernest Marwick who was instrumental in the resurgence of poetry in post-war Orkney, through his friendships with Robert Rendall, George Mackay Brown and the dialect writer, Christina Costie. He also published *An Anthology of Orkney Verse* in 1949, which gathered the poetry of the islands from the Norse period, with skaldic verse from Earl Rognvald Kolsson and Bishop Bjarni Kolbeinsson, through to modern times, including poems from Robert Rendall and, for the first time in print, George Mackay Brown.[1053]

The son of an Evie crofter and denied a secondary education because of illness, Ernest was too humble for his own good. According to his friend, Dr Ray Fereday, he was so rigorously self-critical that he was embarrassed by the possibility of being given a memorial in St Magnus Cathedral, even expressing an objection in his will to being so commemorated. It is to be hoped that in due course the humility of this reluctant local hero can be overridden and he be given the honour he deserves in the building he loved.

120. J. Storer Clouston 1870-1944

This bronze plaque, mounted on polished wood and designed by Stanley Cursiter, was unveiled by Provost Mrs Leitch in June 1971.[1054]

J. STORER CLOUSTON
1870-1944
HISTORIAN AUTHOR ANTIQUARY

On Sir Thomas Clouston's plaque (106) are the words, "a loyal Orcadian". Sir Thomas certainly instilled in his son, Joseph Storer Clouston, a love of and loyalty to Orkney. Storer Clouston was actually born in Cumberland, in 1870, while his father was Superintendant of the local asylum. He was educated at Merchiston Castle School in Edinburgh and Magdalen College, Oxford. At both school and college, Storer Clouston was very athletic, being captain of the rugby team and winning many medals as a sprinter. He, along with Lord Lovat, introduced curling to Oxford.[1055] With his father having ambitions for him to become a doctor, Storer Clouston studied medicine in his first year at Oxford, but the squeamish student, who could not stand the sight of blood, soon rebelled. At his father's insistence, he switched to law and completed his BA before being called to the English Bar at the Inner Temple in 1895.

J. Storer Clouston, pictured here outside Smoogro House in Orphir, might have had a glittering law career had he not discovered another talent - writing. He became a successful novelist, with one of his books, A Spy in Black, being made into a film, but his passion was historical research, especially Norse history. *Orkney Library Photographic Archive*

A glittering legal career might have followed, had he not discovered another talent, writing. His novel, *Lunatic at Large*, published in 1899 and undoubtedly influenced by his father's expertise, made him widely known in Britain and America. Because of public demand, there were several sequels to the book and it was made into a film in 1928. His First World War spy thriller, *The Spy in Black*, was also made into a film, being directed by Michael Powell in 1938 and world premiered in the Albert Kinema, Kirkwall, with both the writer and the director present.[1056] His 1912 novel, *His First Offence*, was set to film by director Marcel Carné, in collaboration with screen writer Jacques Prévert, as the 1937 French comedy, *Drôle de Drame*. Storer Clouston produced a large number of novels and plays, being admired by P. G. Wodehouse, among others.[1057]

While writing was his bread and butter, historical research, especially into the Norse history of Orkney, was his passion. At first, Storer Clouston worked with

Alfred W. Johnston in collecting and transcribing old records. The two men, however, fell out badly after Storer Clouston published his *Records of the Orkney Earldom* in 1914. In a series of letters to the local press, Johnston berated Clouston for not acknowledging his help in interpreting old documents and poured scorn over Clouston's attempts at tracing the origins of the Clouston family name.[1058]

It was, however, Storer Clouston who proved to be the brilliant researcher, with his work on medieval Orkney being unsurpassed at the time. For a relatively small community, Orkney produced a formidable array of historians in the first half of the twentieth century. A group of them formed the Orkney Antiquarian Society in 1922, with Storer Clouston as its president for much of its existence. The Society published 15 volumes of *Proceedings*, to which he contributed a large number of papers. His greatest achievement was the much admired *History of Orkney*, published in 1932. A criticism of Storer Clouston, however, is his dismissal of Orkney history after 1611, an accusation he openly acknowledged, admitting that he had treated the last 300 years in "what may seem a somewhat cavalier fashion".[1059] It is also recognised today that his interpretation of Orkney's earlier history was rather romanticised, but it nevertheless remains a most readable account.

Storer Clouston also dabbled in archaeology, taking part in digs at Clouston in Stenness, the Bu in Cairston, the Round Church in Orphir, Westness in Rousay and Cubbie Roo's Castle in Wyre. He was often consulted during the renovation of St Magnus Cathedral and it was his suggestion to include old Orkney coats-of-arms in the stained glass windows of the south transept and in the wheel of the great east window.[1060]

Storer Clouston married his cousin, Winifred Clouston, in 1903.[1061] Prior to the start of the First World War, Storer Clouston made his home in Orkney, living at Smoogro, in Orphir. Towards the end of the First World War, he worked for the Government, being a Sub-Commissioner in the National Service Department (Scotland) Agricultural Section. He entered Orkney County Council in 1919, becoming Convener of the newly constituted County Council in 1930 and Chairman of Orkney Harbours Commission from 1933. He was also Chairman of the Police Committee of the County Council and was a trustee of Balfour Hospital. During King George V's Silver Jubilee in 1935 he was awarded an OBE.

Storer Clouston died suddenly at his home in 1944 and was buried in the Orphir Churchyard. Six policemen acted as the bearer party for his funeral.[1062]

121. John Mooney 1862-1950

The plaque to John Mooney was unveiled by his son, Rev. Harald Mooney, in 1968.[1063]

JOHN MOONEY
1862-1950 HISTORIAN
A FREEMAN OF THIS ROYAL BURGH

John Mooney never received a university education, but nevertheless overcame many difficulties to become one of Orkney's most prominent historians. He was Kirkwall born and retained a deep love of the city for all of his life. While his work is not now so well regarded as that of his fellow antiquarians, Storer Clouston and Hugh Marwick, his researches gave local people an understanding of and pride in Kirkwall's city status, along with the unique public ownership of Orkney's most important building.

John Mooney's early life involved a constant struggle against poverty. He was born illegitimate on 17th July 1862 at Main Street in Kirkwall. His mother, who was illiterate at the time of his birth, was Betsy Burgess, an agricultural servant.[1064] His father, John Mooney, was a stoneware merchant, who, along with his parents and siblings, had come from Buckie.[1065] Young John received his early education at the old Glaitness School, but his schooldays were brief and none too happy.[1066] Being of small stature, he no doubt had to endure many taunts from his fellow pupils. He had, however, a determination to learn and received the backing of some important benefactors, such as B. H. Hossack (98) and Alfred Baikie's father, William Layman Cowan.[1067]

After leaving school, Mooney was first employed with a seeds merchant on Junction Road. This experience brought him into contact with the farming community and acquainted him with the problems of Orkney agriculture. A spell as a reporter on the *Orkney and Shetland Telegraph* followed, during which time he witnessed the visit of William Gladstone and Alfred Tennyson to Kirkwall.

In 1884, Robert Garden (102) asked Mooney to help him expand his business. John Mooney started as Robert Garden's confidential clerk, some ten years after Garden had started up in Orkney. Much of Robert Garden's success can be attributed to the work of John Mooney. He had a good understanding of the problems facing farmers, was tactful with customers and was able to look after the office side of the expanding business. In 1916, Mooney became a director and secretary of the firm when it was set up as a limited company. He had the highest regard for Robert Garden and was very proud of the social role Garden's travelling shops played in Orkney, particularly by bringing good reading material to the remoter parts.[1068] He continued in his role with the company for more than half a century.

John Mooney was active in public affairs from a relatively young age, being elected to the school board for Kirkwall in 1897. Within a few years he became a member of Kirkwall Town Council and represented that body on the Kirkwall Educational Trust. He was re-elected to the Town Council in 1911 and missed out topping the poll by receiving one less vote than P. C. Flett (117). During his time on the Council, there was some debate on the merits of sending a representative to the antiquated Convention of Royal Burghs. Mooney said he looked forward to the time when Kirkwall would have a representative in a Home Rule Parliament for Scotland, but until then, he thought the Convention currently did good work.[1069] It was through Mooney's initiative, while a member of the Town Council, that Kirkwall became regarded as a City and Royal Burgh. It was a theme that would consume his later years.

With strong Christian convictions, Mooney was a member of the Cathedral congregation and became ordained as a lay preacher. His religious convictions also saw him as an advocate of total abstinence and he was very prominent in the Temperance Movement.

In his younger days, Mooney dabbled in poetry, winning a *Boy's Own Paper* Award of Merit in 1881 for his poem, *One Volunteer Worth Three Pressed Men*.[1070] Some of his verses appeared later in a Scottish anthology.[1071] In 1894, he co-wrote, with J. Wilson, a witty, dramatic burlesque in verse, which was produced as a comedy drama in the Temperance Hall, Kirkwall. Serious historic research, however, took precedence over this light-hearted work and, unsurprisingly, Mooney was one of the founding members of Orkney Antiquarian Society, contributing many articles to its *Proceedings*. He wrote a number of books, the first of which was *Eynhallow, the Holy Island of the Orkneys* in 1924. His strong belief in the essential holiness of St Magnus was examined in *St Magnus-Earl of Orkney*, published in 1935. *The Cathedral and Royal Burgh of Kirkwall*, in which he examined how King James III of Scotland was able to convey St Magnus Cathedral to the Magistrates and Community of Kirkwall, followed in 1943, with a second edition published in 1949. While in his eighties, Mooney embarked on the ambitious task of editing Kirkwall's burgh charters, which was published by Aberdeen's Third Spalding Club. It was an unfulfilled ambition of his to see a memorial erected to Patrick Craigie, the seventeenth century member of Kirkwall Town Council, who bankrupted himself defending Kirkwall's rights and privileges from the attacks of the Earl of Morton. Mooney was also keen to see a suitable memorial erected in St Magnus Churchyard for those removed from the Cathedral in the nineteenth and twentieth century renovations. He pointed out that the dust of earls, bishops and other Orcadians of high lineage and accomplishments mingled there with the dust of other worthy islanders.

John Mooney was elected a Fellow of the Society of Scottish Antiquarians in 1922 and, in 1945, he was rewarded, appropriately, for all his work on behalf of his beloved Kirkwall when he was made an Honorary Burgess and Freeman of the Burgh. The other recipients on the day were ex Provost John White and Rev Andrew Campbell (115). Mooney was too frail to attend the ceremony, which was held in the Town Hall, and his son, Rev. Harald Mooney, attended on his behalf. After the ceremony, Provost P. C. Flett personally delivered the scrolls to Mooney's home at Cromwell Cottage.

John Mooney had married Isabella Jane Barron, from St Margaret's Hope, in 1902. Three sons and a daughter were the product of this happy marriage. Their son, Erlend, was chosen from over a thousand applicants to be cabin boy on Ernest Shackleton's 1921 Antarctica expedition. Unfortunately, seasickness got the better of the boy and he was sent home from Madeira. The Mooneys received a telegram from Shackleton saying, "regret necessary action solely in boy's interest, he was always willing". Erlend predeceased his father when he met an accidental death in Nigeria. Isabella died in 1945 and John was survived by his sons, the long-serving Deerness minister, Rev. Harald Mooney, and ICI research scientist, Ronald Mooney, plus his daughter, Embla, who had looked after him in his last years.

122. Hugh Marwick 1881-1965

This bronze plaque, designed by Stanley Cursiter and mounted on polished wood, was unveiled by Provost Mrs Leitch in June 1971.[1072]

HUGH MARWICK D. Lit
1881-1965
Scholar and Philologist

Hugh Marwick was born in Rousay in 1881 and was brought up at the cottage of Guidhall in the district of Sourin. His father, also Hugh, had spent time abroad, being apprenticed as a shipwright in New Zealand. Young Hugh was educated at Sourin Public School and his academic ability allowed him to become a pupil-teacher in his home school before setting off to Aberdeen, to the United Free Church Training College. After two years training, he acted as assistant master for three years at Newbattle Public School in Midlothian, where he earned his teacher's diploma and enough money to fund himself through university.

Hugh Marwick receiving the Freedom of Kirkwall from Provost James Flett, the author's great uncle.

He started at Edinburgh University in the autumn of 1905 and graduated four years later with MA Honours in English Language and Literature. This was despite ill health and the lack of finance to attend his final year in Edinburgh. Instead, he was able to study at home in Orkney thanks to the help of a university friend, who sent him lecture notes and loaned him books. Despite the difficulties he faced, he returned to Edinburgh in 1909 to sit his final exams and was one of only three students who obtained a First Class Honours degree in English that year.

In October 1910, Marwick took up the appointment of English master in the Burnley Grammar School, Lancashire. Three years later, he was asked by the Oxford University Press to edit a school version of George Elliot's *Silas Marner* and he followed this up with Tennyson's *Enoch Arden*, in 1914. It was in Burnley that he met Jane Barrit, who became his wife in 1914, about the time he was appointed to the post of headmaster of Kirkwall Grammar School (then called the Burgh School). He took up his post, which had an annual salary of £260, just after the outbreak of war. This was a difficult time, with many of his staff volunteering to join the army. Of six male teachers in the Secondary Department in 1914, only one survived the war.[1073] Marwick's wife took some time to settle in Orkney, not helped by a difficult pregnancy, which affected her health thereafter. Tragically, their only child, also called Hugh, died in an accident when still a boy.[1074]

Shortly after graduating from Edinburgh University, Marwick was awarded a Carnegie Research Scholarship to study the Orkney Dialect. After many years of collecting material and working on his own thesis, Marwick was rewarded with a Doctorate of Literature from Edinburgh University in 1926. The thesis, entitled *The Orkney Norn*, was published by the Clarendon Press in 1929.[1075] This was also the year he was appointed as Orkney's Director of Education.

Marwick was one of the co-founders of the Orkney Antiquarian Society and fulfilled the role of secretary for the lifetime of the society. He contributed a large number of papers to the 15 volumes of *Proceedings*, which the society published between 1922 and 1939. He saw seven of his books published during his lifetime and another was published posthumously. Along with his study of the Orkney Norn, his most important work related to the place names of Orkney. While much of his historic work on Orkney institutions has now been discredited, his study on Orkney words and place names still provides the bedrock of modern research.[1076]

The Orkney Antiquarian Society did not survive the Second World War, but Dr Marwick kept the flame of historic research alight in post war Orkney through the Orkney Record and Antiquarian Society, which published papers in its *Orkney Miscellany*. Realizing the importance of studying Norwegian sources to help interpret Orkney place names, he was in constant communication with Scandinavian scholars, some of whom came to Orkney to seek him out.

Dr Marwick received many honours during his lifetime. He was appointed Honorary Sheriff-substitute for Orkney in 1936, was admitted Companion of the Order of the British Empire (OBE) in 1938 for services to education, was conferred an Honorary LL.D by Aberdeen University in 1956 and was awarded an Honorary Fellowship by the Society of Antiquaries of Scotland. After retiring in 1946, he was granted the Knighthood of the Norwegian Order of St Olaf by King Haakon of Norway and, in 1964, the University of Bergen gave him an Honorary D. Phil., the first person outside of Norway to be accorded this honour.[1077] In addition, the Freedom of Kirkwall was conferred on him in 1954. His portrait was painted by Stanley Cursiter (126) and was hung in the gym hall of the then Grammar School.

Dr Marwick resided at Alton House in Kirkwall. After suffering a stroke, he died in Eastbank Hospital on 21st May 1965. He received a civic funeral, with the service taking place in St Magnus Cathedral.

123. Edwin Muir 1887-1959

The plaque to the memory of Edwin Muir, which was designed by Stanley Cursiter (126), was the first of the plaques in Poets' Corner, being unveiled in October 1961.

EDWIN MUIR
POET 1887-1959

Edwin Muir became one of the central figures in the

Scottish literary renaissance of the interwar years, which sought to revive Scottish writing. He, however, fell out with its other leading exponents, such as Hugh MacDairmid, over Muir's rejection of the use of the Scots language and his promotion of English as the language of literature.

Muir was born in Deerness in 1887. He was two when his parents, James Muir from Sanday and Elizabeth Cormack from Deerness, left their farm, called the Folly, and moved to the Bu in the island of Wyre. Muir would later look back on his time in Wyre as something of an idyllic Eden. This was apart from his experience of school, which he hated; a school inspector had described him as "a particularly stupid boy".[1078] Increasing rents forced the family to move from the Bu to the less fertile neighbouring farm of Helzigartha and then out of Wyre altogether, to the Mainland farm of Garth, near the present day airport. Here the land was poor, needing constant draining, and the dwelling-house was damp. Muir's mother was constantly ill and his father's health broke down trying to work the farm. Gradually, most of his brothers and sisters left for jobs in Kirkwall, Glasgow or Edinburgh. His father gave up Garth, when Muir was 13 and, after a year in Kirkwall, the family moved to the slums of Glasgow in 1901. Apart from the deeply traumatic effect this had on the sensitive, young Muir, the move was a disastrous one for the family. Within a few years, both his parents and two of his brothers were dead.[1079] Muir had no doubts about the original cause of their descent into the squalor of the Glasgow slums. Their landlord in Wyre had been General Burroughs (100). Muir wrote, "He was a bad landlord and in a few years drove my father out of the farm by his exactions".[1080]

Muir experienced a better time at school in Kirkwall than the start he had made in Wyre, soon developing a passion for reading and realising that he wanted to be an author. After moving to Glasgow, he worked in a series of menial and unfulfilling office jobs and soon became attracted to Socialism and developed an infatuation with the German philosopher, Nietzsche.

After the outbreak of the First World War, Muir was refused entry into the army owing to ill health, but he secured work in a shipbuilding office.[1081] By 1916, he was contributing poetry to a magazine called *New Age* under the pseudonym Edward Moore, and he published his first book, *We Moderns*, in 1918. This was the year he met Willa Anderson, whose parents came from Shetland.[1082] She had studied classics at St Andrews and was then a lecturer in a women's college in London. After the two married in the summer of 1919, Willa had to give up her teaching job. Muir later wrote that their marriage was the most fortunate event of his life.[1083]

Edwin Muir was born in Deerness and became a poet on an international stage. He was appointed Norton Professor of English at Harvard University in 1955 and was made a CBE in the Coronation Honours List.

Orkney Library Photographic Archive

Being exiles from their respective island backgrounds, the Muirs never settled down anywhere to make roots. In 1921, the pair gave up their jobs and headed for the Continent, travelling extensively in Europe over the next few years. During that time, they started translating from German to English works from writers such as Frank Kafka, Heinrich Mann and Hermann Broch. Muir also began to gain a reputation as a literary critic and poet, with his *First Poems* being published in 1925. More volumes of poetry followed over the next thirty years, along with three novels, a description of John Knox, some travel writing, a number of critical works and, probably most well known, his autobiography. It was in his critical piece *Scott and Scotland* (1936) that Muir enraged his friend, Hugh MacDiarmid, by declaring that Scots, as a literary language, was dead and that Scotland could only create a national literature by writing in English.

Their son, Gavin Anderson Cormack Muir, was born in Surrey in 1927. Following a long holiday in Orkney to help Gavin recover from an accident, the family settled in St Andrews, Fife in 1934.

During the war years, Muir started to give lectures to soldiers and refugees from the Continent on behalf of the British Council. This led to Muir becoming, in the immediate post war years, Director of the British Institute in Prague and later in Rome. During his time in Prague, he witnessed the Communist seizure of power in Czechoslovakia. In 1950, Muir accepted the post of Warden of Newbattle Abbey College, near Edinburgh, which had been set up to give working class adults a second chance to gain an education. Among his students were fellow Orcadians, George Mackay Brown (127) and Ernest Marwick.

In 1955 Muir was made Norton Professor of English at Harvard University in the USA, an appointment that lasted one year. He retired to Swaffham Prior in Cambridge, where, in 1959, he died and was buried. During his life, he received honorary degrees from the Universities of Prague, Edinburgh, Rennes and Leeds, was given a number of poetry prizes and was made a CBE in the 1953 Coronation Honours List.[1084] A memorial bench to Muir was erected in the small village of Swanston, near Edinburgh, where Muir spent time in the 1950s.

124. Robert Rendall 1898-1967

ROBERT RENDALL
1898-1967
POET AND CONCHOLOGIST

Robert Rendall was one of those multitalented individuals who appear from time to time in small communities such as Orkney. As well as being an outstanding poet, his Orkney dialect poems capturing the very essence of Orkney, and an expert on sea shells, he was also an archaeologist, discovering the Broch of Gurness in Evie, an artist, a travel writer and a theologian.

Robert was born in Glasgow to Westray parents, his father coming from a family of weavers going back six generations. Forced to leave Westray as a result of economic hardship, his father went to sea and obtained his master's ticket by the time he was thirty three. His wife, Barbara Craigie Garrioch, moved to Glasgow to be near him when his ship was in port. Born into the city tenements and pollution of Glasgow, young Robert was a sickly child. When he was seven, he was not expected to live another year and so his mother took him back to Orkney to settle in Kirkwall, a move that Robert was convinced saved his life.[1085]

Long separation from his family, the hard life at sea and lack of promotional prospects had taken their toll on Robert's father. He became increasingly depressed and one day young Robert found him shortly after

Robert Rendall had a very difficult upbringing and rose to become one of the stars in the Orkney literary world. His dialect poetry was extremely popular and he also became an expert in shells and nature.

Orkney Library Photographic Archive

having attempted to cut his throat. He was admitted to the Royal Mental Hospital in Aberdeen, where he died three years later. His committal to a mental institution led to his son leaving school at the age of thirteen and taking employment in the Kirkwall drapery business of George Rendall & Co., which had been founded by an uncle of Robert's father.[1086] Starting off as an apprentice, he eventually succeeded to a third share of the business.

Robert was called up in 1916 and joined the navy, being posted as an officer's steward on HMS *Imperieuse*, which was anchored in Longhope Bay, and acted as a supply vessel and post office for the Grand Fleet in Scapa Flow. It was about this time that Robert began a systematic study of Orkney sea shells, having been encouraged by botanist and schoolmaster, Magnus Spence of Deerness. Robert continued his study for forty years, becoming the recognised authority on the marine life of Orkney and receiving the recognition of the wider scientific community when his researches were published in the *Proceedings of the Royal Society of Edinburgh* in 1956, under the title, *Mollusca Orcadensia*.

After the First World War, Robert was drawn into the work of Orkney Antiquarian Society by John Mooney and developed an interest in archaeology. He was taught the rudiments by William Traill of Holland, the laird of Papa Westray, who showed him how to make plans of an archaeological site.[1087] In 1930, he presented a paper to the Society on a survey he had carried out on a newly ploughed field near Quanterness, St Ola, in which he had discovered a Stone Age 'factory' for making flint implements. A painting expedition led to the discovery of Orkney's best preserved Iron Age broch, at Gurness, when the leg of his easel sank into a hole in the ground.

Having attended night school to learn German, Robert made a number of trips to Germany in the 1930s. Initially, it was his involvement with the European missionary work of the Christian Brethren (more commonly known as the 'Plymouth Brethren') that took him to that country. He was a committed Christian, having been influenced by his mother. During his visits to Germany, he witnessed the rise of fascism and the suppression of evangelical groups like the Brethren.

By the outbreak of the Second World War, Robert had become a pacifist, being influenced, not only by Brethren belief, but also by discussions with John Mooney, who had portrayed St Magnus as an early Christian pacifist. Robert was anti-fascist, however, and being too old for active service, he bought a croft, Northbank, at Scapa, to cultivate the land and contribute to the war effort in his own way. By this stage, he was becoming hard of hearing, giving him a reason to leave the running of his drapery business to another partner.[1088] Having never learnt to drive, nor even ride a bicycle, his attempts at farming were very small scale.[1089] It was a life he enjoyed, however, and out of this experience of crofting came his first book of poems, *Country Sonnets*, published after the war. Robert had long been keen on poetry and, as early as 1915, had produced advertisements in verse form, extolling the virtues of his drapery firm.[1090] Hugh Marwick wrote a foreword to *Country Sonnets* and Stanley Cursiter encouraged him to send a copy to James Ferguson of *The Glasgow Herald*, who ensured Robert's poems were read by a much wider audience. Ferguson declared in a broadcast that "his first book contains more promise than any first book of poems I have seen published since Hugh MacDiarmid's *Sangscaw*".

Robert's next book of poems, *Orkney Variants* (1951), included some of his best dialect poems, such as *Cragsman's Widow* and *Salt i' the Bluid*. It was followed, in 1957, by *Shore Poems*, which included *Renewal*, described by George Mackay Brown as one of the most perfect sonnets ever written.[1091] Once Robert and his mother moved into Kirkwall from Scapa, he was able to discuss his poetry with his near neighbour and friend, Ernest Marwick. Near the end of his life, he gathered some other poems he wished to preserve and published them in a slim volume called *The Hidden Land*. After publication of his *Mollusca Orcadensia*, he wrote a semi-autobiographical book, *The Orkney Shore*, which described his early life, the influences which led him to the study of shells and the way his interests in nature, literature and religion were united on the shores of Orkney.

His lifelong interest in Christian doctrine saw expression in numerous articles for various religious journals and magazines. He also wrote two religious books, the first, *History, Prophecy and God* (1954), examining his thoughts on the Christian interpretation of history. The second, a collection of his religious writing, was published in 1956 as *The Greatness and Glory of Christ*.[1092] Despite being a theologian, Robert had a wicked sense of humour, frequently getting up to what Orcadians would call 'devilment'.

After his mother died in 1949, he began travelling again in Europe, visiting Italy for the first time in 1950. He was drawn by a wish to see its classical monuments and works of art. The Adriatic port of Pesaro became the base for his travels in Italy during the nine visits he made, the last of which was in 1964.[1093]

After his health deteriorated in 1965, he moved into St Peter's Home in Stromness, where he was able to resume his friendship with George Mackay Brown and also enjoy the company of the artist and teacher, Ian MacInnes, who painted Robert's portrait. During the last year of his life, he was recognised with a pension on the Civil List, an honour granted by the Queen. It was Stanley Cursiter and Lord Birsay who had made the arrangements to secure this deserved honour.

125. Eric Linklater 1899-1974

ERIC LINKLATER
1899-1974
AUTHOR

As well as being a novelist with an international reputation, Eric Linklater was an essayist, poet, biographer, historian, playwright and broadcaster. He also travelled extensively and, as a soldier, witnessed the horrors of war at first hand.

Although born in Penarth, Wales, Eric Robert Russell Linklater was always proud of his Orkney roots. His father, Robert Linklater of Mosseter in Dounby, was a master mariner who had married Elizabeth Young, the daughter of a sea captain. She wrote of her early life on sailing ships in her book, *A Child Under Sail*.[1094]

Eric Linklater, with his wife, Marjorie, in 1933, was a best-selling novelist and proud of his Orkney roots. A school teacher's report once stated he was doing fine "but was handicapped with a sense of humour".

Orkney Library Photographic Archive

When Eric was young, the family moved back to Orkney, where he spent much of his childhood. He was educated at Aberdeen Grammar School and entered the University of Aberdeen in 1916 to study medicine, after failing to enlist at the tender age of fifteen. He loved to quote from one of his early school reports, which stated that, on the whole, he was doing fairly well, "but is handicapped by a sense of humour".[1095] His career was to prove otherwise.

His studies were soon interrupted by military service, initially serving with a yeomanry unit, which used bicycles instead of horses, and subsequently with the Black Watch as a sniper in the trenches of the Western Front. His glittering career in literature very nearly did not happen when he narrowly missed getting his head blown off. A German bullet from a machine gun went through his helmet and made a neat dent in the back of his skull, resulting in a scar he carried for the rest of his life.[1096]

After demobilisation, he went back to Aberdeen University to continue with medicine but, after failing anatomy four times, switched to English Literature, in which he excelled. He became the editor of the university magazine, *Alma Mater,* and graduated with distinction in 1925. Taking up journalism and fulfilling his ambition to travel, he became assistant editor of *The Times of India* in Bombay. Travelling through Baghdad, Persia and the Caucasis, he returned to Aberdeen two years later as an assistant to the professor of English. In 1929, he published his first novel, *Whitemaa's Saga*, which was partly set in Orkney and caused considerable excitement in the islands.[1097]

Linklater spent two years in America, then in the grip of Prohibition, as a Commonwealth Fellow at Cornell and Berkeley. His experience across the Atlantic provided the inspiration for the novel which established his reputation, *Juan in America.* As well as being a best seller in the UK, it was regarded in some quarters as somewhat 'naughty' and his reputation as a risqué writer endured in Orkney for some time.[1098] It also annoyed the Commonwealth Foundation, who accused Linklater of showing disrespect to the institutions of the United States. *Juan in America* was followed by the Orcadian-themed, *The Men of Ness,* reflecting his fascination with Old Norse literature and culture.

Being an ardent Scottish nationalist, he stood unsuccessfully as a parliamentary candidate in the 1933 East Fife by-election, losing his deposit in the process. Eric was incapable of giving the same speech more than twice and soon realised he was not cut out for politics. The experience, however, provided the stimulus for his brilliantly creative satire, *Magnus Merriman.*

1933 was also the year he married Marjorie McIntyre, daughter of Ian McIntyre, a Unionist MP, Scottish international rugby player and Writer to the Signet. After a period in Italy, followed by visits to India and China, the couple settled in Harray, where Eric had spent much of his childhood, and renovated the house at Merkister. It was during this spell in Orkney that he provided the narrative for the octocentenary pageant celebrating the founding of St Magnus Cathedral. Being a restless individual, he continued to travel.

In 1938, Linklater was commissioned as a captain into the newly formed Orkney (Fortress) Company Royal Engineers. This Territorial Army unit, made up of local volunteers, was to man the searchlights in support of the coastal defence guns of Scapa Flow. By the time war broke out, he was in command of the unit, having risen to the rank of major. To help maintain morale among the tens of thousands of service men and women in Orkney during World War Two, it was Linklater's idea to have a printed newspaper, dedicated entirely to the troops. Acting as its first editor, *The Orkney Blast* was launched on 17th January 1941 and continued to be printed each week at *The Orcadian* for the next four years.[1099] Shortly before its first publication, Linklater was transferred to the Directorate of Public Relations at the War Office, where he was able to travel fairly widely, considering the restrictions of wartime. He produced a pamphlet, *Northern Garrisons,* covering both Orkney and the Faroes. For the radio, he composed a series of imaginary conversations between ordinary servicemen and past greats, such as Lincoln, Lenin, Socrates and Beethoven.[1100] He went back to Italy and witnessed some of the hard fighting there, later writing an official history of the campaign. He also helped to rediscover the art treasures of Florence, lost during the war. His experiences gave him the idea for a novel, *Private Angelo*, which was an immediate success and was made into a film in 1949, starring Peter Ustinov.

After the war, Linklater briefly returned to Orkney before moving the family (which now included two sons and two daughters) to Pitcalzean House near Nigg. Orkney still remained important to him and he returned often to meet old friends and fish the Harray Loch. In 1951, he went to Korea, with the temporary rank of lieutenant-colonel, to write the official accounts of the war. He went on to visit Australia, New Zealand and New Guinea.

Many honours came his way, serving as Rector of Aberdeen University between 1945 and 1948, and receiving an honorary doctorate during this time. He was awarded a CBE in 1954, became deputy lieutenant for Ross and Cromarty from 1968 to 1973 and was elected a Fellow of the Royal Society of Edinburgh in 1971. Linklater died in Aberdeen on 7th November 1974 and was buried in the Harray Kirkyard.

126. Stanley Cursiter 1887-1976

STANLEY CURSITER
1887-1976
HER MAJESTY'S PAINTER & LIMNER
A FREEMAN OF THIS ROYAL BURGH

Stanley Cursiter was an artist of distinction, who accumulated a huge list of honours and who fully deserves a special place in the history of Scottish art. He was born into a relatively well-off Kirkwall family, spending his first four years at East Road, before the family moved out of town to Alton House. His father, John Cursiter, was a Kirkwall merchant and his mother, Mary Thomson, was the daughter of a Sanday farmer. Stanley's father having died when he was only nine, he developed a close relationship with his uncle, the antiquarian, James W. Cursiter. He was a sickly child, missing a lot of early schooling because of asthma and bronchitis.[1101]

Stanley Cursiter was an outstanding Orcadian artist who, proposed and designed, St Rognvald Chapel in the Cathedral. His paintings of Orkney landscapes are unrivalled and he was once the King's Painter and Limner in Scotland. *Orkney Library Photographic Archive*

While at school in Kirkwall, where one of his fellow pupils was Edwin Muir (123), Cursiter developed an ambition to become an architect. Leaving school in 1904, he sought an apprenticeship with Kirkwall architect, T. S. Peace, who turned him down and advised him to widen his horizons by seeking an apprenticeship in Edinburgh. Soon after arriving in the capital, he found there was insufficient money to fund an architectural apprenticeship. Instead, he found training with a firm of printers and lithographers, where he learned skills that provided a foundation for his painting and mapping skills. After attending a short course at the Royal College of Art in London, he returned to Edinburgh to study at the School of Art, making ends meet as a freelance designer. The heavy workload led to a breakdown before sitting his final diploma. Not wanting to continue another year as a student, he established himself as a designer, his main focus being to earn enough money to return to Orkney (or occasionally Shetland) each summer to paint.[1102]

Cursiter was soon making a living from his paintings. He was not frightened to experiment and, in 1913, embarked on a series of 'Futurist' paintings, having seen the first Post Impressionist Exhibition in London some years previously.[1103] Continuing to return home in the summer, he was witness to the restoration work in St Magnus Cathedral, which provided a source of inspiration for a number of his works.

The outbreak of war saw the artist volunteer for active service and, after initially being rejected on health grounds, he was eventually accepted into the Officer

The Stanley Cursiter-designed badge and chain of office for the Provost of Kirkwall, in the mid 1950s.

Training Corps, before being posted to the 1st Battalion of the Scottish Rifles, known as the Cameronians. On October 14th 1916, while on leave, he married Phyllis Hourston, whom he had first met in Kirkwall in 1910. A week later he was sitting in a front line trench on the Somme. He would not see Phyllis for another two years. The conditions in the trenches soon affected his health and he had to be hospitalised after contracting bronchitis and suffering a severe bout of asthma. He convalesced in the South of France, where he was able to do some painting and sketching. After succumbing to his illness a second time and being told he was of no further use to the British Army in France, he pleaded to be kept, actively seeking a position he could undertake. He drew up a list of his skills, pointing out that he had lithographic training and knew about printing. This eventually led to a transfer to the 4th Field Survey Battalion, where he soon excelled in map making. Cursiter devised a system of creating maps that was much quicker and more accurate by using a 'magic lantern' that he had inherited from his father to project the aerial photograph on to a map mounted on a board. One of the discoveries made during this mapping work was the identification of the 'Hindenburg Line', a massive defensive position built by the Germans in the winter of 1916-17 some distance back from the front. After a poor start to his military career, Cursiter had made a significant wartime contribution. He was rewarded with a military OBE and two mentions in dispatches.[1104]

Cursiter was demobbed in 1919 and returned to Phyllis in Edinburgh, resuming life as an artist. He purchased a house and studio in Royal Circus, in the New Town, and became President of the Society of Scottish Artists. In 1920, still suffering chest problems, he spent six months with Phyllis in the South of France to recuperate and to paint. Making life as an artist in the post war depression was very uncertain. Accordingly, he applied for the post of Keeper at the Scottish National Galleries in 1925, but initially accepted the job with a degree of reluctance, having been set on the idea of leasing a cottage on Fair Isle. He soon made a difference at the National Portrait Gallery, devising new heating and lighting systems to prevent damaging condensation emitting from the old steam radiators. He also redesigned the Gallery's interior after damage caused by a fire in a neighbouring building. More importantly, in partnership with a Dutch picture restorer, Martin de Wild, he developed new scientific methods of picture repair, establishing a restoration department at the National Gallery.[1105]

In 1930, Cursiter became Director of the National Galleries of Scotland, a post he held until 1948. Throughout this period, he advocated the urgent need for a gallery of modern art, which would also be a centre for Scottish craft and design. It was a major disappointment to him that he did not see this progressive idea realised during his time in office.[1106]

During this time, he continued to paint, producing more Orkney landscapes as well as some fine portraits, notably of Eric and Marjory Linklater (1933), which were presented as a wedding present to the couple. Having painted the houses at Shore Street, in Kirkwall, a number of times, he described their demolition to make way for oil storage tank, as a 'scandalous desecration' of the forefront of the town.[1107]

With the outbreak of war in 1939, the National and Portrait Galleries were closed, the paintings being moved to six country houses for safe keeping. Cursiter was given leave of absence to go to Southampton, where his services were required by the Ordnance Survey. He was put in charge of the drawing offices, overseeing nearly a thousand draughtsmen. By December 1940, he was back in Edinburgh to reopen the National Gallery for temporary exhibitions to illustrate the art of the British Allies. He arranged some eighty exhibitions during the war years, a quarter of them being for children. He was rewarded by the Educational Institute of Scotland for this work with children by an Honorary Fellowship. With the ending of the war in 1945, Cursiter oversaw the reopening of the Galleries and the return of the evacuated paintings.

A general view of St Rognvald Chapel.

In 1948, he was given a series of honours, including a CBE, Freeman of the City and Royal Burgh of Kirkwall and Fellow of the Royal Society of Edinburgh. He was also appointed as His Majesty's Painter and Limner in Scotland. In the same year, frustration at the lack of progress for a gallery of modern art influenced his decision to resign as Director of the National Galleries and return to Orkney to paint full time.

In Orkney, he converted an old boatyard in Stromness into his home and studio. Once he had finished converting his house, Stenigar, he embarked on a career as a portrait painter, using Henry Raeburn's old studio in Edinburgh.[1108]

There were also royal duties to perform and, in 1953, he painted the Queen receiving the Honours of Scotland in St Giles Cathedral. Later that year, he designed a new chain of office for the Provost of Kirkwall, along with other badges of office for the Town Council. This led to a disagreement with the Lord Lyon, who objected to the use of heraldic symbols taken from many old Kirkwall families and trades whose coats-of-arms had never been registered.[1109]

Increasing pain in his wrists and hands meant he had to give up painting. The Cursiters downsized, moving into a smaller house in Stromness in 1965. However, he was still able to do something special for the building that meant so much to him. Concerned that there was no memorial to St Rognvald, he proposed and designed St Rognvald Chapel at the east end of the choir of St Magnus Cathedral. His designs included a pulpit, communion table and lectern, all incorporating sixteenth and seventeenth century wooden panels which had been used previously to decorate the pews of important Orkney families. He also created plans for the figures of Kol, Rognvald and Bishop William. Wood found in the Cathedral by Cursiter was used for the carvings, which were produced by local master craftsman, Reynold Eunson. Finance was provided by the Society of the Friends of St Magnus, of which Cursiter was an Honorary President.[1110] A few years later, he played his part in raising funds for the 'Save St Magnus Cathedral Appeal', using his contacts around the world to publicise the Cathedral's plight.

Cursiter died in 1976, just short of his 89th birthday and was buried alongside his wife in the Finstown cemetery.

127. George Mackay Brown 1921-1996

GEORGE MACKAY BROWN
1921-1996
POET

George Mackay Brown became one of Scotland's greatest twentieth century writers, with a wide international reputation. He was born in Stromness on 17th October 1921, the youngest of six children. His mother, Mhairi Sheena Mackay, a native Gaelic speaker, came from Strathy in Sutherland. Her grandfather had been cleared out of Strathnaver by the Duke of Sutherland and forced north to become a crofter fisherman. She came to Orkney to work in the Stromness Hotel, then owned by a relative of her father. She married local man John Brown, a tailor by trade, but who had to supplement his income as a part-time postman. He also delivered laundry in Stromness for the Glaitness Laundry Company.[1111] The family lived at 80 Victoria Street until George was six, when their 'mad' landlady evicted them, the family moving a couple of hundred yards down the street to a dark, damp house in Melvin Place.[1112] This move proved very detrimental to the health of his father and, seven years later, the family moved into a modern council house in Well Park, where it was hoped his health would recover. This was not to be, however, and two years later, John Brown was forced to retire from the Post Office. With no pension, life became much harder for the family.

George showed a talent for writing from an early age, starting, when only seven, his own comic, *The Celt,* named after his favourite football team. Football at this stage was his passion and he himself was a natural at the game, scoring many goals for his Boys' Brigade team and also scoring, at the age of 13, for Stromness in a match against archrivals, Kirkwall. His footballing days were cut short, however, when he contracted measles at the age of 15. The illness had a lasting effect, leaving him physically and mentally damaged.

After failing his first attempt at Highers, George stayed on at school for an extra year, before taking a job sorting mail in Stromness Post Office. With war having broken out, he also joined the Home Guard. His call-up papers arrived in March 1941, but, instead of receiving a uniform, he was sent straight to Eastbank Hospital, after being diagnosed with tuberculosis at his medical examination. He spent six months in the sanatorium, his condition adding to the depression that developed in his teens. During his convalescence, he was able to read a great deal and it was at this time that he first encountered the *Orkneyinga Saga*, the story of St Magnus creating a deep impression on George.

The author George Mackay Brown, pictured here with his mother, Mhairi. GMB, as he is known, was an unassuming Orkney writer, from Stromness, who developed an international reputation and later collaborated with the isles-based composer, Peter Maxwell Davies. *Orkney Library Photographic Archive*

Towards the end of the war, he was employed as the Stromness correspondent for *The Orkney Herald*. His contributions developed into a weekly column, signed 'Islandman', in which he poured out his views on the state of the world in general and Orkney in particular, railing against, what he termed, the cancer of progress. He was effusive about the beauty and splendour of Rackwick, after a visit to Hoy, but was convinced the community which had survived in that valley for centuries declined owing to the influence of the outside world.

About this time, George's ambition to become a poet was in danger of being drowned in the whisky and beer he was consuming. After being 'dry' since the 1920s, Stromness voted in 1947 to reopen its pubs. George's first taste of alcohol was a revelation to him, finding it washed away all his cares and shyness.[1113] He began to drink heavily and regularly had to be helped home to his disapproving mother by friends.

A chance meeting in Kirkwall with a shop assistant in Leonard's bookshop helped to keep him on the writing track. In Ernest Marwick, George found a kindred spirit, who was able to encourage him in his poetry and to help him develop as a writer. Marwick was the first to publish some of George's poems (1949) and remained an important influence, particularly through his collection of Orkney folk tales, of which George would make extensive use in his writing.

In 1951, George was encouraged to enrol as a mature student at Newbattle Abbey College, under the tutelage of fellow Orcadian, Edwin Muir (123), the two having met in Stromness in the summer of that year. The secluded Midlothian abbey was to be the perfect environment for the fledgling writer to broaden his horizons and Muir the ideal tutor to help realise his potential. George's first year at Newbattle was one of the happiest periods of his life, but a recurrence of tuberculosis prematurely ended his second year at the college. It was another four years before George resumed his studies, but he had not been idle in the intervening period publishing his first book of poems. His time at Newbattle earned him entry into Edinburgh University to study English Literature.

While at Edinburgh, George often spent his Friday and Saturday evenings drinking in the pubs of Rose Street with several of the major Scottish poets of his time. Here, he also met Stella Cartwright, with whom he was briefly engaged and kept up a lifelong correspondence. Despite these distractions, George graduated in 1960. To comply with the conditions of his grant, he was obliged to follow his degree with teacher training, the thought of which appalled him. Ill health came to the rescue when he contracted chronic bronchitis. The teaching authorities eventually gave up on him and, after a period of unemployment, he obtained a grant to carry out postgraduate research on the English nineteenth century poet, Gerard Manley Hopkins. Although the research proved an unmitigated failure, the postgraduate period allowed him breathing space. He worked on a volume of poems set in Orkney, which was accepted for publication as *The Year of the Whale* and was well received on release. By 1965, with his verse appearing in various publications, he was able to support himself for the first time in years.[1114] A book of short stories, *A Calendar of Love*, followed, again receiving widespread praise. He cemented his reputation as one Scotland's most critically acclaimed poets and writers with a second volume of short stories, *A Time to Keep*.

After contemplating his religious beliefs for many years, George converted to Catholicism in 1961. He had long become disillusioned with the austere Calvinistic faith in which he had been brought up.[1115] Much to the disgust of his mother, his conversion did not lead to a change of lifestyle and she would chastise him for being a poor example of a Catholic as he recovered from yet another hangover.[1116]

After his mother died in 1967, he began work on another collection of essays about Orkney, to be published as *An Orkney Tapestry,* followed by his first novel, *Greenvoe*, set in a fictional Orkney community menaced by a vast unnamed industrial project.[1117] He then started on his most ambitious work of prose and also the most arduous to produce, a novel about the life of St Magnus. It describes the life and execution of Magnus before switching from twelfth century Orkney to Nazi Germany and the torture of the Lutheran pastor, Dietrich Bonhoeffer. This baffled some critics but had a profound effect on many, most notably, the composer Peter Maxwell Davies, who viewed *Magnus* as George's greatest achievement.[1118] Davies began work on an opera based on the novel. Keen to establish a new arts festival in Orkney, he used this opera, *The Martyrdom of St Magnus,* as the centrepiece of the first St Magnus Festival, held in 1977. Many more collaborations between the two followed and the festival went from strength to strength.

In 1974, George was awarded the OBE, but the period after the writing of *Magnus* had exerted a psychological toll and he suffered one of his severest bouts of mental illness. Nevertheless, he still managed to keep writing, with more poems, children's stories, a collection of short stories and a weekly column in *The Orcadian* (*The Orkney Herald* having closed down in 1961), which continued for some twenty five years.

Despite developing bowel cancer in 1990, which required two major operations and a long stay in hospital, the last ten years of his life were his most productive. His output during this time included two novels, *Vinland*, published in 1992 and *Beside the Ocean of Time*, which won the Scottish Saltire Book of the Year Award for 1994. It was also shortlisted for the Booker Prize, which caused George a great deal of stress, hating the publicity which the nomination generated and dreading the thought of having to wear a 'revolting' dinner jacket for the award ceremony.[1119] It was with quiet relief that he watched on TV, at home, James Kelman being announced as the winner.

George's health deteriorated in the spring of 1996, being taken to Balfour Hospital, where he slipped away in the early evening of April 13th. He was buried alongside his parents in Warbeth Cemetery after being given a funeral service in St Magnus Cathedral. His funeral was only the second occasion in which a Catholic priest had celebrated a Requiem Mass in the Cathedral since the Reformation, happening, as if ordained, on St Magnus Day. It was a most fitting farewell to Orkney's most famous bard.

Vanity motif panels from the graves of James Black (60) John Kaa (63) and George Liddell (69). These were intended to be reminders of mortality as shown by the coffin, deid bell, spade or turfing iron; the passage of earthly life as shown by the hour glass or sundial/clock; and the future of the corporal body, as represented by the skull and cross bones.

Glossary

Apprising: legal process whereby lands of a debtor were sold to pay debt due to creditor.

Commendator: an ecclesiastic who holds an abbey *in commendam,* drawing its revenues but not exercising any authority over its inner monastic discipline.

Horn (being put to the horn): being proclaimed an outlaw for debt, so called as it was signalled by three blasts of the horn at the mercat cross.

Lawting: the head court.

Lawburrows: term used to describe obtaining security against injuring a third party.

Merk: £13 4s Scots money. Originally the amount of land that could be bought for one merk.

Prebend: an ecclesiastical endowment commonly intended for the service of an altar dedicated to a saint.

Roithman: one of the 'best landed men' who composed the Lawting.

Tack: a lease - a fixed sum of money paid for the privilege of collecting tax and other revenue.

Teinds: the tenth part of annual produce of land due to the church

Abbreviations

NHO:	New History of Orkney
NOAJ:	New Orkney Antiquarian Journal
OA:	Orkney Archives
ODNB:	Oxford Dictionary of National Biography 2004
OH:	Orkney Heritage
OIC:	Orkney Islands Council
OM:	Orkney Miscellany
POAS:	Proceedings of Orkney Antiquarian Society
PSAS:	Proceedings of the Society of Antiquaries of Scotland
RCAMS:	Royal Commission on Ancient Monuments Scotland, 12th Report Vol. II, Inventory of Orkney, 1946.
SND:	Scottish National Dictionary

Appendix 1

The Windows of St Magnus Cathedral

Starting at the north side of the nave at the west end and progressing round the building in a clockwise direction the following is a list of the figures depicted in the stained-glass windows of the Cathedral.[1120]

North Aisle of the Nave (west to east)
1. St Francis of Assisi - Italian Catholic friar, who founded the Franciscan Order and who died in 1226.
2. St Augustine - early Christian philosopher and theologian, who was Bishop of Hippo Regius in what is now Algeria.
3. St Nicholas - fourth century Greek Christian Bishop of Myra in Lycia in what is now Turkey. He had a reputation for secretly bestowing gifts, which led to the story of Santa Claus.
4. St Christopher - possible third century Greek Christian martyr, who became associated with travellers.
5. Joseph of Arimathea - wealthy Jew, who gave up his prepared tomb for Jesus after the Crucifixion.
6. Memorial Window for James David Marwick (see 101), installed in 1912 by the Marwick family, showing Christ as a boy holding the scroll of prophecy and crushing the adder under his left foot. The text says, "Every valley shall be exalted and every mountain and hill shall be made low." (Isaiah 40.4)
7. Memorial Window for Rev. Charles Clouston (see 96), installed by the Clouston family in 1886, showing Elijah standing on Mount Carmel, when he prophesied to Ahab that there would be an abundance of rain. The text says, "Behold there ariseth a little cloud out of the sea". (Kings 18:44)

North Nave Triforium – West End
8. The Ark during the flood with the Latin words "dies irae" (the day of wrath).

North Nave Clerestory (upper level, west to east)
9. St Margaret - English princess, who became Queen of Scotland after marrying Malcolm III. She died in 1093.
10. Anthony - early Greek Christian, who is reputed to have founded monasticism.
11. Molach – aged figure with walking stick in right hand and extremely large book in the other hand.
12. St Patrick - a Roman Briton, who was captured by Irish raiders and went on to become a Christian missionary to Ireland.
13. St Ninian – fourth to fifth century Christian missionary among the Pictish people of southern Scotland.
14. Martin of Tours - fourth century Roman born in Hungary and brought up in Italy who converted to Christianity and became bishop of Tours in France.
15. St Columba - sixth century Gaelic Irish missionary, who spread Christianity among the Picts.
16. Simeon - one of Jacob's sons and patriarch of the tribe of Simeon, one of the twelve tribes of Israel.

North Transept
17. Lower level, west side, Thorkel Fostri - foster father of Earl Thorfinn the Mighty.
18. Lower level, north side, Harald Hardrada - King of Norway, killed at Battle of Stamford Bridge in 1066.
19. Triforium level, west side, Kolus, (see 3.)
20. Triforium level, north side, St Magnus (see 2.)
21. Clerestory level, west side, St Rognvald (see 4.)
22. Clerestory level west side, Earl Paul, Earl of Orkney 1122-1137.
23. Clerestory level, north side, St Triduana, early Christian woman, who lived in Scotland between the fourth and eighth centuries and who tore out her eyes to stop the unwanted attentions of a Pictish king.
24. Clerestory level, north side, Earl Thorfinn - the most powerful of the Earls of Orkney 1020-1064.
25. Clerestory level, east side, Earl Rognvald I - Earl of Orkney c1037-c1045 and possible founder of Kirkwall.
26. Clerestory level, east side, Olaf Tryggvasson - King of Norway 995-1000, who played an important part in forcibly converting the Norse to Christianity.
27. Top of north gable, Coat-of-Arms of the City and Royal Burgh of Kirkwall. This window was installed in September 1976, the previous one having been blown out in a gale.

North Choir Aisle (west to east)
28. James Theeder standing in a boat clasping a staff in his right hand. This window, which dates from 1913, was originally placed here as a specimen window, the plan being to have all the windows finished in this leaded style without colour, to allow as much light as possible.
29. St Jude - one of the twelve disciples of Jesus.
30. St Thomas - also called 'Doubting Thomas' was one of the twelve disciples of Jesus.
31. St Bartholomew - one of the twelve disciples of Jesus.
32. St Philip - one of the twelve disciples of Jesus.
33. James Bishop - known as James the Just, first bishop of Jerusalem. He is depicted with a club, the symbol of his martyrdom.

North Choir Clerestory (west to east)
34. Phoebe of Cenchrea - mentioned in Romans 16:1 as deaconess of the church at Cenchrea in Greece
35. Veronica - fictional character not mentioned in the Gospels, who is said to have wiped Jesus' face with a handkerchief, while on the way to be crucified.
36. Mary Magdalene - one of Jesus' followers, who is said to have been the first to see Jesus after he rose from the dead.
37. Elizabeth - mother of John the Baptist.
38. Virgin Mary - mother of Jesus.
39. Anna - aged Jewish prophetess mentioned in Luke and who prophesied about Jesus at the Temple of Jerusalem.

The East Windows
40. North side depicting St Paul, one of the most prominent and influential leaders of the early Christian church.
41. Centre Memorial Window to Sheriff Thoms, which depicts the Crucifixion. The lower part shows the three

crosses on Golgotha, the two Marys, the Disciples and the Roman Centurion. The upper part shows the Ascension with the Disciples looking on. The Rose window has twelve petals, with the Seal of the Chapter of Orkney in the trefoil centre. There are shields in the petals, with those at three, six, nine and twelve o'clock being Crucifixion symbols and the remaining containing coats-of-arms with the following descriptions written round the shields, (moving in a clockwise direction) 'Earl of Orkney of Auld', 'Earls Angus', 'Earls Stratherne', 'Earls Sinclair', 'Ernglise Svensson', 'Haakon Jonsson', 'Bishop Thomas Tulloch' and 'Bishop William Tulloch'.

42. South side depicting St Peter, leader of the twelve disciples of Jesus, who was eventually crucified in Rome with his head downwards.

South Choir Aisle (east to west)

43. St Andrew - brother of St Peter and one of the twelve disciples of Jesus, who became patron saint of Scotland, among other countries.
44. St James - one of the first disciples of Jesus.
45. St John - one of the disciples of Jesus and author of the Gospel of John.
46. St Matthew - one of the disciples of Jesus and author of the Gospel of Matthew.
47. Above the previous two windows, which are side by side, is a window with the words, "In the Beginning was the Word. The Book of the Generation of Jesus Christ".
48. Memorial Window to P. C. Flett (see 117) showing St Simon, the Patron Saint of Ironmongers. This window was chosen by Kirkwall Town Council as a memorial to P. C. Flett, as the Provost was a prominent ironmonger in his day.
49. St Mark - founder of Christianity in Africa and author of the Gospel of Mark.

South Choir Clerestory (east to west)

50. Thekla - woman commissioned by Paul to teach and evangelise.
51. St Helena - mother of Constantine the Great and legendary discoverer of the True Cross at Golgotha in 326AD.
52. Monica - born in North Africa in the fourth century AD, mother of St Augustine.
53. St Catherine - fourth century Christian convert, born in Alexandria and condemned to death on an instrument of torture called the breaking wheel.
54. St Cecilia - second century female Roman Christian Martyr, who became patron saint of musicians.
55. Thinaw – figure of a woman with boat in right hand and scroll in left hand.

South Transept Chapel (Custodian's Office)

56. Window showing coats-of-arms of families with a Norse origin, starting from the top, Paplay, Ayrland. Cloustuth, Flett and Hacro.
57. Window showing coats-of-arms of families from Scotland, Sinclair, Cragy, Yirwing, Tulloch and Fresell. The words "Justice", "Lawman" and "Roithman" denote the position each family held in the High Courts of Arbitration in the Thing or Norse Parliament. Both windows designed by J. S. Clouston (120).

South Transept

58. South side lower level, Torf Einar, Earl of Orkney c893-c946.
59. West side lower level, King Belus, legendary King of Assyria.
60. South side triforium level, Cormac - Irish King 901-907 and bishop of Munster, killed by the Danes in Battle of Moy Albe.
61. West side triforium level, Gaius, S.P.Q.R (Senatus Populusque Romanus, Latin for the Senate and people of Rome)
62. South side clerestory level east, Thorfinn I, known as Skull-Splitter, Earl of Orkney c963-c976.
63. South side clerestory level west, Sigurd the Stout, Earl of Orkney 991-1014, killed at Battle of Clontarf in Ireland.
64. East side clerestory level, Harald Harfager – reputedly first king of a united Norway.
65. East side clerestory level, Sigurd I, one of the first Norse Earls of Orkney.

South Aisle of Nave (east to west)

66. John the Baptist, with text, "Repent ye, for the Kingdom of Heaven is at hand".
67. Isaiah – prophet in eighth century BC kingdom of Judah, who prophesied the virgin birth of Jesus.
68. Memorial Window to Thomas Peace (see 97), installed by the Peace family in 1897 and showing the parable of the Good Samaritan.
69. Memorial Window to Buckham Hugh Hossack (see 98), installed by Mrs Hossack and showing the parable of the Sower.
70. King Solomon - son of David and King of Israel c971-931BC.
71. King David – King of Israel c1003-970BC.
72. Isaac – son of Abraham and one of the three patriarchs of the Israelites.
73. Adam – first man created by God.

South Nave Triforium – West End

74. The Creation with the Latin words, "Fiat Lux" (Let there be light).

The four windows which are on display in the south triforium depict St Stephen, Timothy, Ezekiel and Daniel.

South Nave Clerestory Level (east to west)

75. Zechariah – prophet of the kingdom of Judah (or could be father of John the Baptist).
76. Jonah – prophet of the northern kingdom of Israel, famous for being swallowed by a whale.
77. Nehemiah – governor of Judah, who rebuilt the walls of Jerusalem and purified the Jewish community.
78. Malachi – Jewish prophet and author of the Book of Malachi.
79. Ruth – great-grandmother of David and therefore ancestor of Jesus.
80. Melchizedek – High Priest, who blesses Abraham (Genesis 14:18-20)
81. Jesse – grandson of Ruth and father of David.
82. Eve – first woman and second person to be created by God.

West Front

850th Anniversary Memorial Window designed by Crear McCartney.

Index of Names

Adamson, James, mason, 49, 61-62
Adamson, Patrick, mason, 62
Adome, John, 63
Adolphus, Gustavus, King of Sweden, 42
Alexander, Kenneth, Private, 134
Alexander, Halen, wife of George Sinclair of Rapness, 52
Allardyce, Janet, mistress of Earl Robert Stewart, 33
Anderson, Isobel, 3rd wife of Patrick Smyth of Braco, 53-54
Andrew (Pictoris), Bishop of Orkney, 17, 18-19, 23
Arnott, Sir John, 38, 48
Amundsen, Roald, explorer, 117
Anderson, Willa, wife of Edwin Muir, 153, note 1083
Asleifsson, Sweyn, 6, 7
Aytoun, William, Sheriff, 109

Baikie, Alfred, 141-142
Baikie, Andrew, landwaiter, 99, 101
Baikie, Anna, 2nd wife of George Traill, 74
Baikie, Christina, wife of Rev. John Yule, 101
Baikie, Elizabeth, wife of William Irving of Kirbuster, 73
Baikie, Hugh of Burness, 70, 82
Baikie, James of Burness, 69-70, 74
Baikie, James (1st) of Tankerness, 49-51, 70, 72
Baikie, Jean, wife of Captain Peter Winchester, 70, 72
Baikie, John, lieutenant in RN, 101, 113
Baikie, John, Landwaiter, 89
Baikie, Katherine, wife of Edward Pottinger, 51
Baikie, Magnus, brother-in-law of Edward Pottinger, 51
Baikie, Magnus, ancestor of James Baikie (1st) of Tankerness, 72
Baikie, Samuel, 113
Baikie, Rev. Thomas, 70, 101
Baikie, Thomas, minister of Rousay and Egilsay, 68-69
Baikie, Thomas, father of James Baikie (1st) of Tankerness, 72
Baikie, William Balfour, 112-115, 140
Baillie, Hugh, Customs Collector, 91
Baird, John, married to Margaret Groat, 61
Balfour, Alison, alleged witch, 44
Balfour, David, note 850, 125
Balfour, Gilbert, 33
Balfour, Mary, wife of John Traill, 91
Balfour, William of Trenaby, 91
Banks, Alastair, 46-47
Banks, Alexander, 46-47
Bannatyne, John, father of William, 44
Bannatyne, William, 36, 44-55
Barclay, Rev. William, 144-145
Barnett, Edwin, Private, 134

Barrit, Jane, 152
Barron, Isabella Jane, 151
Barry, Rev. George, 102
Barth, Heinrich, explorer, 113-114
Beaton, Cardinal David, 25
Bell, Dr B. D. C., 130-131, 139
Bellenden, Ann, wife of Provost Craigie, 66
Bellenden, Espet, 82
Bellenden, Isobel, wife of Robert Richan, 65-66
Bellenden, Katherine, mother of Bishop Adam Bothwell, 66
Bellenden, Patrick of Stenness, 32, 34, 44
Bellenden, Sir John of Auchinoull, 32, 34
Black, Henry, Captain of Kirkwall Castle, 65
Black, Isobel, eldest daughter of James Black, 65
Black, James, 61, 65, 68
Black Jean, daughter of James Black, 65
Black, John, son of James Black, 65
Black, Thomas, chamberlain of Orkney, 65
Black, William, 65
Blair, Patrick of Little Blair, 55-57, 64, 75
Blaw, Barbara, mother of Laings 103
Blaw, Rev. William, 87, 103
Bonar, Margaret, wife of Wm. Henryson, 32
Borthwick, Robert, 24
Boswell, Grizell, wife of Bishop Law, 38
Bothwell, Adam, Bishop of Orkney, 21, 24, 30, 33, 34, 56, 66
Bothwell, Janet, sister of Bishop Bothwell, 56
Boyle, Marion, wife of Bishop James Law, 39
Brand, Alexander, tacksman, 72, 85
Breakspear, Cardinal Nicholas, 26
Brown, George Mackay, 154, 155, 160-161
Brown, John, 34
Brown, Thomas, diarist, 64, 78
Bruce, Lawrence of Cultmalindie, 32
Brusisson, Rognvald 1, 2, 5
Bryce, David, architect, 96, 126
Buchanan, Arthur of Sound, 49, 50, 58, 76, 77
Buchanan, Margaret, mother of James Spence 87
Buchanan, Sir Alexander, 58
Buchanan, Sir John, 58
Buchanan, Sir Walter, 58
Burroughs, Frederick W. T. 107, 124-126, 153

Calcrit, Isobel, 44
Campbell, Rev., Andrew James, 142-144, 151
Campbell, Margaret, mother of J. Rae, 115
Canute the Great, King of Denmark and England, 2
Carmichal, Marjory, wife of John Sinclair, 61-62

Carnegie, Margaret Dempster, 104
Cartwright, Stella, 161
Chalmaer, Margaret, wife of John Cuthbert, 58
Chamberlain, Joseph, MP, 119
Charles I, King of Great Britain, 50, 54
Charles II, King of Great Britain, 55, 57, 61, 66
Charles VII, King of France, 22, 58
Chisholm, Agnes, 2nd wife of John Napier of Merchiston, 56
Christison, E. C., wife of Dr Bell, 130
Christison, Sir Robert, 131, 138
Clere, Sir John, 30
Clouston, Rev. Charles, 118-119
Clouston, Hugh, 79
Clouston, Joseph Storer, 14, 22, 27, 28, 46, 52, 64, 119, 121,132, 149-150
Clouston, Thomas Smith, 131-132, 149
Clouston, Rev. William, 118
Clouston, Winifred, 150
Cobb, Margaret, wife of Donald Groat, 88
Cok, Jean, 81
Cok, Rev. Thomas, 81
Colville, Henry, Parson of Orphir, 45
Cooper, James, Private, 134
Corrigal, John, HBC employee, 179
Corse, James, Corporal, 134
Couper, Robert, 46
Couper, William, carpenter, 46
Covingtrie, David, 77, 80-81
Covingtrie, John, 81
Cracroft, Sophie, Lady Franklin's companion 111
Craigie, Anna, 77, 83
Craigie, Catherine, wife of Magnus Pottinger, 45
Craigie, David of Oversanday, 49, 70, 77, 81-83
Craigie, George, 92
Craigie, Hugh of Gairsay, 49, 57, 58, 82
Craigie, Isobel, 3rd wife of Hew Halcro of that Ilk, 48
Craigie, Patrick, Provost, 66, 80 and notes 189 & 561
Craigie, Magnus, father of Sir William Craigie, 48
Craigie, Robert, *SS Express*, 135
Craigie, Sir William of Gairsay, 48-49, 82
Craven Rev J. B. 22
Crichton, Marion, wife of Bishop Graham, 39
Cromarty, John of Cara, 28
Cromwell, Oliver, 18, 50, 57
Crowther, Samuel, freed slave, note 854
Cullace, Captain, 55
Cunningham, Euphan, wife of Bishop Honeyman, 41
Cunningham, Rev Samuel, 41
Cursiter, Stanley, 122, 149, 155, 157-159
Cuthbert, Elizabeth, wife of Rev. James Wallace 79-80
Cuthbert, Margaret, daughter of John, 58
Cuthbert, John, Girnell-keeper, 58-59, 80

Cutt, John, Corporal, 135
Cutt, Thomas, Gunner, 135

Darnley, Lord, husband of Mary Queen of Scots, 33
David, King of Scotland, 7
Davidson, Alexander, 101
Davis, Peter Maxwell, 161
De Ruyter, Dutch Admiral, 64
Davidson, Jean, married to Robert Nicholson, 63
Dennison, Richard, skipper, 72
Dennison, Walter Traill, 37
Dick, Sir Andrew Dick, Sheriff of Orkney, 50, 51, 56, note 638
Dick, John, Sheriff of Orkney, 49, 50
Dick, Isobel, 2nd wife of George Richan, 67
Dick, Sir William Dick of Braid, 58
Dickens, Charles, 117
Dishington, Andrew, father of Thomas, 60
Dishington, John, chamberlain to Earl Robert Stewart, 60
Dishington, John, master of the Grammar School, 50, 60
Dishington, Margaret, wife of Edward Sinclair, 29
Dishington, Thomas, 59-60, 68
Dolgfinn, Bishop of Orkney, 27
Douglas, George, 13th Earl of Morton, 86
Douglas, James 14th Earl of Morton, 85, 86
Douglas, Rev. James, 69
Douglas, Robert, 8th Earl of Morton, 55, 56
Douglas, Robert, minister in Edinburgh, 55
Douglas, William, 7th Earl of Morton, 50, 56
and note 250
Douglas, William, 9th Earl of Morton, 50, 57, 75, 85
Drummond, Agnes, daughter of George Drummond and Agnes Napier, 54-55
Drummond, David, Baillie, 55, 82
Drummond, John, apprentice, 66
Drummond, John, young Drummond of Balloch, 54
Drummond, George of Balloch and Blair, 39, 54-55, 56
Drummond, George of Lidcrieff, 55
Drummond, George, son of George of Balloch and Blair, 55
Drummond, Katherine, daughter of George Drummond and Agnes Napier, 55
Drummond, Margaret, 2nd wife of Patrick Monteith of Egilsay, 55
Drummond, Mary, wife of Patrick Blair of Little Blair, 55-56
Dryden, Sir Henry, 11, 14, 15, 25-28, 110
Dundas, Marion, wife of Bishop Law, 38
Dundas, Sir Lawrence, 85
Dunnet, James, Corporal, 135

Eccles, George, Gunner, 135
Edgar, King of Scotland, 3
Edmondstone, Anna, wife of Arthur Murray, 76
Edmondstone, John, 75
Edward VI, King of England, 26

Index of Names

Einarsson Thorfinn (Thorfinn Sull-Splitter) 1
Elphinstone, Elizabeth, 72
Elphinstone, Euphemia, mother of Earl Robert Stewart, 33
Elphinstone, John of Lopness, 72
Elphinstone, Margaret, 2nd wife to Thomas Dishington, 60
Elphinstone, Col Robert, 72 and note 535
Erik, King of Norway, 22
Erlendsson, Erling, brother of St Magnus 3
Eunson, Reynold, cabinet maker, 4, 159
Eystein, King of Norway, 7
Eysteinsson, Sigurd 1

Farquahar, William, glover, married to Jean Nicholson, 64
Fea, Christian, wife of Walter Sandison, 52
Fea, Helen, 61
Fea, James of Clestrain, 86, 92
Fea, Elizabeth, 70
Fea, Peter of Dunatoun, 86
Finlayson, David, *SS Express*, 135
Finlayson, John, 38
Flett, George, HBC employee, 116
Flett, Kolbein, 22
Flett, Peter C., 145-146, 151
Flett, Magnus, 22
Flett, William of Hobbister, 22
Forbes, David, 61, 77-78, 80
Forbes, Elizabeth, 78
Foulis, George, *SS Express*, 135
Foulzie, Gilbert, 49
Foulzie, Ursula, 49
Fox, Charles James, MP, 86-87, 103
Fox, James, *SS Express*, 135
Frakok of Dale, 6, 7
Franklin, Sir John, 111, 115-118
Fremy, Claudius, bell caster, 24, 43
Frisken, Adam, Chief Petty Officer, 135
Frisken, William, Private, 135
Fullerton, Revd. Thomas of Westray, 70

Garden, Dora, 144-145
Garden, Robert, 90, 127-129, 144, 150
Geddes, Alexander, 43, 79
Geddes, Eliza, wife of General Burroughs, 124, 126-127
Gerrald, Joseph, 'Scottish Martyr', 103
Gifford, Adam, Sheriff, 109
Gifford, Marjorie, 1st wife of Rev. Leigh, 79
Gilli, Harald, King of Norway, 5
Gillies, Lord Adam, 103
Gladstone, William Ewart, PM 100, 119-120, 150
Good, Katherine, wife of Alastair Banks, 46
Goodfellow, Rev. Alexander, 111-112
Gordon, David, Gunner, 135

Gordon, James of Cairston, 86, 101
Gow, Pirate, 91
Graham, Alexander, 85, 88
Graham, Barbara, wife of Patrick Blair, 57
Graham, Beatrix, sister of Bishop Graham, 54
Graham, Catherine, 1st wife of Patrick Smyth of Braco, 40, 53
Graham, Christane, daughter of Patrick of Rothiesholme, wife of David Drummond, 55
Graham, David of Gorthie, 40, 55
Graham, George, Bishop of Orkney, 39-40, 49, 53-54
Graham, Jean, 77, 80-83
Graham, John, Marquis of Montrose, 50, 54, 55, 57, 60, 69
Graham, John of Breckness, 40
Graham, Margaret Mason, 139-140
Graham, Marjorie, wife of George Drummond, 40, 55
Graham, Patrick of Rothiesholme, 40, 55, 82
Gray, Janet, mistress of Earl Robert Stewart, 33
Grenske, Harald, 2
Griffin, Jane, Lady Franklin, 111, 117
Groat, Donald of Newhall, 88-89
Groat, John of Elsness, 51
Groat, M., wife of David MacLellan, 77, 78
Groat, Malcolm, 88
Groat, Margaret, wife of Patrick Prince, 61
Groat, Robert, 89
Groat, William, 89
Groat, Malcolm of Tankerness, 45, 61
Gudbrandsdatter, Asta, mother of St Olaf, 2
Gullion, Albert, Lance Corporal, 135
Gunnhild, mother of St Rognvald, 4, 5

Hakonsson, Hakon, King of Norway, 10-11
Hakonsson, Harald, 7
Hakonsson, Paul, 5-7
Halcro, David of Thurregar, 27
Halcro, Henry, father of Hew Halcro, 32, 48
Halcro, Hew of that Ilk, 48, 70
Halcro, Jean, sister of Sibillia Halcro, 54, 70
Halcro Magnus, note 150
Halcro, Margaret, wife of Sir Wm. Craigie, 48-49, 82
Halcro, Nicholas, 27-28
Halcro, Sibillia, 54, 69-70, 79
Halcro, William, 28
Halcro, William of Aikers, 28
Hall, Captain, 54
Haraldsson, Erlend, 6, 7
Haraldsson, David, 9
Haraldsson, John, 9
Hardrada, Harald, King of Norway 2
Harcus, Thomas, Private, 135
Harrold, James W., Private, 135
Hartside, Margaret, wife of Sir John Buchanan, 58

Harvey, Emma, 93
Hay, George, 3rd Earl of Kinnoul, 55
Hay, Sir George of Kinfauns, 1st Earl of Kinnoul, 18, 58
Hay, Robert, Private, 135
Hay, William, Private, 135
Heart, Rev. James, 61
Heddle, Charles, Sierra Leone, 115, note 860
Heddle, Henrietta Moodie, 93
Helga, mother of Harald Hakonsson, 7
Hepburn, James, Earl of Bothwell, 33
Henderson, Margaret, 77
Henry, Bishop of Orkney, 9, 11, 26
Henry IV, King of England, 18
Henry V, King of England, 22
Henry VIII, King of England, 26
Henryson, Cuthbert, brother of William Henryson, 32
Henryson, Robert of Holland, 49
Henryson, William, 32, 34, 40
Hlodvirsson, Sigurd (Sigurd the Stout), 1
Hog, Bessie, wife of William Kincaid, 35
Holland, James W., Private, 135
Honeyman, Andrew, Bishop of Orkney, 41-42, 57, 78, 80
Honeyman, George, brother of Bishop Honeyman, 80
Honeyman, Robert of Graemsay, 42
Hossack, B. H., 45, 48, 54, 59, 61, 65, 71, 74, 121-122, 150
Hourston, Phyllis, wife of Stanley Cursiter, 158
Hruga, Kolbein, 9
Hutton, Isabella, mother of W. B. Baikie, 113

Ingagerth, owner of Horrie, 47
Irvine, John, blacksmith, 2nd husband of Christian Fea, 79
Irving, Alison, daughter of Captain Robert Irving, 64-65
Irving, Barbara, wife of Mitchell Rendall of Breck, 61, 72-74
Irving, Elizabeth, wife of George Traill of Quendale, 73, 76-77
Irving, Captain Robert, 64-65
Irving, Edward, brother of William Irving senior of Sebay, 47
Irving, Gilbert, brother of Wm. senior of Sebay, 47
Irving, James, father of Wm. senior of Sebay, 47
Irving, Margaret, daughter of Captain Robert Irving, 64-65
Irving, Magnus, brother of Wm. senior of Sebay, 47
Irving, Mary, daughter of Captain Robert Irving, 64-65
Irving, Patrick, son of Wm. senior of Sebay, 47
Irving, William of Kirbuster, 73, 76
Irving, William of Sebay, 47-48
Irving, William senior of Sebay, 47-48
Isabella, mother of Earl Henry I Sinclair, 13

James III, King of Scotland, 17, 46
James IV, King of Scotland, 19
James V, King of Scotland, 21, 24, 29, 31, 33, 34, 47
James VI, King of Scotland, 34, 38, 39
James VII, King of Scotland, James II of England and Ireland, 73, 83

Joan of Arc, 22
Jofrey, Bishop of Orkney, 10, 27
Jolly, Margaret, 129, 144

Kaa, Margaret, 2nd wife of David Covingtrie, 68, 81
Kaa, James, 43
Kaa, James, son of John Kaa, 68, 73
Kaa, John, 68, 72, 81
Kaa, Robert, father of John Kaa, 68
Kalisson, Kol, father of St Rognvald, 4-5
Kelly, Agnes, wife of Samuel Laing, 105
Kennedy, Jean, wife of Earl Robert Stewart, 33
Kennedy, David, minister of Birsay and Harray, 50
Kincaid, John, 35
Kincaid, William of Falkirk, 35
King, David of Warbister, note 175, 48 note 308
Kinnaird, Elspeth, wife of Gilbert Foulzie, 49
Kinnoul, Earls of, see Hay
Kirkness, Jane, mother of David Covingtrie, 81
Klerk, Thorbjorn, killer of St Rognvald, 6
Knox, John, note 216
Kolbeinsson, Bjarni, Bishop of Orkney, 9-10, 14, 26-27, 149
Kolbeinsson, Sigvat, 14
Kolbeinsson, Einar, Abbot of Munkeliv Abbey, 14
Kristian, King of Denmark, 17, 18

Laing, Gilbert Meason, 92, 104-105
Laing Malcolm, 92, 103-106
Laing, Robert, 103
Laing, Samuel, 93, 98-99, 103-106
Laird, George M., Private, 135
Law, James, Bishop of Orkney, 37-39, 48
Learmonth, James A., Private 135
Leask, Alexander M., Private, 136
Lees, Elizabeth, 120
Leigh, Rev. Hugh, 78
Leigh, Robert, 78
Leslie, Harald, Lord Birsay, 146-147, 155
Liddell, George of Hammer, 74-75
Liddell, William of Hammer, 74-75, 91
Lifolf, killer of St Magnus, 14
Linay, Anna, wife of Patrick Murray, 79
Linay, Oliver, 36, 79
Linklater, Andrew, 65
Linklater, David S., Private, 136
Linklater, Eric, 121, 155-157, 158
Linklater, Patrick, skipper, 65
Linklater, William, merchant, 65
Logie, Harriet, wife of *JR*, 111
Logie, Dr James, 107, 120, 130, 131, 138-139
Logie, Rev. William, 107-108, 110, 111, 138
Loutit, Agnes, wife of John Kaa, 68

Index of Names

Loutit, Janet, wife of John Richan, 67
Loutit, Thomas of Lyking, 68, 72
Loutit, Thomas, Provost, 72
Low, Charles, 120
Lyell Sir Leonard, MP, 122 note 904

MacDairmid, Hugh, 153, 155
Mackay, James, Private, 136
Mackay, Mhairi Sheena, 160-161
Mackenzie, Alexander of Broomhill, 79, 82
Mackenzie, John, father of Bishop Mackenzie, 42
Mackenzie, Margaret, mother of Mary Young, 86
Mackenzie, Murdoch, Bishop of Orkney, 42-43, 80, 81, 82, 86
Mackenzie, Murdoch, mapmaker, 87
Mackintosh, W. R., 54
Macintyre, Marjorie, wife of Eric Linklater, 156, 158
MacLey, Margaret, wife of Bishop Mackenzie, 42
MacLellan, David, 50-51
Macrae, R. A. A. S. 147-148
Maddadsson, Harald, 3, 6, 7, 9, 10
Madelaine de Valois, wife of King James V, 26
Magnus Barelegs, King of Norway 3, 4
Maich, Marie, married to Robert Nicholson, younger, 64
Maine, Thomas, 36, 79
Maine, William, 35-36
Malise, Earl of Strathearn, 13
Manson, William 99-101, note 755
Margaret, daughter of Earl Hakon, 3, 6
Margaret, Maid of Norway, 9
Margaret, Danish wife of King James III, 17, 18
Marjoribanks, Thomas, 47
Marwick, Ernest W., 149 note 1053, 154, 155
Marwick, Hugh, 44, 90, note 1066, 151-152, 155
Marwick, Hugh, Saddler, 136
Marwick, James David, 127
Marwick, Rena, 147
Mary I, Queen of England, 26
Mary, Queen of Scots, 26, 31, 33
Maxwell, Robert, Bishop of Orkney, 24-25
Maxwell. Sir John of Pollock, 24
McKinlay, Jean wife of George Omond, 100
Melrose, Adam, 124
Menzies, David, Governor of Orkney, 17, 47
Miller, Hugh, geologist, 119
Milne, Francis I., 136
Milne, William, Private, 136
Mitchell, Andrew, Dean of Guild, 59, 82
Mitchell, James, 63
Mitchell, John, Edinburgh merchant, 58
Moncrieff, Margaret, 2nd wife of Mitchell Rendall, 77
Moncrieff, David, 2nd husband of Isobel Anderson, 54, note 365, 80

Monmouth, Duke of, 77 note 590
Monroe, David, litster, 78-79
Monteith, James of Saltcoats, 34-35
Monteith, Patrick of Egilsay, 35, 44, 50, 55
Monteith, Patrick of Fair Isle, 34-35
Monteith, Robert of Egilsay, 55
Monteith, Sybla, wife of B. H. Hossack, 122
Moodie, Benjamin of Melsetter, 85, 86, 88, 91-92
Moodie, Captain James, 88
Moodie, Francis of Breckness, 48
Mooney, John, 144, 150-151, 155
Morton, Earls of, see Douglas
Mowbray, Elizabeth, 75
Mowbray, Matthew, 75
Muat, Alexander, 48
Mudie, Elspeth, 1st wife of George Richan, 67
Muir, Edwin, 152-153, 157
Murray, Arthur, 75-76
Murray, Francis, 79
Murray, James of Clerdane, 59
Murray, Isobel, daughter of Arthur, 76
Murray, Magnus, 23-24
Murray, Patrick, 76, 79
Murray, Thomas of Garth, 23-24

Napier, Alexander, father of John Napier, 56
Napier, John of Merchiston, 54, 56
Neaves, Charles, Sheriff, 109
Nicholson, Andrew, Private, 136
Nicholson, James, son of Robert Nicholson, 64
Nicholson, Jean, daughter of Robert, 64
Nicholson, Robert, glazier, 63-64, 67
Nicholson, Robert, son of Robert, 64
Nicholson, Ursula, daughter of Robert Nicholson, 64, 74
Nisbet, Elizabeth, 2nd wife of Thomas Baikie, 70
Norton Smith, H. L., 21
Novell, Ralph, 7 note 34

Omond, George, 99-100
Orem, William, notary public, 65
Ospaksson, Sumerlidi, grandfather of St Magnus, 3
Osburne, Alfred, Private, 136

Paplay, Magnus, weaver, 75
Paplay, Elizabeth, wife of Magnus Craigie, 48
Paplay, Kathleen, mother of Thomas Murray of Garth, 24
Paplay, Steven, 14
Paterson, Rev. Robert, 110
Paulsson, Hakon, 3, 4, 8
Peace, Thomas, 119-120
Peter, Bishop of Orkney, 27
Peterkin, Alexander, 95, 104

Peterson, William Thomas, 22-23
Petrie, Rev. Peter, 108
Phankouth, Henry, 18-19, 28, 30
Phillippa, Queen of Denmark, 17
Pollexfen, Henry, 102
Pollexfen, Thomas, 102
Pope Clement VII, 23
Pottinger, Alexander, roithman, 59
Pottinger, Edward of Howbister, 45, 51, 59
Pottinger, Janet, wife of Thomas Taylor, 59
Pottinger, John, merchant, 45, 51, 55, 59
Pottinger, Magnus, 45, 51
Pottinger, Marable, daughter of Magnus Pottinger and Catherine Craigie, 45
Pottinger, Marion, daughter of Magnus Pottinger and Catherine Craigie, 45
Pottinger, Marjorie, wife of Thomas Dishington, 59-60
Pottinger, Robert of Howbister, 59, 61
Prince, Catherine, daughter of Patrick, 61
Prince, Edward, son of Patrick, 61
Prince, Henry, father of Patrick, 61
Prince, Magnus, Lord Provost of Edinburgh, 61 note 433, 94
Prince, Patrick, 60-61, 111

Queen Victoria, 115, 125, 127

Rae, John, 115-118
Rae, John senior, 104, 115
Reid, Andrew, roithman, 66
Reid, George, grandfather of George Omond, 99
Reid, James, Private, 136
Reid, John, father of Bishop Robert Reid, 25
Reid, John, Kirkwall merchant, 99-100
Reid, Marion, mother of John Richan, 67
Reid, Robert, Bishop of Orkney, 6, 10, 21, 25-26, 28, 30, 32, 43
Reid, Tomas, 43
Reid, Wat, 44
Rendall, George, RN Reserve, 136
Rendall George I., *SS Express*, 136
Rendall, John, carpenter, 68
Rendall, Margaret, daughter of Mitchell, 77
Rendall, Marjory, daughter of Mitchell, 77
Rendall, Mitchell of Breck, 61, 76-77
Rendall, Robert, 154-155
Rendall, William of Breck, 77, 83
Reoch, Elspeth, alleged witch, 45
Richan, George, son of Robert Richan and Isobel Bellenden, 67
Richan, Helen, wife of James Black, 65
Richan, Jean, daughter of Robert Richan and Mary Rowsay, 66
Richan, Jean, wife of David Monroe, 78-79
Richan, John, 67-68
Richan, John, son of John Richan and Janet Loutit, 68

Richan, Margaret, wife of James Kaa, 66, 68
Richan, Robert, father of John Richan, 67
Richan, Robert of Caldale, 66
Richan, Robert of Linklater, 61, 66-67
Richardson, Sir John, 117
Riddoch, Margaret, 102
Riddoch, James, 100-101, 102, 104
Riddoch, John, 85-87, 89, 100, 102
Ritchie, Ann, 3rd wife of George Richan, 66
Ritchie, George, Chamberlain, 82
Ritchie, Marion, 79
Robert II, King of Scotland, 23
Robertson, Archibald Garden, 132-133
Robertson, Christian, 98-99
Robertson, Duncan J., 94, 109, 111, 132-133
Robertson, James, Gunner, 136
Robertson, James, Sheriff, 94, 108-111, 125, 132
Rognvaldsson, Einar (Turf-Einar) 1
Rosie, John, Private, 136
Rosta, Olvir, 6
Rowsay, Mary, 1st wife of Robert Richan, 65
Rynd, Edward, weaver, 80

Saebjarnarsson, Kali, father of Kol, 4
Saint-Clair, Roland, 52 note 355
Sandilands, Marjorie, mistress of Earl Robert Stewart, 33
Sarle, Harriet, 93
Sandison, George, Private, 136
Sandison, John, weaver, 52
Sandison, Thomas, son of Walter, 51-52
Sandison, Walter, son of John Sandison, 51-52
Scarth, Robert, factor, 107, 126
Scollay, David of Tofts, 33
Scollay, Mitchel, 51
Scollay, James, of Tofts, 51
Scollay, Marjorie, 47
Scott, Donald M., Assistant Paymaster, 137
Scott, Sir Walter, 15, 103, 104, 115
Scott, Rev William, 36
Seatter, Jean, 74
Shackelton, Ernest, 151
Sharp, James, Archbishop of St Andrews, 42, note 590
Shearer, Pat, 129-130
Shilps, John, master of the Grammar School, 60
Sibbald, Sir Robert, 80
Sigurd of Paplay, 27
Sigurdsson, Thorfinn 'the Mighty', 2, 3
Sigvatsson, Sigurd, 14
Simison, James, Private, 137
Sinclair, Barbara, daughter of George Sinclair of Rapness, 53
Sinclair, Edward of Essonquoy, 49
Sinclair, Edward of Strome, 21, 28-30

Sinclair, George, Earl of Caithness, 39, 48 Sinclair, George of Rapness, 52-53
Sinclair, George W., Private, 137
Sinclair, Gilbert, son of Edward of Essonquoy, 49
Sinclair, Henry I, Earl of Orkney, 13
Sinclair, Henry, son of Edward Sinclair, 30
Sinclair, James, victor of Summerdale, 21, 29
Sinclair, James of Quendale, 80
Sinclair, James, eldest son of John Sinclair of Quendale, 52-53
Sinclair, John, married to Marjory Carmichal, 61-62
Sinclair, John of Quendale, 53
Sinclair John W. S., Sapper, 137
Sinclair, Isobel, wife of James Adamson, 62
Sinclair, Lawrence, 30-31
Sinclair, Lord Henry, 17, 18, 19, 21, 29
Sinclair, Lord William, 21, 25, 29
Sinclair, Malcolm of Quendale, 53
Sinclair, Magnus of Warsetter, 29
Sinclair, Robert, son of Edward Sinclair, 30
Sinclair, Sir David of Sumburgh, 19, 22, 29
Sinclair, Sir John of Ulbster, 133-134
Sinclair, Sir William of Warsetter, 21, 29
Sinclair, William, Earl of Orkney, 17-18, 27
Sinclair, William of Houss, 30
Sinclair, William of Tolhop, 48
Sinclair, William J., Lance Corporal, 137
Skea, James, heretic, 27
Skea, Janet, possible wife of William Halcro, 28
Slater, David, beadle, 70
Smith, Robert M. Lance Corporal, 137
Smith, Thomas, land waiter, 99
Smyth, Andrew of Rapness, 39, 53
Smyth, Beatrix, daughter of Patrick of Braco, 53
Smyth, Marjorie, daughter of Patrick of Braco, 53
Smyth, Patrick of Braco, 39-40, 53-55
Smyth, Patrick, son of Patrick of Braco, 54
Spence, Caroline Cumming, 142-143
Spence, Graeme, 87-88
Spence, James & Janet, 87
Spence, B. S., wife of Dr Logie, 138-139
St. Magnus Erlendsson, 3-5, 7-8, 14, 26
St. Michael, 22-23, 61
St. Olaf II Haraldsson, King and patron saint of Norway 1-2
St Rognvald Kali Kolsson, 3-8, 9-10, 27
St. Peter, 22
Stewart, Archibald of Brugh, 91
Stewart, Barbara, daughter of Lord Adam Stewart, 31-32, 48
Stewart, Edward, Bishop of Orkney, 19, 23
Stewart, Helen, 2nd wife of Capt. Winchester, 72
Stewart, Helenor, mother of Lord Adam Stewart, 32
Stewart, Henry of Graemsay, 48
Stewart, James of Burray, 86, 91

Stewart, James of Graemsay, 42, 48, 52
Stewart, John, Master of Orkney, 44-45
Stewart, Jean, 2nd wife of Hew Halcro, 48
Stewart, Isobel, 3rd wife of Edward Pottinger, 51
Stewart, Lord Adam, 31-32
Stewart, Margaret, wife of John Richan, younger, 68
Stewart, Margaret, 2nd wife of Patrick Smyth of Braco, 54
Stewart, Margaret, wife of Thomas Baikie, 69
Stewart, Martha, possible 1st wife of George Sinclair, 52
Stewart, Patrick, Earl of Orkney, 35, 37-39, 44-45, 47-48, 65
Stewart, Patrick, sailor, 71
Stewart, Robert, Earl of Orkney, 34, 32-37, 44, 46, 47, 52, 65
Stewart, Robert, son of Earl Patrick Stewart, 38-39
Stewart, William, brother of Bishop Edward Stewart, 23
Stewart, Revd. Walter, 72
Steuart, Charles, Stewart Clerk of Orkney, 65
Stuart, Rev James, 111-112
Strang, Janet, wife of Lawrence Sinclair, 31
Striveling, Elizabeth, 1st wife of John Napier of Merchiston, 56
Sturlasson, Snorri, 11
Sutherland, Anderson, Major, 137
Sutherland, David of Windbreck, 77
Sutherland, Goodwin, 2nd Lieutenant, 137
Sydserff, Thomas, Bishop of Orkney, note 245

Taylor, Alexander, 45
Taylor, Elspeth, 2nd wife of Magnus Pottinger, 45
Taylor, Thomas, 49
Tennyson, Alfred, Lord, 119-120, 150
Thompson, 'Kate', wife of J. Rae, 115, 117
Thomson, Elizabeth, wife of William Irving senior of Sebay, 47
Thomson, Esther, 1st wife of Hew Halcro, 48,
Thomson, Mariore, wife of William Maine, 35
Thoms, George, Sheriff, 109, 121, 122-124, 139
Thora, mother of St Magnus, 3, 4, 14
Thorfinnsson, Erlend, father of St Magnus, 3, 4
Thorfinnsson, Paul, 3, 9
Thordarsson, Sturla, 11
Traill, David of Sebay, 70
Traill, Elizabeth, 3rd wife of Rev. Thomas Baikie, 70
Traill, Elizabeth, daughter of George Traill of Quendale, 74
Traill, Elizabeth, wife of George Liddell of Hammer, 74
Traill, Elspeth, 2nd wife of Ed. Pottinger, 51
Traill, George of Quendale, 72-74, 81, 83
Traill, George William, 106-107, 124
Traill, James of Woodwick 90-91, 128
Traill, James of Westove, 73, 81
Traill, James, son of George Traill of Quendale, 73-74
Traill, John (Jack) of Woodwick, 92
Traill, John of Elsness, 72, 91
Traill, John of Westness, 91-92
Traill, Margaret, 91

Traill, Marjorie, 2nd wife of Tho. Loutit, 72
Traill, Nicola, 80-81
Traill of Holland, 87
Traill of Woodwick, 92-94
Traill, Patrick, brother-in-law of Edward Pottinger, 51, 57, 59, 71
Traill, T. S., 93, 95 note 722, 99, 102, 113
Tryggvasson, Olaf, King of Norway, 1-2
Tulloch, Begis, 22
Tulloch, Elizabeth, wife of Andrew Dishington, 60
Tulloch(k), James W. Private, 137
Tulloch, Thomas, Bishop of Orkney, 17-18, 26, 42
Tulloch, William, Bishop of Orkney, 18, 31

Ungi, Hanef, 9

Van Bassan, 48

Wallace, Rev. James, 43, 78, 79-80
Warwick, Thomas, 66
Watson, George Mackie, architect, 121
Watson, James, 98-99
Watson, William Baikie, 133-134, 137
Watt, Jane, 127
Watt, William G. T., 133
Webster, J. Duncan, Private, 137
Wick, John, Private, 138
Willets, James, Private, 138
William I the Old, Bishop of Orkney, 4-8
William II, Bishop of Orkney, 9
William III, Bishop of Orkney, 14 note 70, 27
William IV, Bishop of Orkney, 14 note 70
William of Orange, 74, 85
Williamson, Barbara, wife of Captain Robert Irving, 64-65
Williamson, Elizabeth, 2nd wife of Hugh Leigh, 78
Wilson, Rev. John, 70
Winchester, Captain Peter, 70-72
Winchester, Sibillia, 72

Yenstay, Andrew, 52
Yenstay, Elene, 52
Yenstay, Gilbert, 52
Young, Andrew of Castleyards, 64, 67, 85
Young, James, 77-78
Young, Janet, wife of James Riddoch, 100-101
Young, Mary, 78, 85-86, 100
Yule, Rev. John, 70, 101
Yule, Rev. Robert, 70, 99, 101-102, 107

ENDNOTES

Prelims
1. Hossack, B. H. 1900, *Kirkwall in the Orkneys* 1986 reprint P55.
2. People had lived in the area long before the Vikings arrived. The area around the present day Royal Bank of Scotland was, for example, an Iron Age settlement, probably including a broch (Olwyn, O. (Ed) 2005, *The World of Orkneyinga Saga* P186). It was Rognvald Brusisson, however, who was responsible for the 'Kirk' in Kirkwall.
3. It has to be said there are no certainties in this. Crawford points out that it is possible that the 'Kirk' refers to the Cathedral and that mention of Kirkwall in the saga at the time of Rognvald Brusisson was in fact retrospective. See Crawford, B. E. 2012, *The Northern Earldoms Orkney and Caithness from AD870-1470* P206 note 25
4. Mooney, J. 1947, *The Cathedral and Royal Burgh of Kirkwall* P94.
5. Palsson, H. & Edwards, P. 1978, *Orkneyinga Saga* Chapter 29.

The Eleventh Century – Early Beginnings of Kirkjuvagr
6. Thomson, W. P. L. 2001, *The New History of Orkney* P74-75.
7. ODNB Volume 36 P130.
8. Palsson, H. & Edwards, P. 1996, *Magnus' Saga, The Life of St Magnus, Earl of Orkney* P15.
9. Palsson, H. & Edwards, P. 1978, *Orkneyinga Saga* Chapter 50.
10. Ibid. Chapter 52.
11. Jesch, J. & Molleson, T. 2005, *The Death of Magnus Erlendsson and the relics of St Magnus* in *The World of Orkneyinga Saga* Ed Owen, O. P137.
12. Palsson, H. & Edwards, P. 1978, *Orkneyinga Saga* Chapter 45.
13. Palsson, H. & Edwards, P. 1978, *Orkneyinga Saga* Chapter 42.
14. Ibid. Chapter 68.
15. Prescott, J. 2009, *Earl Rognvaldr Kali: Crisis and Development in Twelfth Century Orkney* University of St Andrews MPhil Thesis.
16. Palsson, H. & Edwards, P. 1978, *Orkneyinga Saga* Chapter 65.
17. Ibid. Chapters 69, 70 and 71.
18. Ibid. Chapter 76.
19. There is disagreement as to what is meant by "buying back their odal lands". See Thomson, W. P. L. 2001, *The New History of Orkney* P108 for an explanation.
20. Palsson, H. & Edwards, P. 1978, *Orkneyinga Saga* Chapter 58. He described himself in his own words: "At nine skills I challenge - a champion at chess: runes I rarely spoil, I read books and write: I'm skilled at skiing and shooting and sculling and more!-I've mastered music and verse".
21. Palsson, H. & Edwards, P. 1978, *Orkneyinga Saga* Chapter 61.
22. Ibid. Chapter 75.
23. These endowments became known as the Prebend of St John. Mooney, J. 1947, *The Cathedral and Royal Burgh of Kirkwall* P51.
24. Palsson, H. & Edwards, P. 1978, *Orkneyinga Saga* Chapter 103.
25. Crawford, B. E. 2012, *The Northern Earldoms Orkney and Caithness from AD870-1470* P218-219.
26. Jesch, J. & Molleson, T. 2005, *The Presumed Relics of St Rognvald* in *The World of Orkneyinga Saga*, Ed Owen O. P139.
27. Palsson, H. & Edwards, P. 1978, *Orkneyinga Saga* Chapter 58.
28. Ibid. Chapter 92.
29. Ibid. Chapter 94 P176-177.
30. Ibid. Chapter 94 P177.
31. Mooney, J. 1925, *Notes on Discoveries in St Magnus Cathedral, Kirkwall* PSAS May 11 1925 P245, POAS vol III. P73.
32. Mooney, J. 1947, *The Cathedral and Royal Burgh of Kirkwall* P86.
33. *Orkneyinga Saga* says he was a kinsman of Sweyn Asleifsson of Gairsay, who sought the Bishop's help after Sweyn had murdered Sweyn Breast-Rope in Orphir – Palsson, H. & Edwards, P. 1978, *Orkneyinga Saga* Chapter 67. Johnston, A. W. & Johnston, A. (Ed) 1907, *Orkney & Shetland Old Lore Series* No 1 P12 says he came from Melrose.
34. Crawford, B. E. 2009, *The Bishopric of Orkney*, NOAJ Vol 4 P48. Around 1109, the Archbishop of York had installed Ralph (or Radulph) Novell of York as Bishop of Orkney. Ralph continued to have the support of the Papacy after Magnus's death. See Johnston, A. W. & Johnston, A. (Ed) 1907, *Orkney & Shetland Old Lore Series* No 1 P14-15.
35. Thomson, W. P. L. 2001, *The New History of Orkney* P94-95
36. Palsson, H. & Edwards, P. 1978, *Orkneyinga Saga* Chapters 66, 76 and 77.
37. ODNB Volume 59 P38.
38. Palsson, H. & Edwards, P. 1978, *Orkneyinga Saga* Chapter 57.
39. Evan MacGillivray hypothesised that this was not built for the Bishop but was, in fact, Earl Rognvald's hall and court. *The Orcadian* July 30th 1987.
40. Mooney, J. 1925, *Notes on Discoveries in St Magnus Cathedral, Kirkwall* PSAS May 11 1925 P242-243, Callaghan, S. & Wilson, B. 2001, *The Unknown Cathedral* P25.

The Twelfth Century – Construction begins
41. Mooney, J. 1929, *Internments and Excavations in St Magnus Cathedral* POAS Volume VII P29.
42. See, for example, Thomson, W. P. L. 2001, *The New History of Orkney* P135.
43. Crawford, B. E. (Ed) 1988, *St Magnus Cathedral and Orkney's Twelfth Century Renaissance* P109.
44. Palsson, H. & Edwards, P. 1978, *Orkneyinga Saga* Chapter 84.
45. Lamb, G. 2004, *Orcadiana* P218.
46. Crawford, B. E. 2009, *The Bishopric of Orkney*, NOAJ Vol 4 P52.
47. Thomson, W. P. L. 2001, *The New History of Orkney* P128.
48. Crawford, B. E. (Ed) 1988, *St Magnus Cathedral and Orkney's Twelfth Century Renaissance* P223. There is considerable doubt that Bjarni is the author of *Malshattakvaedi*, but most experts agree with his authorship of the *Jomsvikings*. See Frank, R. 2004, *Sex, Lies and Malshattakvaedt: a Norse Poem from Medieval Orkney*
49. Schei, L. K. 1985, *The Orkney Story* P66, Thomson W. P. L. 2001, *The New History of Orkney* P412.
50. The early endowments of this prebend also consisted of the teinds of land in Midhouse, Evie, Nistahowe and Cottiscarth in Rendall, Langskaill in Rousay and 12 merks in Fair Isle. The most valuable were the teinds of Wyre. See Clouston, *Old Prebends of Orkney*, POAS Vol IV P34. .
51. Stefansson, J. 1907, Bishop *Biarne Kolbeinsson, the Skald, Orkney and Shetland Old Lore No1* P46.
52. Crawford, B. E. (Ed) 1988, *St Magnus Cathedral and Orkney's Twelfth Century Renaissance* P129.
53. Stefansson, J. 1907, *Bishop Biarne Kolbeinsson, the Skald, Orkney and Shetland Old Lore No1* P47.
54. Sinclair, James 2000, *Images in Time* Vol 3.
55. Wikipedia, Haakon IV of Norway.
56. Palsson, H. 1973, *Hakonar Saga-Portrait of a King* OM Vol 5 P51.
57. Thomson, W. P. L. 2001, *The New History of Orkney* P138-141.
58. Information provided by Cathedral custodian. The sarcophagus is thought more likely to date from the fourteenth century.
59. Thomson, A. 1954, *Masons Marks in St Magnus Cathedral* OM Vol 2 P 66.
60. Dryden, Sir H. E. L. 1878, *Description of the Church Dedicated to St Magnus and the Bishop's Palace* P58.

The Thirteenth Century – Norse Power Wanes
61. RCAMS 1946 P130.
62. Thomson, W. P. L. 2001, *The New History of Orkney* P187.
63. Ibid. P190.

64 Anderson, P. D. 2003, *Cathedral, Palace and Castle* in Waugh, D.J., *Stones, Skalds & Saints*, P81-93. Crawford, B. E. 2012, *The Northern Earldoms Orkney and Caithness from AD870-1470* P75.

65 Clouston, J. S. 1918, *Some Early Orkney Armorials* PSAS 5th Series Vol IV P182-185.

66 Dryden, Sir H. E. L. 1878, *Description of the Church Dedicated to St Magnus and the Bishop's Palace* P57.

67 Clouston, J. S. 1918, *Some Early Orkney Armorials* PSAS 5th Series Vol IV P183.

68 RCAMS 1946 Vol II, P126.

69 For more information on the family, see Ugulen J. R. 2006, *A study of the social composition of the landowning elite in the Westland in the Middle Ages* PhD Thesis, University of Bergen P 405-407 and P677. Sigvat was likely made Lawman of Orkney because of his interest in the islands' trade, see Helle, K. 1988, *Orknoyne I norsk historie* P23.

70 The Norwegian crown had great difficulties with the Orkney bishops in the fourteenth century. Bishop William III was investigated on a number of occasions for various misdemeanours, such as misappropriating funds, employing foreigners and apostates, laxity in rooting out heresy, witchcraft and idolatry, and participating in the boisterous pastime of hunting. His successor, William IV, became involved in the bitter dispute, mentioned above, with crown officials.

71 Ballantyne, J. H. & Smith, B. (Ed) 1999, *Shetland Documents 1195-1579* no.12, Clouston, J. S. 1914, *Records of the Earldom of Orkney* P15-18 (no. VIII).

72 See Thomson, W. P. L. 2001, *The New History of Orkney* P156-157.

The Fourteenth Century – The Black Death

73 Loudon, Dr J. B. 2006, *The Journal of James Robertson 1842-1853* 17th November 1847.

74 Smith, B. 2011, *When did Orkney and Shetland become part of Scotland?* NOAJ Vol 5 P52.

75 Mooney, J. 1952, *Kirkwall Charters* P16.

76 Ibid. P18. There is a letter from c1460, written to the Danish king by Thomas of Kyrknes and John Mager, describing themselves as 'burgesses and bailies of your burgh of Kirkwall'- Crawford, B. E. 2012, *The Northern Earldoms Orkney and Caithness from AD870-1470* P375.

77 Cuthbert, O. D. 1998, *A Flame in the Shadows Robert Reid Bishop of Orkney 1541-1558* P85.

78 Crawford, B. E. 2009, *The Bishopric of Orkney*, NOAJ Vol 4 P61.

79 Thomson, W. P. L. 2001, *The New History of Orkney* P175.

80 Clouston, J. S. 1914, *Records of the Earldom of Orkney 1299-1614* P36-45 (no XVIII).

81 Ibid. P45-48 (no XIX).

82 Ibid. P49-51 (no XXI).

83 Crawford, B. E. 2009, *The Bishopric of Orkney*, NOAJ Vol 4 P63.

84 Thomson, W. P. L. 2001, *The New History of Orkney* P190.

85 Crawford, B. E. 2009, *The Bishopric of Orkney*, NOAJ Vol 4 P62-63.

86 Cant, W. & Firth, H. (Ed) 1989, *Light in the North* P 121-122.

87 Thomson, W. P. L. 2001, *The New History of Orkney* P248.

88 Clouston, J. S. 1914, *Records of the Earldom of Orkney* P53.

89 Callaghan, S. 2001, *The Unknown Cathedral* P27.

90 Norton Smith, H. L. 1902, *Orkney Armorials* P65.

91 Olwyn, O. and Lowe, C. (eds.) 1999, *Kebister, the four-thousand-year-old story of one Shetland township* P215-219.

92 Smith, B. 1989, *In the Tracks of Bishop Andrew Pictoris and Henry Phankouth, Archdeacon of Shetland* Innes Review Vol XL no 2 P92-93.

93 Ibid. Vol XL no 2 P94.

94 Crawford, B. E. (Ed) 1988, *St Magnus Cathedral and Orkney's Twelfth Century Renaissance* P109.

The Fifteenth Century – A Change of Ownership

95 Brian Smith has come across what seems to be Andrew's university matriculation, which suggests he might have been younger.

96 Thomson, W. P. L. 2001, *The New History of Orkney* P230-232.

97 Mackay, R. 1829, *History of the House and Clan Mackay* P110.

98 While the king owned earldom land in Sanday and Stronsay, he certainly did not own all of the land within these islands. For an assessment of this charter see Thomson, W. P. L. 2001, *The New History of Orkney* P241-242.

99 No memorial for Adam Bothwell exists in the Cathedral. This is a pity, considering the important role he played in the story of the Cathedral.

100 Berry, R. J. & Firth, H. N. 1998, *The People of Orkney* P220.

101 Norton Smith, H. L. 1902, *Orkney Armorials*.

102 Norton Traill, H. L. 1922, *Use of Armorial Bearings in Orkney Families* PSAS 1921-22 Vol LVI P311-318.

103 Clouston, J. S. 1918, *Some Early Orkney Armorials* PSAS 5th Series Vol IV P185-186. For further evidence of Fletts using the device of three trefoils, see Clouston J. S.1932, POAS Vol X P37.

104 An illegitimate son of Earl William Sinclair, Sir David Sinclair of Sumburgh had a very successful career in the service of both the kings of Scotland and of Norway. He was very wealthy and owned estates in both Orkney and Shetland.

105 Clouston, J. S. 1919, *Some Further Early Orkney Armorials* PSAS 5th series Vol 5 P183.

106 Clouston, J. S. 1914, *Records of the Earldom of Orkney* P 78 & 95.

107 His sons, Thomas and Andrew completed a land deal concerning Ness in that year. Clouston, J. S. 1914, *Records of the Earldom of Orkney* P189. See P460 for a family tree.

108 Clouston, J. S. 1937, *Orkney and the Archer Guards* POAS Vol XV P31-32.

109 Clouston, J. S. 1914, *Records of the Earldom of Orkney* P95.

110 Clouston, J. S. 1948 (2002 reprint), *The Family of Clouston* P36-37 and 41-44.

111 Craven, J. B. 1901, *The Blazon of Episcopacy in Orkney 1421-1688* P5.

112 On a charter found in the Skaill Charter Chest, dated 7th July 1523, is affixed part of the seal of William Stewart, 'bruyther germane and bailze till ane Reverend fader in God, Edward, Bishop of Orkney'. See Craven, J. B. 1901, *History of the Church in Orkney Prior to 1588* P133 and Clouston, J. S. 1914, *Records of the Earldom of Orkney* P207.

113 Craven, J. B. 1901, *History of the Church in Orkney Prior to 1588* P132-133.

114 Ibid. P134-136.

115 Johnston, A. W. 1908, *Orkney and Shetland Records* Vol 1 P257.

116 Ibid.Vol 1 P265.

117 Clouston, J. S. 1914, *Records of the Earldom of Orkney* P335.

118 Ibid. P274-276.

119 Donaldson, G. *Some Shetland Parishes at the Reformation* in Crawford, B. Ed 1984, *Essays in Shetland History*, P143.

120 Ibid.P157-158.

121 Dryden, Sir H. E. L., 1878, *Description of the Church Dedicated to St Magnus and the Bishop's Palace* P51-56.

122 The Cathedral also has a smaller bell, with a 1 foot 8 inch diameter, called 'the Skellat Bell'. There is no date or inscription on this bell. It was used for many purposes, chiefly to give the alarm in cases of fire, but was also used as the school bell. It tolled for the departing soul and was rung at funerals and festivals. The bell is now on display in the triforium.

123 Hewison, W. S. 1998, *Who Was Who in Orkney* P106.

124 Thomson, W. P. L. 2001, *The New History of Orkney* P248.

125 Craven, J. B. 1901, *History of the Church in Orkney Prior to 1588* P146.

126 Cameron, J. 1998, *James V, The Personal Rule 1528-1542* P144.

127 Cuthbert, O. D. 1998, *A Flame in the Shadows Robert Reid Bishop of Orkney 1541-1558* P17, Hewison, W. S. 1998, *Who Was Who in Orkney* P125.

128 Cuthbert, O. D. 1998, *A Flame in the Shadows Robert Reid Bishop of Orkney 1541-1558* P75-76.

129 Hossack, B. H. 1900, *Kirkwall in the Orkneys* 1986 reprint P307.

130 www.orkneyjar.com/history/stmagnus/magcath.htm.

131 Clouston, J. S. 1914, *Records of the Earldom of Orkney 1299-1614* P363-371.

132. Wilson, B. 2003, *Profit Not Loss, the Story of the Baikies of Tankerness* P10-11.
133. Thomson, W. P. L. 2001, *The New History of Orkney* P249-251.
134. Mooney, J. 1947, *The Cathedral and Royal Burgh of Kirkwall* P52-53.
135. Cuthbert, O. D. 1998, *A Flame in the Shadows Robert Reid Bishop of Orkney 1541-1558* P85.
136. Hewison, W. S. 1998, *Who Was Who in Orkney* P125.
137. Craven, J. B. 1901, *The Blazon of Episcopacy in Orkney 1421-1688* P11.
138. Lyon, Rev W. T. 1917, *Arms of the Scottish Bishoprics* Chapter IX.
139. Crawford, B. E. (Ed) 1988, *St Magnus Cathedral and Orkney's Twelfth Century Renaissance* P128.
140. Donaldson, G. in Crawford, B. E. (Ed) 1995, *Northern Isles Connections* P107.
141. Crawford, B. E. 2009, *The Bishopric of Orkney*, NOAJ Vol 4 P53.
142. Crawford, B. E. (Ed) 1988, *St Magnus Cathedral and Orkney's Twelfth Century Renaissance* P137.
143. Cant, R. G. 1972, *The Church in Orkney and Shetland and its Relations with Norway and Scotland in the Middle Ages.* Gray & Withrington (Ed) *Northern Scotland* Vol 1 P13.
144. See 10. Paplay Tomb. Two Orkney clerics, who were part of this arbitration, had Scottish names; William of Buchan was the Archdeacon of Orkney and Walter of Buchan was a canon belonging to the chapter.
145. Donaldson, G. 1987, *Reformed by Bishops* P20. It was assumed that the two individuals were the same person, suggesting Kaa was an alternative for the well-known Orkney surname, Skea. Given the prevalence in Kirkwall in centuries past of the name Kaa, this is perhaps doubtful (see 63).
146. Clouston, J. S. 1918, *Some Early Orkney Armorials* PSAS 5th Series Vol IV P186.
147. Clouston J. S. 1914, *Records of the Earldom of Orkney* P84.
148. Ibid. P364.
149. Ibid. P338.
150. Clouston, J. S. 1918, *Some Early Orkney Armorials* PSAS 5th Series Vol IV P188. The possibility of Aikers being a son is very feasible as celibacy was certainly not followed by many of the Cathedral clerics. For example, Nicholas Halcro's successor as precentor, Magnus Halcro, had a number of illegitimate children and later married the daughter of James Sinclair of Brecks (brother of Edward Sinclair-22). He was excommunicated from the reformed church for adultery. Donaldson G. 1987, *Reformed by Bishops* P28-29.
151. Clouston, J. S. 1918, *Some Early Orkney Armorials* PSAS 5th Series Vol IV P187.
152. Ibid. Vol IV P188.
153. Clouston, J. S. 1914, *Records of the Earldom of Orkney* P113-117.
154. Clouston, J. S. 1918, *Some Early Orkney Armorials* PSAS 5th Series Vol IV P189-190.
155. Clouston, J. S. 1919, *Some Further Early Orkney Armorials* PSAS 5th series Vol 5 P184.
156. Thomson, W. P. L. 2001, *The New History of Orkney* P237-238.
157. Thomson, W. P. L. 2001, *The New History of Orkney* P239. As Thomson states, most of what we know about Summerdale is very one sided, coming from Lord William Sinclair's subsequent complaint to the King. See Ballantyne, J. H. & Smith, B. (Ed) 1999 *Shetland Documents 1195-1579* no 51.
158. James Sinclair lived at Linksness in Tankerness and is reputed to have jumped into the nearby Gloup of Linksness. See Thomson, W. P. L. 2001, *The New History of Orkney* P242.
159. Thomson, W. P. L. 2001, *The New History of Orkney* P243.
160. Ibid. P246, Anderson, P. D. 1982, *Robert Stewart* P32.
161. Clouston, J. S. 1914, *Records of the Earldom of Orkney* P370.
162. Cuthbert, O. D. 1998, *A Flame in the Shadows Robert Reid Bishop of Orkney 1541-1558* P109.
163. Their marriage contract is dated 10th September 1539.
164. Smith, B. 1989, *In the Tracks of Bishop Andrew Pictoris and Henry Phankouth, Archdeacon of Shetland* Innes Review Vol XL no 2 P102.
165. Edward is last mentioned in court records concerning a dispute over land in Shetland, dating from July 1563. See Ballantyne, J. H. & Smith, B. (Ed) 1999, *Shetland Documents 1195-1579* no. 136 & 138.
166. Grant, F. J. 1893, *The County Families of the Shetland Islands* P257.
167. Clouston, J. S. 1932, *Our Ward Hills and Ensigns* POAS Vol X P38, Clouston J. S. 1919 *Some Further Early Orkney Armorials* PSAS 5th series Vol 5 P185.
168. For a full list of names see Low, G. *Orkney and Schetland 1774* P208.
169. Ballantyne, J. H. & Smith, B. (Ed) 1999, *Shetland Documents 1195-1579* no 120, dated 3rd July 1560.
170. Ibid. no 149.
171. Ibid. no 254.
172. Loudon, Dr J. B. 2006, *The Journal of James Robertson 1842-1853* Thursday 5th October 1848.
173. Johnston, L. 1994, *St Magnus Cathedral Gravestones* P56.
174. ODNB Volume 29 P627.
175. Anderson, P. D. 1982, *Robert Stewart* P156-158. Another daughter married David King of Warbister (see 41).
176. On a number of records from the time, William Henryson is described as "Dingwall pursuivant", an officer of the Court of the Lord Lyon. See Ballantyne, J. H. & Smith, B. (Ed) 1999, *Shetland Documents 1195-1579* no145.
177. Hewison, W. S. 1998, *Who Was Who in Orkney* P74.
178. Anderson, P. D. 1982, *Robert Stewart* P176.
179. For the terms of reference for the commission see Ballantyne, J. H. & Smith, B. (Ed) 1999, *Shetland Documents 1195-1579* no 233 and no 237 for the commission's report.
180. See Anderson, P. D. 1982, *Robert Stewart* P96-101 for a detailed description of the complaints.
181. Clouston, J. S. 1914, *Records of the Earldom of Orkney* P320.
182. Dennison, W. T. 1995, *Orkney Folklore & Sea Legends* P158. See also the start of Chapter 7.
183. *Memorial Catalogue, Heraldic Exhibition*, Edinburgh 1892.
184. Omand, D. (Ed) 2003, *The Orkney Book* P86.
185. Anderson, P. D. 1982, *Robert Stewart* P131.
186. Thomson, W. P. L. 2001, *The New History of Orkney* P263.
187. Ibid. P264-265.
188. Mooney, J. 1952, *Kirkwall Charters* P80.
189. Anderson P. D. 2012, *The Stewart Earls of Orkney* P79 and 104. It was Provost Patrick Craigie who, in the middle of the following century, accused Robert of perpetrating this deed.
190. Hewison, W. S. 1998, *Who Was Who in Orkney* P154.
191. Hewison, W. S. 1998, *Who Was Who in Orkney* P155.
192. Thomson, W. P. L. 2001, *The New History of Orkney* P275.
193. Norton Smith, H. L. 1902, *Orkney Armorials* P102.
194. Anderson, P. D. 1982, *Robert Stewart* P180.
195. Ibid. P57-58. Also Anderson, P. D. 2012, *The Stewart Earls of Orkney* P65.
196. Anderson, P. D. 1982, *Robert Stewart* P62.
197. Ibid. P95.
198. Willsher, B. & Hunter, D. 2006, *Stones, a Guide to Some Remarkable Eighteenth Century Gravestones* P56
199. Anderson, P. D. 1982, *Robert Stewart* P179.
200. Hossack, B. H. 1900, *Kirkwall in the Orkneys* 1986 reprint P222.
201. Black, J. 1946, *The Surnames of Scotland* P574.
202. Clouston, J. S. 1914, *Records of the Earldom of Orkney* P160. There is a possibility that this William Maine is not the same William Maine on the gravestone. Attached to the document are twelve seals, including one belonging to a William Maine. This seal shows a different coat-of-arms to that on the gravestone and consists of a mullet on a fess between three loaves.
203. Ibid. P351-353.
204. Clouston, J. S. 1926, *An Old Kirkwall House* POAS Vol V.
205. Hossack, B. H. 1900, *Kirkwall in the Orkneys* 1986 reprint P51

The Sixteenth Century – Trouble and Strife

206. Clouston, J. S. 1926, *An Old Kirkwall House* POAS Vol V.
207. Tarlow, S. A. 1995, *Metaphors of Death in Orkney 1560-1945AD* P119. Vanity had the meaning of futility in the seventeenth century.

208 Ibid. P112.
209 Olcott, C. S. *The Orkneys and Shetlands – A Mysterious Group of Islands*, from *National Geographic Magazine* Vol XXXIX no. 2, Feb 1921. Tarlow disagrees with this assertion and believes it to be an attempt for more anatomical accuracy, with the incision on the side of the skull, depicting the zygomatic arch. See Tarlow, S. A. 1995, *Metaphors of Death in Orkney 1560-1945AD* P111.
210 Dennison, W. T. 1995, *Orkney Folklore & Sea Legends* P153.
211 Ibid. P154.
212 This screen had to be torn down in 1671 for fear of catching fire when the steeple was struck by lightning – Hossack, B. H. 1900, *Kirkwall in the Orkneys* 1986 reprint P40.
213 Anderson, P. D. 1999, *Earl Patrick and his Enemies* NOAJ P45.
214 Hossack, B. H. 1900, *Kirkwall in the Orkneys* 1986 reprint P45.
215 ODNB says Agnes Strang was his mother.
216 John Knox would have approved - he liked a round of golf on the Sabbath as a means of helping him compose the evening sermon.
217 ODNB Volume 32 P757.
218 He would not be consecrated as Bishop until 1611. Scott, H 1928, *Fasti Ecclesiae Scoticanae* Vol VII P322.
219 Thomson, W. P. L. 2001, *The New History of Orkney* P291.
220 Bardgett, F. D. 2000, *Two Millennia of Church and Community in Orkney* P74.
221 Thomson, W. P. L. 2001, *The New History of Orkney* P291.
222 Hewison, W. S. 1998, *Who Was Who in Orkney* P153.
223 Thomson, W. P. L. 2001, *The New History of Orkney* P295.
224 Another court was held in the great hall of the Bishop's Palace. Courts were also held in Rousay and Stronsay. See Barclay, R. S. 1967, *The Court Books of Orkney and Shetland 1614-1615* PXXI.
225 Thomson, W. P. L. 2001, *The New History of Orkney* P321.
226 Thomson, W. P. L. 2001, *The New History of Orkney* P297.
227 Ibid. P298.
228 The guns included "Thrawn Mou", which was taken from Edinburgh Castle.
229 Anderson, P. D. 1992, *Black Patie* P122.
230 Thomson, W. P. L. 2001, *The New History of Orkney* P298.
231 Bardgett, F. D. 2000, *Two Millennia of Church and Community in Orkney* P75.
232 Norton Smith, H. L. 1902, *Orkney Armorials* P53.
233 Sir Robert had been one of Earl Patrick Stewart's creditors and had represented Patrick in an arbitration case against Robert Monteith of Egilsay-see Anderson, P. D. 1992, *Black Patie* P67 & 104.
234 The Bishop's wife died in 1633 and was buried in St Magnus Cathedral – Hossack, B. H. 1900, *Kirkwall in the Orkneys* 1986 reprint P79, Graeme, L. G. 1903, *Or and Sable, a book of the Graemes and Grahams* P60.
235 Scott, H 1928, *Fasti Ecclesiae Scoticanae* Vol VII P353. Graeme, L. G. 1903, *Or and Sable, a book of the Graemes and Grahams* P41. Braco is a village about 5 miles from Dunblane
236 Graeme, L. G. 1903, *Or and Sable, a book of the Graemes and Grahams* P46.
237 Irvine, J. M. 2009, *The Breckness Estate* P36.
238 Graeme, L. G. 1903, *Or and Sable, a book of the Graemes and Grahams* P52.
239 Irvine, J. M. 2009, *The Breckness Estate* P34.
240 Scott, H 1928, *Fasti Ecclesiae Scoticanae* Vol VII P353.
241 The city had fallen in 1628 before the money could be put to its intended use.
242 Fereday, R. F. 1976, *From Sang School to Burgh School*.
243 Thomson, W. P. L. 2001, *The New History of Orkney* P308, Irvine, J. M. 2009, *The Breckness Estate* P34.
244 Irvine, J. M. 2009, *The Breckness Estate* P35.
245 Irvine, J. M. 2009, *The Breckness Estate* P36-37. Thomas Sydserf was actually the next Bishop of Orkney, but because of his age, he never visited Orkney and he died in 1663.
246 Mackintosh, W. R. 1885, *Glimpses of Kirkwall in Olden Time* P227.
247 Norton Smith, H. L. 1902, *Orkney Armorials* P73.
248 Scott, H 1928, *Fasti Ecclesiae Scoticanae* Vol VII P353.
249 Honeyman, A. 1909, *The Honeyman Family in Scotland and America 1548-1908*, Chapter II.
250 The 7th Earl of Morton had been granted the earldom of Orkney by King Charles I in 1643 and had taken a 19-year lease of the Palace from the city of Edinburgh, which had been assigned the revenues of the bishopric. See Pringle, D. *The Houses of the Stewart Earls in Orkney and Shetland* NOAJ Volume 1 P38.
251 Hossack, B. H. 1900, *Kirkwall in the Orkneys* 1986 reprint P84.
252 The full title is actually, *A survey of the insolent and infamous libel, entitled Naphtali & wherin several things falling in debate in these times are considered, and some doctrines in Lex Rex and the Apolog. Narration (called by this author martyrs) are brought to the touchstone* (Part 1, 1668 and Part 2, 1669).
253 Hewison, W. S. 1998, *Who Was Who in Orkney* P75.
254 Scott, H 1928, *Fasti Ecclesiae Scoticanae* Vol VII P353.
255 Mooney, J. 1925, *Notes on Discoveries in St Magnus Cathedral, Kirkwall* PSAS May 11 1925 P243.
256 Scott, H 1928, *Fasti Ecclesiae Scoticanae* Vol VII P354.
257 Smith, J. 1907, *The Church in Orkney* P39.
258 Hewison, W. S. 1998, *Who Was Who in Orkney* P97.
259 Craven, J. B. 1893, *History of the Church in Orkney 1662-1688* P80.
260 Craven, J. B. 1893, *History of the Church in Orkney 1662-1688* P91.
261 The Diary of Thomas Brown says, "Friday at 6hrs at night or yrby the 17th Febry 1688 Murdoch, Bishop of Orkney & Zetland, depairted this lyfe, being near ane hundreth yeiris of adge or yrby, and wes interned in St Magnus Kirk in Kirkwall, within the comone place of the samyne, commonly called the counsell houss, qr no persone haith been interred heitherto". The last Bishop of Orkney was Andrew Bruce, who signed a loyal address to King James VII in 1688. He was deposed without ever having visited Orkney, following the proclamation of William and Mary and the abolition of Episcopacy in April 1689.
262 Johnston, L. 1994, *St Magnus Cathedral Gravestones* P66.
263 Clouston, J. S. 1914, *Records of the Earldom of Orkney* P81. This record is from a decree of the Lawman of Orkney (John Craigie) and Roithmen regarding the boundaries of Sebay and rights of the owners.
264 Anderson, P. D. 1982, *Robert Stewart* P190.
265 Clouston, J. S. 1919, *Some Further Early Orkney Armorials* PSAS 5th series Vol 5 P188.
266 Johnston, L. 1994, *St Magnus Cathedral Gravestones* P30.
267 Clouston, J. S. 1919, *Some Further Early Orkney Armorials* PSAS 5th series Vol 5. P190.
268 Johnston, L. 1994, *St Magnus Cathedral Gravestones* P30.
269 Clouston, J. S. 1919, *Some Further Early Orkney Armorials* PSAS 5th series Vol 5. P190.
270 Smith, B. & Ballantyne, J. H. (Ed) 1994, *Shetland Documents 1580-1611* no 412.
271 Marwick, H. Unpublished, *William Bannatyne of Gairsay* OA D29/1/15. As well as his sons, Gilbert and John, William had an illegitimate son, called Robert.
272 Marwick, H. Unpublished, *William Bannatyne of Gairsay* OA D29/1/15.
273 Clouston, J. S. 1914, *Records of the Earldom of Orkney* P160.
274 Anderson, P.D. in Omand, D. (Ed) 2003, *The Orkney Book* P87.
275 Thomson, W. P. L. 2001, *The New History of Orkney* P278.
276 Anderson, P. D. 1992, *Black Patie* P52.
277 Tudor, J. R. 1883, *The Orkneys and Shetland* P545 & 622.
278 Marwick, H. Unpublished, *William Bannatyne of Gairsay* OA D29/1/15. Ballantyne, J. H. & Smith, B. (Ed) 1994, *Shetland Documents 1580-1611* no 229 & 507.
279 Anderson, P. D. 1992, *Black Patie* P57.
280 Ibid. P122.
281 Tudor, J. R. 1883, *The Orkneys and Shetland* P273.
282 Johnston, L. 1994, *St Magnus Cathedral Gravestones* P96.
283 OA D31/14/1 Roland St Clair typescript, "Orcadian Families-Pottinger". Barclay, R. S. 1977, *Orkney Testaments and Inventories 1573-1615* P123.
284 Hossack, B. H. 1900, *Kirkwall in the Orkneys* 1986 reprint P335.

285 This John Pottinger is likely to be the merchant, who supplied weapons to the Royalist cause (see 50) and was father of Marjorie Pottinger (55)
286 Flett, J. 1929, *Kirkwall Incorporated Trades* POAS Vol VII, P48.
287 Clouston, J. S. 1919, *Some Further Early Orkney Armorials* PSAS 5th series Vol 5 P190.
288 Ibid. Vol 5 P190.
289 Hossack, B. H. 1900, *Kirkwall in the Orkneys* 1986 reprint P318, street plan, though Clouston disagreed and places the Hall of Banks slightly to the north. See Clouston, J. S. 1926, *An Old Kirkwall House* POAS P9-14.
290 Anderson, P. D. 1982, *Robert Stewart* P166.
291 See Barclay, R. S. 1967, *The Court Books of Orkney and Shetland 1614-1615* P73, 77, 78, 81 & 93.
292 Dryden, Sir H. E. L. 1878, *Description of the Church Dedicated to St Magnus and the Bishop's Palace* P59 Johnston, L. 1994, *St Magnus Cathedral Gravestones* P54.
293 Clouston, J. S. 1914, *Records of the Earldom of Orkney* P45.
294 Sebay is in the parish of St Andrews, in the East Mainland.
295 Hossack, B. H. 1900, *Kirkwall in the Orkneys* 1986 reprint P155.
296 Clouston, J. S. 1932, *History of Orkney* P275.
297 Manson, A. 1999, *Horrie Farm and its Neighbourhood 1500-1924* P4. For copies of the charters referring to Horrie see Ballantyne, J. H. & Smith, B. (Ed) 1999, *Shetland Documents 1195-1579* nos 40, 43 & 179).
298 Manson, A. 1999, *Horrie Farm and its Neighbourhood 1500-1924* P5, Anderson, P. D. 1982, *Robert Stewart* P177.
299 OA D8/1/14 dated 1594 – "charge of disobedience of the King's writ and warrant for putting Gilbert Irving of Sebay, Edward Irving, his brother, Margaret Irving, their sister and Alexander Flett, her husband, in possession of the lands and mill of Sebay from which they were dispossessed by William Irving".
300 Barclay, R. S. 1977, *Orkney Testaments and Inventories 1573-1615* P165-166, Manson, A. 1999, *Horrie Farm and its Neighbourhood 1500-1924* P6.
301 Anderson, P. D. 1982, *Robert Stewart* P177-178.
302 Anderson, P. D. 1992, *Black Patie* P45. A bronze canon recovered from the wreck site in 1970 was recently restored and is now on display in Shetland Museum.
303 Ibid. P96
304 Ibid. P122-123.
305 Clouston, J. S. 1914, *Records of the Earldom of Orkney* P448.
306 Ibid. P448.
307 Johnston, A. W. & Johnston, A. 1908, *Orkney & Shetland Records Vol III Orkney Sasines 1617-1621* P63-64.
308 David King of Warbister (Hoy) was one of Earl Patrick Stewart's Sheriffs-Depute and legal advisers, along with his brother and nephew (see Anderson, P. D. 1992, *Black Patie* P160). He was married to another daughter of Adam Stewart (25) and so was related by marriage to Hew Halcro. Interestingly, David King's son was James King, Lord Eythin, who had a successful career fighting in the Thirty Years War, before a less successful spell as one of the leaders of the Royalists during the Civil War. James King died in Stockholm in 1652 and was given a state funeral.
309 Clouston, J. S. 1924, *Old Orkney Houses III* POAS Volume II P9.
310 Johnston, A. W. & Johnston, A. 1908, *Orkney & Shetland Records Vol III Orkney Sasines 1617-1621* P109, OA D23/6/108 Instrument of sasine dated 25 Jan 1644, in favour of Hew Halcro younger of that ilk for the lands and teinds of Braebuster disponed to him by Hew Halcro elder.
311 Anderson, P. D. 1992, *Black Patie* P96.
312 Ibid. P102-103.
313 Clouston, J. S. 1914, *Records of the Earldom of Orkney* P449.
314 Ibid. P lx, Anderson, P. D. 1982, *Robert Stewart* P190.
315 Clouston, J. S. 1914, *Records of the Earldom of Orkney* P399 & 448.
316 See photograph in RCAMS opposite P131.
317 Hossack, B. H. 1900, *Kirkwall in the Orkneys* 1986 reprint P137
318 Thomson, W. P. L. 2001, *The New History of Orkney* P352.
319 RCAMS 1946 P150.
320 Hossack, B. H. 1900, *Kirkwall in the Orkneys* 1986 reprint P182.
321 Barry, Rev G. 1805, *The History of the Orkney Islands* 1975 reprint P473.
322 Craven, J. B. *History of the Church in Orkney 1558-1662* P146.
323 Hossack, B. H. 1900, *Kirkwall in the Orkneys* 1986 reprint P185.
324 Son of Sir William Dick of Braid. For more information see Thomson, W. P. L. 2001, *The New History of Orkney* P303-304.
325 Hossack, B. H. 1900, *Kirkwall in the Orkneys* 1986 reprint P330 and Clouston, J. S. 1927, *The Orkney Parishes* P189.
326 Hossack, B. H. 1900, *Kirkwall in the Orkneys* 1986 reprint P131.
327 Clouston, J. S. 1927, *The Orkney Parishes* P143, 189, 239, 251 & 334.
328 Clouston, J. S. 1932 *History of Orkney* P333.
329 The garrison of English troops was established in Kirkwall, where they were quartered in the Cathedral and the Earl's Palace. They fortified the town's defences by building batteries on either side of the bay, using the kirkyard dyke round the Cathedral as a source of stone and some of the pews in the Cathedral to furnish the batteries. They also vandalised the tomb of Thomas Tulloch. The metal rings driven into some of the pillars of the Cathedral are thought to date from this period and were used to tether their horses.
330 Craven, J. B. 1897, *History of the Church in Orkney 1558-1662* P213.
331 Ministers of the time were good at switching sides, when circumstances changed. Indeed, David Kennedy became Archdeacon of Orkney after Episcopacy was re-established.
332 See Mooney, J. 1952, *Kirkwall Charters* P83-84 and Mooney, J. 1939, OAS Vol XV *St Magnus Cathedral: Proprietorship and Maintenance* P72.
333 Hossack, B. H. 1900, *Kirkwall in the Orkneys* 1986 reprint P265-266.
334 Fereday, R. F. 1976, *From Sang School to Burgh School*.
335 Shaw, F. J. 1980, *The Northern and Western Islands of Scotland* P150 & 237.
336 Smith, J. S. 1898, *The Grange of St Giles* P93.
337 All the major nobles of Scotland were in a similar state of debt, see Lynch, M. 1992, *Scotland, A New History* P291.
338 Marshall, D. 1889, *Notes of the Connection of the Earls of Morton and Dick of Braid* PSAS P284, Douglas, Sir R. 1798, *The Baronage of Scotland* P271.
339 Marshall D. 1889, *Notes of the Connection of the Earls of Morton and Dick of Braid* PSAS May 13th 1889 P307.
340 Norton Smith, H. L. 1902, *Orkney Armorials* P58.
341 Johnston, L. 1994, *St Magnus Cathedral Gravestones* P80.
342 Hossack, B. H. 1900, *Kirkwall in the Orkneys* 1986 reprint P357.
343 Johnston, A. W. & Johnston, A. 1908 *Orkney & Shetland Records Vol III Orkney Sasines 1617-1621* P67 and OA D2/27/16, "discharge by Edward Pottinger, skipper in Kirkwall, under marriage-contract, 13 December 1615, with later Katherine Baikie, daughter of Thomas Baikie and sister of James Baikie (of Tankerness)".
344 Clouston, J. S. 1914, *Records of the Earldom of Orkney* P444. Robert of Hobbister also transferred land in Orphir to Robert Richan (61) – OA D23/4/101 – extract of disposition, dated 15th March 1633, by Robert Flett of Howbuster to Robert Richan of four merk lands in Orphir.
345 Ritchie, E. 2009, *A Collected History of the Traill/Trail Family* P259.
346 Hossack, B. H. 1900, *Kirkwall in the Orkneys* 1986 reprint P129, Ritchie E. 2009, *A Collected History of the Traill/Trail Family* P260-261. See also 51 and the case of the *Kenmerland*.
347 Johnston, L. 1994, *St Magnus Cathedral Gravestones* P22.
348 Kirkwall was divided into the Burgh in the north, the Laverock in the south and Midtown between the two.
349 Pottinger, M. 2000, *The Minutes of the Town Council of Kirkwall in the Orkneys 1669-1700* P44.
350 Hossack, B. H. 1900, *Kirkwall in the Orkneys* 1986 reprint P119.
351 Black, G. F. 1946, *The Surnames of Scotland* P827.
352 Clouston, J. S. 1914, *Records of the Earldom of Orkney* P470.
353 Clouston, J. S. 1919, *Some further Early Orkney Armorials* PSAS 5th Series Vol 5 P192.
354 Johnston, L. 1994, *St Magnus Cathedral Gravestones* P70.

355 Saint-Clair, R. W. 1898, *The Saint-Clair of the Isles*. Roland William Saint-Clair (not his birth name) wrote the book in New Zealand and included any information sent to him without checking his facts.

356 Johnston, A. W. & Johnston, A. 1908, *Orkney & Shetland Records Vol III Orkney Sasines 1617-1621* P81

357 Craven, J. B. *History of the Church in Orkney* Vol II P149, Peterkin, A. 1820, *Rentals of the Ancient Earldom and Bishoprick of Orkney* P65

358 OA D31/14/1 Roland St Clair typescript, "Orcadian Families-Sinclair of Rapness".

359 Commissioners of Supply consisted of the principal landowners in each area and provided local administration in the counties of Scotland until the creation of County Councils in 1890.

360 Johnston, L. 1994, *St Magnus Cathedral Gravestones* P76.

361 Hossack, B. H. 1900, *Kirkwall in the Orkneys* 1986 reprint P251.

362 His brother was Sir John Stewart of Killeith, Lord Ochiltree, and was a former unpopular tacksman of Orkney – see Thomson, W. P. L. 2001, *The New History of Orkney* P302.

363 Hossack, B. H. 1900, *Kirkwall in the Orkneys* 1986 reprint P255.

364 Ibid. P251.

365 Ibid. P125-126. Moncrieff was a keen golfer, which was played at that time on land adjacent to Papdale.

366 The full list of signatories were Robert, Earl of Morton, Patrick Smyth of Braco, David MacLellan of Woodwick (44), James Baikie of Tankerness (66), Hew Sinclair of Damsay, Edward Sinclair of Gyre, William Sinclair of Sebay, John Graham of Breckness, Patrick Gordon of Cairston, James Mudie of Melsetter, David Beaton in Cairston, Robert Sinclair fear of Sebay, David Kincaid of Yenstay and Harie Henderson of Clett.

367 Marwick, H. 1930, *A Glimpse of the Great Marquis* POAS Vol VIII, OA D29/1/13.

368 Irvine, J. M. 2009, *The Breckness Estate* P39.

369 Hossack, B. H. 1900, *Kirkwall in the Orkneys* 1986 reprint P251.

370 Graeme, L. G. 1903, *Or and Sable, a book of the Graemes and Grahams* P532. Many of the letters Smyth wrote to his son, Patrick, during the time of Cromwell's occupation of Kirkwall are recorded in Hossack.

371 Mackintosh, W. R. 1885, *Glimpses of Kirkwall in Olden Time* P311

372 Hossack, B. H. 1900, *Kirkwall in the Orkneys* 1986 reprint P255.

373 Johnston, L. 1994, *St Magnus Cathedral Gravestones* P2.

374 Graeme, L. G. 1903, *Or and Sable, a book of the Graemes and Grahams* P115.

375 Johnston, A. W. & Johnston, A. 1908, *Orkney & Shetland Records Vol III Orkney Sasines 1617-1621* P108-109.

376 Wishart, Rev. G. 1893, *The Memoirs of James Marquis of Montrose 1639-1650* P109.

377 Drummond, W. 1681, *Genealogy of the Most Noble and Ancient House of Drummond* 1831 reprint P282.

378 Graeme, L. G. 1903, *Or and Sable, a book of the Graemes and Grahams* P538, OA D31/14/1 Roland St Clair typescript, "Orcadian Families-Graham". Note that different sources give different lists of off spring from George Drummond's two marriages.

379 Steuart, A. F. (ed) 1898, *Diary of Thomas Brown 1675-1693* P14.

380 Hossack, B. H. 1900, *Kirkwall in the Orkneys* 1986 reprint P467 and Craven J. B. 1897 *History of the Church in Orkney 1558-1662* P241 say 1647-50. Mackintosh, W. R. 1892, *Curious Incidents from the Ancient Records of Kirkwall* P304 says 1648-50.

381 Wishart, Rev. G. 1893, *The Memoirs of James, Marquis of Montrose 1639-1650* P292.

382 Ibid. P257.

383 Wishart, Rev. G. 1893, *The Memoirs of James, Marquis of Montrose 1639-1650* P293. If young George was the son of George's second marriage, it would make him very young indeed to have such a promoted position. At least one source says he is a son of the first marriage - Drummond W. 1681 *Genealogy of the Most Noble and Ancient House of Drummond* 1831 reprint P61.

384 Son of Magnus Pottinger and Catherine Craigie (see 36 and 45).

385 Wishart, Rev. G. 1893, *The Memoirs of James, Marquis of Montrose 1639-1650* P293.

386 Ibid. P497.

387 Mackay, R. 1829, *History of the House and Clan of Mackay* P344.

388 All the Orkney ministers had been deposed as a result of their loyal address to Montrose, except for two, James Morrison of Evie and Rendall and Patrick Waterstoun of Stronsay and Eday – see Hossack P8.

389 Drummond, W. 1681, *Genealogy of the Most Noble and Ancient House of Drummond* 1831 reprint P282-283.

390 Graeme, L. G. 1903, *Or and Sable, a book of the Graemes and Grahams* P539.

391 Johnston, L. 1994, *St Magnus Cathedral Gravestones* P26.

392 Anderson, P. D. 1982, *Robert Stewart* P35.

393 www.clannapier.org, www.gordonamacgregor.com

394 Mackintosh, W. R. 1892, *Curious Incidents from the Ancient Records of Kirkwall* P304.

395 Marshall, D. 1889, *Notes of the Connection of the Earls of Morton and Dick of Braid* PSAS May 13th 1889, P300-312. The Earl's Palace in Kirkwall was also surveyed at this time.

396 OA D16/2/16.

397 The seventeenth century saw the Dutch become a global superpower and rivalry in trade led to a series of Anglo-Dutch wars in the latter half of the seventeenth century, which ended in victory for the Dutch. While Kirkwall traders continued to trade with Norway, Amsterdam became an important port of call, where all sorts of luxury goods, such as silks and spices, could be obtained.

398 The beacons were built of peats and heather, the householders of each parish being bound, under penalty, to always have them ready. *John O'Groats Journal* 12th December 1851.

399 OA D16/2/16 Feb./March 1667. This certainly confirms that the Wideford Hill beacon was the main trigger for all other beacons to be lit. Outlying beacons could be lit to give warning of impending attack and the direction from which the danger was approaching, the general alarm would only go out when Wideford Hill was lit. See J. S. 1932, *Our Ward Hills and Ensigns* POAS Vol X P34 and Barry, Rev. G. 1805, *The History of the Orkney Islands* 1975 reprint P468.

400 At the start of the next war, in 1673, the Dutch moved quickly to eliminate this fort before it could be rearmed and garrisoned. A landing party came ashore and burnt Fort Charlotte, along with many of the houses in Lerwick.

401 Thomson, W. P. L. 2001, *The New History of Orkney* P307.

402 Ritchie, E., 2009, *A Collected History of the Traill/Trail Family* P260-261.

403 It would appear that the Earl of Morton was in fact telling the truth. See Thomson, W. P. L. 2001 *The New History of Orkney* P307.

404 The 7th Earl of Morton obtained a 19-year lease of the Earl's Palace in 1643 from the city of Edinburgh, which held the tack of the Bishopric estate. Ross, J. 1977, *Orkney and the Earls of Morton 1643-1707* P4.

405 Craven, J. B. 1893, *History of the Church in Orkney 1662-1688*, P52.

406 Johnston, L. 1994, *St Magnus Cathedral Gravestones* P110.

407 Hossack, B. H. 1900, *Kirkwall in the Orkneys* 1986 reprint P247.

408 Thomson, W. P. L. 2001, *The New History of Orkney* P303.

409 Johnston, L. 1994, *St Magnus Cathedral Gravestones* P4.

410 Hossack, B. H. 1900, *Kirkwall in the Orkneys* 1986 reprint P125.

411 Thomson, W. P. L. 2001 *The New History of Orkney* P304.

412 Pottinger, M. 2000, *The Minutes of the Town Council of Kirkwall in the Orkneys 1669-1700* P3.

413 Johnston, L. 1994, *St Magnus Cathedral Gravestones* P24.

414 Hossack, B. H. 1900, *Kirkwall in the Orkneys* 1986 reprint P334.

415 Pottinger, M. 2000, *The Minutes of the Town Council of Kirkwall in the Orkneys 1669-1700* P107.

416 Hossack, B. H. 1900, *Kirkwall in the Orkneys* 1986 reprint P358.

417 Ritchie, E., 2009, *A Collected History of the Traill/Trail Family* P260.

418 Johnston, L. 1994, *St Magnus Cathedral Gravestones* P38.

419 OA D31/14/1 Roland St Clair typescript, "Orcadian Families-Pottinger". Her grandfather was Magnus Pottinger (see 36).

420 Black, G. F. 1946 *The Surnames of Scotland* P670.

421 Pottinger, G. 1983 *The Afghan Connection, the Extraordinary Adventures of Major Eldred Pottinger* P1.

422 Scott, H. 1928 *Fasti Ecclesiae Scoticanae* Vol VII P255.
423 Hossack, B. H. 1900, *Kirkwall in the Orkneys* 1986 reprint P431 and 165
424 Ibid. P122.
425 Harrison, K. *Kirkwall Families* www.orkneyfhs.co.uk. Dishington Family baptismal record on June 17th 1673 reads, "Thomas Dishingtoune lawful sonne to Thomas Dishingtoune praecentor and Margaret Elphinstone was baptized be Mr James Wallace minister".
426 Hossack, B. H. 1900, *Kirkwall in the Orkneys* 1986 reprint P120.
427 Craven, J. B. 1893, *History of the Church in Orkney 1662-1688* P63.
428 Pottinger, M. 2000, *The Minutes of the Town Council of Kirkwall in the Orkneys 1669-1700* P180.
429 Hossack, B. H. 1900, *Kirkwall in the Orkneys* 1986 reprint P266.
430 Craven, J. B. 1893, *History of the Church in Orkney 1662-1688* P99.
431 Scott, H. 1928, *Fasti Ecclesiae Scoticanae* Vol VII P255 gives a death date of 2nd June 1682.
432 Johnston, L. 1994, *St Magnus Cathedral Gravestones* P106.
433 Hossack, B. H. 1900, *Kirkwall in the Orkneys* 1986 reprint P230. Magnus Prince went on to become a very prominent citizen in Edinburgh, being appointed treasurer of Edinburgh Town Council in 1680, before rising to become the city's Lord Provost during the turbulent period, 1687-1689, at the end of the reign of King James VII. Hossack suggests that the name Prince was Danish in origin.
434 Hossack, B. H. 1900, *Kirkwall in the Orkneys* 1986 reprint P198.
435 Ibid. P328.
436 Pottinger, M. 2000, *The Minutes of the Town Council of Kirkwall in the Orkneys 1669-1700* P2.
437 Hossack, B. H. 1900, *Kirkwall in the Orkneys* 1986 reprint P113. This same year saw a new constitution, resulting in a "great Counsell" consisting of 16 members, not including the Provost and four Bailies. The Dean of Guild and Treasurer were chosen out of the 16 members of the "great Counsell". In addition, the trades were to elect three persons, being the only representative members on the Council – Pottinger, M. 2000, *The Minutes of the Town Council of Kirkwall in the Orkneys 1669-1700* P22.
438 OA D31/14/1 Roland St Clair typescript, "Orcadian Families-Groat"
439 Hossack, B. H. 1900, *Kirkwall in the Orkneys* 1986 reprint P117.
440 Steuart, A. F. (ed) 1898, *Diary of Thomas Brown 1675-1693* P3. The minutes of Kirkwall Town Council say that Margaret Groat was spouse to John Baird since 2nd February 1677, Pottinger, M. 2000, *The Minutes of the Town Council of Kirkwall in the Orkneys 1669-1700* P162.
441 Pottinger, M. 2000, *The Minutes of the Town Council of Kirkwall in the Orkneys 1669-1700* P161.
442 Hossack, B. H. 1900, *Kirkwall in the Orkneys* 1986 reprint P231.
443 OA D31/14/1 Roland St Clair typescript, "Orcadian Families–Prince".
444 Hossack, B. H. 1900, *Kirkwall in the Orkneys* 1986 reprint P198.
445 Johnston, L. 1994, *St Magnus Cathedral Gravestones* P10.
446 Pottinger, M. 2000, *The Minutes of the Town Council of Kirkwall in the Orkneys 1669-1700* P82.
447 Hossack, B. H. 1900, *Kirkwall in the Orkneys* 1986 reprint P185.
448 Ibid. P34.
449 Pottinger, M. 2000, *The Minutes of the Town Council of Kirkwall in the Orkneys 1669-1700* P124-125.
450 Hossack, B. H. 1900, *Kirkwall in the Orkneys* 1986 reprint P55
451 Tarlow, S. A. 1995, *Metaphors of Death in Orkney 1560-1945AD* P106 note 45. The board was carried at a funeral, then hung outside the dead person's house for up to a year, after which it would often be hung in the local church (villagenet.co.uk/reference/hatcment.php).
452 RCAMS 12th Report 1946 P139-140.
453 Hossack, B. H. 1900, *Kirkwall in the Orkneys* 1986 reprint P358.
454 Ibid. P118.
455 Ibid. P359.
456 Steuart, A. F. (ed) 1898, *Diary of Thomas Brown 1675-1693* P26.
457 Ibid. P3, 29 & 33.
458 Johnston, L. 1994, *St Magnus Cathedral Gravestones* P44.
459 Clouston, J. S. 1918, *Some Early Orkney Armorials* PSAS 5th Series Vol IV P191. He was possibly from Aberdeenshire as only that branch of the family used the three sheaves of holly as opposed to three single leaves – information from James Irvine.
460 OA D16/2/16 30th August 1661.
461 Steuart, A. F. (ed) 1898, *Diary of Thomas Brown 1675-1693* P7.
462 Irvine, J. M. 2009 *The Breckness Estate* P52.
463 Marshall, D. 1889, *Notes of the Connection of the Earls of Morton and Dick of Braid* PSAS May 13th 1889 P300-303.
464 *Gleanings from Ancient Records* Orkney Room 941YZ P2-3.
465 Johnston, L. 1994, *St Magnus Cathedral Gravestones* P14.
466 Anderson, P. D. 1982, *Robert Stewart* P166 & 181.
467 Anderson, P. D. 1992, *Black Patie* P60
468 Ibid. P120.
469 Hossack, B. H. *1900 Kirkwall in the Orkneys* 1986 reprint P348.
470 Pottinger, M. 2000, *The Minutes of the Town Council of Kirkwall in the Orkneys 1669-1700* P3.
471 Hossack, B. H. 1900, *Kirkwall in the Orkneys* 1986 reprint P297.
472 Steuart, A. F. (ed) 1898, *Diary of Thomas Brown 1675-1693* P51.
473 Ibid. P36 & 56.
474 Ibid. P65.
475 Clouston, J. S. 1919, *Some further Early Orkney Armorials* PSAS 5th series Vol 5 P193.
476 Johnston, L. 1994, *St Magnus Cathedral Gravestones* P8.
477 Black, G. F. 1946, *The Surnames of Scotland* P692.
478 Robert Richan's father died in 1642 and was buried at the Round Church in Orphir, where his gravestone was found to be a re-use of a fourteenth century warrior gravestone. For more on his genealogy see Clouston, J. S. 1914, *Records of the Earldom of Orkney* P322.
479 Hossack B. H. 1900, *Kirkwall in the Orkneys* 1986 reprint P348.
480 Pottinger M. 2000, *The Minutes of the Town Council of Kirkwall in the Orkneys 1669-1700* P16.
481 Ibid. P5.
482 Ibid. P84.
483 OA D31/14/1 Roland St Clair typescript, "Orcadian Families-Bellenden".
484 Hossack, B. H. 1900, *Kirkwall in the Orkneys* 1986 reprint P348.
485 Ibid. P351, Steuart, A. F. (ed) 1898, *Diary of Thomas Brown 1675-1693* P32.
486 OA D31/14/1 Roland St Clair typescript, "Orcadian Families-Richan".
487 Hossack, B. H. 1900, *Kirkwall in the Orkneys* 1986 reprint P358, OA D8/1/23 for drawing.
488 Ibid. P250.
489 Ibid. P211.
490 Ibid. P351.
491 Johnston, L. 1994, *St Magnus Cathedral Gravestones* P14.
492 Harrison, K. *Kirkwall Families* www.orkneyfhs.co.uk – Richan Family.
493 Rogers, Rev. C., 1883, *Social life in Scotland* Volume 1 Chapter 9.
494 Hossack, B. H. 1900, *Kirkwall in the Orkneys* 1986 reprint P98-101.
495 Ibid. P436.
496 Ibid. P297-298.
497 Steuart, A. F. (ed) 1898*, Diary of Thomas Brown 1675-1693* P29.
498 Johnston, L. 1994, *St Magnus Cathedral Gravestones* P18.
499 Lamb, G. 2003, *Orkney Family Names* P74.
500 The siblings of John Kaa are recorded on letters of horning and poinding. The letters are dated 18th January 1645 and say that the legal action was taken by Robert, James, John, Jean and Helen Kaa, children of the deceased Robert Kaa, notary public, against Ursula Fulsie, relict of Edward Sinclair of Essonquoy (43). OA D24/9/46.
501 Hossack, B. H. 1900, *Kirkwall in the Orkneys* 1986 reprint P122.
502 Ibid. P180 and OA D31/14/1 Roland St Clair typescript, "Orcadian Families-Loutit".
503 Pottinger, M. 2000, *The Minutes of the Town Council of Kirkwall in the Orkneys 1669-1700* P64.
504 Ibid. P122.
505 Ibid. P78-79.

506 Pottinger, M. 2000, *The Minutes of the Town Council of Kirkwall in the Orkneys 1669-1700* P110.
507 Ibid. P290.
508 Steuart, A. F. (ed) 1898, *Diary of Thomas Brown 1675-1693* P56.
509 Johnston, L. 1994, *St Magnus Cathedral Gravestones* P90.
510 Scott, H. 1928, *Fasti Ecclesiae Scoticanae* Vol VII P222 & 267, Craven, J. B. 1897, *History of the Church in Orkney 1558-1662* P220.
511 Johnston, L. 1994, *St Magnus Cathedral Gravestones* P92.
512 Hossack, B. H. 1900, *Kirkwall in the Orkneys* 1986 reprint P238.
513 Pottinger, M. 2000, *The Minutes of the Town Council of Kirkwall in the Orkneys 1669-1700* P93.
514 Ibid.P143. In July 1706, it took the Magistrates and Councillors two days to complete the circuit of the burgh's lands.
515 Hossack, B. H. 1900, *Kirkwall in the Orkneys* 1986 reprint P183.
516 Mooney, J. 1976, *Eynhallow: The Holy Island of the Orkneys* P136.
517 Ibid. P238.
518 Pottinger, M. 2000, *The Minutes of the Town Council of Kirkwall in the Orkneys 1669-1700* P318.
519 Scott, H. 1928, *Fasti Ecclesiae Scoticanae* Vol VII P223.
520 Rendall, J. 2009, *Steering the Stone Ships* P98.
521 Scott, H. 1928, *Fasti Ecclesiae Scoticanae* Vol VII P224.
522 Hossack, B. H. 1900, *Kirkwall in the Orkneys* 1986 reprint P239.
523 Johnston, L. 1994, *St Magnus Cathedral Gravestones* P94.
524 OA D14/6/8, D14/3/10 and D24/8/390.
525 Hossack, B. H. 1900, *Kirkwall in the Orkneys* 1986 reprint P122.
526 OA D14/6/7. Among the papers relating to Captain Peter Winchester is a 1672 inventory of the furnishings and rigging of the frigate *St Peter*, along with an obligation by her officers, seamen, and soldiers with their names and signatures. See also Hossack B. H. 1900 *Kirkwall in the Orkneys* 1986 reprint P142, which shows that Winchester's wife, Helen Stewart, had the ownership of the stores of the frigate, *St Peter*, following her husband's death.
527 OA D29/1/15. Among papers belonging to Hugh Marwick is a 1675 letter of obligation by the owners of the frigate, *Sound* of Orkney, to Patrick Fea.
528 OA D16/2/16 Nov 19th 1670.
529 Hossack, B. H. 1900, *Kirkwall in the Orkneys* 1986 reprint P140.
530 Hossack, B. H. 1900, *Kirkwall in the Orkneys* 1986 reprint P141
531 *Gleanings from Ancient Records* Orkney Room 941YZ P7-8.
532 RCAMS 12th Report 1946 Vol. II P151.
533 Johnston, L. 1994, *St Magnus Cathedral Gravestones* P12.
534 Steuart, A. F. (ed) 1898, *Diary of Thomas Brown 1675-1693* P11.
535 Hewison, W. S. 1998, *Who Was Who in Orkney*. Robert Elphinstone had married a Dutch lady, Clara van Overmear, and it was widely assumed she was the source of his good fortune in obtaining the tack of both the earldom and bishopric, now that a Dutch King was on the throne. See also Steuart, A. F. (ed) 1898, *Diary of Thomas Brown 1675-1693* P60-63 and Thomson, W. P. L. 2001, *The New History of Orkney* P309-310.
536 Steuart, A. F. (ed) 1898, *Diary of Thomas Brown 1675-1693* P21.
537 Pottinger, M. 2000, *The Minutes of the Town Council of Kirkwall in the Orkneys 1669-1700* P122.
538 Ibid. P158.
539 Hossack, B. H. 1900 *Kirkwall in the Orkneys* 1986 reprint P328.
540 Johnston, L. 1994, *St Magnus Cathedral Gravestones* P78.
541 Irvine, W. 1977, *Isle of Shapinsay* P44-47.
542 Barclay, R. S. 1977, *Orkney Testaments and Inventories 1573-1615* P53.
543 Hossack, B. H. 1900, *Kirkwall in the Orkneys* 1986 reprint P185, Clouston, J. S. 1914, *Records of the Earldom of Orkney 1299-1614* P455.
544 Transcript of Marriage Contract found on freepages.genealogy.rootsweb.ancestry.com.
545 Irvine, James M, *The Genealogy of Washoington Irving* (forthcoming).
546 His initial appointment as Provost was by royal decree – see 78 and Pottinger M. 2000, *The Minutes of the Town Council of Kirkwall in the Orkneys 1669-1700* P268.
547 Mackintosh, W. R. 1892 *Curious Incidents from the Ancient Records of Kirkwall* P88.
548 Pottinger, M. 2000, *The Minutes of the Town Council of Kirkwall in the Orkneys 1669-1700* P277.
549 Lynch, M. 1992, *Scotland, A New History* P302.
550 Pottinger, M. 2000, *The Minutes of the Town Council of Kirkwall in the Orkneys 1669-1700* P275.
551 Hossack, B. H. 1900, *Kirkwall in the Orkneys* 1986 reprint P177.
552 Pottinger, M. 2000, *The Minutes of the Town Council of Kirkwall in the Orkneys 1669-1700* P342.
553 Steuart, A. F. (ed) 1898, *Diary of Thomas Brown 1675-1693* P17.
554 Both Hossack (P177) and Wm. Traill's *A Genealogical Account of the Traills* mistakingly say James Baikie of Tankerness.
555 Steuart, A. F. (ed) 1898, *Diary of Thomas Brown 1675-1693* P21.
556 Hossack, B. H. 1900, *Kirkwall in the Orkneys* 1986 reprint P177.
557 Harrison, K. *Kirkwall Families* www.orkneyfhs.co.uk – Liddell Family.
558 Traill, W. 1883, *A Genealogical Account of the Traills*.
559 Johnston, L. 1994, *St Magnus Cathedral Gravestones* P108.
560 Harrison, K. *Kirkwall Families* www.orkneyfhs.co.uk – Liddell Family.
561 After resuming operation in 1654, Kirkwall Town Council had sent Patrick Craigie of Wasdale to Edinburgh to negotiate with Cromwell's Scottish Parliament for restitution of Kirkwall's rights. Craigie was successful and obtained an act, "discharging the Justices of Peace and uthers in Orkney and Zetland from incroaching on the said burgh and (its) liberties". This only led the burgh into more trouble as, following the Restoration, the 9th Earl of Morton alleged the burgh had collaborated with Commonwealth authorities. Craigie and his fellow Councillors were declared rebels and were threatened with confiscation of their goods and property. Craigie was again sent to Edinburgh, this time to fight Morton's charges and eventually succeeded in obtaining a new Royal Charter for Kirkwall (1661) followed by ratification by the Scottish Parliament in 1670.
562 Hossack, B. H. 1900, *Kirkwall in the Orkneys* 1986 reprint P340. See also OA D16/2/13/2 legal papers concerning action of horning by George Liddell of Hammer against Patrick Craigie of Wasdale, DA/7/117 27th Jan 1680, charter by the Provost, Bailies and Council of Kirkwall to George Liddell and D24/7/118 instrument of sasine in favour of George Liddell for tenements in Kirkwall, taken from Patrick Craigie, and granted to him by the Provost, Bailies and Council of Kirkwall.
563 Steuart, A. F. (ed) 1898, *Diary of Thomas Brown 1675-1693* P18.
564 Hossack, B. H. 1900, *Kirkwall in the Orkneys* 1986 reprint P149.
565 Johnston, L. 1994, *St Magnus Cathedral Gravestones* P96.
566 Hossack, B. H. 1900 *Kirkwall in the Orkneys* 1986 reprint P332.
567 Mackintosh, W. R. 1892 *Curious Incidents from the Ancient Records of Kirkwall* P303.
568 Lamb, G. 2006, *The Place Names of South Ronaldsay and Burray* P58. See also Johnston, A. W. & Johnston, A. 1907-1908, *Orkney and Shetland Old Lore Miscellany* Vol 1P255 for a description of Matthew Mowbray's gravestone by Rev. A. Goodfellow (93).
569 Hossack, B. H. 1900, *Kirkwall in the Orkneys* 1986 reprint P333.
570 Mackintosh, W. R. 1892, *Curious Incidents from the Ancient Records of Kirkwall* P5.
571 Hossack, B. H. 1900, *Kirkwall in the Orkneys* 1986 reprint P331.
572 Mackintosh, W. R. 1892, *Curious Incidents from the Ancient Records of Kirkwall* P304.
573 OA D24/7/82 – extract from an instrument of sasine in favour of Arthur and Patrick Murray for lands in Kirkwall (Laverock) disponed to them by their father, Francis Murray, 28th August 1666.
574 Hossack, B. H. 1900, *Kirkwall in the Orkneys* 1986 reprint P334.
575 Steuart, A. F. (ed) 1898, *Diary of Thomas Brown 1675-1693* P35.
576 Hossack, B. H. 1900, *Kirkwall in the Orkneys* 1986 reprint P286 & 426.
577 Thomson, W. P. L. 2005, *Orkney Land and People* P181.
578 OA D31/14/1 Roland St Clair typescript "Orcadian Families-Murray".
579 Johnston, L. 1994, *St Magnus Cathedral Gravestones* P84.
580 Steuart, A. F. (ed) 1898, *Diary of Thomas Brown 1675-1693* P24.

581 OA D23/6/60.
582 Henry Rendall was, for example, Lawman of Orkney in 1446.
583 Fenton, A. 1978, *The Northern Isles: Orkney and Shetland* P475-483 and Thomson, W. P. L. 2005, *Orkney Land and People* P164.
584 Fenton, A. 1978, *The Northern Isles: Orkney and Shetland* P472-475.
585 Mitchell's mark was, "*ane rip out of both the lugs and ax behind in the right lug and ax before in the left lug………whilk desire the said Sheriff thought reasonable and thairfore has ordained the samen to be the said Mitchell his sheep mark in all time coming*". A rip was a single slit in the ear, while an axe was a right angled notch.
586 It was very near the house belonging to the Sandisons (see 46). Hossack, B. H. 1900, *Kirkwall in the Orkneys* 1986 reprint P119.
587 Pottinger, M. 2000, *The Minutes of the Town Council of Kirkwall in the Orkneys 1669-1700* P64.
588 Ibid. P136.
589 Ibid. P154.
590 These events are recorded in the diary of Thomas Brown, who makes clear to which side he belonged. 3rd May 1679, being Saturday, James Sharp, Archbishop of St Andrews "was barboslie murdered by some fanatical persones within a myle or two of ye sd citie." 22nd June 1679, being a Sabbath morning, the Duke of Monmouth "hath battell with the wigges in ye wast of Scotland, neir Bothwell Briggs, and he with his arme (glorie be to the Almighty) hade the victorie yt day." Steuart, A. F. (ed) 1898, *Diary of Thomas Brown 1675-1693* P9.
591 Pottinger, M. 2000, *The Minutes of the Town Council of Kirkwall in the Orkneys 1669-1700* P246.
592 Hossack, B. H. 1900, *Kirkwall in the Orkneys* 1986 reprint P119.
593 Steuart, A. F. (ed) 1898, *Diary of Thomas Brown 1675-1693* P37.
594 Hossack, B. H. 1900, *Kirkwall in the Orkneys* 1986 reprint P314
595 Steuart, A. F. (ed) 1898, *Diary of Thomas Brown 1675-1693* P49.
596 Clouston, J. S. 1923, *Norse Heraldry in Orkney* PSAS Vol IX P312.
597 Johnston, L. 1994, *St Magnus Cathedral Gravestones* P16
598 Craven, J. B. 1893, *History of the Church in Orkney 1662-1688* P79.
599 Pottinger, M. 2000, *The Minutes of the Town Council of Kirkwall in the Orkneys 1669-1700* P189.
600 Craven, J. B. 1893, *History of the Church in Orkney 1662-1688* P50.
601 Pottinger, M. 2000, *The Minutes of the Town Council of Kirkwall in the Orkneys 1669-1700* P220.
602 Johnston, L. 1994, *St Magnus Cathedral Gravestones* P114.
603 Johnston, A. W. & Johnston, A. 1907, *Orkney and Shetland Old Lore* P124.
604 Pottinger, M. 2000, *The Minutes of the Town Council of Kirkwall in the Orkneys 1669-1700* P135.
605 Scott, H. 1928, *Fasti Ecclesiae Scoticanae* Vol VII P280.
606 Johnston, L. 1994, *St Magnus Cathedral Gravestones* P28.
607 Steuart, A. F. (ed) 1898, *Diary of Thomas Brown 1675-1693* P32.
608 Pottinger, M. 2000, *The Minutes of the Town Council of Kirkwall in the Orkneys 1669-1700* P271.
609 Johnston, L. 1994, *St Magnus Cathedral Gravestones* P62.
610 Pottinger, M. 2000, *The Minutes of the Town Council of Kirkwall in the Orkneys 1669-1700* P285.
611 Lamb, G. 2003, *Orkney Family Names* P53.
612 Steuart, A. F. (ed) 1898, *Diary of Thomas Brown 1675-1693* P6.
613 Hossack, B. H. 1900, *Kirkwall in the Orkneys* 1986 reprint P205.
614 Harrison, K. *Kirkwall Families* www.orkneyfhs.co.uk – Traill of Holland.
615 Steuart, A. F. (ed) 1898, *Diary of Thomas Brown 1675-1693* P17.
616 Johnston, L. 1994, *St Magnus Cathedral Gravestones* P102, RCAMS 1946 P137
617 Craven, J. B. 1893 *History of the Church in Orkney 1662-1688* P27.
618 Ibid. P50.
619 Hossack, B. H. 1900 *Kirkwall in the Orkneys* 1986 reprint P38.
620 Ibid. P170-171.
621 Steuart, A. F. (ed) 1898, *Diary of Thomas Brown 1675-1693* P18, Craven, J. B. 1893 *History of the Church in Orkney 1662-1688* P97.
622 Pottinger, M. 2000, *The Minutes of the Town Council of Kirkwall in the Orkneys 1669-1700* P34.
623 Scott, H. 1928, *Fasti Ecclesiae Scoticanae* Vol VII P222.
624 Johnston, L. 1994, *St Magnus Cathedral Gravestones* P86.
625 Steuart, A. F. (ed) 1898, *Diary of Thomas Brown 1675-1693* P51.
626 Hossack, B. H. 1900, *Kirkwall in the Orkneys* 1986 reprint P135.
627 Pottinger, M. 2000, *The Minutes of the Town Council of Kirkwall in the Orkneys 1669-1700* P64, 76 & 82.
628 Steuart, A. F. (ed) 1898, *Diary of Thomas Brown 1675-1693* P56.
629 Harrison, K. *Kirkwall Families* www.orkneyfhs.co.uk – Covingtrie Family.
630 Johnston, L. 1994, *St Magnus Cathedral Gravestones* P100.
631 Hossack, B. H. 1900, *Kirkwall in the Orkneys* 1986 reprint P190.
632 Ibid. P238.
633 As a Royal Burgh, Kirkwall had its own representative in the Scottish Parliament until the 1707 Act of Union, when Kirkwall became part of the Northern Burghs. Hossack B. H. 1900 *Kirkwall in the Orkneys* 1986 reprint P467.
634 OA D16/2/16 Nov 22nd 1665.
635 Pottinger, M. 2000, *The Minutes of the Town Council of Kirkwall in the Orkneys 1669-1700* P158.
636 *Gleanings from Ancient Records* Orkney Room 941YZ P9-10. The other gentlemen were Magnus Mowat of Balquhallie, James Murray of Pennyland, William Carmichell and James Boog, Edinburgh merchants, David Murray of Cleardain and John Murray, writer in Edinburgh.
637 Pottinger, M. 2000, *The Minutes of the Town Council of Kirkwall in the Orkneys 1669-1700* P218, 251.
638 Andrew Dick was the son of John Dick, Sheriff of Orkney and was appointed Stewart Principal and Chamberlain of Orkney and Shetland in 1669. He successfully bid for the tacks for both the Stewartry and bishopric in 1675 (Irving, *The Breckness Estate* P49). In 1685, he was accused of "many great malversations and oppressions" including having delivered 100 men to a Dutch captain for his country's wars. He was banished from Orkney the following year, sailing to Shetland, where he had acquired some land round the Lerwick area (*Diary of Thomas Brown* P38).
639 Steuart, A. F. (ed) 1898, *Diary of Thomas Brown 1675-1693* P13, Pottinger, M. 2000, *The Minutes of the Town Council of Kirkwall in the Orkneys 1669-1700* P179, 190, 251 & 255.
640 Pottinger, M. 2000, *The Minutes of the Town Council of Kirkwall in the Orkneys 1669-1700* P250.
641 Steuart, A. F. (ed) 1898, *Diary of Thomas Brown 1675-1693* P45-46.
642 Pottinger, M. 2000, *The Minutes of the Town Council of Kirkwall in the Orkneys 1669-1700* P244, 245 256 and 257.
643 Pottinger, M. 2000, *The Minutes of the Town Council of Kirkwall in the Orkneys 1669-1700* P265, 266 & 268.

The Seventeenth Century – 'Thou shalt not make false idols'
644 Hossack, B. H. 1900, *Kirkwall in the Orkneys* 1986 reprint P238.
645 Ross, J. 1977, *Orkney and the Earls of Morton 1643-1707* P9.
646 Ibid. P10.
647 Ibid. P14.
648 Known as the Pundlar Process, which dragged on from 1733-1759. A charge of tampering with the weights was not a new issue. Similar accusations had been made among the bishopric tenents in the time of Bishop Robert Reid some two centuries before. See Anderson, P. D. 2012, *The Stewart Earls of Orkney* P15-16.
649 As an active president of the Royal Society, Morton was deeply involved in the preparation for Captain Cook's voyage to Tahiti and was happy to be rid of his troublesome islands. Thus, in 1766, Sir Lawrence Dundas of Kerse paid £63,000 for the Earldom estate in Orkney and the Lordship of Shetland.
650 Flett, J. 1976, *Lodge Kirkwall Kilwinning No 38² The story from 1736* P24.
651 Ibid. P95.
652 His father, Captain James Moodie, was shot by supporters of Sir James Stewart in Broad Street, in 1725.
653 Thomson, W. P. L., 2001, *The New History of Orkney* P374.
654 Macinnes, I. 1981, *The Alexander Graham Case*, OH Volume 1 P128.

655 Sir Alexander Brand, an Edinburgh arms dealer, had the tack of the earldom from 1693-5. Young's salary was £226 13s 4d. See Hossack, B. H. 1900, *Kirkwall in the Orkneys* 1986 reprint P210 and Mackintosh, W. R. 1885 *Glimpses of Kirkwall in Olden Time* P73.
656 Hossack, B. H. 1900, *Kirkwall in the Orkneys* 1986 reprint P210-213.
657 Ibid. P213, Burgher, L., 1991 *Orkney, an Illustrated Architectural Guide* P14.
658 Hossack, B. H. 1900, *Kirkwall in the Orkneys* 1986 reprint P214.
659 Account by Earl of Morton, quoted in Fereday, R. P. 1980, *Orkney Feuds and the '45* P42-45. Work finally started on the new Tolbooth in 1743, the Earl of Morton giving permission for stone to be used from the ruins of Kirkwall Castle as well as slate from the Earl's Palace. Its first prison inmate was ironically Sir James Stewart.
660 Fereday, R. P. 1980, *Orkney Feuds and the '45* P52.
661 Fereday, R. P. 1980, *Orkney Feuds and the '45* P89.
662 Pundlar Process, 1757, *Earl of Galloway and Udallers of Orkney versus Earl of Morton* P190.
663 Mackintosh, W. R. 1892, *Curious Incidents from the Ancient Records of Kirkwall* P244-248.
664 Fereday, R. P. 1990, *The Orkney Balfours 1747-1799* P100. Sir John Sinclair went on to produce the first Statistical Account of Scotland.
665 Fereday, R. P. 1980, *Orkney Feuds and the '45* P48.
666 OA D16/1/2 'Spences in Early Orkney Records', compiled by William Spence.
667 Pundlar Process, 1757, *Earl of Galloway and Udallers of Orkney versus Earl of Morton* P150 & 156.
668 Scott, H. 1928, *Fasti Ecclesiae Scoticanae* Vol VII P277.
669 Rendall, J. 2009, *Steering the Stone Ships* P95.
670 Ibid. P96.
671 Graeme had many siblings, not all of whom survived to adulthood. Preserved in Orkney Archives is a fascinating letter Graeme wrote to an old school friend in Kirkwall about two of his brothers. He also mentions a sister living with his mother, OA46/2/6.
672 OA D2/49/12. Quoted from a letter from Murdoch Mackenzie in Poole to Captain William Manson on 11th December 1785.
673 Hewison, W. S. 1998, *Who Was Who in Orkney* P147, Hewison, W. S. 1985, *This Great Harbour Scapa Flow* P23.
674 Fereday, R. P. 1980, *Orkney Feuds and the '45* P34.
675 Ibid. P78, Hewison W. S. 1998, *Who Was Who in Orkney* P96.
676 Fereday, R. P. 1980, *Orkney Feuds and the '45* P78-79.
677 Macinnes, I. 1981, *The Alexander Graham Case*, OH Volume 1 P129.
678 Hossack, B. H. 1900, *Kirkwall in the Orkneys* 1986 reprint P192.
679 Pundlar Process, 1757, *Earl of Galloway and Udallers of Orkney versus Earl of Morton* Orkney Room 333Y, P187. The 6th Earl of Galloway, Alexander Stewart, had inherited Sir James Stewart's Burray estates and continued the litigation against the Earl of Morton, started by Sir James, in the Pundlar Process.
680 Pundlar Process, 1757 P190.
681 Ibid. P196.
682 Pundlar Process, 1757 P199.
683 Mackintosh, W. R. 1885, *Glimpses of Kirkwall in Olden Time* P129.
684 Thomson, W. P. L. 1983, *KelpMaking in Orkney* P75.
685 James Baikie, 6th of Tankerness, was Provost of Kirkwall (1737-64) and one of Orkney's leading men in the mid eighteenth century.
686 OA D24/4/99 January 6th 1737.
687 OA D1/182/2/11.
688 OA D23/4/63, Marwick, H. 1936, *Merchant Lairds of Long Ago* P142.
689 Wenham, S. 2001, *A More Enterprising Sprit* P264.
690 A.Francis Steuart, Orkney News from the Letter Bag of Charles Steuart in Johnston, A. W. & Johnston, A. 1907-1932, *Orkney and Shetland Old Lore Miscellany* Vol 6 P47.
691 Sutherland Graeme, P. N. 1954, *Health and Healing in the 17th and 18th Centuries* OM Volume 2 P45-46.
692 OA D24/4/10. 1763 tack by James Baikie of the seashores of the Tankerness estate for the manufacture of kelp for nine years.
693 Great grandfather of William Balfour Baikie (94).
694 OA D24/9/64 and D24/9/65. Copy of answers to William Groat's protests against Janet Douglas, John Baikie and John Riddoch.
695 Berry, R. J. & Firth, H. N. 1998, *The People of Orkney* P231.
696 Harrison K. *Kirkwall Families* www.orkneyfhs.c.uk – Traill of Westness. See also Traill, W. 1883, *A Genealogical Account of the Traills*.
697 Marwick, H. 1936, *Merchant Lairds of Long Ago*.
698 An account of John Gow was published by Daniel Defoe, the author of *Robinson Crusoe* and *Moll Flanders*. Sir Walter Scott subsequently heard about the story when he visited Orkney in 1814 and used it as the basis for his novel, *The Pirate*.
699 Mackintosh, W. R. 1892, *Curious Incidents from the Ancient Records of Kirkwall* P232.
700 Hossack, B. H. 1900, *Kirkwall in the Orkneys* 1986 reprint P346 and Mackintosh, W. R. 1885, *Glimpses of Kirkwall in Olden Time* P113-115.
701 See Marwick, H. 1936, *Merchant Lairds of Long Ago*.
702 OA D24/9/57 Letter to Mrs Margaret Traill from Alexander Mowat, Nottar public.
703 Traill, W. 1883, *A Genealogical Account of the Traills*.
704 Hossack, B. H. 1900, *Kirkwall in the Orkneys* 1986 reprint P157-158.
705 Fereday, R. P. 1980, *Orkney Feuds and the '45* P95.
706 Fereday, R. P. 1980, *Orkney Feuds and the '45* P101.
707 Ibid. P108-111.
708 Traill, W. 1883, *A Genealogical Account of the Traills* P XIII, Thomson, W. P. L. 2000, *The Little General and the Rousay Crofters* P22.
709 Fereday, R. P. 1990, *The Orkney Balfours 1747-1799* P128-129.
710 Ibid. P163.
711 Ibid. P185.
712 A.Francis Steuart, Orkney News from the Letter Bag of Charles Steuart in Johnston, A. W. & Johnston, A. 1907-1932, *Orkney and Shetland Old Lore Miscellany* Vol 6 P105.
713 Ritchie, E. 2009, *A Collected History of the Traill/Trail Family* P308
714 Ibid. P308-309.
715 Ibid. P309.
716 Hossack, B. H. 1900, *Kirkwall in the Orkneys* 1986 reprint P354, Fereday, R. P. 2000, *The Autobiography of Samuel Laing of Papdale* P225-228. The overall result was 107 votes for George Traill, 96 votes for Samuel Laing and 9 votes for Robert Hunter.

The Eighteenth Century – An Acrid Smell

717 Ritchie, E. 2009, *A Collected History of the Traill/Trail Family* P314 & 315.
718 Logie and Petrie 1832, *Representations on St Magnus Cathedral*.
719 Tarlow, S. A. 1995, *Metaphors of Death in Orkney 1560-1945AD* P129, Baikie S. 2001, *Reminiscences of the Cathedral Church of St Magnus Since 1846 by an Eye Witness* P5
720 Mooney, J. 1937, POAS Vol XIV *St Magnus Cathedral: Proprietorship and Maintenance (First Paper)* P68.
721 Mooney, J. 1929, POAS vol VII, *Interments and Excavations in St Magnus Cathedral*, POAS Vol VII P27-32.
722 There was certainly some opposition to the digging up of the graves. During a visit to Orkney, in 1847, Professor T. S Traill wrote about a conversation he had had with the Clerk of Works, Mr Kerr, "The floor is to be lowered to its former level. He (Mr Kerr) stated that he hoped no opposition would now be made to this by the inhabitants. I believed not. He informed me that my address to the people in the churchyard, the other day, had produced the best effects; and now found their objections to disturbing the graves have subsided". Traill T. S., *A Visit to Orkney, 1847*, Professor Thomas Stewart Traill's Journal from 19th August to 9th September 1847, edited by R. P. Fereday (unpublished).
723 OA K1/1 Kirkwall Town Council Minutes 29th April 1850.
724 OA K1/1 Kirkwall Town Council Minutes 1st December 1849. 876 was the number of seats available prior to the Government intervention.
725 *John O'Groat's Journal* 6th December 1850.
726 OA K1/1 Kirkwall Town Council Minutes 13th November 1850.
727 OA K1/1 Kirkwall Town Council Minutes 26th August 1851.
728 OA K1/1 Kirkwall Town Council Minutes 6th April 1852.

729 In 1972, when the west end of the Cathedral was in danger of collapse, some people, describing themselves as "The Kirkwall Citizens' Association", enquired about the possibility of the Crown taking over the building to avoid the cost of maintenance. Callaghan, S. 2001, *The Unknown Cathedral* P78.

730 OA D/13/6/4. Contract of partnership between George Duncan, writer in Dumfries, and James Watson, also residing there.

731 Thomson, W. P. L. 2001, *The New History of Orkney* P343. OA D13/6/12 The circular was written in 1805 by Rev. Francis Liddell against James Watson, "a broken down pedlar of Dumfries" and entitled, "To the Humane and Generous Inhabitants of Britain; the Groans of the Poor Oppressed Clergy of the Orkney Islands". As factor of the principal heritor of Orkney, James Watson received frequent letters from ministers regarding their stipends.

732 Mackintosh, W. R. 1885, *Glimpses of Kirkwall in Olden Time* P217.

733 Fraser, J. 1935, *Some Transactions of the Vice-Admiral Depute of Orkney in 1801-1803* POAS Vol XIII P33. This situation continued in Scotland until 1831, when civil control of maritime affairs was placed under the jurisdiction of the Court of Session and the County Sheriffs. The rights of Vice-Admirals to a share of unclaimed wrecks were repealed in 1846, but the title of Honorary Vice-Admiral was bestowed on the Sheriff-Principals of Orkney and Shetland (see 99).

734 Fraser, J. 1935, *Some Transactions of the Vice-Admiral Depute of Orkney in 1801-1803* POAS Vol XIII P37.

735 Fereday, R. P. 1995, *Saint-Faust in the North 1803-1804* P52.

736 Ibid. P87-92.

737 Ibid. P92-96. While Sanday had a bad reputation for coveting shipwrecks, William Clouston, in his Statistical Account of Sanday and North Ronaldsay (see Clouston J. S. (ed) 1927, *The Orkney Parishes* P283-284), defended the people of Sanday and especially their treatment of shipwrecked sailors.

738 OA D1/46/48. Draft letter to William Marsden, Admiralty Office from James Watson, Vice Admiral Depute of Orkney and Shetland, summarising the proceedings regarding the wreck and salvage of the *Utrecht*.

739 Fraser, J. 1937, *Three Years of Shipwreck* POAS Vol XIV P28.

740 Fereday, R. P. 2000, *The Autobiography of Samuel Laing of Papdale* P180.

741 Fereday, R. P. 2000, *The Autobiography of Samuel Laing of Papdale* P43.

742 Ibid. P44.

743 Ibid. P180-181.

744 Whittaker, I. G. 1998, *Off Scotland, A Comprehensive Record of Maritime and Aviation Losses in Scottish Waters*. It was little wonder that, in 1789, one of the first lighthouses in Scotland was built at the north east end of North Ronaldsay. This beacon proved ineffectual and the light was transferred to Sanday's Start Point in 1806.

745 There is ample evidence for this, with, for example, James Riddoch following his father as Collector and then handing the position over to his nephew, Thomas Pollexfen. Andrew Baikie's father was Collector before he too became a Custom's officer.

746 OA D2/18/1. The brigantine, *Pallas* of New York, had been on a voyage from Amsterdam to Surinam, but grounded on Sanday before being taken into Kirkwall, where she was delayed for over a month. During this time much valuable cargo was landed and then carried south without any clearance from the customs. See Fereday, R. P. 1990, *The Orkney Balfours 1747-1799* P177.

747 OA CE55/4/39, Officer's declarations.

748 Fraser, J. 1937, *Three Years of Shipwreck* POAS Vol XIV P24.

749 Hossack, B. H. 1900, *Kirkwall in the Orkneys* 1986 reprint P270.

750 Mooney, R. B. 1969, *A Business Journey from Orkney to Liverpool in 1789*.

751 Light horse-drawn carriage.

752 Hossack, B. H. 1900, *Kirkwall in the Orkneys* 1986 reprint P214.

753 Fereday, R. P., 1990, *The Orkney Balfours 1747-1799* P127.

754 Hossack, B. H. 1900, *Kirkwall in the Orkneys* 1986 reprint P390-393.

755 William Manson had a fascinating career in America, being in charge of the last colonial venture before the outbreak of the American War of Independence. He fought against the rebels, accepted the surrender of one of their leaders in Georgia and caused the destruction of America's third oldest town, in South Carolina. After service in the Jamaica trade, he returned to Kirkwall, married Elizabeth Balfour, daughter of William Balfour of Trenaby, bought the property, 'Hell', once owned by Patrick Prince (56) and secured the sinecure of Comptroller of Customs. See Fereday, R. P. 1990, *The Orkney Balfours 1747-1799* P120-127.

756 The Navigation Act of 1786 was intended to encourage British merchant shipping and give incentive to fishing by fixing new premiums and bounties for British registered fishing vessels. See Fereday, R. P. 1990, *The Orkney Balfours 1747-1799* P124.

757 Flett, J. 1976, *Lodge Kirkwall Kilwinning No 38² The story from 1736* P156.

758 OA D2/18/1.

759 Fereday, R. P. 1990, *The Orkney Balfours 1747-1799* P177.

760 OA D2/18/1. Letter from James Riddoch 10th February 1796.

761 OA D2/18/1. Customs Minutes 5/10/1796.

762 OA D2/36/8 Letter signed by James Riddoch and William Manson to William Balfour, WS, Edinburgh, concerning the capture by the enemy of the brigantines, *Pomona* and *Edinburgh*, owned by William Balfour's brother, Col Thomas Balfour, 15th January 1807. Also see Fereday R. P. 1995, *Saint-Faust in the North 1803-1804* P97-98 for letter from Riddoch and Manson to Commissioners of Customs, deploring the lack of a defence force in Orkney.

763 Fereday, R. P. 1990, *The Orkney Balfours 1747-1799* P188.

764 OA D28/3/35.

765 Hossack, B. H. 1900, *Kirkwall in the Orkneys* 1986 reprint P396-398. John Rae senior was sworn in as a landwaiter by William Manson on 8th June 1801. See OA CE55/4/39.

766 OA, SC11/86/1/4.

767 Wilson, B. 2003, *Profit Not Loss, the Story of the Baikies of Tankerness*, family tree of the Baikies.

768 Johnston, A. W. & Johnston, A. 1913, *Orkney and Shetland Old Lore Miscellany* Vol VI P141.

769 House of Lords Journal March 1785, "….and that Margaret and Janet Young, lawful children of the deceased Andrew Young, and James Gordon and James Riddoch, their husbands,......".

770 Scott, H 1928, *Fasti Ecclesiae Scoticanae* Vol VII P224. Mrs Yule was one of the last people to be buried within the nave of St Magnus Cathedral (1835). Mooney, J. POAS Vol 7 P32.

771 Fereday, R. P. 1990, *The Orkney Balfours 1747-1799* P118. Thomas Balfour was son of William Balfour of Trenaby, one of the fugitive lairds that went into hiding after the failure of the 1745 rising.

772 Fereday, R. P., 1990, *The Orkney Balfours 1747-1799* P150.

773 Flett, J. 1976, *Lodge Kirkwall Kilwinning No 38² The story from 1736* P72-73.

774 Thomson, A. 1987, *Windows in St Magnus* in The Orkney View - St Magnus Cathedral 850 years – A Celebration P45.

775 *St Magnus Cathedral Law Papers 1758-1920 – Answers for the Rev William Logie to the Reasons of Suspension for James Baikie of Tankerness, William Traill of Frotoft, Lieutenant Gilbert Traill of Hatston and the Trustees of James Stewart, late Merchant of Kirkwall* P5. Orkney Room 274.1Y.

776 Hossack, B. H. 1900, *Kirkwall in the Orkneys* 1986 reprint P215.

777 Irvine, J. M. 2009, *The Breckness Estate* P169.

778 Translation kindly provided by Victoria Whitworth.

779 Traill, T. S., *A Visit to Orkney, 1847*, Professor Thomas Stewart's Journal from 19th August to 9th September 1847, edited by R. P. Fereday (unpublished). Professor Traill was given the responsibility of arranging the erection of the monument to his relative.

780 Fereday, R. P. 2000, *The Autobiography of Samuel Laing of Papdale* P40-41.

781 The Roman calendar was based on the first three phases of the moon. The new moon was the day of the Kalends and over time it came to mean the first day of each month. Instead of counting days after the start of the month, the Romans counted forward to these named days. Thus the 17th of Kalends of December was 17 days before the 1st of December.

782 Fereday, R. P. 2000, *The Autobiography of Samuel Laing of Papdale* P56-57.

783   Ibid. P35.
784   Hossack (P206 and 395) is wrong in saying 1805 as the year Robert died. See Fereday, R. P. 2000, *The Autobiography of Samuel Laing of Papdale* P178.
785   www.gravestonephotos.com/public/cemetery.
786   OA D3/346.
787   Mackintosh, W. R. 1885, *Glimpses of Kirkwall in Olden Time* P229-233.
788   Hossack, B. H. 1900, *Kirkwall in the Orkneys* 1986 reprint P397.
789   Dr T. S. Traill, 1781-1862, Professor of Medical Jurisprudence at Edinburgh University (see 83).
790   Fereday, R. P. 2000, *The Autobiography of Samuel Laing of Papdale* P57.
791   Ibid. P76.
792   Ibid. P186. Peace of Amiens - a preliminary treaty was signed, between Britain and France, in October 1801, which saw the lifting of the naval blockade. The Treaty of Amiens was signed in March 1802, but hostilities resumed in May 1803.
793   Ibid. P205.
794   Fereday, R. P. 2000, *The Autobiography of Samuel Laing of Papdale* P206.
795   Slavery was abolished throughout the British Empire in 1833. Other markets in Britain and Europe opened up instead.
796   Fereday, R. P. 2000, *The Autobiography of Samuel Laing of Papdale* P210.
797   Ibid. P242.
798   Fereday, R. P. 2000, *The Autobiography of Samuel Laing of Papdale* P254.
799   *The Orcadian*, Book Review.
800   Fereday, R. P. 2000, *The Autobiography of Samuel Laing of Papdale* P271. In 1848, the Germans of Holstein and southern Slesvig rebelled against Danish rule, hostilities ending after a Danish victory at Idstedt in 1851. The victory was short lived and Denmark ultimately lost the two Duchees, when the Prussians invaded in 1864.
801   Ibid. P276.
802   Marwick, E. W. 1991, *An Orkney Anthology* J. D. M. Robertson (ed) P465.
803   Hossack, B. H. 1900, *Kirkwall in the Orkneys* 1986 reprint P159.
804   Ibid. P158.
805   Pant, S. N. D. *A Historical Retrospect of the Administration of Justice in Kumaun*.
806   Ibid.
807   Thomson W. P. L. 2000, *The Little General and the Rousay Crofters* P11-14.
808   Thomson, W. P. L. 2000, *The Little General and the Rousay Crofters* P47.
809   Loudon, Dr J. B. 2006, *The Journal of James Robertson 1842-1853* Tuesday 14th July 1846. Liverless meant lacking in liveliness.
810   Thomson, W. P. L. 2000, *The Little General and the Rousay Crofters* P14.
811   Hossack, B. H. 1900, *Kirkwall in the Orkneys* 1986 reprint P 137 & 298
812   Logie, Rev W. 1857, *Sermons and Sevices of the Church* Pxii.
813   Elizabeth's nephew was Robert Scarth of Binscarth. See Irvine J. M. 2009, *The Breckness Estate* P205 for a family tree.
814   Hossack, B. H. 1900, *Kirkwall in the Orkneys* 1986 reprint P383.
815   Ibid. P135.
816   Logie and Petrie 1832, *Representations on St Magnus Cathedral*.
817   Smith, J. 1907, *The Church in Orkney* P82-83, Bardgett, F. D. 2000, *Two Millennia of Church and Community in Orkney* P132.
818   In order to aid the work of the enumerators, the Town Council started officially to name Kirkwall streets, following a suggestion by Sheriff-substitute, Charles Shireff.
819   Scott, H 1928, *Fasti Ecclesiae Scoticanae* Vol VII P224.
820   www.jamesirvinerobertson.co.uk.
821   It is interesting to note while reading *JR's* journal that, when travelling south, one went 'up' to Edinburgh or 'up' to London, while coming back to Orkney from south was travelling 'down' to the islands.
822   Captain William Balfour died just before *JR* arrived in Orkney. *JR* shared the house for a time with Captain Balfour's second surviving son, William, who had Berstane House rebuilt in 1850.
823   Hossack, B. H. 1900, *Kirkwall in the Orkneys* 1986 reprint P203 and Wilson, B. 2003 *Profit Not Loss, the Story of the Baikies of Tankerness* P37. Dr Robert Baikie was a surgeon in India and built Buttquoy House when he returned to Britain to live in Kirkwall. He, however, did not enjoy the climate and went to live in Edinburgh.
824   Loudon, Dr J. B. 2006, *The Journal of James Robertson 1842-1853* eg Sunday 14th January 1849, see footnote. A post office had first been established in Kirkwall in 1747. During the next hundred years, communication relied on open boats across the Pentland Firth, which naturally led to considerable delays and cancellations in times of bad weather.
825   Loudon, Dr J. B. 2006, *The Journal of James Robertson 1842-1853*. The Meeting of Commissioners of Supply, which ratified *JR's* Memorial concerning the Earl's Palace, was held on 22nd January 1849. OA D2/2/14. Letter to David Balfour, 1863, concerning Earl's Palace.
826   Loudon, Dr J. B. 2006, *The Journal of James Robertson 1842-1853* Thursday 20th May 1847.
827   The name referred to Sir Hugh Halcro, Canon of St Magnus Cathedral and Rector of Ronaldsay (died 1554), who, on his way to Kirkwall, could look back to South Ronaldsay and have a last look at his home.
828   Loudon, Dr J. B. 2006, *The Journal of James Robertson 1842-1853* Friday 21st May 1847.
829   Sutherland, P. J. 2013, *Mirth, Madness & St Magnus* P3.
830   Loudon, Dr J. B. 2006, *The Journal of James Robertson 1842-1853* Tuesday 11th September 1849.
831   Loudon, Dr J. B. 2006, *The Journal of James Robertson 1842-1853* Monday 2nd October 1848.
832   Ibid. Tuesday 26th December 1848.
833   Robertson J. D. M. 2005, *The Kirkwall Ba' Between the Water and the Wall* P88, Hossack, B. H. 1900, *Kirkwall in the Orkneys* 1986 reprint P465.
834   Loudon, Dr J. B. 2006, *The Journal of James Robertson 1842-1853* Tuesday 2nd June 1846.
835   Ibid. Friday 4th August 1848.
836   Loudon, Dr J. B. 2006, *The Journal of James Robertson 1842-1853* Monday 3rd September 1849.
837   It was during this visit that Kirkwall Town Council gave him the petition offering to give up ownership of the Cathedral in return for funding towards a new church. *John O'Groats Journal* 5th September 1851.
838   Unknown to Lady Franklin at this time, her husband and the other members of his expedition had in fact perished in 1847. It would take Orcadian, Dr. John Rae (95), to discover the fate of the expedition.
839   He met John Rae for the first time in Stromness on 14th January 1853 and described him as "a very good fellow".
840   Loudon, Dr J. B. 2006, *The Journal of James Robertson 1842-1853* Monday 29th January 1849 & Thursday 1st March 1849. It was not until 1871 that Episcopalians had access to a venue for worship in Kirkwall. A new church was eventually built a few years later in Dundas Crescent by Samuel Baikie of Kirkwall, with Alexander Ross as architect.
841   Flett, J. 1976, *Lodge Kirkwall Kilwinning No 38² The story from 1736* P78. Prior to *JR's* arrival in Orkney, the Lodge had been in abeyance for 24 years, resuming again in 1844.
842   Kirkwall & St Ola 1871 Census. The family at this stage was living in Buttquoy House.
843   Ewing, Rev W. (ed) 1914, *Annals of the Free Church of Scotland 1843-1900 Vol 1* P334.
844   *Sixty Years A Holy Place: A History of the King Street Congregation*, 1953 Orkney Room 285Y.
845   *The Orcadian* September 29th 1927.
846   Picken, S. D. B. 1972, *The Soul of an Orkney Parish* P102-103.
847   Thomson, W. P. L. 2000, *The Little General and the Rousay Crofters* P146.
848   *The Orcadian* September 24th 1910.
849   Reid, J. T. 1881, *Pictures from the Orkney Islands* P IV.

850 The epitaph was composed by David Balfour of Balfour and Trenabie, the builder of Balfour Castle, Hossack, B. H. 1900, *Kirkwall in the Orkneys* 1986 reprint P56.
851 Baikie, S. 2001, *Reminiscences of the Cathedral Church of St Magnus Since 1846 by an Eye Witness* P19, Wilson, B. 2003 *Profit Not Loss, the Story of the Baikies of Tankerness* P73-74. For Samuel Baikie's appointment as contractor for the Covenanters Memorial see *The Orcadian* 5th May 1888. For parentage see www.orkneyfhs.co.uk – Baikie family.
852 Both sisters of Captain John Baikie married Balfours. The cousins were David Balfour, builder of Balfour Castle in Shapinsay, and James William Balfour. Marwick, H. 1957, *The Baikies of Tankerness* OM Vol 4 P46. See also article in *The Orcadian* of 2nd January 2003.
853 Marwick, E. W. 1965, *William Balfour Baikie Explorer of the Niger* P7.
854 Ibid. P8. Among the Europeans was a John Harcus, almost certainly an Orcadian, who acted as chief mate and later master of the vessel when Baikie became unhappy with the ability of the original master. The expedition also included the freed African slave, Samuel Crowther, who went on to become the first Bishop of the Niger.
855 Marwick, E. W. 1965, *William Balfour Baikie Explorer of the Niger* P9.
856 Gramont, S. de 1975, *The Strong Brown God* P233.
857 Marwick, E. W. 1965, *William Balfour Baikie Explorer of the Niger* P9-10, Pedraza, H. J. 1960, *Borrioboola-Gha, the story of Lokoja, the first British Settlement in Nigeria* P52.
858 Gramont, S. de 1975, *The Strong Brown God* P235-238.
859 Pedraza, H. J. 1960, *Borrioboola-Gha, the story of Lokoja, the first British Settlement in Nigeria* P54-60.
860 Charles William Maxwell Heddle, son of John Heddle and a native Senegalese woman, was the leading trader in Sierra Leone. See Hewison, W. S. 1998, *Who Was Who in Orkney* P72.
861 Gramont, S. de 1975, *The Strong Brown God* P239.
862 Marwick, E. W. 1965, *William Balfour Baikie Explorer of the Niger* P7.
863 *The Orcadian* August 28th 2008.
864 Richards, R. L. 1994, *Dr John Rae* P219 note 54.
865 Richards Ibid. P2, McGoogan, K. 2002, *Fatal Passage* P13.
866 Richards, R. L. 1994, *Dr John Rae* P11.
867 McGoogan, K. 2002, *Fatal Passage* P37.
868 Ibid. P75.
869 Ibid. P81.
870 McGoogan, K. 2002, *Fatal Passage* P267-270
871 Ibid. P305. Lady Franklin's campaign on behalf of her dead husband eventually paid off and Sir John Franklin was credited, erroneously, with being the discoverer of the Northwest Passage. See McGoogan K. 2006, *Lady Franklin's Revenge*.
872 McGoogan, K. 2002, *Fatal Passage* P276-277.
873 McGoogan, K. 2002, *Fatal Passage* P279-288.
874 Richards, R. L. 1994, *Dr John Rae* P169, McGoogan, K. 2002, *Fatal Passage* P299
875 Quoted in McGoogan, K. 2002, *Fatal Passage* P301-302.
876 *The Orkney Herald* August 2nd 1893. The pall-bearers were the Crown Chamberlain, J. Barnett, the Vice Convener of the County, Andrew Gold, the Sheriff-Clerk, T. W. Rankin, the County-Clerk, Duncan Robertson (107), the Cathedral Minister, Rev. James Walker, Provost Spence, R. G. Irvine and Samuel Baikie.
877 *Scottish Leader*, Feb 3rd 1887, OA D1/610/5
878 Hewison, W. S. 1998, *Who Was Who in Orkney* P28.
879 Irvine, J. M. 2009, *The Breckness Estate* P166-167 & P184. The building of the church was achieved in a decade which saw a run of bad harvests.
880 Rendall, J. 2009, *Steering the Stone Ships* 154.
881 OA D1/610/2. Letter enclosing a receipt for his Registration Fee to the General Council of Medical Education and Registration, 1859. The Medical Act of 1858 required Physicians, Surgeons and Medical Officers to be registered under the Act. Rev. Charles Clouston duly sent his application to be registered.
882 OA D1/610/4 Biography of Rev. Charles Clouston LLD.
883 Miller, H. 1861, *Rambles of a Geologist* in *The Cruise of the Betsey* P464-467.
884 Scott, H. 1928, *Fasti Ecclesiae Scoticanae* Vol VII P249. Two sons and two daughters survived him.
885 Hazell, H. 2000, *The Orcadian Book of the 20th Century* P37.
886 *The Orkney Herald* 29th June 1892. Duncan Maclaren was a former City Treasurer and Lord Provost of Edinburgh, who had rescued the city finances from ruin and had pioneered free education for all in the city. In 1824, he had set up his own draper business in Edinburgh and, by the time Thomas Peace came to work for him, he was a Liberal MP for Edinburgh.
887 1881 Census Record for Kirkwall.
888 Hazell, H. 2000, *The Orcadian Book of the Twentieth Century*
889 They graduated to the Territorial Army in 1908.
890 Rollo, D. 1958, *The History of the Orkney and Shetland Volunteers and Territorials 1793-1958* P7-15.
891 *The Orkney Herald* 29th June 1892.
892 Evidence of Mrs Elizabeth Peace in the Thoms Trustees case, 1904. Orkney Room 274.1Y.
893 Mooney, J. *Famous Visitors to Orkney* OA D49/9/3.

The Nineteenth Century – Cathedral Ownership Questioned

894 *The Orkney Herald* 29th June 1892.
895 See Sutherland, P. J. 2013, *Mirth, Madness & St Magnus*.
896 Mooney, J. 1929, *Notes on Discoveries in St Magnus Cathedral, Kirkwall* POAS vol VII P29.
897 Hazell, H. 2000, *The Orcadian Book of the Twentieth Century* P102.
898 Long, P. *A Great Triumph – The 1937 Kirkwall Pageant, Living Orkney* Issue 80 July 2012 P21.
899 OA D1/280. Elizabeth Seabrook, *Study of 19th Century Stronsay families, Davidsons and Hossacks*.
900 *The Orcadian* January 11th 1902.
901 OA D31/20/3/90. Notes by Ernest Marwick on B. H. Hossack.
902 *The Orkney Herald* 31st August 1892.
903 *The Orkney Herald* 8th January 1902.
904 Sir Leonard Lyell, 1850-1926 was a Scottish Liberal politician, who succeeded Samuel Laing the Younger as MP for Orkney and Shetland from 1885 to 1900.
905 *The Orkney Herald* 4th November 1903.
906 Callaghan, S. & Wilson, B. 2001, *The Unknown Cathedral* P86.
907 *Evidence in the Thom's Trustees Case*, 8th February 1905, Orkney Room 274.1Y.
908 Callaghan, S. & Wilson, B. 2001, *The Unknown Cathedral* P86, Sutherland, P. J. 2013, *Mirth, Madness & St Magnus* P20.
909 Fraser, J. 1935, *Some Transactions of the Vice-Admiral Depute of Orkney in 1801-1803* POAS Vol XIII P33.
910 Sutherland, P. J. 2013, *Mirth, Madness & St Magnus* P9.
911 *The Orkney Herald* 4th November 1903.
912 See Sutherland, P. J. 2013, *Mirth, Madness & St Magnus* P24-25 for details of their bequest.
913 Evidence of David Yellowlees MD of Edinburgh University in the Thoms Trustees case, "I am aware that Mr Thoms suffered from gout severely and for many years he suffered gravely from syphilis". Also, evidence from James Ormiston Affleck MD, "I remember about five years before his death, some sores broke out on his body due to syphilis".
914 Thomson, W. P. L. 2000, *The Little General and the Rousay Crofters* P61-62.
915 Loudon, Dr J. B. 2006, *The Journal of James Robertson 1842-1853* Saturday 15th July 1848.
916 Loudon, Dr J. B. 2006, *The Journal of James Robertson 1842-1853* Friday 11th August 1848. A few weeks later *JR* received a letter from Burroughs returning the money.
917 Thomson, W. P. L. 2000, *The Little General and the Rousay Crofters* P100.
918 Thomson, W. P. L. 2000, *The Little General and the Rousay Crofters* P100-102.
919 Ibid. P59.

920 Thomson, W. P. L. 2000, *The Little General and the Rousay Crofters* P86-87.
921 Ibid. P142.
922 Ibid. P85.
923 Ibid. P163.
924 *The Orkney Herald* February 10th 1892.
925 Thomson W. P. L. 2000, *The Little General and the Rousay Crofters* P210-211.
926 *The Orcadian* April 12th 2012.
927 Thomson, W. P. L. 2000, *The Little General and the Rousay Crofters* P90. *The Orkney Herald* February 12th 1908.
928 Burroughs gifted the ancient font from the long disused St Mary's Church at Westness to St Olaf's Episcopal Church.
929 ODNB James Marwick.
930 Hazell, H. 2000, *The Orcadian Book of the 20th Century* P29.
931 Hewison, W. S. 1998, *Who Was Who in Orkney* P105, Wikepedia, James David Marwick.
932 Sinclair, James 2000, *Images in Time Volume 3* No 89.
933 His birth certificate says, "born in uncleanness". His father married another woman a few years later.
934 Cormack, A. & A. 1971, *Days of Orkney Steam* P148-149.
935 According to anecdotal evidence, he arrived in Kirkwall with a barrowload of onions. See Hazell, H. 2010, *The Orcadian Book of the Twentieth Century Volume 2* P281.
936 Board of Trade Inquiry, *Lizzie Bain* and *Queen*, 3rd December 1888.
937 Hewison, W. S. 1998, *Who Was Who in Orkney* P54
938 *The Orcadian* September 7th 1912, obituary of Robert Garden.
939 Hazell, H. 2010, *The Orcadian Book of the Twentieth Century Volume 2* P113.
940 *The Orcadian* April 27th 1933.
941 In 2005, Kirkwall & St Ola Community Council had the building taken down and rebuilt in Tankerness House Gardens, thus making it publically accessible and restoring it to its original garden setting.
942 *The Orkney Herald* April 13th 1892, minutes of Police Commission.
943 *The Orcadian* November 4th 1905. Robert Garden took the samples in the presence of local officials, including Dr Bell (105).
944 OA D49/9/14/1.
945 *The Orkney Herald* May 25th 1938, obituary of Margaret Jolly.
946 Hazell, H. 2000, *The Orcadian Book of the 20th Century* P43.
947 *The Orkney Herald* March 9th 1938.
948 Ibid. February 23rd 1938.
949 Kirkwall and St Ola Census 1891.
950 *The Orcadian* August 30th 1913.
951 Hazell, H. 2000, *The Orcadian Book of the 20th Century* P55.
952 As told to one of the Cathedral custodians in 2011.
953 *The Orkney Herald* January 6th 1915.
954 *The Star* (Auckland) September 24th 1889.
955 *The New York Times* May 2nd 1916.
956 *Shetlopedia* – The Shetland Encyclopaedia, Robert Bell. Sheriff Bell was a contemporary of James Robertson (92) and the two corresponded with one another on official business.
957 Hazell, H. 2000, *The Orcadian Book of the Twentieth Century* P17.
958 *The Orkney Herald* 12th September 1883. The Orkney Combination was formed around 1880 and comprised the parishes of Birsay, Harray, Cross and Burness, Lady, Eday, Holm, Kirkwall, Orphir, South Ronaldsay, Rousay and Egilsay, Shapinsay, Stronsay and Westray. Once the new poorhouse was built, inspectors, whose parochial boards were under the combination, could send in the paupers from their area who needed poorhouse accommodation.
959 *The Orkney Herald* April 7th 1915, obituary of Dr Bell. His gravestone is the first to be found in the north west corner of the cemetery, against the boundary wall.
960 *The Orcadian*, April 24th 1915.
961 *The Orkney View* No 47, April/May 1993 P28 – Muir, M. *Sir Thomas Smith Clouston*.
962 *The British Medical Journal*, April 24th 1915.
963 ODNB Volume 12 P211-212.
964 ODNB Volume 12 P211.
965 Burgher, L. 1991 *Orkney, an Illustrated Architectural Guide* P46.
966 *The British Medical Journal*, April 24th 1915.
967 ODNB Volume 12 P212.
968 On 1st April 1918, the Royal Flying Corps became independent of the army and was renamed the Royal Air Force.
969 *Flight*, August 9th 1917.
970 *The Orkney Herald* June 5th 1941.
971 *The Orkney Herald* June 5th 1941. His father was *JR*.
972 Irvine, J. M. 2009, *The Breckness Estate* P199. The other trustees were Alfred Baikie (113) and Robert Scarth, son of the factor, Robert Scarth of Binscarth. The trustees were reduced to two, following the death of Robert Scarth in 1916.
973 This appeared as a regular column in *The Orcadian* in 1932-33.
974 George Mackay Brown (126) thought him Orkney's most underrated poet. (Hazell, H. 2010, *The Orcadian Book of the Twentieth Century Volume 2* P191).
975 *The Orcadian* August 31st 1922.
976 *The Orcadian* September 27th 1922.
977 *The Orkney Herald* December 3rd 1924.
978 *The Orcadian* November 25th 1905 – advert on P3.
979 Kirkwall & St Ola Census 1901 and 1911.
980 Walls and Flotta Census 1871.
981 Kirkwall & St Ola Census 1911.
982 Kirkwall & St Ola Census 1911.
983 *The Orcadian* December 1st 1917. More detailed information supplied by Brian Budge. See also *Supplement to the London Gazette* 22nd March 1918.
984 *The Orcadian* April 13th 1918.
985 Most of the information, unless otherwise footnoted, is provided by war historian, Brian Budge.
986 *The Orcadian* Sptember 11th 1915.
987 *The Orcadian* November 28th 1918.
988 SS *Express* was a 138ft steamer belonging to Messrs William Cooper and Sons of Kirkwall. She was en route to Kirkwall with a cargo from Leith when she was sunk in a collision with the destroyer HMS *Grenville* ten miles south east of Copinsay, with all hands lost. *The Orcadian* February 16th 1918.
989 *The Orcadian* August 15th and 22nd 1918.
990 HMS *Swiftsure* was a pre-dreadnought battleship built in 1903. At the start of the war, she escorted troop convoys in the Indian Ocean, prior to being transferred to the Suez Canal Patrol in December 1914. She saw action in the Dardenelles Campaign, bombarding Ottoman defences. Shortly after the death of Adam Frisken, she was transferred to convoy duty in the Atlantic.
991 Royal British Legion, Kirkwall website.
992 *The Orcadian* March 11th 1916.
993 Orkney Image Library no 22730.
994 *The Orcadian* March 24th 1917.
995 Michael was codename for one of four separate German attacks on allied line in the spring of 1918.
996 *The Orcadian* May 25th 1918.
997 *The Orcadian* October 16th 1915.
998 *The Orcadian* September 23rd 1916.
999 Information gleaned from 1911 Kirkwall and Edinburgh Census, death certificate from Arizona State Board of Health and excerpt from local newspaper.
1000 William Milne's death certificate is on the RBL, Kirkwall/Memorial website.
1001 *The Orcadian* June 8th 1918.
1002 *The Orcadian* May 12th 1917.
1003 *The Orcadian* April 13th 1918.
1004 *The Orcadian* October 6th 1917, *The London Gazette* August 25th 1917.
1005 *The Orcadian* November 14th 1918.
1006 *The Orcadian* May 5th 1917.
1007 On the plaque, 'Tulloch' should have been spelt 'Tullock'.

1008 *The Orcadian* February 6th 1915.
1009 Sir Robert Christison's granddaughter married Dr Logie's future partner, Dr Bell.
1010 *Dr James S. S. Logie of Kirkwall, Orkney, Scotland*, Extracts from T*he Orcadian* May 12th 1920, Orkney Room 610Y. Professor Syme (1799-1870) treated Dr Logie's friend, James Robertson (92), while *JR* was ill with a fever during a visit to Edinburgh in September 1847.
1011 *The Orkney Herald* July 21st 1920.
1012 Loudon, Dr J. B. 2006, *The Journal of James Robertson 1842-1853* Monday 8th January 1849.
1013 *Dr James S. S. Logie of Kirkwall, Orkney, Scotland*, Extracts from T*he Orcadian* May 12th 1920, Orkney Room 610Y.
1014 Sutherland, P. J. 2013, *Mirth, Madness & St Magnus* P14.
1015 *The Orcadian* October 22nd 1964.
1016 Orphir Census 1861.
1017 *The Orkney Herald* October 25th 1933.
1018 *Islander* 1994 P28.
1019 The *Derflinger* was part of the German High Seas Fleet interred in Scapa Flow after the end of the First World War and subsequently sunk in "the Grand Scuttle". She was raised just before the start of World War 2 and spent the next six years moored upside down off Rysa.
1020 Hewison, W. S. 1985, *This Great Harbour Scapa Flow* P380-381. *The Orcadian* December 5th 1957.
1021 In contrast there was no opposition to extensive salvage work being carried out on HMS *Vanguard*.
1022 Wilson, B. 2003, *Profit Not Loss, the Story of the Baikies of Tankerness* P38. It was Dr Robert Baikie who built Buttquoy House.
1023 *The Orcadian* October 30th 1947.
1024 Among the pall-bearers at William Baikie's funeral were Dr Bell (105) and Dr Logie (110). funeral was Dr Bell at William Baikie'
1025 Information provided by Carrie's niece, Mrs Elizabeth Miller.
1026 1891 and 1901 Kirkwall Census.
1027 Statement by Carrie's niece, Mrs Elizabeth Miller.
1028 *Shetland Times* September 9th 1902.
1029 The couple lived at 220 West Regent Street.
1030 *The Orcadian* November 26th 1936.
1031 OA D31/20/3/96, *The Scottish Field*, May 1945 - 37
1032 *The Orcadian*, October 23rd 1915.
1033 *The Orcadian* May 1950.
1034 Scott, H 1928, *Fasti Ecclesiae Scoticanae* Vol VII P225.
1035 Callaghan, S. 2001, *The Unknown Cathedral* P72-73.
1036 *The Orkney Herald* June 14th 1933.
1037 *The Glasgow Herald* July 10th 1958.
1038 *The Orcadian* July 17th 1958.
1039 Hazell, H. 2010, *The Orcadian Book of the Twentieth Century Volume 2* P287.
1040 *The Orcadian* January 28th 1960.
1041 *The Edinburgh Gazette* August 21st 1984.
1042 Harald Leslie opened Kirkwall Salvation Army Hall on Junction Road in August 1960. He also opened Sanday Secondary School in 1964.
1043 ODNB Volume 33 P451.
1044 Hewison, W. S. 1998, *Who Was Who in Orkney* P91.
1045 Hazell, H. 2000, *The Orcadian Book of the Twentieth Century* P177.
1046 ODNB Volume 33 P451.
1047 Hewison, W. S. 1998, *Who Was Who in Orkney* P91.
1048 ODNB Volume 33 P452.
1049 Irvine, J. M. 2009, *The Breckness Estate* P211.
1050 See family tree, Irvine, J. M. 2009, *The Breckness Estate* P205.
1051 *The Orcadian* November 25th 1999.
1052 Irvine, J. M. 2009, *The Breckness Estate* P211, *The Herald* November 27th 1999.
1053 In 1975, Ernest published *The Folklore of Orkney and Shetland*. He wrote prolifically for *The Orkney Herald* and *The Orcadian*, and some of his articles are reproduced in *Volumes I* (1990) and *II* (2012) of *An Orkney Anthology*. He was also instrumental in saving the Italian Chapel and Papdale House, and in organising protests against the mining of uranium. He was a founder member and later Chairman of Orkney Heritage Society. He was awarded the Freedom of the City and Royal Burgh of Kirkwall in 1975 and an Honorary Master of Arts by Edinburgh University in the following year. Ernest was tragically killed in a car accident in 1977 and was buried in St Olaf's Cemetery after a memorial service in the Cathedral.
1054 *The Orcadian* June 24th 1971.
1055 Marwick, E. W. *Storer-Clouston and his work – a fresh look*, The *Orcadian* May 21st 1970.
1056 Thomson, K., *Orkney Cinema History*.
1057 See the foreword to P. G. Wodehouse's *The Girl on the Boat*.
1058 See both *The Orcadian* and *Orkney Herald* of January and February 1915 and Smith, B. 2003, *Holy Moses! Orkney Historians on Medieval Orkney*, NOAJ Volume 3 P3-14..
1059 Marwick, E. W. *Storer Clouston and his work – a fresh look*, *Orcadian* May 21st 1970. Clouston's most famous quote concerning 1611 and the events thereafter can be found in Clouston, J. S. 1932, *History of Orkney* P317 "It was the history of the Country of Orkney which ended here and the annals of a Scottish county which began instead".
1060 *The Orkney Herald* June 27th 1944.
1061 Winifred was a granddaughter of Rev. Charles Clouston (96).
1062 *The Orcadian* June 29th 1944.
1063 Sinclair, James 2000, *Images in Time Volume 3* No 88.
1064 On his birth certificate, his mother signed with her mark.
1065 The family lived in Victoria Street. See 1861 Kirkwall & St Ola Census.
1066 Hugh Marwick made the following comment regarding an account Mooney wrote for his family about his own early life, "I think you have done wisely in compiling this account, even though it is destined to meet the eyes only of your own family and one or two others, of whom I, speaking for myself, may say that your confidence touches me to the heart. Such an experience as you had might well have soured and embittered anyone not inspired with the highest faith in God and man, and I can believe that even to set it down in words now long afterward must have been a trying experience." OA D49/1/7, dated 12th April 1946.
1067 *The Orcadian* March 29th 1945.
1068 *The Orcadian* October 12th 1950.
1069 *The Orcadian* January 22nd 1910.
1070 OA D49/10/3.
1071 *The Orcadian* October 12th 1950, obituary by Hugh Marwick.
1072 *The Orcadian* June 24th 1971.
1073 *The History of KGS* from the *Kirkwallian Magazine* 1974.
1074 Dickens, B. *An Orkney Scholar: Hugh Marwick 1881-1965* Saga-Book of the Viking Society Vol. XVII 1966-1969 P3.
1075 *The Orkney Herald* January 3rd 1938.
1076 For a critical assessment of Marwick and other Orkney historians see Smith, B. 2003, *Holy Moses! Orkney Historians on Medieval Orkney*, NOAJ Volume 3
1077 Dickens, B. *An Orkney Scholar: Hugh Marwick 1881-1965* Saga-Book of the Viking Society Vol. XVII 1966-1969 P4.
1078 Muir, E. 1980, *An Autobiography* P41.
1079 Muir, E. 1980, *An Autobiography* P63.
1080 Ibid. P15.
1081 Ibid. P146.
1082 Wilhelmina Johnston Anderson was born in Montrose in 1890 of Shetland parents, both from Unst. Along with Carrie Spence (114), she was among the first women to study for a university degree. She outlived her husband by eleven years, dying in May 1970
1083 Muir, E. 1980, *An Autobiography* P154.
1084 *The Orcadian*, January 8th 1959.
1085 Dickson, N. 1990, *An Island Shore, The Life and Work of Robert Rendall* P17-21.
1086 Ibid. P22.
1087 Dickson, N. 1990, *An Island Shore, The Life and Work of Robert Rendall* P27 and 181.
1088 Marwick, E. W. 2012, *An Orkney Anthology Vol 2* Ed. Robertson, Irvine and Sutherland P195.

1089 Ibid. P186.
1090 An example is *Rendall's Bazaar*, the first two lines of which are, "Friends, Yamils, Orkneymen – Look for your cash! I'm back with goods from Rendall's, let me praise them". See Brown, J. F. & Murray, B. (Ed) 2012 *Robert Rendall Collected Poems* P304.
1091 Fergusson, M., 2006, *George Mackay Brown, The Life* P125.
1092 *The Orcadian* June 15th 1967.
1093 Dickson, N. 1990, *An Island Shore, The Life and Work of Robert Rendall* P40 and P127.
1094 Elizabeth Linklater celebrated her 90th birthday in January 1957 (*The Orkney Herald* January 29th 1957). She died in November 1957.
1095 *The Orcadian* November 14th 1974.
1096 The helmet, complete with bullet hole can be seen in the Orkney Museum in Tankerness House. For an account of the incident, see *The Orcadian* May 8th 2014 P10.
1097 Hall, S. W. 2010, *The History of Orkney Literature* P81-82.
1098 Marwick, E. W. 2012, *An Orkney Anthology Vol 2* Ed. Robertson, Irvine and Sutherland P232.
1099 Hewison, W. S. 1985, *This Great Harbour Scapa Flow* P351.
1100 Marwick, E. W. 2012, *An Orkney Anthology Vol 2* Ed. Robertson, Irvine and Sutherland P232.
1101 Beasant, P. 2007, *Stanley Cursiter, a life of the artist* P1-12.
1102 Ibid. P13-14.
1103 *Stanley Cursiter Centenary Exhibition* 1987, Pier Arts Centre P11-12.
1104 Shearer, J. 2012, *Stanley Cursiter and his contribution to mapping*, The Journal of the Charles Close Society P12.
1105 Beasant, P. 2007, *Stanley Cursiter, a life of the artist* P39-49.
1106 Ibid. P71. It would not be until 1960 when the Scottish National Gallery of Modern Art was first opened.
1107 Hazell, H. 2000, *The Orcadian Book of the Twentieth Century* P143. The building of oil tanks on Shore Street in 1937 is a legacy that persists to this day, despite several attempts to have the tanks relocated. To be fair to the members of Kirkwall Town Council of the time, the transport of oil in barrels was no longer acceptable and therefore there was a need for a bulk storage facility near the pier. Added to this was the scathing report by Dr Bannerman, Kirkwall's Medical Officer, on the standard of housing in Shore Street, which he thought should be 'absolutely condemned and wiped out' (*Rural Housing* Orkney Agricultural Discussion Society 1932).
1108 Beasant, P. 2007, *Stanley Cursiter, a life of the artist* P88.
1109 Ibid. P97. For the story of the provost's chain, see Marwick, E. W. 1991, *An Orkney Anthology* Ed. J. D. M. Robertson P90-91.
1110 Marwick, E. W. 1991, *An Orkney Anthology* Ed. J. D. M. Robertson P457-462.
1111 Fergusson, M., 2006, *George Mackay Brown, The Life* P4-7.
1112 Ibid. P23.
1113 Ibid. P89-90.
1114 Fergusson, M., 2006, *George Mackay Brown, The Life* P181.
1115 Ibid. P40.
1116 Ibid. P170.
1117 *Greenvoe* is viewed as prophesising the coming of oil to Flotta, as well as the threat Orkney faced with uranium mining.
1118 Fergusson, M., 2006, *George Mackay Brown, The Life* P232.

The Twentieth Century – Cathedral Future Secured
1119 Ibid. P284.

Appendix 1
1120 Much of the information in this Appendix is from Albert Thomson, *Windows in St Magnus* 1987 in *St Magnus Cathedral 850 years-a celebration* published by *The Orkney View*.